NTC's
Pocket Guide
for
DOUBTFUL
SPELLERS

David Downing

NTC's
Pocket Guide
for
DOUBTFUL SPELLERS

David Downing

Printed on recyclable paper

 National Textbook Company
a division of *NTC Publishing Group* • Lincolnwood, Illinois USA

1995 Printing

Contents

To the User   vii

How to Use This Dictionary   ix

Pocket Guide for Doubtful Spellers   1

Appendix: Guidelines for American English Spelling   311

To the User

If you don't know how to spell a word, you are supposed to look it up in a dictionary. But how can you look it up if you don't know how to spell it?

For example, if you are not sure how to spell the word for a compulsive thief, you might try looking up "cleptomaniac." In a regular dictionary all your searching in the *c*'s would be in vain, because the word you need begins with a *k*: *kleptomaniac*. And if you gave up on the fancy word and started looking for "theif," you would have just as little success: *Thief* is one of those "*i* before *e*" words.

NTC's Pocket Guide for Doubtful Spellers is designed to help you discover the correct spelling of a word quickly and easily. It includes over 7,000 commonly misspelled words and over 17,000 ways in which those words are most likely to be misspelled. It also includes many words that are commonly confused.

The *Pocket Guide* is easy to use. Simply look up a word under your best guess at its correct spelling. In the alphabetical word list, you will find an entry that

- identifies the spelling as correct;
- identifies the spelling as incorrect and provides the correct spelling; or
- distinguishes between two or more words commonly confused.

English spelling can be quite illogical. Some of the irregularities can be traced to the language's checkered (or is it *chequered*?) past, especially its many borrowings from other languages. Differences between American and British usage add a bit of craziness. The few "rules" that do help make sense of American English spelling are listed in the Appendix at the end of the *Pocket Guide*.

How to Use This Dictionary

NTC's Pocket Guide for Doubtful Spellers is designed to help you quickly resolve questions of spelling and usage. Here's how it works:

1. Correct spellings are printed in **boldface type** and syllabified. For example:

   pre·scrip·tion

2. Incorrect spellings appear in lightface type without syllabication. They are followed by a colon and the correct spelling printed in **boldface type** and syllabified. For example:

   perscription : **pre·scrip·tion**

3. Spellings that are acceptable British variants appear in lightface type without syllabication. They are followed by the designation *Brit.* in parentheses, then by the preferred American spelling printed in **boldface type** and syllabified. For example:

   acknowledgement (*Brit.*) : **ac·knowl·edg·ment**

4. Entries for easily confused words provide additional information so that you can readily identify the word you need. Entries for easily confused words include brief definitions or synonyms and parts of speech in parentheses. If an incorrect spelling might lend itself to more than one correct spelling, all possible words (and their definitions) are offered. For example:

   ad·vice (*noun*); **ad·vise** (*verb*)
   dear (precious); **deer** (animal)
   it's (it is); **its** (belonging to it)
   per·ish (to cease to exist); **par·ish** (church community)
   exept : **ac·cept** (to receive) *or* **ex·cept** (to exclude)

5. Because English spelling is so arbitrary, often more than one form (or variant) of a word is in current usage. Variants of a word that are used with essentially the same frequency are listed in alphabetical order in the word list. However, an incorrect spelling refers only to the variant that comes first alphabetically or that is in slightly more frequent use in American English. Less commonly used variants are listed as incorrect spellings. For example:

    levaled : **lev·eled**
    lev·eled *or* **lev·elled**
    lev·elled *or* **lev·eled**
    Ju·go·sla·via *or* **Yu·go·sla·via**
    Yugaslovia : **Yu·go·sla·via**
    Yu·go·sla·via *or* **Ju·go·sla·via**

A Note on Syllabication

The words listed in this *Pocket Guide* have dots (·) to indicate where each word may be hyphenated if it is divided at the end of a line. In general, you should follow these guidelines when hyphenating words:

1. Do not divide one-syllable words. If a one-syllable word will not fit at the end of a line, type the whole word on the next line.

2. Do not leave only one letter at the end of one line (*o·ver, i·dea*) or at the beginning of the next (*word·y, Ohi·o*).

3. Avoid hyphenating the last word on a page.

4. If a word already contains a hyphen, divide it at the hyphen (*self-· esteem,* not *self-es·teem*).

5. In general, words with double consonants may be divided between the consonants (*ar·rogant, fal·lible*). However, when a suffix is added to a root word ending in double consonants, the hyphen comes after both consonants (*kiss·ing, stroll·ing*).

Terms and Abbreviations

adj.	adjective	*noun*	
adv.	adverb	*past of*	past tense of verb
Brit.	British variant spelling	*plur.*	plural form of noun
fem.	feminine form of word	*sing.*	singular form of noun
masc.	masculine form of word	*verb*	

A

abait : **abate**
abalish : **abol·ish**
ab·a·lo·ne
abaloney : **ab·a·lo·ne**
abanden : **aban·don**
aban·don
abarigine : **ab·o·rig·i·ne**
abarrance : **ab·er·rance**
abate
abayance : **abey·ance**
abbandon : **aban·don**
abbate : **abate**
abberance : **ab·er·rance**
ab·bess (head of convent);
   abyss (bottomless pit)
abbet : **ab·bot**
ab·bey
abblaze : **ablaze**
abboard : **aboard**
ab·bot
ab·bre·vi·ate
abbrieviate : **ab·bre·vi·ate**
abbuse : **abuse**
abby : **ab·bey**
abcess : **ab·scess**
   (inflammation) *or* **ob·sess** (to
   preoccupy)
abdecate : **ab·di·cate**
ab·di·cate
ab·do·men
abdomenal : **ab·dom·i·nal**
abdomin : **ab·do·men**
ab·dom·i·nal
abducion : **ab·duc·tion**
ab·duc·tion
aberence : **ab·er·rance**
ab·er·rance
ab·er·rant
aberrent : **ab·er·rance**
abey·ance

abeyence : **abey·ance**
abhominable : **abom·i·na·ble**
ab·hor
abhorance : **ab·hor·ence**
ab·hor·ence
abil·i·ty
abillity : **abil·i·ty**
abismal : **abys·mal**
abiss : **abyss**
ab·jure (to renounce); **ad·jure**
   (to ask)
ablaize : **ablaze**
ablaze
abley : **ably**
ablivion : **obliv·i·on**
ably
abnagate : **ab·ne·gate**
ab·ne·gate
abnigate : **ab·ne·gate**
ab·nor·mal
abnormel : **ab·nor·mal**
abnoxious : **ob·nox·ious**
aboard
abol·ish
abolission : **ab·o·li·tion**
ab·o·li·tion
abollish : **abol·ish**
abolone : **ab·a·lo·ne**
abomanable : **abom·i·na·ble**
abom·i·na·ble
abor : **ab·hor**
abord : **aboard**
aborence : **ab·hor·ence**
ab·o·rig·i·ne
aboriginnie : **ab·o·rig·i·ne**
aboriginy : **ab·o·rig·i·ne**
abracive : **abra·sive**
abrade
abraid : **abrade**
abra·sive

1

abreast
abregate : **ab·ro·gate**
abrest : **abreast**
abreviate : **ab·bre·vi·ate**
abridgement (*Brit.*) :
  abridg·ment
abridg·ment
abrieviate : **ab·bre·vi·ate**
ab·ro·gate
abrubt : **abrupt**
abrupt
absalute : **ab·so·lute**
absalutely : **ab·so·lute·ly**
abscence : **ab·sence**
ab·scess (inflammation) *or*
  ob·sess (to preoccupy)
ab·sence
absensce : **ab·sence**
absense : **ab·sence**
ab·sen·tee
absentie : **ab·sen·tee**
absenty : **ab·sen·tee**
abserd : **ab·surd**
absess : **ab·scess**
  (inflammation) *or* **ob·sess** (to
  preoccupy)
ab·so·lute
ab·so·lute·ly
absoluty : **ab·so·lute·ly**
ab·sorb
absorbant : **ab·sorb·ent**
ab·sorb·ent
absorbtion : **ab·sorp·tion**
ab·sorp·tion
abstainence : **ab·sti·nence**
abstanence : **ab·sti·nence**
abstinance : **ab·sti·nence**
ab·sti·nence
ab·surd
abun·dance
abun·dant
abundence : **abun·dance**

abundent : **abun·dant**
abuse
abut·ment
abuttment : **abut·ment**
abuze : **abuse**
abys·mal
abyss (bottomless pit); **ab·bess**
  (head of convent)
abyssmal : **abys·mal**
abzerd : **ab·surd**
aca·cia
ac·a·dem·ic
ac·a·dem·i·cal·ly
academicly : **ac·a·dem·i·cal·ly**
acasha : **aca·cia**
accademy : **acad·em·y**
accasion : **oc·ca·sion**
ac·cede (to agree reluctantly);
  ex·ceed (to go beyond)
acceed : **ac·cede**
accelarate : **ac·cel·er·ate**
ac·cel·er·ate
accelerater : **ac·cel·er·a·tor**
ac·cel·er·a·tor
ac·cent
ac·cept (to receive); **ex·cept** (to
  exclude)
ac·cept·able
ac·cept·ance
acceptible : **ac·cept·able**
accesory : **ac·ces·so·ry**
ac·cess
accessable : **ac·ces·si·ble**
accessery : **ac·ces·so·ry**
ac·ces·si·ble
ac·ces·sion
ac·ces·so·ry
accidant : **ac·ci·dent**
ac·ci·dent
ac·ci·den·tal·ly
accidently : **ac·ci·den·tal·ly**
ac·claim

ac·cli·ma·tize
accommadate :
    ac·com·mo·date
ac·com·mo·date
accomodate : **ac·com·mo·date**
ac·com·pa·ni·ment
accompanyment :
    ac·com·pa·ni·ment
ac·com·plice
accomplis : **ac·com·plice**
ac·com·plish
ac·cord
accordien : **ac·cor·di·on**
ac·cor·di·on
ac·count·able
ac·count·ant
accountent : **ac·count·ant**
ac·cou·ter·ment *or*
    ac·cou·tre·ment
accoutrament : **ac·cou·tre·ment**
ac·cou·tre·ment *or*
    ac·cou·ter·ment
accross : **across**
accummulate : **ac·cu·mu·late**
ac·cu·mu·late
ac·cu·mu·la·tion
ac·cu·ra·cy
ac·cu·rate
accurisy : **ac·cu·ra·cy**
accurite : **ac·cu·rate**
ac·cu·sa·tion
ac·cuse
ac·cus·tom
ac·cus·tomed
accustommed : **ac·cus·tomed**
accutrement : **ac·cou·tre·ment**
acedemic : **aca·dem·ic**
acelerate : **ac·cel·er·ate**
acent : **ac·cent**
acept : **ac·cept**
acer·bic
acertain : **as·cer·tain**

acess : **ac·cess**
acessible : **ac·ces·si·ble**
acession : **ac·ces·sion**
acessory : **ac·ces·so·ry**
acetic : **as·cet·ic**
acheive : **achieve**
achieve
achieve·ment
acident : **ac·ci·dent**
acknowledgement (*Brit.*) :
    ac·knowl·edg·ment
ac·knowl·edg·ment
acknowlege : **ac·knowl·edge**
ackumen : **acu·men**
aclaim : **ac·claim**
aclimatize : **ac·cli·ma·tize**
acompaniment :
    ac·com·pa·ni·ment
acomplice : **ac·com·plice**
acomplish : **ac·com·plish**
acord : **ac·cord**
acordion : **ac·cor·di·on**
acountent : **ac·count·ant**
acousticks : **acous·tics**
acous·tics
acoutrement : **ac·cou·tre·ment**
ac·quain·tance
acquaintence : **ac·quain·tance**
acquaintense : **ac·quain·tance**
acquatic : **aqua·tic**
ac·qui·esce
acquiese : **ac·qui·esce**
acquiesse : **ac·qui·esce**
ac·quire
ac·qui·si·tion
ac·quit
acquited : **ac·quit·ted**
ac·quit·tal
ac·quit·ted
acquittel : **ac·quit·tal**
acrage : **acre·age**

acre
acre•age
acrebat : acro•bat
acrige : acre•age
across
actavate : ac•ti•vate
acter : ac•tor
acteress : ac•tress
ac•ti•vate
ac•tor
actoress : ac•tress
ac•tress
ac•tu•al
ac•tu•al•ly
actule : ac•tu•al
actully : ac•tu•al•ly
acu•men
acumin : acu•men
acummulation :
  ac•cu•mu•la•tion
acumulate : ac•cu•mu•late
acumulation : ac•cu•mu•la•tion
acuracy : ac•cu•ra•cy
acurate : ac•cu•rate
acusation : ac•cu•sa•tion
acuse : ac•cuse
acustics : acous•tics
acustom : ac•cus•tom
ad (advertisement); add (to
  combine)
ad•age
ad•a•mant
adament : ad•a•mant
adapt (to modify); adept
  (skilled); adopt (to accept)
adapt•able
adapt•er
adaptible : adapt•able
adaptor : adapt•er
adaquacy : ade•qua•cy
adaquate : ade•quate

add (to combine); ad
  (advertisement)
add hoc : ad hoc
add lib : ad lib
addage : ad•age
addative : ad•di•tive
ad•den•da (plur.); ad•den•dum
  (sing.)
ad•den•dum (sing.); ad•den•da
  (plur.)
addept : ad•ept
addick : ad•dict
ad•dict
ad•dic•tion
ad•di•tion (adding); e•di•tion
  (book)
ad•di•tive
addopt : adopt
addrenalin : ad•ren•a•line
ad•dress
addulation : ad•u•la•tion
addult : adult
addulterer : adul•ter•er
addulteress : adul•ter•ess
addultery : adul•ter•y
adeau : adieu
adeiu : adieu
adelescence : ad•o•les•cence
adendum : ad•den•dum
adept (skilled); adapt (to
  modify); adopt (to accept)
adequasy : ade•qua•cy
ade•quate
adequit : ade•quate
adhear : ad•here
adherance : ad•her•ence
ad•her•ence (quality of
  adhering); ad•her•ents
  (followers)
ad hoc
adhoc : ad hoc
adhock : ad hoc

adict : **ad·dict**
adiction : **ad·dic·tion**
adieu (good-bye); **ado** (fuss)
adige : **adage**
ad·ja·cent
adjasent : **ad·ja·cent**
ad·jec·tive
ad·join
ad·journ
ad·ju·di·cate
ad·jure (to ask); **ab·jure** (to renounce)
adjurn : **ad·journ**
ad·just
ad·just·able
adjustible : **ad·just·able**
ad·ju·tant
adjutent : **ad·ju·tant**
ad-lib
admaral : **ad·mir·al**
admendment : **amend·ment**
admeration : **ad·mi·ra·tion**
adminester : **ad·min·is·ter**
ad·min·is·ter
administerate : **ad·min·is·trate**
ad·min·is·trate
administrater : **ad·min·is·tra·tor**
adminition : **ad·mo·ni·tion**
adminster : **ad·min·is·ter**
ad·mi·ral
ad·mir·er
admirerer : **ad·mir·er**
admiror : **ad·mir·er**
admision : **ad·mis·sion**
admissable : **ad·mis·si·ble**
ad·mis·si·ble
admitance : **ad·mit·tance**
admited : **ad·mit·ted**
ad·mit·tance
ad·mit·ted
admittence : **ad·mit·tance**

admittense : **ad·mit·tance**
ad·mo·ni·tion
ado (fuss); **adieu** (good-bye)
ado·be
adobie : **ado·be**
adoby : **ado·be**
adolecense : **ado·les·cence**
adolecent : **ado·les·cent**
ado·les·cence
ado·les·cent
adolesence : **ado·les·cence**
adolesense : **ado·les·cence**
adolesent : **ado·les·cent**
adom : **atom**
adoo : **adieu** (good-bye) *or* **ado** (fuss)
adopt (to accept); **adapt** (to modify); **adept** (skilled)
ador·able
adorible : **ador·able**
adorn
adorn·ment
adourn : **adorn**
adournment : **adorn·ment**
adrenalin : **ad·ren·a·line**
ad·ren·a·line
adrenlin : **ad·ren·a·line**
adrenolin : **ad·ren·a·line**
adres : **ad·dress**
adress : **ad·dress**
adrinalin : **ad·ren·a·line**
adsorb : **ab·sorb**
adsorption (*Brit.*) : **ab·sorp·tion**
adu·la·tion
adult
adultarate : **adul·ter·ate**
adul·ter·er
adul·ter·ess
adulteror : **adul·ter·er**
adul·ter·y
adultrer : **adul·ter·er**

adultress : **adul·ter·ess**
adultry : **adul·ter·y**
advacate : **ad·vo·cate**
advacator : **ad·vo·ca·tor**
ad·vance
advanse : **ad·vance**
ad·van·tage
ad·van·ta·geous
advantagious : **ad·van·ta·geous**
advantige : **ad·van·tage**
advenchure : **ad·ven·ture**
ad·ven·ture
ad·ven·tur·er
adventuror : **ad·ven·tur·er**
adventurur : **ad·ven·tur·er**
adversarry : **ad·ver·sary**
ad·ver·sary
ad·verse (unfavorable); **averse**
   (disinclined)
ad·ver·tise·ment
ad·ver·tis·er
advertisor : **ad·ver·tis·er**
advertize (*Brit.*) : **ad·ver·tise**
advertizer (*Brit.*) : **ad·ver·tis·er**
advertizing (*Brit.*) :
   ad·ver·tis·ing
ad·vice (*noun*); **ad·vise** (*verb*)
ad·vis·able
ad·vise (*verb*); **ad·vice** (*noun*)
ad·vis·ed·ly
ad·vis·er *or* **ad·vis·or**
advisible : **ad·vis·able**
advisidly : **ad·vis·ed·ly**
ad·vis·or *or* **ad·vis·er**
advizable : **ad·vis·able**
advizer : **ad·vis·er**
ad·vo·cate
advocater : **ad·vo·ca·tor**
ad·vo·ca·tor
aeleron : **ai·le·ron**
aer·ate
aer·i·al

ae·rie (nest); **airy** (relating to
   air); **ee·rie** (weird)
aero·dy·na·mic
aerodynamick : **aero·dy·nam·ic**
aeronatic : **aero·nau·tic**
aero·nau·tic
aeronawtic : **aero·nau·tic**
aeronotic : **aero·nau·tic**
aeronottic : **aero·nau·tic**
aero·sol
aes·thet·ic *or* **es·thet·ic**
afability : **af·fa·bil·i·ty**
afable : **af·fa·ble**
afadavit : **af·fi·da·vit**
afair : **af·fair**
afare : **af·fair**
afect : **af·fect**
afection : **af·fec·tion**
af·fa·bil·i·ty
affabillity : **af·fa·bil·i·ty**
af·fa·ble
affadavet : **af·fi·da·vit**
affadavid : **af·fi·da·vit**
affadavit : **af·fi·da·vit**
af·fair
affare : **af·fair**
af·fect (to influence); **ef·fect**
   (result; to bring about
   results)
affense : **of·fense**
affibility : **af·fa·bil·i·ty**
affible : **af·fa·ble**
af·fi·da·vit
af·fil·i·ate
affilliate : **af·fil·i·ate**
af·fin·i·ty
af·fir·ma·tive
affirmitive : **af·fir·ma·tive**
affluance : **af·flu·ence**
affluant : **af·flu·ent**
af·flu·ence

af·flu·ent (prosperous);
   ef·flu·ent (flowing out)
affraid : **afraid**
Afgan : **Af·ghan**
Afganistan : **Af·ghan·i·stan**
Af·ghan
Afghanastan : **Af·ghan·i·stan**
Af·ghan·i·stan
afiliate : **af·fil·i·ate**
afinity : **af·fin·i·ty**
afirm : **af·firm**
afirmative : **af·fir·ma·tive**
afluent : **af·flu·ent**
afore·said
aforism : **aph·o·rism**
aforsaid : **afore·said**
afrade : **afraid**
afraid
against
aganize : **ag·o·nize**
agany : **ag·o·ny**
agast : **aghast**
agate
agatt : **agate**
aged
ageing : **aging**
agen·cy
agensy : **agen·cy**
agetate : **ag·i·tate**
agete : **agate**
aggile : **ag·ile**
aggility : **agil·i·ty**
aggitate : **ag·i·tate**
aggnostic : **ag·nos·tic**
aggnosticism : **ag·nos·ti·cism**
aggonize : **ag·o·nize**
aggony : **ag·o·ny**
aggragate : **ag·gre·gate**
aggrandise (*Brit.*) :
   ag·gran·dize
ag·gran·dize
ag·gra·vate

ag·gra·vat·ed
aggreave : **ag·grieve**
aggreeable : **agree·able**
ag·gre·gate
ag·gre·ga·tion
ag·gress (to attack); **egress**
   (exit)
aggresser : **ag·gres·sor**
ag·gres·sion
ag·gres·sor
aggrevate : **ag·gra·vate**
aggreve : **ag·grieve**
aggriculture : **ag·ri·cul·ture**
ag·grieve
agground : **aground**
aghast
agid : **aged**
agile
agilety : **agil·i·ty**
agil·i·ty
agill : **ag·ile**
agillity : **agil·i·ty**
agincy : **agen·cy**
aging
aginst : **against**
agi·tate
agnastic : **ag·nos·tic**
agnasticism : **ag·nos·ti·cism**
agnaustic : **ag·nos·tic**
agnausticism : **ag·nos·ti·cism**
ag·nos·tic
agnostick : **ag·nos·tic**
agnosticysm : **ag·nos·ti·cism**
agnostischism : **ag·nos·ti·cism**
agnostisism : **ag·nos·ti·cism**
agoanize : **ag·o·nize**
agoany : **ag·o·ny**
agonie : **ag·o·ny**
agonise (*Brit.*) : **ag·o·nize**
ag·o·nize
agonnize : **ag·o·nize**
agonny : **ag·o·ny**

agraculture : **ag·ri·cul·ture**
agrandize : **ag·gran·dize**
agravate : **ag·gra·vate**
agreable : **agree·able**
agreave : **ag·grieve**
agreculture : **ag·ri·cul·ture**
agreeabal : **agree·able**
agreeabel : **agree·able**
agree·able
agreeible : **agree·able**
agregate : **ag·gre·gate**
agress : **ag·gress** (to attack) *or* **egress** (exit)
agression : **ag·gres·sion**
agriculchure : **ag·ri·cul·ture**
agricullture : **ag·ri·cul·ture**
ag·ri·cul·ture
agrieve : **ag·grieve**
agrikulture : **ag·ri·cul·ture**
aground
agrownd : **aground**
aid (to help); aide (helper)
aid-de-camp : **aide-de-camp**
aide (helper); aid (to help)
aide-de-camp
ailaron : **ai·ler·on**
ai·ler·on
ailerron : **ai·ler·on**
aim·less
aimliss : **aim·less**
airasol : **aero·sol**
airboarn : **air·borne**
airborn : **air·borne**
air·borne
aireate : **aer·ate**
aireborne : **air·borne**
airial : **ae·ri·al**
airiate : **aer·ate**
airodinamic : **aero·dy·nam·ic**
airodynamic : **aero·dy·nam·ic**
airodynammic : **aero·dy·nam·ic**
aironautic : **aero·nau·tic**

aironawtic : **aero·nau·tic**
airosol : **aero·sol**
airplain : **air·plane**
air·plane
airy (relating to air); **ae·rie** (nest)
ais·le (walkway); **is·le** (small island)
ajacent : **ad·ja·cent**
ajective : **ad·jec·tive**
ajile : **ag·ile**
ajitate : **ag·i·tate**
ajoin : **ad·join**
ajourn : **ad·journ**
ajudicate : **ad·ju·di·cate**
ajust : **ad·just**
akacia : **aca·cia**
aknowledge : **ac·knowl·edge**
aknowledgment : **ac·knowl·edg·ment**
akre : **acre**
akrobat : **ac·ro·bat**
Al·a·ba·ma
Alabamma : **Al·a·ba·ma**
alabasster : **al·a·bas·ter**
al·a·bas·ter
alabi : **al·i·bi**
alacritty : **alac·ri·ty**
alac·ri·ty
alakrity : **alac·ri·ty**
alamony : **al·i·mo·ny**
Alasca : **Alas·ka**
Alas·ka
alay : **al·lay**
albam : **al·bum**
Albanea : **Al·ba·ni·a**
Al·ba·ni·a
Albaquerque : **Al·bu·quer·que**
albatros : **al·ba·tross**
al·ba·tross
albeat : **al·be·it**
al·be·it

albem : **al·bum**
albetross : **al·ba·tross**
albiet : **al·be·it**
albim : **al·bum**
al·bi·no
albinoes : **al·bi·nos**
al·bi·nos
albinow : **al·bi·no**
Albiquerque : **Al·bu·quer·que**
albitross : **al·ba·tross**
alblum : **al·bum**
al·bum
Al·bu·quer·que
Albuquirque : **Al·bu·quer·que**
alcahol : **al·co·hol**
alcali : **al·ka·li**
alcemy : **al·che·my**
al·che·my
alchohol : **al·co·hol**
alcohal : **al·co·hol**
al·co·hol
alebasster : **al·a·bas·ter**
alebaster : **al·a·bas·ter**
alebi : **al·i·bi**
aledge : **al·lege**
alegation : **al·le·ga·tion**
alege : **al·lege**
Aleghenies : **Al·le·ghe·nies**
alegiance : **al·le·giance**
alegory : **al·le·go·ry**
alegro : **al·le·gro**
alein : **alien**
alergy : **al·ler·gy**
aleron : **ai·ler·on**
aleus : **ali·as**
Aleu·tians
aleviate : **al·le·vi·ate**
alfabet : al·**pha·bet**
al·fal·fa
alfallfa : **al·fal·fa**
alfalpha : **al·fal·fa**
al·ga (*sing.*); **al·gae** (*plur.*)

algabra : **al·ge·bra**
al·gae (*plur.*); **al·ga** (*sing.*)
algaebra : **al·ge·bra**
al·ge·bra
algibra : **al·ge·bra**
aliance : **al·li·ance**
alias
Alibama : **Al·a·ba·ma**
al·i·bi
aliby : **al·i·bi**
alien
aliess : **alias**
aligator : **al·li·ga·tor**
align *or* **aline**
alimmony : **al·i·mo·ny**
alimoney : **al·i·mo·ny**
al·i·mo·ny
aline *or* **align**
aliteration : **al·lit·er·a·tion**
alitteration : **al·lit·er·a·tion**
alkahol : **al·co·hol**
al·ka·li
alkalie : **al·ka·li**
alkeli : **al·ka·li**
alkemy : **al·che·my**
alkohol : **al·co·hol**
Allabama : **Al·a·ba·ma**
allabaster : **al·a·bas·ter**
allacate : **al·lo·cate**
allacrity : **alac·ri·ty**
allagation : **al·le·ga·tion**
allagator : **al·li·ga·tor**
Allaghenies : **Al·le·ghe·nies**
allagorry : **al·le·go·ry**
allagory : **al·le·go·ry**
allagro : **al·le·gro**
allamony : **al·i·mo·ny**
Allaska : **Alas·ka**
al·lay
allaygro : **al·le·gro**
Allbania : **Al·ba·ni·a**
allbatross : **al·ba·tross**

allbeit : **al·be·it**
allbino : **al·bi·no**
allbum : **al·bum**
Allbuquerque : **Al·bu·quer·que**
allchemy : **al·che·my**
allcohol : **al·co·hol**
alleaviate : **al·le·vi·ate**
alledge : **al·lege**
alledgedly : **al·leg·ed·ly**
allegance : **al·le·giance**
al·le·ga·tion
allegator : **al·li·ga·tor**
al·lege
allegence : **al·le·giance**
Al·le·ghe·nies
al·le·giance
allegorey : **al·le·go·ry**
allegorry : **al·le·go·ry**
al·le·go·ry
al·le·gro
allegroe : **al·le·gro**
alleiviate : **al·le·vi·ate**
allergie : **al·ler·gy**
al·ler·gy
allerjy : **al·ler·gy**
alleron : **ai·ler·on**
Alleutians : **Aleu·tians**
al·le·vi·ate
al·ley (road); **al·ly** (friend)
allfalfa : **al·fal·fa**
allgebra : **al·ge·bra**
al·li·ance
allias : **alias**
allibi : **al·i·bi**
allience : **al·li·ance**
alligater : **al·li·ga·tor**
alligation : **al·le·ga·tion**
al·li·ga·tor
alligattor : **al·li·ga·tor**
Allighenies : **Al·le·ghe·nies**
allimony : **al·i·mo·ny**
allirgy : **al·ler·gy**

al·lit·er·a·tion
alliterration : **al·lit·er·a·tion**
allitiration : **al·lit·er·a·tion**
allitteration : **al·lit·er·a·tion**
allkali : **al·ka·li**
allmanac : **al·ma·nac**
allmighty : **al·mighty**
allmond : **al·mond**
allmost : **al·most**
al·lo·cate
alloha : **alo·ha**
al·lot (to assign a portion) **a
  lot** (many)
al·lot·ment
al·lot·ted
al·low
al·low·able
al·low·ance
allowence : **al·low·ance**
allowible : **al·low·able**
allpaca : **al·pa·ca**
allphabet : **al·pha·bet**
all ready or **already**
allready : **all ready** or **al·ready**
all right
alltercation : **al·ter·ca·tion**
allthough : **al·though**
alltimeter : **al·tim·e·ter**
allto : **al·to**
all to·geth·er (all in one place);
  al·to·geth·er (totally, wholly)
alltruism : **al·tru·ism**
al·lude (to refer); **e·lude** (to
  escape)
alluminum : **alu·min·um**
allurgy : **al·ler·gy**
al·lu·sion (reference); **elu·sion**
  (evasion); **il·lu·sion** (false
  idea or image)
al·lu·sive (making references);
  elu·sive (avoiding); **il·lu·sive**
  (deceptive)

allways : **al·ways**
al·ly (friend); **al·ley** (road)
al·ma·nac
almanack : **al·ma·nac**
almenace : **al·ma·nac**
almend : **al·mond**
al·mighty
alminac : **al·ma·nac**
almity : **al·mighty**
al·mond
al·most
almund : **al·mond**
alocate : **al·lo·cate**
alo·ha
aloominum : **alu·min·um**
a lot (many); **al·lot** (to assign a portion)
alot : **al·lot** (to assign a portion) or **a lot** (many)
alotment : **al·lot·ment**
alottment : **al·lot·ment**
aloud
alow : **al·low**
alowable : **al·low·able**
alowd : **aloud**
alowha : **alo·ha**
al·pa·ca
alpacka : **al·pa·ca**
al·pha·bet
alphalfa : **al·fal·fa**
alphebet : **al·pha·bet**
alphibet : **al·pha·bet**
al·ready or **all ready**
alright : **all right**
al·tar (table used in worship); **al·ter** (to change)
altarcation : **al·ter·ca·tion**
al·ter (to change); **al·tar** (table used in worship)
al·ter·ca·tion
alterkation : **al·ter·ca·tion**
alternater : **al·ter·na·tor**

al·ter·na·tor
altho : **al·though**
al·though
al·tim·e·ter
altimiter : **al·tim·e·ter**
al·to
altoes : **al·tos**
al·to·geth·er (totally); **all to·geth·er** (all in one place)
al·tos
altrueism : **al·tru·ism**
altruesm : al·tru·ism
al·tru·ism
alude : **al·lude** (to refer) or **elude** (to escape)
Aluetians : **Aleu·tians**
alumanum : **alu·min·um**
alumenem : **alu·min·um**
alumenum : **alu·min·um**
alu·min·um
alusion : **al·lu·sion** (reference) or **elu·sion** (evasion) or **il·lu·sion** (false idea or image)
alusive : **al·lu·sive** (making references) or **elu·sive** (avoiding) or **il·lu·sive** (deceptive)
al·ways
amal·gam
amalgem : **amal·gam**
amallgam : **amal·gam**
amarous : **amor·ous**
amass
am·a·teur
amathist : **ame·thyst**
amatoor : **am·a·teur**
amatuer : **am·a·teur**
amature : **am·a·teur**
amaze·ment
amazemint : **amaze·ment**
amazment : **amaze·ment**

ambaguity : **am·bi·gu·i·ty**
ambasador : **am·bas·sa·dor**
ambassader : **am·bas·sa·dor**
am·bas·sa·dor
ambassator : **am·bas·sa·dor**
ambedextrous : **am·bi·dex·trous**
ambeguity : **am·bi·gu·i·ty**
ambent : **am·bi·ent**
ambersand : **am·per·sand**
ambiant : **am·bi·ent**
ambideckstrous :
   am·bi·dex·trous
ambidexterous :
   am·bi·dex·trous
am·bi·dex·trous
ambidextrus : **am·bi·dex·trous**
am·bi·ent
ambigooity : **am·bi·gu·i·ty**
ambiguety : **am·bi·gu·i·ty**
am·bi·gu·i·ty
ambint : **am·bi·ent**
ambivalant : **am·biv·a·lent**
am·biv·a·lent
ambivelent : **am·biv·a·lent**
ambivilent : **am·biv·a·lent**
ambroasia : **am·bro·sia**
ambrosa : **am·bro·sia**
ambrosha : **am·bro·sia**
am·bro·sia
am·bu·lance
ambulence : **am·bu·lance**
ambyent : **am·bi·ent**
ameable : **ami·a·ble**
ameago : **ami·go**
amealiorate : **ame·lio·rate**
ameanable : **ame·na·ble**
ameba : **amoe·ba**
ameeba : **amoe·ba**
ameeliorate : **ame·lio·rate**
amego : **ami·go**
ameleorate : **ame·lio·rate**
ameliarate : **ame·lio·rate**

amelierate : **ame·lio·rate**
ameliorait : **ame·lio·rate**
ame·lio·rate
ame·na·ble
amenaty : **amen·i·ty**
amend (to change or add to);
   emend (to correct)
amend·ment
ameneble : **ame·na·ble**
amenety : **amen·i·ty**
amenible : **ame·na·ble**
ame·ni·ty
amennable : **ame·na·ble**
ameoba : **amoe·ba**
amerous : **amor·ous**
ameteur : **am·a·teur**
amethist : **ame·thyst**
ame·thyst
amfibian : **am·phib·ian**
amfitheater : **am·phi·the·a·ter**
amiabal : **ami·a·ble**
amiabel : **ami·a·ble**
ami·a·ble
amicabal : **am·i·ca·ble**
am·i·ca·ble
amiceble : **am·i·ca·ble**
amicible : **am·i·ca·ble**
amickable : **am·i·ca·ble**
amieble : **ami·a·ble**
amiggo : **ami·go**
ami·go
aminable : **ame·na·ble**
Amish
amithyst : **ame·thyst**
ammass : **amass**
ammeba : **amoe·ba**
ammendment : **amend·ment**
ammenity : **amen·i·ty**
ammethyst : **ame·thyst**
ammigo : **ami·go**
Ammish : **Amish**
ammliorate : **ame·lio·rate**

ammonea : **am·mo·nia**
am·mo·nia
ammonition : **am·mu·ni·tion**
ammonnia : **am·mo·nia**
ammonya : **am·mo·nia**
ammoral : **amor·al**
ammorphus : **amor·phous**
ammortize : **amor·tize**
ammount : **amount**
ammulet : **amu·let**
ammulit : **amu·let**
ammunishin : **am·mu·ni·tion**
am·mu·ni·tion
ammusement : **amuse·ment**
amnasty : **am·nes·ty**
amneasia : **am·ne·sia**
amneesia : **am·ne·sia**
amnesha : **am·ne·sia**
am·ne·sia
amnessty : **am·nes·ty**
amnestie : **am·nes·ty**
am·nes·ty
amoarous : **am·o·rous**
amoartize : **amor·tize**
amoe·ba
among
amonia : **am·mon·ia**
amonya : **am·mo·nia**
amoorous : **amor·ous**
amor·al
amorale : **amor·al**
amorfous : **amor·phous**
amorfus : **amor·phous**
amorish : **am·o·rous**
am·o·rous
amorphis : **amor·phous**
amor·phous
amortise (*Brit.*) : **amor·tize**
amor·tize
amorus : **am·o·rous**
amoung : **among**
amount

amourous : **am·o·rous**
amourphous : **amor·phous**
amourtize : **amor·tize**
ampasand : **am·per·sand**
ampeer : **am·pere**
ampeir : **am·pere**
ampeire : **am·pere**
amper : **am·pere**
am·pere
am·per·sand
ampesand : **am·per·sand**
ampezand : **am·per·sand**
amphatheater :
   am·phi·the·a·ter
amphebian : **am·phib·i·an**
amphetheater :
   am·phi·the·a·ter
am·phib·i·an
amphibien : **am·phib·i·an**
amphibyan : **am·phib·i·an**
am·phi·the·a·ter
amphitheatre (*Brit.*) :
   am·phi·the·a·ter
amphithiater : **am·phi·the·a·ter**
amplefy : **am·pli·fy**
am·pli·fy
am·pu·tee
amputiy : **am·pu·tee**
amputy : **am·pu·tee**
am·u·let
amulette : **am·u·let**
amund : **al·mond**
amunition : **am·mu·ni·tion**
amuse·ment
amusemint : **amuse·ment**
amuzement : **amuse·ment**
amyable : **ami·a·ble**
amythist : **ame·thyst**
anach·ro·nism
anachronnism : **anach·ro·nism**
anachronysm : **anach·ro·nism**
anackronism : **anach·ro·nism**

anacronism : **anach·ro·nism**
anagesic : **an·al·ge·sic**
anagraham : **ana·gram**
ana·gram
anagramm : **ana·gram**
analegy : **anal·o·gy**
analgeasic : **an·al·ge·sic**
analgeesic : **an·al·ge·sic**
analgeezic : **an·al·ge·sic**
an·al·ge·sic
analgesick : **an·al·ge·sic**
analgezic : **an·al·ge·sic**
analigy : **anal·o·gy**
analisees : **anal·y·ses**
analises : **anal·y·ses**
analisis : **anal·y·sis**
analisiss : **anal·y·sis**
analisys : **anal·y·sis**
analitic : **an·a·lyt·ic**
analitick : **an·a·lyt·ic**
analityc : **an·a·lyt·ic**
analize : **an·a·lyze**
analjesic : **an·al·ge·sic**
anallogy : **anal·o·gy**
anallyses : **anal·y·ses**
anallysis : **anal·y·sis**
anallytic : **an·a·lyt·ic**
analoge : **anal·o·gy**
analogee : **anal·o·gy**
analoggy : **anal·o·gy**
analogie : **anal·o·gy**
anal·o·gy
analoje : **anal·o·gy**
analyse (*Brit.*) : **an·a·lyze**
anal·y·ses (*plur.*); **anal·y·sis** (*sing.*)
anal·y·sis (*sing.*); **anal·y·ses** (*plur.*)
an·a·lyt·ic
an·a·lyze
anamosity : **an·i·mos·i·ty**
ananymity : **an·o·nym·i·ty**

Anapolis : **An·nap·o·lis**
anarchie : **an·ar·chy**
an·ar·chy
anarcky : **an·ar·chy**
anasthesia : **an·es·the·sia**
anatamy : **anat·o·my**
anatome : **anat·o·my**
anatomie : **anat·o·my**
anat·o·my
ancer : **an·chor**
ancerage : **an·chor·age**
ancesstor : **an·ces·tor**
ancester : **an·ces·tor**
ancesteral : **an·ces·tral**
ancestir : **an·ces·tor**
an·ces·tor
ancestoral : **an·ces·tral**
an·ces·tral
ancestrall : **an·ces·tral**
ancestree : **an·ces·try**
ancestrel : **an·ces·tral**
ancestrie : **an·ces·try**
an·ces·try
anchant : **an·cient**
anchar : **an·chor**
ancharage : **an·chor·age**
anchent : **an·cient**
ancher : **an·chor**
ancherage : **an·chor·age**
anchint : **an·cient**
an·chor
an·chor·age
anchoredge : **an·chor·age**
anchorege : **an·chor·age**
anchorige : **an·chor·age**
an·cient
anciety : **an·xi·ety**
ancilary : **an·cil·lary**
an·cil·lary
ancillery : **an·cil·lary**
ancilliary : **an·cil·lary**
ancilliery : **an·cil·lary**

anckor : **an·chor**
anckorage : **an·chor·age**
andiran : **and·iron**
andiren : **and·iron**
andirn : **and·iron**
and·iron
anecdoat : **an·ec·dote**
an·ec·dote (story); **an·ti·dote**
  (remedy)
aneckdote : **an·ec·dote**
aneemia : **ane·mia**
anegesic : **an·al·ge·sic**
anegram : **ana·gram**
anekdote : **an·ec·dote**
anelgesic : **an·al·ge·sic**
anemea : **ane·mia**
ane·mia
anem·o·ne
anemoney : **anem·o·ne**
anemonne : **anem·o·ne**
anemony : **anem·o·ne**
anemosity : **an·i·mos·i·ty**
an·es·the·sia
anesthessia : **an·es·the·sia**
anesthisia : **an·es·the·sia**
anesthsya : **an·es·the·sia**
an·gel (spiritual being); **an·gle**
  (figure in geometry)
an·gel·ic
angelick : **an·gel·ic**
angellic : **an·gel·ic**
an·gle (figure in geometry);
  an·gel (spiritual being)
An·go·ra
Angorra : **An·go·ra**
angxiety : **an·xi·ety**
anhemia : **ane·mia**
anihilate : **an·ni·hi·late**
an·i·mal
animall : **an·i·mal**
animel : **an·i·mal**
animocity : **an·i·mos·i·ty**

animone : **anem·o·ne**
animony : **anem·o·ne**
animositty : **an·i·mos·i·ty**
an·i·mos·i·ty
animossity : **an·i·mos·i·ty**
animul : **an·i·mal**
aniversary : **an·ni·ver·sa·ry**
aniversery : **an·ni·ver·sa·ry**
anjelic : **an·gel·ic**
ankel : **an·kle**
anker : **an·chor**
ankerage : **an·chor·age**
an·kle
annachronism : **anach·ro·nism**
annagram : **ana·gram**
annalogy : **anal·o·gy**
annalyses : **anal·y·ses**
annalysis : **anal·y·sis**
annalytic : **an·a·lyt·ic**
annalyze : **an·a·lyze**
An·nap·o·lis
annarchy : **an·ar·chy**
annatation : **an·no·ta·tion**
annatomy : **anat·o·my**
annaversary : **an·ni·ver·sa·ry**
annaversery : **an·ni·ver·sa·ry**
annesthesia : **an·es·the·sia**
anneversary : **an·ni·ver·sa·ry**
annihalate : **an·ni·hi·late**
an·ni·hi·late
annilate : **an·ni·hi·late**
an·ni·ver·sa·ry
anniversery : **an·ni·ver·sa·ry**
annivursery : **an·ni·ver·sa·ry**
annoint : **anoint**
annomaly : **anom·a·ly**
an·no·ta·tion
announser : **an·nounc·er**
an·noy·ance
annoyence : **an·noy·ance**
an·nu·al
anoint

anomale : **anom•a•ly**
anomally : **anom•a•ly**
anom•a•ly
anommaly : **anom•a•ly**
anonimity : **an•o•nym•i•ty**
anonimous : **anon•y•mous**
an•o•nym•i•ty
anon•y•mous
anonymus : **anon•y•mous**
anotation : **an•no•ta•tion**
anounce : **an•nounce**
anouncer : **an•nounc•er**
anounse : **an•nounce**
anoyance : **an•noy•ance**
anser : **an•swer**
ansestor : **an•ces•tor**
ansestral : **an•ces•tral**
ansestry : **an•ces•try**
anshent : **an•cient**
ansiety : **an•xi•ety**
ansilary : **an•cil•lary**
ansillary : **an•cil•lary**
ansor : **an•swer**
an•swer
ant (insect); **aunt** (female relative)
antaganist : **an•tag•o•nist**
antaggonist : **an•tag•o•nist**
antaginist : **an•tag•o•nist**
an•tag•o•nist
antamology : **en•to•mol•o•gy** (study of insects) *or* **et•y•mol•o•gy** (study of words)
ant•arc•tic
antartic : **ant•arc•tic**
antecedant : **an•te•ced•ent**
an•te•ced•ent
anteceedent : **an•te•ced•ent**
antemology : **en•to•mol•o•gy** (study of insects) *or*

et•y•mol•o•gy (study of words)
antena : **an•ten•na**
an•ten•na
antesedent : **an•te•ced•ent**
antham : **an•them**
an•them
anthim : **an•them**
antholagy : **an•thol•o•gy**
anthollogy : **an•thol•o•gy**
an•thol•o•gy
anthum : **an•them**
antic (clownish); **an•tique** (old)
anticedent : **an•te•ced•ent**
anticepate : **an•ti•ci•pate**
anticipait : **an•ti•ci•pate**
an•ti•ci•pate
an•ti•dote (remedy); **an•ec•dote** (story)
an•tique (old); **an•tic** (clownish)
antisipate : **an•ti•ci•pate**
antissipate : **an•ti•ci•pate**
antomology : **en•to•mol•o•gy** (study of insects) *or* **et•y•mol•o•gy** (study of words)
anual : **an•nu•al**
anxiaty : **an•xi•ety**
an•xi•ety
anxioty : **an•xi•ety**
any•body (any person); **any body** (any body at all)
any•one (any person); **any one** (any item)
Apache
Apachee : **Apache**
apachure : **ap•er•ture**
Apalachian : **Ap•pa•la•chian**
apalogize : **apol•o•gize**
Apamattox : **Ap•po•mat•tox**
aparatus : **ap•pa•ra•tus**
aparel : **ap•par•el**

aparent : **ap·par·ent**
aparint : **ap·par·ent**
apart
aparteid : **apart·heid**
apart·heid
aparthide : **apart·heid**
aparthied : **apart·heid**
apartide : **apart·heid**
apastasy : **apos·ta·sy**
Apatche : **Apache**
ap·a·thet·ic
apathetick : **ap·a·thet·ic**
apa·thy
apatite : **ap·pe·tite**
apature : **ap·er·ture**
apeace : **apiece**
apeal : **ap·peal**
apease : **ap·pease**
apeice : **apiece**
Apelachian : **Ap·pa·la·chian**
apendage : **ap·pend·age**
apendectomy :
    ap·pen·dec·to·my
apendege : **ap·pend·age**
apera : **op·era**
aperchure : **ap·er·ture**
ap·er·ture
apethetic : **ap·a·thet·ic**
apethy : **apa·thy**
apetite : **ap·pe·tite**
apeture : **ap·er·ture**
aphasea : **apha·sia**
aphasha : **apha·sia**
apha·sia
apherism : **aph·o·rism**
aphirism : **aph·o·rism**
aph·o·rism
apiece
apindectomy :
    ap·pen·dec·to·my
apithy : **apa·thy**
apitite : **ap·pe·tite**

aplaud : **ap·plaud**
apliance : **ap·pli·ance**
apocalips : **apoc·a·lypse**
apocalipse : **apoc·a·lypse**
apoc·a·lypse
apocelypse : **apoc·a·lypse**
apockalypse : **apoc·a·lypse**
apockriphal : **apoc·ry·phal**
apockryphal : **apoc·ry·phal**
apocrifal : **apoc·ry·phal**
apocriphal : **apoc·ry·phal**
apocryfal : **apoc·ry·phal**
apoc·ry·phal
apointe : **ap·poin·tee**
apolagise : **apol·o·gize**
apolagize : **apol·o·gize**
apolegize : **apol·o·gize**
apologise (*Brit.*) : **apol·o·gize**
apol·o·gize
apolojize : **apol·o·gize**
Apomattox : **Ap·po·mat·tox**
aposle : **apos·tle**
apossel : **apos·tle**
apossle : **apos·tle**
aposstasy : **apos·ta·sy**
aposstle : **apos·tle**
apostacy : **apos·ta·sy**
apos·ta·sy
aposticy : **apos·ta·sy**
apostisy : **apos·ta·sy**
apos·tle
apos·tro·phe
appairel : **ap·par·el**
appairent : **ap·par·ent**
Appalachan : **Ap·pa·la·chian**
Appalachen : **Ap·pa·la·chian**
Ap·pa·la·chian
Appalachin : **Ap·pa·la·chian**
Appamattox : **Ap·po·mattox**
apparal : **ap·par·el**
apparant : **ap·par·ent**
apparatis : **ap·pa·ra·tus**

ap·pa·ra·tus
ap·par·el
ap·par·ent
apparil : **ap·par·el**
appart : **apart**
appartheid : **apart·heid**
appathetic : **ap·a·thet·ic**
appatite : **ap·pe·tite**
appatizing : **ap·pe·tiz·ing**
appeace : **ap·pease**
ap·peal
ap·pear·ance
appearanse : **ap·pear·ance**
appearant : **ap·par·ent**
appearence : **ap·pear·ance**
appearense : **ap·pear·ance**
ap·pease
appeerance : **ap·pear·ance**
appeil : **ap·peal**
appeirance : **ap·pear·ance**
appele : **ap·peal**
ap·pend·age
appendecktomy :
  ap·pen·dec·to·my
appendectome :
  ap·pen·dec·to·my
ap·pen·dec·to·my
appendege : **ap·pend·age**
appendidge : **ap·pend·age**
appendige : **ap·pend·age**
apperture : **ap·er·ture**
appetight : **ap·pe·tite**
appetising (*Brit*.) : **ap·pe·tiz·ing**
ap·pe·tite
ap·pe·tiz·ing
appettite : **ap·pe·tite**
appettizing : **ap·pe·tiz·ing**
appiece : **apiece**
appiese : **ap·pease**
appindage : **ap·pend·age**
appindectomie :
  ap·pen·dec·to·my

appindige : **ap·pend·age**
appitite : **ap·pe·tite**
appitizing : **ap·pe·tiz·ing**
ap·plaud
applawd : **ap·plaud**
ap·pli·ance
applianse : **ap·pli·ance**
applicabel : **ap·pli·ca·ble**
ap·pli·ca·ble
applicabul : **ap·pli·ca·ble**
appliceble : **ap·pli·ca·ble**
applicible : **ap·pli·ca·ble**
applickable : **ap·pli·ca·ble**
applience : **ap·pli·ance**
appliense : **ap·pli·ance**
applod : **ap·plaud**
applodd : **ap·plaud**
applyance : **ap·pli·ance**
appocryphal : **apoc·ry·phal**
ap·point·ee
appointie : **ap·poin·tee**
appointy : **ap·poin·tee**
appologize : **apol·o·gize**
Appomatox : **Ap·po·mat·tox**
Ap·po·mat·tox
appostasy : **apos·ta·sy**
appostrophe : **apos·tro·phe**
ap·praise (to assess); **ap·prise**
  (to inform); **ap·prize** (to
  value)
appreceate : **ap·pre·ci·ate**
ap·pre·ci·ate
ap·pre·ci·a·tion
appreeciate : **ap·pre·ci·ate**
apprentace : **ap·pren·tice**
apprentece : **ap·pren·tice**
ap·pren·tice
apprentiss : **ap·pren·tice**
appreshiate : **ap·pre·ci·ate**
appresiate : **ap·pre·ci·ate**
appricot : **apri·cot**
Appril : **April**

apprintice : **ap·pren·tice**
apprintiss : **ap·pren·tice**
ap·prise (to inform); **ap·praise** (to assess); **ap·prize** (to value)
ap·prize (to value); **ap·praise** (to assess); **ap·prise** (to inform)
ap·proach·able
approachibal : **ap·proach·able**
approachible : **ap·proach·able**
approachibul : **ap·proach·able**
approapriate : **ap·pro·pri·ate**
approchabal : **ap·proach·able**
approchable : **ap·proach·able**
approoval : **ap·prov·al**
appropiate : **ap·pro·pri·ate**
appropreate : **ap·pro·pri·ate**
appropreit : **ap·pro·pri·ate**
ap·pro·pri·ate
ap·prov·al
approvel : **ap·prov·al**
approvil : **ap·prov·al**
approxamate : **ap·prox·i·mate**
approxemate : **ap·prox·i·mate**
approximant : **ap·prox·i·mate**
approximat : **ap·prox·i·mate**
ap·prox·i·mate
approximent : **ap·prox·i·mate**
approximet : **ap·prox·i·mate**
apracot : **apri·cot**
apraise : **ap·praise** (to assess) *or* **ap·prise** (to inform) *or* **ap·prize** (to value)
apreciate : **ap·pre·ci·ate**
aprecot : **apri·cot**
aprentice : **ap·pren·tice**
apri·cot
apricott : **apri·cot**
April
Aprill : **April**

aprise : **ap·prise** (to inform) *or* **ap·prize** (to value)
aproachable : **ap·proach·able**
aprochable : **ap·proach·able**
aprooval : **ap·prov·al**
apropriate : **ap·pro·pri·ate**
aproval : **ap·prov·al**
aproxamate : **ap·prox·i·mate**
aproximate : **ap·prox·i·mate**
apsorb : **ab·sorb**
aptatude : **ap·ti·tude**
aptetude : **ap·ti·tude**
ap·ti·tude
aptutood : **ap·ti·tude**
apurture : **ap·er·ture**
aquaduct : **aq·ue·duct**
aquariam : **aquar·i·um**
aquariem : **aquar·i·um**
aquar·i·um
aquarrium : **aquar·i·um**
aqua·tic
aqueduck : **aq·ue·duct**
aq·ue·duct
aquerium : **aquar·i·um**
aquiduct : **aq·ue·duct**
aquiesce : **ac·qui·esce**
aquire : **ac·quire**
aquisition : **ac·qui·si·tion**
aquit : **ac·quit**
aquittel : **ac·quit·tal**
arabesk : **ar·a·besque**
ar·a·besque
araign : **ar·raign**
arange : **ar·range**
arangement : **ar·range·ment**
arber : **ar·bor**
ar·bor
ar·bo·re·al
arborial : **ar·bo·re·al**
arborreal : **ar·bo·re·al**
arborrial : **ar·bo·re·al**

arc (part of a circle); **ark** (boat or box)

arcaic : **ar·cha·ic**

arcangel : **arch·an·gel**

Arcansas : **Ar·kan·sas**

arceology : **ar·chae·ol·o·gy**

ar·chae·ol·o·gy or **ar·che·ol·o·gy**

ar·cha·ic

archake : **ar·cha·ic**

arch·an·gel

archangil : **arch·an·gel**

archangle : **arch·an·gel**

archanjel : **arch·an·gel**

archaque : **ar·cha·ic**

archatect : **ar·chi·tect**

archealogy : **ar·chae·ol·o·gy**

archeologgy : **ar·chae·ol·o·gy**

ar·che·ol·o·gy or **ar·chae·ol·o·gy**

archepelago : **ar·chi·pel·a·go**

archetect : **ar·chi·tect**

archiology : **ar·chae·ol·o·gy**

ar·chi·pel·a·go

archipelego : **ar·chi·pel·a·go**

archipellago : **ar·chi·pel·a·go**

ar·chi·tect

arcipelago : **ar·chi·pel·a·go**

arcitect : **ar·chi·tect**

arckaic : **ar·cha·ic**

arc·tic

arder : **ar·dor**

ar·dor

areal : **ae·ri·al**

areate : **aer·ate**

arebesk : **ar·a·besque**

arebesque : **ar·a·besque**

are·na

arenna : **are·na**

arest : **ar·rest**

arestocracy : **ar·is·toc·ra·cy**

Arezona : **Ar·i·zo·na**

argasy : **ar·go·sy**

argesy : **ar·go·sy**

argossy : **ar·go·sy**

ar·go·sy

arguement : **ar·gu·ment**

ar·gu·ment

arial : **ae·ri·al**

arid

arie : **ae·rie** (nest) or **airy** (relating to air)

arina : **are·na**

arise

aristockracy : **ar·is·toc·ra·cy**

ar·is·toc·ra·cy

aristocrasy : **ar·is·toc·ra·cy**

aristocricy : **ar·is·toc·ra·cy**

aristocrisy : **ar·is·toc·ra·cy**

arithmatic : **arith·me·tic**

arith·me·tic

arival : **ar·riv·al**

arive : **ar·rive**

Ar·i·zo·na

ark (boat or box); **arc** (part of a circle)

arkaic : **ar·cha·ic**

Arkansah : **Ar·kan·sas**

Ar·kan·sas

Arkansaw : **Ar·kan·sas**

arkeology : **ar·chae·ol·o·gy**

arkitect : **ar·chi·tect**

ar·ma·da

armadda : **ar·ma·da**

ar·ma·dil·lo

armadilo : **ar·ma·dil·lo**

armastice : **ar·mi·stice**

Armeania : **Ar·me·nia**

armedillo : **ar·ma·dil·lo**

Armenea : **Ar·me·nia**

Ar·me·nia

armer : **ar·mor**

armestice : **ar·mi·stice**

armidillo : **ar·ma·dil·lo**

Arminia : **Ar·me·nia**
ar·mi·stice
armistise : **ar·mi·stice**
armistiss : **ar·mi·stice**
ar·mor
armorda : **ar·ma·da**
armordillo : **ar·ma·dil·lo**
armour (*Brit.*) : **ar·mor**
arodinamic : **aero·dy·nam·ic**
arodynamic : **aero·dy·nam·ic**
arogant : **ar·ro·gant**
aro·ma
aronautic : **aero·nau·tic**
arose
arosol : **aero·sol**
around
arouse
aroyo : **ar·royo**
arragant : **ar·ro·gant**
arraighn : **ar·raign**
ar·raign
arrain : **ar·raign**
arraingement : **ar·range·ment**
ar·range
ar·range·ment
arrangemint : **ar·range·ment**
arrangment : **ar·range·ment**
arrena : **are·na**
ar·rest
arrid : **arid**
arrie : **ae·rie** (nest) *or* **airy**
  (relating to air)
arrina : **are·na**
arrise : **arise**
ar·ri·val
ar·rive
arrivel : **ar·riv·al**
arrivil : **ar·riv·al**
arrivle : **ar·riv·al**
arrodinamic : **aero·dy·nam·ic**
arrodynamic : **aero·dy·nam·ic**
ar·ro·gant

arrogent : **ar·ro·gant**
arroio : **ar·royo**
arroma : **aro·ma**
arronautic : **aero·nau·tic**
arrose : **arose**
arrosol : **aero·sol**
arround : **around**
arrouse : **arouse**
ar·royo
arsen : **ar·son**
ar·se·nal
arsenel : **ar·se·nal**
arsenle : **ar·se·nal**
arsin : **ar·son**
arsinal : **ar·se·nal**
arsinel : **ar·se·nal**
ar·son
artachoke : **ar·ti·choke**
artacle : **ar·ti·cle**
artafice : **ar·ti·fice**
artafical : **ar·ti·fi·cial**
artechoke : **ar·ti·choke**
artefice : **ar·ti·fice**
arteficial : **ar·ti·fi·cial**
arterry : **ar·tery**
ar·tery
artharitis : **ar·thri·tis**
arthiritis : **ar·thri·tis**
arthritas : **ar·thri·tis**
ar·thri·tis
arthritus : **ar·thri·tis**
Ar·thur (name); **au·thor**
  (writer)
artic : **arc·tic**
artical : **ar·ti·cle**
articel : **ar·ti·cle**
artichoak : **ar·ti·choke**
ar·ti·choke
ar·ti·cle
ar·ti·fice
ar·ti·fi·cial
artifise : **ar·ti·fice**

artifishal : **ar·ti·fi·cial**
artifisial : **ar·ti·fi·cial**
artifrice : **ar·ti·fice**
artifricial : **ar·ti·fi·cial**
artilary : **ar·til·lery**
artilery : **ar·til·lery**
artillarry : **ar·til·lery**
artillary : **ar·til·lery**
ar·til·lery
artiry : **ar·tery**
ar·tis·ti·cal·ly
artisticly : **ar·tis·ti·cal·ly**
artory : **ar·tery**
asail : **as·sail**
asailant : **as·sail·ant**
asassin : **as·sas·sin**
asault : **as·sault**
as·cend
as·cen·sion
as·cent (act of going upward);
   as·sent (to agree; agreement)
ascerbic : **acer·bic**
ascert : **as·sert**
as·cer·tain
ascertane : **as·cer·tain**
as·cet·ic
asemble : **as·sem·ble**
asend : **as·cend**
aserbic : **acer·bic**
asert : **as·sert**
asertain : **as·cer·tain**
asess : **as·sess**
asessor : **as·ses·sor**
asetic : **as·cet·ic**
asfalt : **as·phalt**
asfault : **as·phalt**
asfixiate : **as·phyx·i·ate**
ashure : **azure**
asign : **as·sign**
asilim : **asy·lum**
asilum : **asy·lum**
asimilate : **as·sim·i·late**

asist : **as·sist**
asistance : **as·sis·tance**
asistant : **as·sis·tant**
asma : **asth·ma**
asociate : **as·so·ciate**
asparagis : **as·par·a·gus**
as·par·a·gus
asparegus : **as·par·a·gus**
asperagus : **as·par·a·gus**
asperin : **as·pi·rin**
asphallt : **as·phalt**
as·phalt
asphault : **as·phalt**
asphixeate : **as·phyx·i·ate**
asphixiate : **as·phyx·i·ate**
asphyxeate : **as·phyx·i·ate**
as·phyx·i·ate
aspicious : **aus·pi·cious**
aspiren : **as·pi·rin**
as·pi·rin
aspren : **as·pi·rin**
asprin : **as·pi·rin**
as·sail
as·sail·ant
assailent : **as·sail·ant**
assalant : **as·sail·ant**
assalent : **as·sail·ant**
assalt : **as·sault**
assasin : **as·sas·sin**
as·sas·sin
as·sas·sin·a·tion
as·sault
as·sem·ble
assend : **as·cend**
as·sent (to agree; agreement);
   as·cent (act of going upward)
as·sert
as·sess
assesser : **as·ses·sor**
assession : **ac·ces·sion**
as·sess·ment
as·ses·sor

as·sign
assimalate : **as·sim·i·late**
as·sim·i·late
assimmilate : **as·sim·i·late**
assine : **as·sign**
as·sist
as·sis·tance
as·sis·tant
assistence : **as·sis·tance**
assistense : **as·sis·tance**
assistent : **as·sis·tant**
assoceate : **as·so·ciate**
as·so·ciate
assosheate : **as·so·ciate**
assoshiate : **as·so·ciate**
asspirin : **as·pi·rin**
assteroid : **as·ter·oid**
assthma : **asth·ma**
asstrology : **as·trol·o·gy**
asstronomer : **as·tron·o·mer**
as·sume
as·sump·tion
assumtion : **as·sump·tion**
as·sur·ance
assurence : **as·sur·ance**
assylum : **asy·lum**
astaroid : **as·ter·oid**
astere : **aus·tere**
asteresk : **as·ter·isk**
as·ter·isk
asterix : **as·ter·isk**
as·ter·oid
asthema : **asth·ma**
asthetic : **aes·thet·ic**
asth·ma
Astralia : **Aus·tral·ia**
astralogy : **as·trol·o·gy**
astranaut : **as·tro·naut**
astranomer : **as·tron·o·mer**
Astria : **Aus·tria**
astrisk : **as·ter·isk**
astroid : **as·ter·oid**

astroknot : **as·tro·naut**
astrollogy : **as·trol·o·gy**
astrologgy : **as·trol·o·gy**
as·trol·o·gy
astronamer : **as·tron·o·mer**
as·tro·naut
astronemer : **as·tron·o·mer**
astronnomer : **as·tron·o·mer**
as·tron·o·mer
astronot : **as·tro·naut**
astronought : **as·tro·naut**
asume : **as·sume**
asumption : **as·sump·tion**
asurance : **as·sur·ance**
asylam : **asy·lum**
asylim : **asy·lum**
asy·lum
atainable : **at·tain·able**
atem : **at·om**
atemology : **en·to·mol·o·gy**
  (study of insects) or
  et·y·mol·o·gy (study of
  words)
atend : **at·tend**
athalete : **ath·lete**
athaletic : **ath·let·ic**
athelete : **ath·lete**
atheletic : **ath·let·ic**
athleet : **ath·lete**
ath·lete
ath·let·ic
athlettic : **ath·let·ic**
athority : **au·thor·i·ty**
atitude : **at·ti·tude**
atmasphere : **at·mo·sphere**
atmesphere : **at·mo·sphere**
atmosfere : **at·mo·sphere**
atmospere : **at·mo·sphere**
atmosphear : **at·mo·sphere**
atmospheer : **at·mo·sphere**
at·mo·sphere
at·om

atonomy : **au·ton·o·my**
atorney : **at·tor·ney**
atrocety : **atroc·i·ty**
atrochious : **atro·cious**
atro·cious
atrocitty : **atroc·i·ty**
atroc·i·ty
atrocius : **atro·cious**
atroshious : **atro·cious**
atrosity : **atroc·i·ty**
attainabal : **at·tain·able**
attainabel : **at·tain·able**
at·tain·able
attaineble : **at·tain·able**
attainible : **at·tain·able**
attanable : **at·tain·able**
attatude : **at·ti·tude**
at·tend
at·tend·ance
at·tend·ant
attendence : **at·tend·ance**
attendent : **at·tend·ant**
atterney : **at·tor·ney**
atterneys : **at·tor·neys**
atternies : **at·tor·neys**
attierney : **at·tor·ney**
at·ti·tude
attom : **at·om**
attornees : **at·tor·neys**
at·tor·ney
at·tor·neys
attornies : **at·tor·neys**
attorny : **at·tor·ney**
atymology : **en·to·mol·o·gy**
  (study of insects) *or*
  et·y·mol·o·gy (study of
  words)
auc·tion·eer
auctioneir : **auc·tion·eer**
auctionier : **auc·tion·eer**
audable : **au·di·ble**
audacety : **au·dac·i·ty**

au·da·cious
audacitty : **au·dac·i·ty**
au·dac·i·ty
audashious : **au·da·cious**
audasious : **au·da·cious**
audasity : **au·dac·i·ty**
audassity : **au·dac·i·ty**
audatious : **au·da·cious**
audiance : **au·di·ence**
aud·i·ble
au·di·ence
auditer : **au·di·tor**
au·di·tor
au·ger (drilling tool); **au·gur**
  (to predict)
au·gur (to predict); **au·ger**
  (drilling tool)
auktioneer : **auc·tion·eer**
aunt (female relative); **ant**
  (insect)
aurthor : **au·thor**
auspichious : **aus·pi·cious**
aus·pi·cious
auspicius : **aus·pi·cious**
auspisious : **aus·pi·cious**
auspitious : **aus·pi·cious**
Ausstralia : **Aus·tral·ia**
Ausstria : **Aus·tria**
austair : **aus·tere**
austare : **aus·tere**
austeer : **aus·tere**
austeir : **aus·tere**
aus·tere
austier : **aus·tere**
Aus·tral·ia (continent);
  Aus·tria (European nation)
Aus·tria (European nation);
  Aus·tral·ia (continent)
autharize : **au·thor·ize**
authenic : **au·then·tic**
au·then·tic
auther : **au·thor**

autherize : **au·thor·ize**
au·thor (writer); **Ar·thur**
  (name)
authoraty : **au·thor·i·ty**
authorety : **au·thor·i·ty**
authorise (*Brit.*) : **au·thor·ize**
authoritty : **au·thor·i·ty**
au·thor·i·ty
au·thor·ize
autioneer : **auc·tion·eer**
au·to·mat·i·cal·ly
automaticly : **au·to·mat·i·cal·ly**
automn : **au·tumn**
autonnomy : **au·ton·o·my**
autonome : **au·ton·o·my**
autonomie : **au·ton·o·my**
au·ton·o·my
autum : **au·tumn**
autumm : **au·tumn**
au·tumn
auxilary : **aux·il·ia·ry**
aux·il·ia·ry
auxilliary : **aux·il·ia·ry**
avacado : **av·o·ca·do**
availabal : **avail·able**
avail·able
availible : **avail·able**
avalable : **avail·able**
avalanch : **av·a·lanche**
av·a·lanche
avaleable : **avail·able**
avant-garde
avant-guard : **avant-garde**
avanue : **av·e·nue**
av·a·rice
avarise : **av·a·rice**
avariss : **av·a·rice**
avaunt-garde : **avant-garde**
aveator : **avi·a·tor**
avecado : **av·o·ca·do**
avelanche : **av·a·lanche**
avenoo : **av·e·nue**

aventurer : **ad·ven·tur·er**
av·e·nue
av·er·age
averedge : **av·er·age**
averege : **av·er·age**
averice : **av·a·rice**
averige : **av·er·age**
averise : **av·a·rice**
averse (disinclined); **ad·verse**
  (unfavorable)
avertise : **ad·ver·tise**
avertising : **ad·ver·tis·ing**
aviater : **avi·a·tor**
aviatir : **avi·a·tor**
avi·a·tor
avid
avilanche : **av·a·lanche**
avinue : **av·e·nue**
avirage : **av·er·age**
avocaddo : **av·o·ca·do**
av·o·ca·do
avoidabel : **avoid·able**
avoid·able
avoid·ance
avoidanse : **avoid·ance**
avoidence : **avoid·ance**
avoidense : **avoid·ance**
avoidible : **avoid·able**
avrage : **av·er·age**
avvid : **avid**
awaikening : **awak·en·ing**
awairness : **aware·ness**
await
awak·en·ing
awakining : **awak·en·ing**
awakning : **awak·en·ing**
aware·ness
awareniss : **aware·ness**
awarness : **aware·ness**
awate : **await**
awesom : **awe·some**
awe·some

awesume : **awe•some**

awsome : **awe•some**

axcel : **ax•le** (wheel shaft) *or* **ex•cel** (to be superior)

axel : **ax•le** (wheel shaft) *or* **ex•cel** (to be superior)

axelerate : **ac•cel•erate**

ax•le (wheel shaft); **ex•cel** (to be superior)

azailea : **aza•lea**

aza•lea

azalia : **aza•lea**

azhure : **azure**

azma : **asth•ma**

azthetic : **aes•thet•ic**

azthma : **asth•ma**

azure

B

Babalon : **Bab·y·lon**
babbies : **ba·bies**
babboon : **ba·boon**
babby : **ba·by**
Babbylon : **Bab·y·lon**
Babelon : **Bab·y·lon**
Babillon : **Bab·y·lon**
ba·boon
babtise : **bap·tize**
babtism : **bap·tism**
Babtist : **Bap·tist**
ba·by
Bab·y·lon
babys : **ba·bies**
bacalaureate : **bac·ca·lau·re·ate**
bacan : **ba·con**
bac·ca·lau·re·ate
baccalaureit : **bac·ca·lau·re·ate**
baccalauriate : **bac·ca·lau·re·ate**
baccaloreate : **bac·ca·lau·re·ate**
baccelaureate :
    bac·ca·lau·re·ate
bacchelor : **bach·el·or**
baccilli : **ba·cil·li**
baccilly : **ba·cil·li**
baccon : **ba·con**
baceball : **base·ball**
baceless : **base·less**
bacement : **base·ment**
bacen : **ba·con**
bachalor : **bach·e·lor**
bacheler : **bach·e·lor**
bachelir : **bach·e·lor**
bach·e·lor
bachelore : **bach·e·lor**
bachteria : **bac·te·ri·a**
bachterium : **bac·te·ri·um**
bacically : **ba·si·cal·ly**
bacili : **ba·cil·li**
bacilica : **ba·sil·i·ca**

ba·cil·li (*plur.*); **ba·cil·lus** (*sing.*)
ba·cil·lus (*sing.*); **ba·cil·li** (*plur.*)
bacilus : **ba·cil·lus**
bacin : **ba·sin**
bacinet : **bas·si·net**
bacis : **ba·sis**
backalaureate :
    bac·ca·lau·re·ate
backen : **ba·con**
backfeild : **back·field**
back·field
backgamen : **back·gam·mon**
backgamman : **back·gam·mon**
backgammen : **back·gam·mon**
backgammin : **back·gam·mon**
back·gam·mon
back·ground
backround : **back·ground**
backterea : **bac·te·ri·a**
backteria : **bac·te·ri·a**
backteriem : **bac·te·ri·a**
backterium : **bac·te·ri·um**
back·ward
backwerd : **back·ward**
backword : **back·ward**
backwurd : **back·ward**
ba·con
bactearia : **bac·te·ria**
bactearium : **bac·te·ri·um**
bacterea : **bac·te·ria**
bactereum : **bac·te·ri·um**
bac·te·ria (*plur.*); **bac·te·ri·um**
    (*sing.*)
bac·te·ri·um (*sing.*); **bac·te·ria**
    (*plur.*)
bacterrea : **bac·te·ria**
bacterreum : **bac·te·ri·um**
bacterrium : **bac·te·ri·um**
bactiria : **bac·te·ria**
bactirium : **bac·te·ri·um**

baddinage : **ba·di·nage**
baddly : **bad·ly**
baddminton : **bad·min·ton**
badely : **bad·ly**
badenage : **ba·di·nage**
badenoge : **ba·di·nage**
badge
badinadge : **ba·di·nage**
ba·di·nage
badinoge : **ba·di·nage**
badlly : **bad·ly**
bad·ly
bad·min·ton
badmiton : **bad·min·ton**
badmitten : **bad·min·ton**
badmitton : **bad·min·ton**
bafel : **baf·fle**
baffel : **baf·fle**
baf·fle
bafful : **baf·fle**
bafle : **baf·fle**
bagage : **bag·gage**
bagaje : **bag·gage**
bage : **badge**
bagege : **bag·gage**
bager : **bad·ger**
baggadge : **bag·gage**
bag·gage
baggaje : **bag·gage**
baggege : **bag·gage**
baggie : **bag·gy**
bag·gy
bagy : **bag·gy**
bail (to get out of jail; to
   remove water); **bale** (hay)
bailef : **bai·liff**
baileff : **bai·liff**
bailif : **bai·liff**
bai·liff
baist : **baste**
bait (lure); **bate** (to subside)
baje : **badge**

bajer : **bad·ger**
bakary : **bak·ery**
bakeing : **bak·ing**
baken : **ba·con**
bak·er
bakerry : **bak·ery**
bak·ing
bakker : **bak·er**
balad : **bal·lad**
bal·ance
balanse : **bal·ance**
balast : **bal·last**
balck : **balk**
bal·co·nies
balconnies : **bal·co·nies**
balconny : **bal·co·ny**
bal·co·ny
baldnes : **bald·ness**
bald·ness
baldnis : **bald·ness**
baldniss : **bald·ness**
bale (hay); **bail** (to get out of
   jail; to remove water)
baled : **bal·lad**
balence : **bal·ance**
balerena : **bal·le·ri·na**
balerina : **bal·le·ri·na**
balet : **bal·let**
balif : **bai·liff**
baliff : **bai·liff**
balist : **bal·last**
balit : **bal·lot**
balk
balkonies : **bal·co·nies**
balkonnies : **bal·co·nies**
balkonny : **bal·co·ny**
balkony : **bal·co·ny**
balkonys : **bal·co·nies**
bal·lad
ballance : **bal·ance**
ballarena : **bal·le·ri·na**
ballarina : **bal·le·ri·na**

bal·last
ballat : **bal·let**
ballay : **bal·let**
balled : **bal·lad**
ballence : **bal·ance**
ballerena : **bal·le·ri·na**
bal·le·ri·na
ballest : **bal·last**
bal·let (dance); **bal·lot** (vote)
balley : **bal·let**
ballid : **bal·lad**
ballist : **bal·last**
ballit : **bal·lot**
bal·loon
bal·lot (vote); **bal·let** (dance)
ballote : **bal·lot**
ballsa : **bal·sa**
ballsah : **bal·sa**
ballsam : **bal·sam**
ballsum : **bal·sam**
Balltimore : **Bal·ti·more**
ballud : **bal·lad**
ballune : **bal·loon**
ballust : **bal·last**
balmy
baloon : **bal·loon**
baloone : **bal·loon**
balot : **ball·let** (dance) or
   bal·lot (vote)
bal·sa
balsah : **bal·sa**
bal·sam
balsum : **bal·sam**
Baltemore : **Bal·ti·more**
Bal·ti·more
bam·boo
bambu : **bam·boo**
bambue : **bam·boo**
bammboo : **bam·boo**
bammy : **balmy**
ba·nal
ba·nana

bananah : **ba·nana**
bananna : **ba·nana**
banche : **ban·shee**
banchee : **ban·shee**
bandadge : **ban·dage**
ban·dage
bandaje : **ban·dage**
ban·dana or **ban·dan·na**
ban·dan·na or **ban·dana**
bandedge : **ban·dage**
bandege : **ban·dage**
bandeje : **ban·dage**
bandet : **ban·dit**
bandetry : **ban·dit·ry**
bandidge : **ban·dage**
bandige : **ban·dage**
ban·dit
banditery : **ban·dit·ry**
banditt : **ban·dit**
bandittry : **ban·dit·ry**
bandwagen : **band·wag·on**
bandwaggen : **band·wag·on**
bandwaggon : **band·wag·on**
band·wag·on
banel : **ba·nal**
baner : **ban·ner**
banesh : **ban·ish**
bangel : **ban·gle**
ban·gle
bangul : **ban·gle**
ban·ish
bankrubt : **bank·rupt**
bankrupcy : **bank·rupt·cy**
bank·rupt
bank·rupt·cy
bankwet : **ban·quet**
bankwit : **ban·quet**
bannal : **ba·nal**
bannana : **ba·nana**
bannanna : **ba·nana**
bannar : **ban·ner**
bannditry : **ban·dit·ry**

ban·ner
banngle : **ban·gle**
bannir : **ban·ner**
bannish : **ban·ish**
ban·quet (feast); **ban·quette**
(bench)
ban·quette (bench); **ban·quet**
(feast)
banquit : **ban·quet**
banqwit : **ban·quet**
banshe : **ban·shee**
ban·shee
banshie : **ban·shee**
banshy : **ban·shee**
ban·tam
bantem : **ban·tam**
bantim : **ban·tam**
bantum : **ban·tam**
ban·zai (cheer); **bon·sai** (dwarf
tree)
banzi : **ban·zai** (cheer) *or*
bon·sai (dwarf tree)
banzie : **ban·zai** (cheer) *or*
bon·sai (dwarf tree)
baonet : **bay·o·net**
Baptest : **Bap·tist**
baptise (*Brit.*) : **bap·tize**
baptisim : **bap·tism**
bap·tism
Bap·tist
baptysm : **bap·tism**
baracade : **bar·ri·cade**
baracks : **bar·racks**
baracuda : **bar·ra·cu·da**
barage : **bar·rage**
baratone : **bar·i·tone**
barbacue : **bar·be·cue**
barbaque : **bar·be·cue**
barbarean : **bar·bar·i·an**
bar·bar·i·an
barbearian : **bar·bar·i·an**
bar·be·cue

barbequ : **bar·be·cue**
barbeque : **bar·be·cue**
barberian : **bar·bar·i·an**
barbicue : **bar·be·cue**
barbique : **bar·be·cue**
bare (uncovered); **bear**
(animal); **bear** (to carry)
bare·back
bare·faced
barefased : **bare·faced**
bare·foot
bare·hand·ed
barel : **bar·rel**
bare·ly (just enough); **bar·ley**
(grain)
baren : **bar·on**
bareness : **bar·on·ess**
(noblewoman) *or*
bar·ren·ness (emptiness)
baretone : **bar·i·tone**
barette : **bar·rette**
bar·gain
bargan : **bar·gain**
barge
bargen : **bar·gain**
bargin : **bar·gain**
bargun : **bar·gain**
barier : **bar·ri·er**
baritoan : **bar·i·tone**
bar·i·tone
barje : **barge**
bar·ley (grain); **bare·ly** (just
enough)
barnacel : **bar·na·cle**
bar·na·cle
barnakel : **bar·na·cle**
barnakle : **bar·na·cle**
barnuckle : **bar·na·cle**
barnukle : **bar·na·cle**
baroak : **ba·roque**
baroke : **ba·roque**
ba·rom·e·ter

baromiter : **ba·rom·e·ter**
bar·on (nobleman); **bar·ren** (unproductive)
bar·on·ess (noblewoman); **bar·ren·ness** (emptiness)
baronness : **bar·on·ess** (noblewoman) *or* **bar·ren·ness** (emptiness)
baroom : **bar·room**
baroqe : **ba·roque**
ba·roque
barracade : **bar·ri·cade**
barracaid : **bar·ri·cade**
bar·racks
barracooda : **bar·ra·cu·da**
bar·ra·cu·da
bar·rage
barrahge : **bar·rage**
barraks : **bar·racks**
barrakuda : **bar·ra·cu·da**
barratone : **bar·i·tone**
barrbarian : **bar·bar·i·an**
barrecade : **bar·ri·cade**
barrecks : **bar·racks**
barreir : **bar·ri·er**
bar·rel
bar·ren (unproductive); **bar·on** (nobleman)
barreness : **bar·on·ess** (noblewoman) *or* **bar·ren·ness** (emptiness)
bar·ren·ness (emptiness); **bar·on·ess** (noblewoman)
barret : **bar·rette**
barrete : **bar·rette**
barrett : **bar·rette**
bar·rette
bar·ri·cade
barricaid : **bar·ri·cade**
barricks : **bar·racks**
bar·ri·er
barrikade : **bar·ri·cade**

barril : **bar·rel**
barritone : **bar·i·tone**
barrometer : **ba·rom·e·ter**
barroness : **bar·on·ess** (noblewoman) *or* **bar·ren·ness** (emptiness)
barronness : **bar·on·ess**
barron : **bar·on**
bar·room
barry : **ber·ry** (fruit) *or* bury (to cover with earth)
bary : **ber·ry** (fruit) *or* **bury** (to cover with earth)
baryl : **ber·yl**
barytone : **bar·i·tone**
ba·salt
basault : **ba·salt**
basball : **base·ball**
base·ball
base·less
baselica : **ba·sil·i·ca**
baseliss : **base·less**
base·ment
basemint : **base·ment**
basen : **ba·sin**
ba·ses (*plur.*); **ba·sis** (*sing.*)
bash·ful
bashfull : **bash·ful**
ba·si·cal·ly
basicaly : **ba·si·cal·ly**
basicly : **ba·si·cal·ly**
basikally : **ba·si·cal·ly**
basileca : **ba·sil·i·ca**
basili : **ba·cil·li**
ba·sil·i·ca
basilika : **ba·sil·i·ca**
basilli : **ba·cil·li**
basillica : **ba·sil·i·ca**
basillus : **ba·cil·lus**
basilus : **ba·cil·lus**
ba·sin
basinet : **bas·si·net**

ba·sis (*sing.*); ba·ses (*plur.*)
Bask : **Basque**
baskette : **bas·ket**
baskit : **bas·ket**
baskitball : **bas·ket·ball**
basless : **base·less**
basment : **base·ment**
basoon : **bas·soon**
Basque
bassalt : **ba·salt**
bassenet : **bas·si·net**
bassili : **ba·cil·li**
bassilus : **ba·cil·lus**
bassin : **ba·sin**
bas·si·net
bassinette : **bas·si·net**
bassis : **ba·sis**
bassket : **bas·ket**
bassketball : **bas·ket·ball**
bas·soon
basstard : **bas·tard**
Basstille : **Bas·tille**
bast : **baste**
bast·ard
baste
Basteel : **Bas·tille**
Bastele : **Bas·tille**
basterd : **bas·tard**
Bas·tille
bastird : **bas·tard**
basune : **bas·soon**
bata : **be·ta**
bataleon : **bat·tal·ion**
batalion : **bat·tal·ion**
batary : **bat·tery**
batchelor : **bach·el·or**
bate (to subside); **bait** (lure)
Baten Rouge : **Ba·ton Rouge**
baten : **ba·ton**
bater : **bat·ter**
batery : **bat·tery**
bath (*noun*); **bathe** (*verb*)

bathe (*verb*); **bath** (*noun*)
Ba·ton Rouge
Baton Ruge : **Ba·ton Rouge**
ba·ton
battal : **bat·tle**
bat·tal·ion
battallion : **bat·tal·ion**
battary : **bat·tery**
battel : **bat·tle**
battelion : **bat·tal·ion**
bat·ter
batterry : **bat·tery**
bat·tery
bat·tle
battleon : **bat·tal·ion**
Batton Rouge : **Ba·ton Rouge**
batton : **ba·ton**
bauball : **bau·ble**
baubble : **bau·ble**
baubel : **bau·ble**
bau·ble
baucite : **baux·ite**
baudy : **bawdy**
bauk : **balk**
bauxcite : **baux·ite**
baux·ite
bawdie : **bawdy**
bawdy
bayenette : **bay·o·net**
bayinet : **bay·o·net**
bay·o·net
bayonnet : **bay·o·net**
bayoo : **bay·ou**
bay·ou
Bayrut : **Bei·rut**
ba·zaar (a fair); bi·zarre (strange)
bazar : **ba·zaar** (a fair) *or* **bi·zarre** (strange)
ba·zoo·ka
bazuka : **ba·zoo·ka**
bazzooka : **ba·zoo·ka**

beacan : **bea·con**
beach (shore); **beech** (tree)
beachead : **beach·head**
beach·head
beachnut : **beech·nut**
beacin : **bea·con**
beacker : **beak·er**
bea·con
beaditude : **be·at·i·tude**
beaf : **beef**
beagel : **bea·gle**
bea·gle
beagul : **bea·gle**
bea·ker
beakon : **bea·con**
beam
bear (animal); **bear** (to carry);
  bare (uncovered)
bearacade : **bar·ri·cade**
bearacuda : **bar·ra·cu·da**
bearback : **bare·back**
beard
bearfaced : **bare·faced**
bearfoot : **barefoot**
bearhanded : **bare·hand·ed**
bearly : **bare·ly**
bearometer : **ba·rom·e·ter**
bearrel : **bar·rel**
bearrier : **bar·ri·er**
beast
beastial : **bes·tial**
beat (to strike or to defeat);
  beet (plant)
beatatude : **be·at·i·tude**
beatician : **beau·ti·cian**
beatitood : **be·at·i·tude**
be·at·i·tude
beatle : **bee·tle**
beattitude : **be·at·i·tude**
beau·ti·cian
beautition : **beau·ti·cian**
beautty : **beau·ty**

beautycian : **beau·ti·cian**
bea·ver
becase : **be·cause**
becauze : **be·cause**
becawse : **be·cause**
becuz : **be·cause**
beddlam : **bed·lam**
Beddouin : **Bed·ou·in**
beddspread : **bedspread**
beddstead : **bed·stead**
bed·lam
bedlem : **bed·lam**
bedlum : **bed·lam**
Bedoin : **Bed·ou·in**
Bed·ou·in
Bedowin : **Bed·ou·in**
bed·spread
bedspred : **bed·spread**
bedsted : **bed·stead**
beech (tree); **beach** (shore)
beechhead : **beach·head**
beech·nut
beecon : **bea·con**
beef
beefs or **beeves**
beegle : **bea·gle**
beeker : **beak·er**
beekon : **bea·con**
beem : **beam**
beer (brewed drink); **bier**
  (funeral stand)
beerd : **beard**
beest : **beast**
beestial : **bes·tial**
beet (plant); **beat** (to strike or
  to defeat)
beetel : **bee·tle**
beet·le
beever : **bea·ver**
beeves or **beefs**
befoar : **be·fore**
befor : **be·fore**

be•foul
befour : **be•fore**
befowl : **be•foul**
beger : **beg•gar**
beg•gar
begger : **beg•gar**
beggin : **be•gin**
begginner : **be•gin•ner**
begginning : **be•gin•ning**
beggotten : **be•got•ten**
begguile : **be•guile**
begial : **be•guile**
begile : **be•guile**
be•gin
beginer : **be•gin•ner**
begining : **be•gin•ning**
beginn : **be•gin**
be•go•nia
begonnia : **be•go•nia**
begonya : **be•go•nia**
begoten : **be•got•ten**
begottin : **be•got•ten**
be•grudge
begrudje : **be•grudge**
begruge : **be•grudge**
be•guile
be•hav•ior
behaviour (*Brit.*) : **be•hav•ior**
beheemoth : **be•he•moth**
be•he•moth
behemuth : **be•he•moth**
beig : **beige**
beige
beighe : **beige**
beije : **beige**
beird : **beard**
Beiroot : **Bei•rut**
Bei•rut
beish : **beige**
beknighted : **be•night•ed**
bekweath : **be•queath**
beleaf : **be•lief**

beleager : **be•lea•guer**
be•lea•guer
beleagur : **be•lea•guer**
beleavable : **be•liev•able**
beleave : **be•lieve**
beleef : **be•lief**
beleeger : **be•lea•guer**
beleevable : **be•liev•able**
beleeve : **be•lieve**
beleif : **be•lief**
beleivable : **be•liev•able**
beleive : **be•lieve**
Belgem : **Bel•gium**
Belgim : **Bel•gium**
Bel•gium
Belgum : **Bel•gium**
belicose : **bel•li•cose**
believabel : **be•liev•able**
be•liev•able
believeble : **be•liev•able**
beligerent : **bel•lig•er•ent**
Beljim : **Bel•gium**
Beljum : **Bel•gium**
belkonies : **bal•co•nies**
belkony : **bal•co•ny**
belleaguer : **be•lea•guer**
bellegerent : **bel•lig•er•ent**
Bellgium : **Bel•gium**
bellicoce : **bel•li•cose**
bel•li•cose
belligerant : **bel•lig•er•ent**
bel•lig•er•ent
belligerint : **bel•lig•er•ent**
belligerent : **bel•lig•er•ent**
bellikose : **bel•li•cose**
bellweather : **bell•weth•er**
bell•weth•er
beloe : **be•low**
be•low
belweather : **bell•weth•er**
belwether : **bell•weth•er**
bemewsed : **be•mused**

bemoosed : **be·mused**
be·mused
bemussed : **be·mused**
bemuzed : **be·mused**
benadiction : **ben·e·dic·tion**
benafactor : **ben·e·fac·tor**
benafit : **ben·e·fit**
benal : **ba·nal**
benall : **ba·nal**
benana : **ba·nana**
be·neath
beneathe : **be·neath**
benedicktion : **ben·e·dic·tion**
ben·e·dic·tion
beneeth : **be·neath**
benefacent : **be·nef·i·cent**
ben·e·fac·tor
benefaktor : **ben·e·fac·tor**
benefet : **ben·e·fit**
be·nef·i·cent
benefiscent : **be·nef·i·cent**
benefisent : **be·nef·i·cent**
ben·e·fit
benevolant : **be·nev·o·lent**
be·nev·o·lent
benidiction : **ben·e·dic·tion**
benificent : **be·nef·i·cent**
benifit : **ben·e·fit**
be·night·ed
benightid : **be·night·ed**
benited : **be·night·ed**
bennediction : **ben·e·dic·tion**
bennefactor : **ben·e·fac·tor**
benneficent : **be·nef·i·cent**
bennefit : **ben·e·fit**
bennzene : **ben·zene**
benzean : **ben·zene**
benzeen : **ben·zene**
ben·zene
benzine : **ben·zene**
beqeath : **be·queath**
be·queath

bequeathe : **be·queath**
bequeeth : **be·queath**
beracuda : **bar·ra·cu·da**
beray : **be·ret**
be·reaved
bereeved : **be·reaved**
bereived : **be·reaved**
be·ret
berey : **be·ret**
berieved : **be·reaved**
beril : **ber·yl**
beroque : **ba·roque**
berrage : **bar·rage**
berrel : **bar·rel**
berrier : **bar·ri·er**
berril : **ber·yl**
ber·ry (fruit); **bury** (to cover
  with earth)
ber·serk
bersirk : **ber·serk**
bersurk : **ber·serk**
berth (bed); **birth** (to be born)
Berut : **Bei·rut**
bery : **ber·ry**
ber·yl
beryll : **ber·yl**
berzerk : **ber·serk**
besalt : **ba·salt**
beseach : **be·seech**
be·seech
beseege : **be·siege**
beseich : **be·seech**
beseige : **be·siege**
beserk : **ber·serk**
besiech : **be·seech**
be·siege
besmearch : **be·smirch**
besmerch : **be·smirch**
be·smirch
besmurch : **be·smirch**
bestal : **bes·tial**
bes·tial

bestoe : **be·stow**
be·stow
bestowe : **be·stow**
be·ta
beter : **bet·ter**
Bethlahem : **Beth·le·hem**
Beth·le·hem
Bethlihem : **Beth·le·hem**
betta : **be·ta**
bet·ter
betwean : **be·tween**
be·tween
betwein : **be·tween**
beuaty : **beau·ty**
beutician : **beau·ti·cian**
beuty : **beau·ty**
beval : **bev·el**
bevarage : **bev·er·age**
bev·el
bevelle : **bev·el**
bev·er·age
beveredge : **bev·er·age**
beverege : **bev·er·age**
bevirage : **bev·er·age**
bevvel : **bev·el**
bevvy : **bevy**
bevy
be·wail
bewair : **be·ware**
bewale : **be·wail**
be·ware
bewear : **be·ware**
bewhale : **be·wail**
bewhich : **be·witch**
bewich : **be·witch**
be·witch
bezooka : **ba·zoo·ka**
bi·as
bi·ased
biassed : **bi·ased**
Bibble : **Bi·ble**
bibbliography : **bib·li·og·ra·phy**

Bibel : **Bi·ble**
Bi·ble
bibleography : **bib·li·og·ra·phy**
bibliografy : **bib·li·og·ra·phy**
bib·li·og·ra·phy
bibliogrephy : **bib·li·og·ra·phy**
bibliogrify : **bib·li·og·ra·phy**
bibliogriphy : **bib·li·og·ra·phy**
bi·cy·cle
bi·cy·clist
biege : **beige**
bier (funeral stand); **beer**
  (brewed drink)
Bierut : **Bei·rut**
bieuty : **beau·ty**
bigonia : **be·go·nia**
bi·o·chem·ist
bious : **bi·as**
bioused : **bi·ased**
birth (to be born); **berth** (bed)
bius : **bi·as**
biused : **bi·ased**
biwitch : **be·witch**
Bizantine : **Byz·an·tine**
boalder : **boul·der**
boar (male pig); **boor**
  (ill-mannered person); **bore**
  (to drill a hole; to cause
  boredom; one who bores)
board
Boardeaux : **Bor·deaux**
board·er (renter); **bor·der**
  (boundary)
boarderline : **bor·der·line**
boardom : **bore·dom**
boast
boatanical : **bo·tan·i·cal**
bobble : **bau·ble**
boddy : **bawdy** (lewd) or **body**
  (corpus)
body
boemian : **bo·he·mi·an**

bogis : **bo·gus**
bo·gus
boheemian : **bo·he·mi·an**
bo·he·mi·an
boicott : **boy·cott**
Boi·se
Boisee : **Boi·se**
boisenbery : **boy·sen·ber·ry**
boiserus : **bois·ter·ous**
Boisie : **Boi·se**
boisonberry : **boy·sen·ber·ry**
bois·ter·ous
boistrous : **bois·ter·ous**
bokay : **bou·quet**
bol·der (more fearless);
  boul·der (rock)
bollsa : **bal·sa**
bollsam : **bal·sam**
bolsa : **bal·sa**
bolsa : **bal·sam**
bombadeer : **bom·bar·dier**
bombadier : **bom·bar·dier**
bombardeer : **bom·bar·dier**
bombardeir : **bom·bar·dier**
bom·bar·dier
bomb·er
bomberdier : **bom·bar·dier**
bomboo : **bam·boo**
bommer : **bomb·er**
bonannza : **bo·nan·za**
bo·nan·za
bon·dage
bondaje : **bond·age**
bondedge : **bond·age**
bondege : **bond·age**
bondige : **bond·age**
bonet : **bon·net**
boney : **bony**
bonis : **bo·nus**
bonnanza : **bo·nan·za**
bon·net
bonnit : **bon·net**

bonnus : **bo·nus**
bon·sai (dwarf tree); **ban·zai**
  (cheer)
bo·nus
bony
bonzai : **ban·zai** (cheer) *or*
  bon·sai (dwarf tree)
bonzi : **ban·zai** (cheer) *or*
  bon·sai (dwarf tree)
boobonic : **bu·bon·ic**
bookeeper : **book·keep·er**
book·keep·er
boomarang : **boom·er·ang**
boom·er·ang
boor (ill-mannered person);
  boar (male pig); **bore** (to
  drill a hole; to cause
  boredom; one who bores)
boor·ish
boo·tee *or* **boo·tie** (baby shoe);
  boo·ty (spoils of war)
boo·ty (spoils of war); **boo·tee**
  (baby shoe)
booz : **booze**
booze
boquay : **bou·quet**
boquet : **bou·quet**
borbon : **bour·bon**
bord : **board**
borde : **board**
Bor·deaux
bor·der (boundary); **board·er**
  (renter)
bor·der·line
Bordeux : **Bor·deaux**
Bordieux : **Bor·deaux**
Bordoe : **Bor·deaux**
bordom : **bore·dom**
bore (to drill a hole; to cause
  boredom; one who bores);
  boar (male pig); **boor**
  (ill-mannered person)

boredem : **bore·dom**
bore·dom
boredum : **bore·dom**
borgeois : **bour·geois** (*adj.*)
borgeoisie : **bour·geoisie** (*noun*)
borish : **boor·ish**
bor·ough (town); **bur·ro** (pack animal); **bur·row** (animal hole)
borow : **bor·row**
borro : **bor·row**
bor·row
bos·om
bosoom : **bos·om**
bossom : **bos·om**
botaney : **bot·a·ny**
bo·tan·i·cal
botanicle : **bo·tan·i·cal**
botanikal : **bo·tan·i·cal**
botannical : **bo·tan·i·cal**
botanny : **bot·a·ny**
bot·a·ny
boteny : **bot·a·ny**
botiny : **bot·a·ny**
botle : **bot·tle**
botom : **bot·tom**
bottal : **bot·tle**
bottanical : **bo·tan·i·cal**
bottel : **bot·tle**
bottem : **bot·tom**
bot·tle
bottocks : **but·tocks**
bot·tom
bottoneer : **bou·ton·niere**
bottum : **bot·tom**
bought
bougt : **bought**
bouil·lon (soup); **bul·lion** (gold blocks)
boukay : **bou·quet**
boulavard : **boul·e·vard**
boul·der

boul·e·vard
boulevarde : **boul·e·vard**
bounce
bound·ary
boundery : **bound·ary**
boundiry : **bound·ary**
boundry : **bound·ary**
bounse : **bounce**
boun·te·ous
boun·ti·ful
bountifull : **boun·ti·ful**
bountious : **boun·te·ous**
bountius : **boun·te·ous**
bountyful : **boun·ti·ful**
bouquay : **bou·quet**
bou·quet
bourben : **bour·bon**
bour·bon
bourgeis : **bour·geois** (*adj.*)
bourgeisie : **bour·geoisie** (*noun*)
bour·geois (*adj.*); **bour·geoi·sie** (*noun*)
bourgeoisee : **bour·geoisie** (*noun*)
bour·geoisie (*noun*); **bour·geois** (*adj.*)
bourgois : **bour·geois** (*adj.*)
bourgoisie : **bour·geoisie** (*noun*)
bourshois : **bour·geois** (*adj.*)
bourshoisie : **bour·geoisie** (*noun*)
bourshwa : **bour·geois** (*adj.*)
bourshwasie : **bour·geoisie** (*noun*)
boutoniere : **bou·ton·niere**
bou·ton·niere
bouttoniere : **bou·ton·niere**
bouyancy : **buoy·an·cy**
bouyant : **buoy·ant**
bouyency : **buoy·an·cy**
bouyensy : **buoy·an·cy**

bouyent : **buoy·ant**
bouyint : **buoy·ant**
bownce : **bounce**
bownteous : **boun·te·ous**
boxite : **baux·ite**
boy (lad); **buoy** (sea marker)
boyancy : **buoy·an·cy**
boyant : **buoy·ant**
boycot : **boy·cott**
boy·cott
boyency : **buoy·an·cy**
boyent : **buoy·ant**
boykott : **boy·cott**
Boyse : **Boi·se**
boy·sen·ber·ry
boysonberry : **boy·sen·ber·ry**
boysterous : **bois·ter·ous**
brace·let
bracelett : **brace·let**
bracelit : **brace·let**
bragart : **brag·gart**
brag·gart
braggert : **brag·gart**
braik : **brake** (to slow or stop)
    or **break** (to shatter)
Brail : **Braille**
Braille
brain
brakable : **break·able**
brake (to slow or stop); **break**
    (to shatter)
brakethrough : **break·through**
Brale : **Braille**
Bralle : **Braille**
brane : **brain**
braselet : **brace·let**
braselit : **brace·let**
Brasil : **Bra·zil**
brauny : **brawn·y**
bra·va·do
bravadoe : **bra·va·do**
bravary : **brav·ery**

braverry : **brav·ery**
brav·ery
bravodo : **bra·va·do**
bravry : **brav·ery**
brawny
Bra·zil
Brazill : **Bra·zil**
breach (to break); **breech**
    (hinder or lower part)
breachcloth : **breech·cloth**
breaches (breaks); **breech·es**
    (trousers)
bread (food); **bred** (raised)
breadth
break (to shatter); **brake** (to
    slow or stop)
breakabel : **break·able**
break·able
break·fast
breakfest : **break·fast**
breakfist : **break·fast**
breakible : **break·able**
break·through
breakthru : **break·through**
breakthrugh : **break·through**
breast
breath (*noun*); **breathe** (*verb*)
breathe (*verb*); **breath** (*noun*)
breathren : **breth·ren**
breath·er
breaze : **breeze**
breazily : **breez·i·ly**
breckfast : **break·fast**
bred (raised); **bread** (food)
bredth : **breadth**
breech (hinder or lower part);
    breach (to break)
breech·cloth
breechclothe : **breech·cloth**
breech·es (trousers); **breaches**
    (breaks)
breef : **brief**

breethe : **breathe**
breether : **breath·er**
breezaly : **breez·i·ly**
breeze
breez·i·ly
bregade : **bri·gade**
breif : **brief**
breivity : **brev·i·ty**
brekfast : **break·fast**
brekfest : **break·fast**
brest : **breast**
breth : **breath**
bretheren : **breth·ren**
breth·ren
brevado : **bra·va·do**
brevety : **brev·i·ty**
brev·i·ty
brewary : **brew·ery**
brewerry : **brew·ery**
brew·ery
brewry : **brew·ery**
bribary : **brib·ery**
brib·ery
bribry : **brib·ery**
brid·al (marriage); **brid·le**
 (harness)
bridge
bridje : **bridge**
brid·le (harness); **brid·al**
 (marriage)
brief
brievity : **brev·i·ty**
bri·gade
brigadeer : **brig·a·dier**
brigadeir : **brig·a·dier**
brig·a·dier
brigaid : **bri·gade**
brige : **bridge**
brigedier : **brig·a·dier**
briggade : **bri·gade**
briggadier : **brig·a·dier**
bright·en

brightin : **bright·en**
briliance : **bril·liance**
briliant : **bril·liant**
brillance : **bril·liance**
bril·liance
brillianse : **bril·liance**
bril·liant
brillience : **bril·liance**
brilliense : **bril·liance**
brillient : **bril·liant**
brissle : **bris·tle**
brisstle : **bris·tle**
bristel : **bris·tle**
bris·tle
Brit·ain (nation); **Brit·on**
 (person)
Britan : **Brit·ain** (nation) *or*
 Brit·on (person)
Britania : **Bri·tan·ni·a**
Bri·tan·ni·a
Britany : **Brit·ta·ny**
Briten : **Brit·ain** (nation) *or*
 Brit·on (person)
briten : **bright·en**
Britesh : **Brit·ish**
Britian : **Brit·ain** (nation) *or*
 Brit·on (person)
Brit·ish
britle : **brit·tle**
Britny : **Brit·ta·ny**
Brit·on (person); **Brit·ain**
 (nation)
Brit·ta·ny
brittel : **brit·tle**
Brittish : **Brit·ish**
brit·tle
Britton : **Brit·ain** (nation) *or*
 Brit·on (person)
broach (to open); **brooch**
 (ornamental pin)
bro·chure
bronny : **brawny**

brooch (ornamental pin);
  broach (to open)
Brooklin : **Brook·lyn**
Brook·lyn
Brooklynn : **Brook·lyn**
broose : **bruise**
broshure : **bro·chure**
brosure : **bro·chure**
broth·er
brouse : **browse**
browse
browze : **browse**
bruise
bruize : **bruise**
bru·net *or* **bru·nette**
bru·nette *or* **bru·net**
brunnette : **bru·net**
bruse : **bruise**
Brusels : **Brus·sels**
brusk : **brusque**
brusqe : **brusque**
brusque
Brussells : **Brus·sels**
Brussels
Brussles : **Brus·sels**
bru·tal
brutel : **bru·tal**
bruther : **broth·er**
brutil : **bru·tal**
brutle : **bru·tal**
Buanos Aires : **Bue·nos Ai·res**
bubbel : **bub·ble**
bub·ble
buble : **bub·ble**
bu·bon·ic
bubonick : **bu·bon·ic**
bubonnic : **bu·bon·ic**
bucanneer : **buc·ca·neer**
buc·ca·neer
buccaneir : **buc·ca·neer**
buccanier : **buc·ca·neer**
buccanneer : **buc·ca·neer**

bucher : **butch·er**
bucholic : **bu·col·ic**
buckaneer : **buc·ca·neer**
buckel : **buc·kle**
buckeneer : **buc·ca·neer**
buc·ket
buckit : **buc·ket**
buc·kle
bucksom : **bux·om**
bu·col·ic
bucolick : **bu·col·ic**
Buda : **Bud·dha**
Budda : **Bud·dha**
Bud·dha
Budd·hist
Buddist : **Budd·hist**
bud·get
budgetarry : **bud·get·ary**
bud·get·ary
budgetery : **bud·get·ary**
budgit : **bud·get**
budgitary : **bud·get·ary**
Budha : **Bud·dha**
Budist : **Budd·hist**
Buenas Aires : **Bue·nos Ai·res**
Bue·nos Ai·res
Buenos Airres : **Bue·nos Ai·res**
Buenos Ires : **Bue·nos Ai·res**
bufalo : **buf·fa·lo**
bufelo : **buf·fa·lo**
bufet : **buf·fet**
buffallo : **buf·fa·lo**
buf·fa·lo
buffat : **buf·fet**
buffay : **buf·fet**
buffelo : **buf·fa·lo**
buf·fet
buffey : **buf·fet**
buf·foon
buffoonary : **buf·foon·ery**
buf·foon·ery
buffune : **buf·foon**

buffunery : **buf•foon•ery**
bufoon : **buf•foon**
bufoonery : **buf•foon•ery**
bugal : **bu•gle**
bugel : **bu•gle**
buget : **bud•get**
bugetary : **bud•get•ary**
buggler : **bu•gler**
buglar : **bu•gler**
bu•gle
bu•gler
build
bukle : **buc•kle**
bukolic : **bu•col•ic**
bulet : **bul•let**
buletin : **bul•le•tin**
bulevard : **boul•e•vard**
bulk•i•er
bulkyer : **bulk•i•er**
bullack : **bul•lock**
bullavard : **boul•e•vard**
bull•doz•er
bulleck : **bul•lock**
bul•let
bulleten : **bul•le•tin**
bullevard : **boul•e•vard**
bul•le•tin
bul•lion (gold blocks);
   bouil•lon (soup)
bullit : **bul•let**
bullitin : **bul•le•tin**
bul•lock
bullrush : **bul•rush**
bullwark : **bul•wark**
bullwerk : **bul•wark**
bullwork : **bul•wark**
bulock : **bul•lock**
bul•rush
bul•wark
bulwerk : **bul•wark**
bulwork : **bul•wark**

bundal : **bun•dle**
bundel : **bun•dle**
bun•dle
bungaloe : **bun•ga•low**
bun•ga•low
bungelow : **bun•ga•low**
bungolow : **bun•ga•low**
bun•ion
bunnion : **bun•ion**
bunyan : **bun•ion**
bunyen : **bun•ion**
bunyon : **bun•ion**
buoy (sea marker); **boy** (lad)
buoy•an•cy
buoyansy : **buoy•an•cy**
buoy•ant
buquet : **bou•quet**
buray : **be•ret**
burben : **bour•bon**
burbon : **bour•bon**
burch : **birch**
burdansom : **bur•den•some**
bur•den
bur•den•some
burdensum : **bur•den•some**
burdonsome : **bur•den•some**
bureacrisy : **bu•reau•cra•cy**
bu•reau
bu•reau•cra•cy
bureaucrasy : **bu•reau•cra•cy**
burgen : **bur•geon**
burgeois : **bour•geois**
burgeoisie : **bour•geoisie**
bur•geon
bur•glar
bur•glary
burgler : **bur•glar**
burglery : **bur•glary**
burglir : **bur•glar**
burglury : **bur•glary**
buri•al
buriel : **buri•al**

burieu : **bu·reau**
burieucracy : **bu·reau·cra·cy**
bur·lap
burlesk : **bur·lesque**
bur·lesque
bur·ley (tobacco); **bur·ly** (muscular)
bur·ly
burreau : **bu·reau**
burreaucracy : **bu·reau·cra·cy**
burret : **bar·rette**
burrette : **bar·rette**
burrey : **bury**
bur·ro (pack animal); **bor·ough** (town); **bur·row** (animal hole)
bur·row (animal hole); **bor·ough** (town); **bur·ro** (pack animal)
bur·sar
burser : **bur·sar**
burserk : **ber·serk**
bur·si·tis
bursitus : **bur·si·tis**
burthday : **birth·day**
burthmark : **birth·mark**
burthplace : **birth·place**
bury (to cover with earth); **ber·ry** (fruit)
buryal : **buri·al**
bus·es *or* **bus·ses**
bushal : **bush·el**
bush·el
bushell : **bush·el**
busi·er
busi·ness (economic activity); **busy·ness** (being busy)
busom : **bos·om**
bus·ses *or* **bus·es**
bussier : **busi·er**

bussle : **bus·tle**
busstle : **bus·tle**
bustel : **bus·tle**
bus·tle
busyier : **busi·er**
busy·ness (being busy); **busi·ness** (economic activity)
butain : **bu·tane**
bu·tane
butchary : **butch·ery**
butch·er
butch·ery
bute : **butte**
buter : **but·ter**
bution : **beau·ti·cian**
butlar : **but·ler**
butocks : **but·tocks**
butress : **but·tress**
butte
but·ter
buttler : **but·ler**
but·tocks
buttonier : **bou·ton·niere**
buttox : **but·tocks**
but·tress
buttriss : **but·tress**
buty : **beau·ty**
bux·om
buxum : **bux·om**
buzard : **buz·zard**
buze : **booze**
buz·zard
buzzerd : **buz·zard**
bycicle : **bi·cy·cle**
byciclist : **bi·cy·clist**
byochemist : **bi·o·chem·ist**
byou : **bay·ou**
Byzanteen : **Byz·an·tine**
Byz·an·tine
Byzentine : **Byz·an·tine**

C

cabage : **cab·bage**
ca·bana
cabanna : **ca·bana**
cabaray : **cab·a·ret**
cab·a·ret
cab·bage
cabbana : **ca·bana**
cabbedge : **cab·bage**
cabbege : **cab·bage**
cabbin : **cab·in**
caben : **cab·in**
cabenet : **cab·i·net**
caberet : **cab·a·ret**
cab·in
cab·i·net
cabinnet : **cab·i·net**
cabnet : **cab·i·net**
cacafony : **ca·coph·o·ny**
cacaphony : **ca·coph·o·ny**
cacheir : **cash·ier**
cachew : **cash·ew**
cachoo : **cash·ew**
cack·le
cacktus : **cac·tus**
cacle : **cack·le**
cacofony : **ca·coph·o·ny**
ca·coph·o·ny
cactos : **cac·tus**
cac·tus
cacus : **cau·cus**
cadance : **ca·dence**
cadanse : **ca·dence**
ca·dav·er
cadavir : **ca·dav·er**
cadavver : **ca·dav·er**
caddet : **ca·det**
ca·dence
cadense : **ca·dence**
ca·det
cadett : **ca·det**

cadette : **ca·det**
cae·sar·e·an
caesarian : **cae·sar·e·an**
cafaterea : **caf·e·te·ria**
cafateria : **caf·e·te·ria**
cafaterria : **caf·e·te·ria**
cafee : **cof·fee**
cafeen : **caf·feine**
cafeine : **caf·feine**
cafene : **caf·feine**
cafetearia : **caf·e·te·ria**
cafeterea : **caf·e·te·ria**
caf·e·te·ria
cafeterria : **caf·e·te·ria**
caff : **cough**
caffateria : **caf·e·te·ria**
caffee : **cof·fee**
caffeen : **caf·feine**
caf·feine
caffene : **caf·feine**
caffeteria : **caf·e·te·ria**
caffiene : **caf·feine**
caffine : **caf·feine**
cagole : **ca·jole**
caidence : **ca·dence**
cainine : **ca·nine**
cairamel : **car·a·mel**
cairful : **care·ful**
cairless : **care·less**
Cai·ro
cairopractor : **chi·ro·prac·tor**
Cairro : **Cai·ro**
cajoal : **ca·jole**
ca·jole
cajolle : **ca·jole**
cakophony : **ca·coph·o·ny**
caktos : **cac·tus**
caktus : **cac·tus**
calaber : **cal·i·ber**
calacko : **cal·i·co**

44

Calafornia : **Cal·i·for·nia**
calamety : **ca·lam·i·ty**
calamitty : **ca·lam·i·ty**
ca·lam·i·ty
calammity : **ca·lam·i·ty**
calamny : **cal·um·ny**
calander : **cal·en·dar** (chart of dates) or **cal·en·der** (pressing machine) or **col·an·der** (drainer)
calaper : **cal·i·per**
calarie : **cal·o·rie** (energy unit) or **cel·ery** (vegetable)
calary : **cal·o·rie** (energy unit) or **cel·ery** (vegetable)
calasthenics : **cal·is·then·ics**
calceim : **cal·ci·um**
calceum : **cal·ci·um**
cal·ci·um
calcuelate : **cal·cu·late**
cal·cu·late
calculis : **cal·cu·lus**
calcullate : **cal·cu·late**
calcullus : **cal·cu·lus**
calculous : **cal·cu·lus**
cal·cu·lus
caleber : **cal·i·ber**
caleco : **cal·i·co**
Calefornia : **Cal·i·for·nia**
caleidascope : **ka·lei·do·scope**
caleko : **cal·i·co**
cal·en·dar (chart of dates); **cal·en·der** (pressing machine);**col·an·der** (drainer)
cal·en·der (pressing machine); **cal·en·dar** (chart of dates); **col·an·der** (drainer)
calenndar : **cal·en·dar** (chart of dates) or **cal·en·der** (pressing machine) or **col·an·der** (drainer)
caleper : **cal·i·per**

calepso : **ca·lyp·so**
calery : **cal·o·rie** (energy unit) or **cel·ery** (vegetable)
cal·i·ber
calibir : **cal·i·ber**
calibre (*Brit.*) : **cal·i·ber**
calicco : **cal·i·co**
calicko : **cal·i·co**
cal·i·co
caliedoscope : **ka·lei·do·scope**
Californea : **Cal·i·for·nia**
Cal·i·for·nia
caliko : **cal·i·co**
calindar : **cal·en·dar** (chart of dates) or **cal·en·der** (pressing machine) or **col·an·der** (drainer)
calinder : **cal·en·dar** (chart of dates) or **cal·en·der** (pressing machine) or **col·an·der** (drainer)
cal·i·per
calipper : **cal·i·per**
calipso : **ca·lyp·so**
calis : **cal·lous** (lack of feeling) or **cal·lus** (hardened skin)
calissthenics : **cal·is·then·ics**
calissthintics : **cal·is·then·ics**
cal·is·then·ics
calisthinics : **cal·is·then·ics**
callaflower : **cau·li·flow·er**
callamity : **ca·lam·i·ty**
callasthenics : **cal·is·then·ics**
callcium : **cal·ci·um**
callculate : **cal·cu·late**
callculus : **cal·cu·lus**
calldran : **caul·dron**
calldren : **caul·dron**
calldron : **caul·dron**
callendar : **cal·en·dar** (chart of dates) or **cal·en·der** (pressing

machine) *or* **col·an·der**
(drainer)
callery : **cal·o·rie** (energy unit)
or **cel·ery** (vegetable)
callesthenics : **cal·is·then·ics**
calliber : **cal·i·ber**
callico : **cal·i·co**
callidoscope : **ka·lei·do·scope**
calliflour : **cau·li·flow·er**
calliflower : **cau·li·flow·er**
Callifornia : **Cal·i·for·nia**
calliper : **cal·i·per**
callipso : **ca·lyp·so**
callis : **cal·lous** (lack of feeling)
or **cal·lus** (hardened skin)
calliss : **cal·lous** (lack of
feeling) *or* **cal·lus** (hardened
skin)
callisthenics : **cal·is·then·ics**
callisthinicks : **cal·is·then·ics**
callisthinics : **cal·is·then·ics**
callorie : **cal·o·rie**
callory : **cal·o·rie**
cal·lous (lack of feeling);
cal·lus (hardened skin)
callumny : **cal·um·ny**
cal·lus (hardened skin);
cal·lous (lack of feeling)
callvary : **Cal·va·ry** (site of the
Crucifixion) *or* **cav·al·ry**
(horse troops)
Callvinist : **Cal·vin·ist**
callypso : **ca·lyp·so**
calocko : **cal·i·co**
caloco : **cal·i·co**
calomny : **cal·um·ny**
calorey : **cal·o·rie**
cal·o·rie
calorrey : **cal·o·rie**
calorrie : **cal·o·rie**
calory : **cal·o·rie**

calous : **cal·lous** (lack of
feeling) *or* **cal·lus** (hardened
skin)
calqulate : **cal·cu·late**
calqulus : **cal·cu·lus**
calseum : **cal·ci·um**
calsium : **cal·ci·um**
caluclate : **cal·cu·late**
calummny : **cal·um·ny**
calumney : **cal·um·ny**
calumnie : **cal·um·ny**
cal·um·ny
calus : **cal·lous** (lack of feeling)
or **cal·lus** (hardened skin)
Cal·va·ry (site of the
Crucifixion); **cav·al·ry** (horse
troops)
calvelry : **Cal·va·ry** (site of the
Crucifixion) *or* **cav·al·ry**
(horse troops)
Calvenist : **Cal·vin·ist**
calvery : **Cal·va·ry** (site of the
Crucifixion) *or* **cav·al·ry**
(horse troops)
Cal·vin·ist
Calvinnist : **Cal·vin·ist**
ca·lyp·so
calypsoe : **ca·lyp·so**
camal : **cam·el**
camara : **cam·era**
ca·ma·ra·de·rie *or* **com·rad·ery**
camarodery : **ca·ma·ra·de·rie**
camealia : **ca·mel·lia**
cameilia : **ca·mel·lia**
cam·el
camelia : **ca·mel·lia**
ca·mel·lia
camelya : **ca·mel·lia**
cam·eo
cam·era
cameraderie : **ca·ma·ra·de·rie**
camerra : **cam·era**

camfor : **cam·phor**
camielia : **ca·mel·lia**
camil : **cam·el**
camill : **cam·el**
camillia : **ca·mel·lia**
camio : **cam·eo**
camioe : **cam·eo**
camira : **cam·era**
cammal : **cam·el**
cammara : **cam·era**
cammel : **cam·el**
cammelia : **ca·mel·lia**
cammeo : **cam·eo**
cammera : **cam·era**
cammerra : **cam·era**
cammillia : **ca·mel·lia**
cammio : **cam·eo**
cammira : **cam·era**
cammirra : **cam·era**
cammouflage : **cam·ou·flage**
cammuflauge : **cam·ou·flage**
camoflage : **cam·ou·flage**
camoflauge : **cam·ou·flage**
camofloge : **cam·ou·flage**
cam·ou·flage
campagne : **cam·paign**
cam·paign
campaigne : **cam·paign**
campain : **cam·paign**
campane : **cam·paign**
campes : **cam·pus**
campfor : **cam·phor**
campher : **cam·phor**
cam·phor
camphur : **cam·phor**
campis : **cam·pus**
camppus : **cam·pus**
cam·pus
campuss : **cam·pus**
camra : **cam·era**
camraderie : **ca·ma·ra·de·rie**
camuflague : **cam·ou·flage**

camuflauge : **cam·ou·flage**
camufloge : **cam·ou·flage**
canabal : **can·ni·bal**
canabel : **can·ni·bal**
canable : **can·ni·bal**
Can·a·da
Canadean : **Ca·na·di·an**
Ca·na·di·an
Canadien : **Ca·na·di·an**
Canaidian : **Ca·na·di·an**
canarry : **ca·nary** (bird) *or*
  can·nery (factory)
ca·nary (bird); **can·nery**
  (factory)
canaster : **can·is·ter**
can·cel
cancelation : **can·cel·la·tion**
can·celed *or* **can·celled**
cancell : **can·cel**
cancellaition : **can·cel·la·tion**
can·cel·la·tion
can·celled *or* **can·celed**
can·cer
cancil : **can·cel**
cancillation : **can·cel·la·tion**
cancilled : **can·celed**
cancor : **can·cer**
cancur : **can·cer**
candal : **can·dle**
candalabra : **can·de·la·bra**
candalstick : **can·dle·stick**
canded : **can·did**
candedacy : **can·di·da·cy**
candedasy : **can·di·da·cy**
candel : **can·dle**
can·de·la·bra
candellabra : **can·de·la·bra**
candelstick : **can·dle·stick**
cander : **can·dor**
can·did
can·di·da·cy
candidasy : **can·di·da·cy**

candidcy : **can·di·da·cy**
candidecy : **can·di·da·cy**
candidicy : **can·di·da·cy**
candidisy : **can·di·da·cy**
candil : **can·dle**
candilabra : **can·de·la·bra**
candilstick : **can·dle·stick**
can·dle
candleabra : **can·de·la·bra**
can·dle·stick
can·dor
candur : **can·dor**
Canecticut : **Con·nect·i·cut**
Caneda : **Can·a·da**
canen : **can·non** (artillery) or
  can·on (list of books; clergy;
  church law)
canery : **ca·nary** (bird) or
  can·nery (factory)
canester : **can·is·ter**
canibal : **can·ni·bal**
Canida : **Can·a·da**
canien : **ca·nine**
canin : **can·non** (artillery) or
  can·on (list of books; clergy;
  church law)
ca·nine
canion : **can·yon**
can·is·ter
cannabal : **can·ni·bal**
cannabel : **can·ni·bal**
cannable : **can·ni·bal**
Cannada : **Can·a·da**
Cannadian : **Ca·na·di·an**
cannary : **ca·nary** (bird) or
  can·nery (factory)
cannaster : **can·is·ter**
cannebal : **can·ni·bal**
canneble : **can·ni·bal**
cannen : **can·non** (artillery) or
  can·on (list of books; clergy;
  church law)

can·nery (factory); **ca·nary**
  (bird)
cannester : **can·is·ter**
Canneticut : **Con·nect·i·cut**
can·ni·bal
cannibel : **can·ni·bal**
cannible : **can·ni·bal**
cannin : **can·non** (artillery) or
  can·on (list of books; clergy;
  church law)
cannine : **ca·nine**
cannister : **can·is·ter**
cannoe : **ca·noe**
can·non (artillery); **can·on** (list
  of books; clergy; church law)
cannu : **ca·noe**
cannue : **ca·noe**
cannun : **can·non** (artillery) or
  can·on (list of books; clergy;
  church law)
cannuster : **can·is·ter**
cannyon : **can·yon**
ca·noe
can·on (list of books; clergy;
  church law); **can·non**
  (artillery)
canoo : **ca·noe**
Cansas : **Kan·sas**
cansel : **can·cel**
cansellation : **can·cel·la·tion**
canselled : **can·celed**
canser : **can·cer**
cansillation : **can·cel·la·tion**
cant (slope; hypocrisy); **can't**
  (cannot)
can't (cannot); **cant** (slope;
  hypocrisy)
cantakerous : **can·tan·ker·ous**
cantaloape : **can·ta·loupe**
cantalope : **can·ta·loupe**
can·ta·loupe
cantankarous : **can·tan·ker·ous**

can·tan·ker·ous
cantankerus : **can·tan·ker·ous**
can·ta·ta
cantatta : **can·ta·ta**
cantean : **can·teen**
can·teen
canteloape : **can·ta·loupe**
cantelope : **can·ta·loupe**
canteloupe : **can·ta·loupe**
cantene : **can·teen**
can·ter (horse trot); **can·tor** (chanter)
cantilope : **can·ta·loupe**
cantiloupe : **can·ta·loupe**
cantine : **can·teen**
can·tor (chanter); **can·ter** (horse trot)
cantota : **can·ta·ta**
cantotta : **can·ta·ta**
canue : **ca·noe**
canun : **can·non** (artillery) or **can·on** (list of books; clergy; church law)
canuster : **can·is·ter**
can·vas (cloth); **can·vass** (to survey)
can·vass (to survey); **can·vas** (cloth)
canves : **can·vas** (cloth) or **can·vass** (to survey)
canvess : **can·vas** (cloth) or **can·vass** (to survey)
canvis : **can·vas** (cloth) or **can·vass** (to survey)
canviss : **can·vas** (cloth) or **can·vass** (to survey)
canvus : **can·vas** (cloth) or **can·vass** (to survey)
canvuss : **can·vas** (cloth) or **can·vass** (to survey)
canyen : **can·yon**
canyin : **can·yon**

can·yon
capabal : **ca·pa·ble**
capabel : **ca·pa·ble**
ca·pa·bil·i·ty
capabillity : **ca·pa·bil·i·ty**
ca·pa·ble
capablety : **ca·pa·bil·i·ty**
capaccity : **ca·pac·i·ty**
capacety : **ca·pac·i·ty**
capachious : **ca·pa·cious**
ca·pa·cious
capacitty : **ca·pac·i·ty**
ca·pac·i·ty
capallary : **cap·il·lary**
capashious : **ca·pa·cious**
capasious : **ca·pa·cious**
capasitty : **ca·pac·i·ty**
capasity : **ca·pac·i·ty**
capatious : **ca·pa·cious**
capchure : **cap·ture**
capcion : **cap·tion**
capcise : **cap·size**
capcize : **cap·size**
capebility : **ca·pa·bil·i·ty**
capeble : **ca·pa·ble**
capellary : **cap·il·lary**
capibility : **ca·pa·bil·i·ty**
capible : **ca·pa·ble**
capilary : **cap·il·lary**
cap·il·lary
capillerry : **cap·il·lary**
capillery : **cap·il·lary**
cap·i·tal (city; property); **cap·i·tol** (statehouse)
cap·i·tal·ism
capitel : **cap·i·tal** (city; property) or **cap·i·tol** (statehouse)
capitelism : **cap·i·tal·ism**
capitle: **cap·i·tal** (city; property) or **cap·i·tol** (statehouse)

cap·i·tol (statehouse); **cap·i·tal**
  (city; property)
capitolism : **cap·i·tal·ism**
capittal : **cap·i·tal** (city;
  property) *or* **cap·i·tol**
  (statehouse)
capitul: **cap·i·tal** (city;
  property) *or* **cap·i·tol**
  (statehouse)
cappellary : **cap·il·lary**
cappillary : **cap·il·lary**
cappital : **cap·i·tal** (city;
  property) *or* **cap·i·tol**
  (statehouse)
cappitalism : **cap·i·tal·ism**
capsel : **cap·sule**
capsell : **cap·sule**
capshen : **cap·tion**
capshun : **cap·tion**
capshure : **cap·ture**
capsil : **cap·sule**
capsill : **cap·sule**
capsise : **cap·size**
cap·size
capsool : **cap·sule**
capsul : **cap·sule**
cap·sule
cap·tain
captan : **cap·tain**
capten : **cap·tain**
capter : **cap·tor**
captian : **cap·tain**
captin : **cap·tain**
cap·tion
captoin : **cap·tion**
cap·tor (*noun*); **cap·ture** (*verb*)
captur : **cap·tor** (*noun*) *or*
  cap·ture (*verb*)
cap·ture (*verb*); **cap·tor** (*noun*)
Carabean : **Car·ib·be·an**
caraboo : **car·i·bou**
carabou : **car·i·bou**

ca·rafe
caraffe : **ca·rafe**
caramal : **car·a·mel**
car·a·mel
caramul : **car·a·mel**
car·at *or* **kar·at** (weight of
  gems); **car·et** (^); **car·rot**
  (vegetable)
carature : **car·i·ca·ture**
car·a·van
carbahydrate : **car·bo·hy·drate**
carban : **car·bon**
carbean : **car·bine**
carbeen : **car·bine**
carbehidrate : **car·bo·hy·drate**
carbehydrate : **car·bo·hy·drate**
carben : **car·bon**
carbene : **car·bine**
carberater : **car·bu·re·tor**
carberator : **car·bu·re·tor**
carberetor : **car·bu·re·tor**
carbihydrate : **car·bo·hy·drate**
carbin : **car·bon**
car·bine
carbohidrait : **car·bo·hy·drate**
carbohidrate : **car·bo·hy·drate**
car·bo·hy·drate
car·bon
carborater : **car·bu·re·tor**
carborator : **car·bu·re·tor**
carboretor : **car·bu·re·tor**
carburator : **car·bu·re·tor**
carbureter : **car·bu·re·tor**
car·bu·re·tor
car·cass
carcus : **car·cass**
carcuss : **car·cass**
cardanal : **car·di·nal**
cardeac : **car·di·ac**
cardegan : **car·di·gan**
cardenal : **car·di·nal**
cardenel : **car·di·nal**

car·di·ac
cardiack : **car·di·ac**
cardiak : **car·di·ac**
car·di·gan
cardiggan : **car·di·gan**
cardiggin : **car·di·gan**
cardigin : **car·di·gan**
car·di·nal
cardinall : **car·di·nal**
cardinel : **car·di·nal**
cardinnal : **car·di·nal**
carear : **ca·reer**
carebou : **car·i·bou**
carecature : **car·i·ca·ture**
ca·reer
care·ful (cautious); **car·ful** (full car)
carefull : **care·ful**
carel : **car·ol** (song) *or* **car·rel** (study table)
care·less
careliss : **care·less**
caremel : **car·a·mel**
carere : **ca·reer**
ca·ress
car·et (^); **car·rot** (vegetable); **kar·at** (weight of gems)
carevan : **car·a·van**
car·ful (full car); **care·ful** (cautious)
cariage : **car·riage**
Ca·rib·be·an
Caribean : **Ca·rib·be·an**
Caribian : **Ca·rib·be·an**
cariboo : **car·i·bou**
car·i·bou
car·i·ca·ture
caricture : **car·i·ca·ture**
carisma : **char·is·ma**
cariture : **car·i·ca·ture**
carkas : **car·cass**
carkass : **car·cass**

carkess : **car·cass**
carmel : **car·a·mel**
carnadge : **car·nage**
car·nage
car·nal
carnavore : **car·ni·vore**
carnedge : **car·nage**
carnege : **car·nage**
carnel : **car·nal**
carnevore : **car·ni·vore**
carnidge : **car·nage**
carnige : **car·nage**
carnil : **car·nal**
carnivor : **car·ni·vore**
car·ni·vore
car·ol (song); **car·rel** (study table)
carosell : **car·ou·sel**
ca·rouse
car·ou·sel
carpat : **car·pet**
car·pen·ter
car·pet
carpinter : **car·pen·ter**
carpit : **car·pet**
Carrabean : **Ca·rib·be·an**
Carrabian : **Ca·rib·be·an**
carradge : **car·riage**
carrafe : **ca·rafe**
carrage : **car·riage**
carramel : **car·a·mel**
carrasel : **car·ou·sel**
carravan : **car·a·van**
carreer : **ca·reer**
car·rel (study table); **car·ol** (song)
carremel : **car·a·mel**
carresel : **car·ou·sel**
carress : **ca·ress**
carrevan : **car·a·van**
car·riage
Carribean : **Ca·rib·be·an**

Carribian : **Ca·rib·be·an**
carribou : **car·i·bou**
carridge : **car·riage**
carrige : **car·riage**
carrivan : **car·a·van**
carrol : **car·rel** (study table) *or*
  car·ol (song)
carrosel : **car·ou·sel**
car·rot (vegetable); **car·et** (^);
  kar·at (weight of gems)
carrouse : **ca·rouse**
carrousel : **car·ou·sel**
carryvan : **car·a·van**
cartalage : **car·ti·lage**
cartalege : **car·ti·lage**
cartalige : **car·ti·lage**
cartan : **car·ton**
cartelage : **car·ti·lage**
cartelige : **car·ti·lage**
carten : **car·ton**
car·ti·lage
cartilege : **car·ti·lage**
cartin : **car·ton**
car·ton
car·toon
cartradge : **car·tridge**
cartrage : **car·tridge**
cartredge : **car·tridge**
car·tridge
cartrige : **car·tridge**
cartune : **car·toon**
caseeno : **ca·si·no**
casel : **cas·tle**
caseno : **ca·si·no**
caserole : **cas·se·role**
casheer : **cash·ier**
casheir : **cash·ier**
cashere : **cash·ier**
cash·ew
cash·ier
cashmear : **cash·mere**
cashmeer : **cash·mere**

cashmeir : **cash·mere**
cash·mere
cashmier : **cash·mere**
cashoo : **cash·ew**
cashou : **cash·ew**
ca·si·no
casock : **cas·sock** (robe) *or*
  cos·sack (Russian cavalry)
cassack : **cas·sock** (robe) *or*
  cos·sack (Russian cavalry)
cassarole : **cas·se·role**
cassaroll : **cas·se·role**
cassel : **cas·tle**
casserio : **ca·si·no**
cas·se·role
casseroll : **cas·se·role**
cassick : **cas·sock** (robe) *or*
  cos·sack (Russian cavalry)
cassino : **ca·si·no**
cassirole : **cas·se·role**
cassoc : **cas·sock** (robe) *or*
  cos·sack (Russian cavalry)
cas·sock (robe); **cos·sack**
  (Russian cavalry)
casstle : **cas·tle**
cast (to throw off); **caste** (social
  system)
cas·ta·net
castanette : **cas·ta·net**
caste (social system); **cast** (to
  throw off)
castel : **cas·tle**
castenette : **cas·ta·net**
castinet : **cas·ta·net**
castinette : **cas·ta·net**
cas·tle
catachism : **cat·e·chism**
cataclism : **cat·a·clysm**
cat·a·clysm
cat·a·comb
catacome : **cat·a·comb**
catagory : **cat·e·go·ry**

catakism : **cat•e•chism**
catalist : **cat•a•lyst**
cat•a•log *or* **cat•a•logue**
cat•a•logue *or* **cat•a•log**
cat•a•lyst
catarpillar : **cat•er•pil•lar**
catasstrophe : **ca•tas•tro•phe**
catastrofe : **ca•tas•tro•phe**
ca•tas•tro•phe
catastrophy : **ca•tas•tro•phe**
catchup : **cat•sup**
cat•e•chism
catechysm : **cat•e•chism**
cateclism : **cat•a•clysm**
cateclysm : **cat•a•clysm**
catecomb : **cat•a•comb**
categorey : **cat•e•go•ry**
cat•e•go•ry
catekism : **cat•e•chism**
catelist : **cat•a•lyst**
catelog : **cat•a•log**
caterpilar : **cat•er•pil•lar**
caterpiler : **cat•er•pil•lar**
cat•er•pil•lar
caterpiller : **cat•er•pil•lar**
cathalic : **cath•o•lic**
cathelic : **cath•o•lic**
cathilic : **cath•o•lic**
catholec : **cath•o•lic**
cath•o•lic
Ca•thol•i•cism
Catholisism : **Ca•thol•i•cism**
Cathollicism : **Ca•thol•i•cism**
catilog : **cat•a•log**
catle : **cat•tle**
catsap : **cat•sup**
catsep : **cat•sup**
catshup : **cat•sup**
catsip : **cat•sup**
cat•sup *or* **ketch•up**
cattagory : **cat•e•go•ry**

cattal : **cat•tle**
cattalist : **cat•a•lyst**
cattalog : **cat•a•log**
cattalyst : **cat•a•lyst**
cattasrophe : **ca•tas•tro•phe**
cattegory : **cat•e•go•ry**
cattel : **cat•tle**
catterpillar : **cat•er•pil•lar**
cat•tle
caucas : **cau•cus**
cauchious : **cau•tious**
cau•cus
cauldran : **caul•dron**
cauldren : **caul•dron**
cauldrin : **caul•dron**
caul•dron
cau•li•flow•er
causalitty : **cau•sal•i•ty**
cau•sal•i•ty
causallety : **cau•sal•i•ty**
causallity : **cau•sal•i•ty**
causeous : **cau•tious**
caushion : **cau•tion**
caushious : **cau•tious**
causion : **cau•tion**
causstic : **caus•tic**
caus•tic
caustick : **caus•tic**
cau•tion
cau•tious
cav•al•cade
cavalcaid : **cav•al•cade**
cavaleer : **cav•a•lier**
cavaleir : **cav•a•lier**
cavalere : **cav•a•lier**
cavalery : **Cal•va•ry** (site of the
    Crucifixion) *or* **cav•al•ry**
    (horse troops)
cav•a•lier
cavalkade : **cav•al•cade**
cavallcade : **cav•al•cade**

cav·al·ry (horse troops);
   Cal·va·ry (site of the
   Crucifixion)
cavelcade : cav·al·cade
cavelier : cav·a·lier
cavellry : Cal·va·ry (site of the
   Crucifixion) or cav·al·ry
   (horse troops)
cavelry : Cal·va·ry (site of the
   Crucifixion) or cav·al·ry
   (horse troops)
cavernis : cav·ern·ous
cav·ern·ous
cavernus : cav·ern·ous
cavilcade : cav·al·cade
cavilere : cav·a·lier
cavilier : cav·a·lier
cavilry : Cal·va·ry (site of the
   Crucifixion) or cav·al·ry
   (horse troops)
cavurnous : cav·ern·ous
cawcus : cau·cus
cawldren : caul·dron
cawldron : caul·dron
cawtion : cau·tion
ceadar : ce·dar (tree) or se·der
   (Passover meal)
ce·dar (tree); se·der (Passover
   meal)
cedaver : ca·dav·er
ceder : ce·dar (tree) or se·der
   (Passover meal)
cedir : ce·dar (tree) or se·der
   (Passover meal)
ceesarean : cae·sar·e·an
cegar : ci·gar
cegarette : cig·a·rette
ceil·ing
cejole : ca·jole
celabate : cel·i·bate
celabrant : cel·e·brant
celabration : cel·e·brate

celabrent : cel·e·brant
celabrity : ce·leb·ri·ty
celar : cel·lar
celary : cel·ery (vegetable) or
   sal·a·ry (wages)
celebet : cel·i·bate
celebit : cel·i·bate
celebrait : cel·e·brate
cel·e·brant
cel·e·brate
celebrent : cel·e·brant
celebrety : ce·leb·ri·ty
celebritty : ce·leb·ri·ty
ce·leb·ri·ty
celerry : cel·ery (vegetable) or
   sal·a·ry (wages)
cel·ery (vegetable); sal·a·ry
   (wages)
celesteal : ce·les·tial
ce·les·tial
cel·i·bate
cellabrate : cel·e·brate
cel·lar (basement); sell·er (one
   who sells)
cellary : cel·ery (vegetable) or
   sal·a·ry (wages)
cellebrant : cel·e·brant
cellebrity : ce·leb·ri·ty
celler : cel·lar (basement) or
   sell·er (one who sells)
cellery : cel·ery (vegetable) or
   sal·a·ry (wages)
cellestial : ce·les·tial
cellibate : cel·i·bate
cel·lo
cellouloid : cel·lu·loid
Celltic : Cel·tic
cel·lu·loid
celo : cel·lo
Celon : Cey·lon
Cel·tic
celuloid : cel·lu·loid

cematary : **cem·e·tery**
cematery : **cem·e·tery**
cemeleon : **cha·me·leon**
cemelion : **cha·me·leon**
cemetarry : **cem·e·tery**
cemetary : **cem·e·tery**
cemeterry : **cem·e·tery**
cem·e·tery
cemettery : **cem·e·tery**
cemical : **chem·i·cal**
cemistry : **chem·is·try**
cencership : **cen·sor·ship**
cenchurion : **cen·tu·ri·on**
cenchury : **cen·tu·ry**
cencus : **cen·sus**
cenema : **cin·e·ma**
cen·ser (incense container);
  cen·sor (to remove
  objectionable material);
  cen·sure (to condemn);
  sen·sor (that which senses)
censership : **cen·sor·ship**
censes : **cen·sus**
cen·sor (to remove
  objectionable material);
  cen·ser (incense container);
  censure (to condemn);
  sen·sor (that which senses)
cen·sor·ship
cen·sure (to condemn); **cen·ser**
  (incense container); **cen·sor**
  (to remove objectionable
  material); **sen·sor** (that
  which senses)
cen·sus
censuss : **cen·sus**
centar : **cen·taur**
cen·taur
centerian : **cen·tu·ri·on**
centerion : **cen·tu·ri·on**
centeripetal : **cen·trip·e·tal**
centermeter : **cen·ti·me·ter**

centerpeace : **cen·ter·piece**
centerpece : **cen·ter·piece**
centerpeice : **cen·ter·piece**
cen·ter·piece
centery : **cen·tu·ry**
cen·ti·me·ter
centimetre (*Brit.*) :
  cen·ti·me·ter
centoorion : **cen·tu·ri·on**
centor : **cen·taur**
centour : **cen·taur**
centrepetal : **cen·trip·e·tal**
centrifecal : **cen·trif·u·gal**
centrifegal : **cen·trif·u·gal**
centriffugal : **cen·trif·u·gal**
centrifical : **cen·trif·u·gal**
centrifigal : **cen·trif·u·gal**
centrifucal : **cen·trif·u·gal**
cen·trif·u·gal
centrifugle : **cen·trif·u·gal**
centrimeter : **cen·ti·me·ter**
cen·trip·e·tal
centripetle : **cen·trip·e·tal**
centripidal : **cen·trip·e·tal**
centripital : **cen·trip·e·tal**
centripittal : **cen·trip·e·tal**
cents (money); **sense**
  (intelligence)
centur : **cen·taur**
centurian : **cen·tu·ri·on**
centurien : **cen·tu·ri·on**
cen·tu·ri·on
centurry : **cen·tu·ry**
cen·tu·ry
cerabellum : **cer·e·bel·lum**
ceramec : **ce·ram·ic**
ce·ram·ic
cerammic : **ce·ram·ic**
ceramony : **cer·e·mo·ny**
cerca : **cir·ca**
cerculate : **cir·cu·late**
cercus : **cir·cus**

ce·re·al (grain); **se·ri·al** (in a series)
cerebellam : **cer·e·bel·lum**
cerebellem : **cer·e·bel·lum**
cer·e·bel·lum
cerebelum : **cer·e·bel·lum**
ce·re·bral
cerebrel : **ce·re·bral**
ce·re·brum
cereebral : **ce·re·bral**
ceremoney : **cer·e·mo·ny**
cer·e·mo·ny
cerial : **ce·re·al** (grain) *or* **se·ri·al** (in a series)
ceribral : **ce·re·bral**
ceribrum : **ce·re·brum**
cerimony : **cer·e·mo·ny**
cerramic : **ce·ram·ic**
cerrebellum : **cer·e·bel·lum**
cerremony : **cer·e·mo·ny**
cerrhosis : **cir·rho·sis**
cerrosis : **cir·rho·sis**
cer·tain
certan : **cer·tain**
certian : **cer·tain**
certifecate : **cer·tif·i·cate**
certifficate : **cer·tif·i·cate**
certificant : **cer·tif·i·cate**
certificat : **cer·tif·i·cate**
cer·tif·i·cate
certin : **cer·tain**
cesairean : **cae·sar·e·an**
cesarean : **cae·sar·e·an**
cesarian : **cae·sar·e·an**
cessarian : **cae·sar·e·an**
cess·pool
cestern : **cis·tern**
Cey·lon
chafeur : **chauf·feur**
chaffer : **chauf·feur**
chaffuer : **chauf·feur**
chaffure : **chauf·feur**

chafure : **chauf·feur**
chaimberlain : **cham·ber·lain**
chaimberlin : **cham·ber·lain**
chairopractor : **chi·ro·prac·tor**
chaist : **chaste**
chalera : **chol·era**
chal·ice
chalise : **chal·ice**
chaliss : **chal·ice**
challice : **chal·ice**
challise : **chal·ice**
cham·ber·lain
chamberlan : **cham·ber·lain**
chamberlin : **cham·ber·lain**
chamealeon : **cha·me·leon**
chamealion : **cha·me·leon**
chameeleon : **cha·me·leon**
chameelion : **cha·me·leon**
cha·me·leon
chamise : **che·mise**
cham·pagne
champaigne : **cham·pagne**
champain : **cham·pagne**
champaine : **cham·pagne**
champane : **cham·pagne**
chanceller : **chan·cel·lor**
chan·cel·lor
chancelor : **chan·cel·lor**
chancillor : **chan·cel·lor**
chandaleer : **chan·de·lier**
chandalier : **chan·de·lier**
chandelear : **chan·de·lier**
chandeleer : **chan·de·lier**
chandelere : **chan·de·lier**
chan·de·lier
chandileer : **chan·de·lier**
chaneled : **chan·neled**
chanelled : **chan·neled**
changable : **change·able**
change·able
changebal : **change·able**
changeble : **change·able**

change•ling
changible : change•able
changling : change•ling
chan•neled or chan•nelled
chan•nelled or chan•neled
chanseller : chan•cel•lor
chansellor : chan•cel•lor
chansillor : chan•cel•lor
cha•os
chaoss : cha•os
chaparone : chap•er•on
chap•el
chapelen : chap•lain
chapelin : chap•lain
chap•er•on or chap•er•one
chap•er•one or chap•er•on
chaperown : chap•er•on
chapil : chap•el
chap•lain
chaplan : chap•lain
chaplin : chap•lain
chappel : chap•el
char•ac•ter
charactor : char•ac•ter
cha•rade
charaid : cha•rade
charatable : char•i•ta•ble
charaty : char•i•ty
char•coal
charcole : char•coal
charecter : char•ac•ter
charector : char•ac•ter
chareot : char•i•ot
chareoteer : char•i•o•teer
charetable : char•i•ta•ble
charety : char•i•ty
chargable : charge•able
chargeabel : charge•able
charge•able
chargible : charge•able
charicter : char•ac•ter
chariet : char•i•ot

charieteer : char•i•o•teer
char•i•ot
char•i•o•teer
chariotere : char•i•o•teer
chariotier : char•i•o•teer
charish : cher•ish
char•is•ma
char•i•ta•ble
chariteble : char•i•ta•ble
charitible : char•i•ta•ble
char•i•ty
charkcole : char•coal
char•la•tan
charlaten : char•la•tan
charlatin : char•la•tan
charletan : char•la•tan
charleten : char•la•tan
charlitan : char•la•tan
charrade : cha•rade
charrcoal : char•coal
charriot : char•i•ot
charrioteer : char•i•o•teer
charrish : cher•ish
charry : cher•ry
char•treuse
chartroose : char•treuse
chartruese : char•treuse
chartruse : char•treuse
charub : cher•ub
chasiss : chas•sis
chasm
chasses : chas•sis
chassey : chas•sis
chas•sis
chassiss : chas•sis
chasstise : chas•tise
chassy : chas•sis
chast : chaste
chaste
chastety : chas•ti•ty
chas•tise
chastitty : chas•ti•ty

chas·ti·ty
chastize : **chas·tise**
Chatannooga : **Chat·ta·noo·ga**
Chatanooga : **Chat·ta·noo·ga**
cha·teau
chatel : **chat·tel**
chatieu : **cha·teau**
chatle : **chat·tel**
chatoe : **cha·teau**
Chat·ta·noo·ga
Chattanuga : **Chat·ta·noo·ga**
chatteau : **cha·teau**
chat·tel
Chattenooga : **Chat·ta·noo·ga**
Chattinooga : **Chat·ta·noo·ga**
chattle : **chat·tel**
chattow : **cha·teau**
chauder : **chow·der**
chauffer : **chauf·feur**
chauf·feur
chauffuer : **chauf·feur**
chauvanism : **chau·vin·ism**
chauvenism : **chau·vin·ism**
chau·vin·ism
chavinism : **chau·vin·ism**
cheaky : **cheeky**
cheap·en
cheapin : **cheap·en**
chearful : **cheer·ful**
cheary : **cheery**
cheatah : **chee·tah**
cheat·er
Checago : **Chi·ca·go**
Chechoslovakia :
   Czech·o·slo·va·kia
check·er
cheeftain : **chief·tain**
cheekey : **cheeky**
cheeky
cheepen : **cheap·en**
cheer·ful
cheerfull : **cheer·ful**

cheery
cheeta : **chee·tah**
chee·tah
cheeter : **cheat·er**
cheiftain : **chief·tain**
cheipen : **cheap·en**
chekey : **cheeky**
Chele : **Chile**
chello : **cel·lo**
chemacal : **chem·i·cal**
chemastry : **chem·is·try**
chemecal : **chem·i·cal**
chemeese : **che·mise**
chemeleon : **cha·me·leon**
chemelion : **cha·me·leon**
chemese : **che·mise**
chemestry : **chem·is·try**
chem·i·cal
chemicle : **chem·i·cal**
che·mise
chemistery : **chem·is·try**
chem·is·try
chentz : **chintz**
chequer (*Brit.*) : **check·er**
cherade : **cha·rade**
Cherakee : **Cher·o·kee**
cherib : **cher·ub**
cheriot : **char·i·ot**
cherioteer : **char·i·o·teer**
cher·ish
cherlish : **churl·ish**
Cher·o·kee
Cherokey : **Cher·o·kee**
cherrish : **cher·ish**
cherrub : **cher·ub**
cher·ry
cher·ub
chery : **cher·ry**
Ches·a·peake
Chesapeeke : **Ches·a·peake**
Chesipeake : **Ches·a·peake**
Chesipeeke : **Ches·a·peake**

chesnut : **chest·nut**
Chessapeake : **Ches·a·peake**
chessnut : **chest·nut**
chest·nut
chetah : **chee·tah**
Cheyanne : **Chey·enne**
Chey·enne
Chicaggo : **Chi·ca·go**
Chi·ca·go
chicainery : **chi·ca·nery**
chicanary : **chi·ca·nery**
chicanerry : **chi·ca·nery**
chi·ca·nery
chickery : **chic·o·ry**
chickory : **chic·o·ry**
chic·o·ry
chief·tain
chieftan : **chief·tain**
chieftin : **chief·tain**
chikanery : **chi·ca·nery**
chikery : **chic·o·ry**
childern : **chil·dren**
chil·dren
Chile
Chille : **Chile**
chimese : **che·mise**
chimnee : **chim·ney**
chim·ney
chimny : **chim·ney**
chimpansey : **chim·pan·zee**
chimpansie : **chim·pan·zee**
chimpansy : **chim·pan·zee**
chim·pan·zee
chimpanzy : **chim·pan·zee**
Chinease : **Chi·nese**
Chineese : **Chi·nese**
Chi·nese
Chineze : **Chi·nese**
chints : **chintz**
chintz
chior : **choir**
chipmonck : **chip·munk**

chipmonk : **chip·munk**
chip·munk
chirapractor : **chi·ro·prac·tor**
chire : **choir**
chiropracktor : **chi·ro·prac·tor**
chiropracter : **chi·ro·prac·tor**
chi·ro·prac·tor
chisal : **chis·el**
chis·el
chisle : **chis·el**
chissel : **chis·el**
chitah : **chee·tah**
chivalery : **chiv·al·ry**
chivalrey : **chiv·al·ry**
chiv·al·ry
chivelry : **chiv·al·ry**
chivilry : **chiv·al·ry**
Chiyenne : **Chey·enne**
chizel : **chis·el**
chizzel : **chis·el**
chloesterol : **cho·les·ter·ol**
chloraform : **chlo·ro·form**
chloreen : **chlo·rine**
chloresterol : **cho·les·ter·ol**
chlo·ride
chloriform : **chlo·ro·form**
chlo·rine
chlo·ro·form
chlouride : **chlo·ride**
chlourine : **chlo·rine**
chluoride : **chlo·ride**
chluorine : **chlo·rine**
chluoroform : **chlo·ro·form**
choake : **choke**
choas : **cha·os**
choir
choiral : **cho·ral**
choireographer :
    cho·re·og·ra·pher
choke
chol·era
cholerra : **chol·era**

cholesteral : **cho·les·ter·ol**
cholesteroil : **cho·les·ter·ol**
cho·les·ter·ol
cholestral : **cho·les·ter·ol**
choot : **chute**
chop sooie : **chop su·ey**
chop sooy : **chop su·ey**
chop su·ey
cho·ral (relating to a choir);
   cho·rale (hymn); **cor·al**
   (reef); **cor·ral** (horse pen)
cho·rale (hymn); **cho·ral**
   (relating to a choir); **cor·al**
   (reef); **cor·ral** (horse pen)
chord (music); **cord** (rope)
chorel : **cho·ral** (relating to a
   choir) *or* **cho·rale** (hymn) *or*
   cor·al (reef) *or* **cor·ral** (horse
   pen)
choreografer :
   cho·re·og·ra·pher
cho·re·og·ra·pher
choriographer :
   cho·re·og·ra·pher
choris : **cho·rus**
choriss : **cho·rus**
cho·rus
chouder : **chow·der**
chovinism : **chau·vin·ism**
chow·der
chrisanthamem :
   chry·san·the·mum
chrisanthamum :
   chry·san·the·mum
chrisanthemum :
   chry·san·the·mum
christhanimum :
   chry·san·the·mum
Chris·tian
Christianety : **Chris·tian·i·ty**
Christianitty : **Chris·tian·i·ty**
Chris·tian·i·ty

Christien : **Chris·tian**
Christienity : **Chris·tian·i·ty**
Christion : **Chris·tian**
Christionity : **Chris·tian·i·ty**
chromeum : **chro·mi·um**
chromiem : **chro·mi·um**
chro·mi·um
chronalogy : **chro·nol·o·gy**
chron·ic
chronical : **chron·i·cle**
chronick : **chron·ic**
chronickal : **chron·i·cle**
chron·i·cle
chronikal : **chron·i·cle**
chronnic : **chron·ic**
chronnicle : **chron·i·cle**
chronnology : **chro·nol·o·gy**
chronollogy : **chro·nol·o·gy**
chronologgy : **chro·nol·o·gy**
chro·nol·o·gy
chrysanthamum :
   chry·san·the·mum
chrysanthemem :
   chry·san·the·mum
chry·san·the·mum
chuckal : **chuck·le**
chuckel : **chuck·le**
chuck·le
chukle : **chuck·le**
churl·ish
churllish : **churl·ish**
chute
cianide : **cy·a·nide**
Ciaro : **Cai·ro**
cibernetics : **cy·ber·net·ics**
cicle : **cy·cle**
ciclone : **cy·clone**
cieling : **ceil·ing**
ciello : **cel·lo**
cifer : **ci·pher**
ci·gar
cigarete : **cig·a·rette**

cig·a·rette
ciger : **ci·gar**
cigerette : **cig·a·rette**
ciggar : **ci·gar**
ciggarette : **cig·a·rette**
cignet : **cyg·net** (swan) *or*
   sig·net (ring)
Ciltic : **Cel·tic**
cilynder : **cyl·in·der**
cimbal : **cym·bal** (brass plate)
   or **sym·bol** (meaningful
   image)
cimball : **cym·bal** (brass plate)
   or **sym·bol** (meaningful
   image)
cimbol : **cym·bal** (brass plate)
   or **sym·bol** (meaningful
   image)
cinama : **cin·e·ma**
cinamin : **cin·na·mon**
cinamon : **cin·na·mon**
Cincanati : **Cin·cin·nati**
Cincenati : **Cin·cin·nati**
Cincennati : **Cin·cin·nati**
Cincinati : **Cin·cin·nati**
Cin·cin·nati
Cincinnatti : **Cin·cin·nati**
Cincinnaty : **Cin·cin·nati**
cin·e·ma
cineman : **cin·na·mon**
cinemon : **cin·na·mon**
cinicism : **cyn·i·cism**
cinnama : **cin·e·ma**
cinnamen : **cin·na·mon**
cinnamin : **cin·na·mon**
cin·na·mon
Cinncinati : **Cin·cin·nati**
Cinncinnati : **Cin·cin·nati**
cinnema : **cin·e·ma**
cinneman : **cin·na·mon**
cinnemon : **cin·na·mon**
Cinsanati : **Cin·cin·nati**

Cinsinnati : **Cin·cin·nati**
ci·pher
cipress : **cy·press**
cir·ca
circamspect : **cir·cum·spect**
circemspect : **cir·cum·spect**
circemstance : **cir·cum·stance**
circis : **cir·cus**
circka : **cir·ca**
cir·cu·late
cir·cum·spect
circumstanse : **cir·cum·stance**
cir·cus
circuss : **cir·cus**
cirhosis : **cir·rho·sis**
cirka : **cir·ca**
cirkus : **cir·cus**
Ciro : **Cai·ro**
ciropractor : **chi·ro·prac·tor**
cirosis : **cir·rho·sis**
cirqulate : **cir·cu·late**
cirrcus : **cir·cus**
cir·rho·ses (*plur.*); **cir·rho·sis**
   (*sing.*)
cir·rho·sis (*sing.*); **cir·rho·ses**
   (*plur.*)
cirrhosiss : **cir·rho·sis**
cirrosis : **cir·rho·sis**
cisstern : **cis·tern**
cisstirn : **cis·tern**
cissturn : **cis·tern**
cis·tern
cistirn : **cis·tern**
cisturn : **cis·tern**
cit·a·del
citadell : **cit·a·del**
citazen : **cit·i·zen**
citecen : **cit·i·zen**
citedel : **cit·a·del**
citezen : **cit·i·zen**
citicen : **cit·i·zen**
citicin : **cit·i·zen**

citidel : **cit·a·del**
cit·ies
cit·i·zen
citrous : **cit·rus**
cit·rus
citties : **cit·ies**
cittizen : **cit·i·zen**
citys : **cit·ies**
cityzen : **cit·i·zen**
civalization : **civ·i·li·za·tion**
civec : **civ·ic**
civelization : **civ·i·li·za·tion**
civ·ic
civick : **civ·ic**
civilisation (*Brit.*) :
   civ·i·li·za·tion
civ·i·li·za·tion
civillization : **civ·i·li·za·tion**
clairet : **clar·et**
clairity : **clar·i·ty**
clair·voy·ance
clairvoyanse : **clair·voy·ance**
clairvoyence : **clair·voy·ance**
clairvoyince : **clair·voy·ance**
clamer : **clam·or**
clamity : **ca·lam·i·ty**
clammer : **clam·or**
clammor : **clam·or**
clam·or
clamour (*Brit.*) : **clam·or**
clarafication : **clar·i·fi·ca·tion**
claranet : **clar·i·net**
clarat : **clar·et**
clarefication : **clar·i·fi·ca·tion**
clarenet : **clar·i·net**
clareon : **clar·i·on**
clar·et
clarety : **clar·i·ty**
clarifacation : **clar·i·fi·ca·tion**
clarifecation : **clar·i·fi·ca·tion**
clarificasion : **clar·i·fi·ca·tion**
clar·i·fi·ca·tion

clar·i·fy
clar·i·net
clar·i·on
clarit : **clar·et**
claritty : **clar·i·ty**
clar·i·ty
clarrion : **clar·i·on**
clarrity : **clar·i·ty**
clarvoyance : **clair·voy·ance**
clasefy : **clas·si·fy**
clasic : **clas·sic**
clasify : **clas·si·fy**
classec : **clas·sic**
classefy : **clas·si·fy**
clas·sic
classick : **clas·sic**
classiffy : **clas·si·fy**
clas·si·fy
clastrophobia :
   claus·tro·pho·bia
Claus (Santa); **clause** (sentence
   part); **claws** (talons)
clause (sentence part); **Claus**
   (Santa); **claws** (talons)
claustraphobia :
   claus·tro·pho·bia
claustrephobia :
   claus·tro·pho·bia
claustrofobia :
   claus·tro·pho·bia
claustrophobea :
   claus·tro·pho·bia
claus·tro·pho·bia
claws (talons); **Claus** (Santa);
   clause (sentence part)
clawstrophobia :
   claus·tro·pho·bia
clean·li·ness
cleanliniss : **clean·li·ness**
cleanlyness : **clean·li·ness**
cleansed
clear·ance

clearanse : **clear·ance**
clearence : **clear·ance**
clearense : **clear·ance**
clearify : **clar·i·fy**
clearrance : **clear·ance**
clearvoyance : **clair·voy·ance**
cleav·age
cleave
cleav·er
cleavidge : **cleav·age**
cleavige : **cleav·age**
cleche : **cli·ché**
cleeche : **cli·ché**
cleerance : **clear·ance**
cleeranse : **clear·ance**
cleerence : **clear·ance**
cleerense : **clear·ance**
cleevage : **cleav·age**
cleeve : **cleave**
cleeveage : **cleav·age**
cleever : **cleav·er**
cleint : **cli·ent**
cleive : **cleave**
cleiver : **cleav·er**
clem·en·cy
clemensy : **clem·en·cy**
clemincy : **clem·en·cy**
cleminsy : **clem·en·cy**
clemmency : **clem·en·cy**
clenliness : **clean·li·ness**
clensed : **cleansed**
cleptomaniac : **klep·to·ma·ni·ac**
cliant : **cli·ent**
cliantele : **cli·en·tele**
cliantell : **cli·en·tele**
clichay : **cli·ché**
cli·ché
click (sound); **clique** (group)
cli·ent
cli·en·tele
clientell : **cli·en·tele**
clientelle : **cli·en·tele**

clieve : **cleave**
cli·mac·tic (of a climax);
  cli·ma·tic (of a climate)
climat : **cli·mate**
cli·mate
cli·ma·tic (of a climate);
  cli·mac·tic (of a climax)
climency : **clem·en·cy**
climet : **cli·mate**
climite : **cli·mate**
climmat : **cli·mate**
climmate : **cli·mate**
climmit : **cli·mate**
clinec : **clin·ic**
clin·ic
clinick : **clin·ic**
clinliness : **clean·li·ness**
clinnic : **clin·ic**
clinsed : **cleansed**
clique (group); **click** (sound)
clishay : **cli·ché**
clishee : **cli·ché**
cloak·room
cloasure : **clo·sure**
cloathing : **cloth·ing**
cloisster : **clois·ter**
clois·ter
clokeroom : **cloak·room**
clokroom : **cloak·room**
cloride : **chlo·ride**
clorine : **chlo·rine**
cloroform : **chlo·ro·form**
close (to shut); **clothes**
  (apparel)
closhure : **clo·sure**
clostrophobia :
  claus·tro·pho·bi·a
clo·sure
clothes (apparel); **close** (to
  shut); **cloths** (fabrics)
cloth·ing

cloths (fabrics); **clothes** (apparel)
clouride : **chlo·ride**
clourine : **chlo·rine**
cloyster : **clois·ter**
coaco : **co·coa**
coaficcient : **co·ef·fi·cient**
coalece : **co·alesce**
co·alesce
coalese : **co·alesce**
coaless : **co·alesce**
coalicion : **co·ali·tion**
coalishion : **co·ali·tion**
co·ali·tion
coalittion : **co·ali·tion**
coarse (rough); **course** (direction)
coaterie : **co·te·rie**
cocaign : **co·caine**
cocain : **co·caine**
co·caine
cocane : **co·caine**
cocanut : **co·co·nut**
cocaonut : **co·co·nut**
coccaine : **co·caine**
cochroach : **cock·roach**
cock·ney
cocknie : **cock·ney**
cockny : **cock·ney**
cock·roach
cockroch : **cock·roach**
cocney : **cock·ney**
cocny : **cock·ney**
co·co (palm); **co·coa** (beverage)
co·coa
cocoanut : **co·co·nut**
co·co·nut
co·coon
cocune : **co·coon**
codafy : **cod·i·fy**
coddafy : **cod·i·fy**

coddefy : **cod·i·fy**
coddify : **cod·i·fy**
codeen : **co·deine**
codefy : **cod·i·fy**
co·deine
codene : **co·deine**
cod·ger
codiene : **co·deine**
cod·i·fy
codine : **co·deine**
coefficiant : **co·ef·fi·cient**
co·ef·fi·cient
coeffisient : **co·ef·fi·cient**
coeffitiant : **co·ef·fi·cient**
coeffitient : **co·ef·fi·cient**
coeficient : **co·ef·fi·cient**
coefisient : **co·ef·fi·cient**
coelesce : **co·alesce**
coelition : **co·ali·tion**
co·erce
coercian : **co·er·cion**
coercien : **co·er·cion**
co·er·cion
coerse : **co·erce**
coersion : **co·er·cion**
coertion : **co·er·cion**
cofee : **cof·fee**
coff : **cough**
cof·fee
coffen : **cof·fin**
cofficient : **co·ef·fi·cient**
cof·fin
cofin : **cof·fin**
co·gen·cy
cogensy : **co·gen·cy**
cogentcy : **co·gen·cy**
cogentsy : **co·gen·cy**
coger : **cod·ger**
co·gnac
cognezant : **cog·ni·zant**
cognisant : **cog·ni·zant**
cog·ni·zant

coharence : **co·her·ence**
coharent : **co·her·ent**
cohecion : **co·he·sion**
coheerence : **co·her·ence**
coheerent : **co·her·ent**
coheesion : **co·he·sion**
coheirence : **co·her·ence**
coheirent : **co·her·ent**
coherance : **co·her·ence**
coheranse : **co·her·ence**
coherant : **co·her·ent**
coherce : **co·erce**
co·her·ence
coherense : **co·her·ence**
co·her·ent
coherse : **co·erce**
co·he·sion
cohhession : **co·he·sion**
cohision : **co·he·sion**
coin·age
coincedence : **co·in·ci·dence**
co·in·cide
co·in·ci·dence
coincidense : **co·in·ci·dence**
coincidince : **co·in·ci·dence**
coincied : **co·in·cide**
coinege : **coin·age**
coinige : **coin·age**
coinsedence : **co·in·ci·dence**
coinside : **co·in·cide**
coinsidence : **co·in·ci·dence**
cokaine : **co·caine**
cokney : **cock·ney**
cokny : **cock·ney**
cokonut : **co·co·nut**
colaborate : **col·lab·o·rate**
colaborator : **col·lab·o·ra·tor**
colan : **col·on**
col·an·der (drainer); **cal·en·dar**
(chart of dates); **cal·en·der**
(pressing machine)
colapse : **col·lapse**

colapsible : **col·laps·ible**
colar : **col·lar**
Colarado : **Col·o·ra·do**
colassal : **co·los·sal**
colateral : **col·lat·er·al**
coldslaw : **cole·slaw**
coleague : **col·league**
colection : **col·lec·tion**
colector : **col·lec·tor**
colege : **col·lege**
colen : **col·on**
colender : **col·an·der**
colera : **chol·era**
cole·slaw
colesterol : **cho·les·ter·ol**
col·ic
coliceum : **col·i·se·um**
colicion : **co·ali·tion**
colick : **col·ic**
col·icky
colicy : **col·icky**
colide : **col·lide**
col·i·se·um (amphitheater);
   Col·os·se·um (amphitheater
   in Rome)
colision : **col·li·sion**
colisium : **col·i·se·um**
colisseum : **col·i·se·um**
colission : **co·a·lition**
colition : **co·a·lition**
collabborate : **col·lab·o·rate**
collabborator : **col·lab·o·ra·tor**
collaberate : **col·lab·o·rate**
collaberator : **col·lab·o·ra·tor**
collabirate : **col·lab·o·rate**
collabirator : **col·lab·o·ra·tor**
col·lab·o·rate
collaborater : **col·lab·o·ra·tor**
col·lab·o·ra·tor
col·lage (composite work);
   col·league (associate);
   col·lege (school)

collander : **col·an·der**
collapce : **col·lapse**
collapsable : **col·laps·ible**
col·lapse
col·laps·ible
col·lar
col·lat·er·al
collaterel : **col·lat·er·al**
colleage : **col·lage** (composite work) *or* **col·league** (associate) *or* **col·lege** (school)
col·league (associate); **col·lage** (composite work); **col·lege** (school)
collecion : **col·lec·tion**
collecktion : **col·lec·tion**
collecter : **col·lec·tor**
col·lec·tion
col·lec·tor
colledge : **col·lage** (composite work) *or* **col·lege** (school)
colleegue : **col·league**
col·lege (school); **col·lage** (composite work); **col·league** (associate)
collegue : **col·league**
colleigue : **col·league**
collender : **col·an·der**
coller : **col·lar**
collerteral : **col·lat·er·al**
collesterol : **cho·les·ter·ol**
collic : **col·ic**
collicky : **col·icky**
col·lide
col·lie
collied : **col·lide**
colliflauer : **cau·li·flow·er**
colliflour : **cau·li·flow·er**
colliflower : **cau·li·flow·er**
collige : **col·lege**
colliseum : **col·i·se·um**

col·li·sion
collisium : **col·i·se·um**
collisseum : **col·i·se·um**
collission : **col·li·sion**
collizion : **col·li·sion**
collocial : **col·lo·qui·al**
collon : **col·on**
collonade : **col·on·nade**
collonel : **col·o·nel**
collonial : **co·lo·nial**
colloqial : **col·lo·qui·al**
colloqueal : **col·lo·qui·al**
col·lo·qui·al
colloquiel : **col·lo·qui·al**
Collorado : **Col·o·ra·do**
collossal : **co·los·sal**
collslaw : **cole·slaw**
collucion : **col·lu·sion**
collumbine : **col·um·bine**
Collumbus : **Co·lum·bus**
collumn : **col·umn**
col·lu·sion
colly : **col·lie**
Co·lom·bia (South American nation); **Co·lum·bia** (federal district)
colombine : **col·um·bine**
Colombus : **Co·lum·bus**
co·lon
colonade : **col·on·nade**
coloneal : **co·lo·nial**
col·o·nel (military officer); **ker·nel** (seed)
co·lo·nial
col·on·nade
colonnaid : **col·on·nade**
colonnel : **col·o·nel**
colonnial : **co·lo·nial**
coloquial : **col·lo·qui·al**
Coloraddo : **Col·o·ra·do**
Col·o·ra·do
coloride : **chlo·ride**

colorine : **chlo·rine**
Colorrado : **Col·o·ra·do**
colosal : **co·los·sal**
co·los·sal
Col·os·se·um (amphitheater in
   Rome); **col·i·se·um**
   (amphitheater)
colum : **col·umn**
Co·lum·bia (federal district);
   Co·lom·bia (South American
   nation)
col·um·bine
Co·lum·bus
Columbuss : **Co·lum·bus**
col·umn
columnade : **col·on·nade**
colusion : **col·lu·sion**
co·ma (unconscious state);
   com·ma (,)
comady : **com·e·dy**
comandant : **com·man·dant**
combenation : **com·bi·na·tion**
com·bi·na·tion
combinnation : **com·bi·na·tion**
combonation : **com·bi·na·tion**
combustable : **com·bus·ti·ble**
com·bus·ti·ble
comecal : **com·i·cal**
comeddy : **com·e·dy**
comedean : **co·me·di·an**
co·me·di·an
com·e·dy
comeedian : **co·me·di·an**
come·ly
comememorate :
   com·mem·o·rate
comemmorate :
   com·mem·o·rate
comemorate : **com·mem·o·rate**
comence : **com·mence**
comendable : **com·mend·able**
coment : **com·ment**

comentary : **com·men·tary**
comerce : **com·merce**
comercial : **com·mer·cial**
comersial : **com·mer·cial**
com·et (celestial body);
   com·mit (to entrust)
comfert : **com·fort**
comfertable : **com·fort·able**
com·fort
com·fort·able
comforteble : **com·fort·able**
comfortible : **com·fort·able**
com·ic
com·i·cal
comick : **com·ic**
comince : **com·mence**
comint : **com·ment**
comintary : **com·men·tary**
comiserate : **com·mis·er·ate**
comissar : **com·mis·sar**
comissary : **com·mis·sary**
comit : **com·et** (celestial body)
   or **com·mit** (to entrust)
comite : **com·mit·tee**
comittee : **com·mit·tee**
com·it·y (civility); **com·mit·tee**
   (task force)
comly : **come·ly**
com·ma (,); **co·ma**
   (unconscious state)
commady : **com·e·dy**
com·man·dant
commandaunt : **com·man·dant**
com·man·deer (to take by
   force); **com·mand·er** (leader)
com·mand·er (leader);
   com·man·deer (to take by
   force)
commant : **com·ment**
commantary : **com·men·tary**
commedian : **co·me·di·an**
commedy : **com·e·dy**

commeidian : **co·me·di·an**

commemerate :
  com·mem·o·rate
com·mem·o·rate
com·mence
com·mend·able
commendeble : **com·mend·able**
commendible : **com·mend·able**
commense : **com·mence**
com·ment
com·men·tary
commenterry : **com·men·tary**
commentery : **com·men·tary**
com·merce
com·mer·cial
commerse : **com·merce**
commershal : **com·mer·cial**
commersial : **com·mer·cial**
commet : **com·et** (celestial
  body) *or* **com·mit** (to
  entrust)
commic : **com·ic**
commical : **com·i·cal**
commince : **com·mence**
commindable : **com·mend·able**
comminse : **com·mence**
commint : **com·ment**
commintary : **com·men·tary**
commisar : **com·mis·sar**
commisary : **com·mis·sary**
com·mis·er·ate
commisirate : **com·mis·er·ate**
com·mis·sar
commissare : **com·mis·sar**
com·mis·sary
commisserate : **com·mis·er·ate**
commisserry : **com·mis·sary**
commissery : **com·mis·sary**
commisurate : **com·mis·er·ate**
commiszar : **com·mis·sar**
com·mit (to entrust); **com·et**
  (celestial body)

commite : **com·mit·tee**
com·mit·tee
committy : **com·mit·tee**
commoddity : **com·mod·i·ty**
commoddore : **com·mo·dore**
com·mode
commodety : **com·mod·i·ty**
commoditty : **com·mod·i·ty**
com·mod·i·ty
commodoar : **com·mo·dore**
commodoor : **com·mo·dore**
commodor : **com·mo·dore**
com·mo·dore
com·mon·er
com·mon·place
commonplaise : **com·mon·place**
commonplase : **com·mon·place**
com·mon·weal
com·mon·wealth
commonweel : **com·mon·weal**
commonweil : **com·mon·weal**
commonwellth :
  com·mon·wealth
commonwelth :
  com·mon·wealth
commoon : **com·mune**
commoonicable :
  com·mu·ni·ca·ble
commoonion : **com·mu·nion**
commoot : **com·mute**
com·mo·tion
com·mune
communety : **com·mu·ni·ty**
communian : **com·mu·nion**
com·mu·ni·ca·ble
com·mu·ni·cate
communiceble :
  com·mu·ni·ca·ble
communickable :
  com·mu·ni·ca·ble
communikate : **com·mu·ni·cate**
com·mu·nion

com·mu·nism
communitty : **com·mu·ni·ty**
com·mu·ni·ty
communiun : **com·mu·nion**
communnity : **com·mu·ni·ty**
communplace : **com·mon·place**
communyon : **com·mu·nion**
commurce : **com·merce**
commurse : **com·merce**
com·mute
comoddity : **com·mod·i·ty**
comode : **com·mode**
comodore : **com·mo·dore**
comoner : **com·mon·er**
comonplace : **com·mon·place**
comotion : **com·mo·tion**
compair : **com·pare**
compairable : **com·pa·ra·ble**
compairative : **com·par·a·tive**
compairison : **com·par·i·son**
com·pan·ion
companiun : **com·pan·ion**
compannion : **com·pan·ion**
companyon : **com·pan·ion**
com·pa·ra·ble
comparason : **com·par·i·son**
com·par·a·tive
com·pare
compareable : **com·pa·ra·ble**
compareble : **com·pa·ra·ble**
compareson : **com·par·i·son**
comparetive : **com·par·a·tive**
comparible : **com·pa·ra·ble**
comparisen : **com·par·i·son**
com·par·i·son
comparisun : **com·par·i·son**
comparitive : **com·par·a·tive**
compas : **com·pass**
compashion : **com·pas·sion**
compasion : **com·pas·sion**
com·pass
com·pas·sion

compatable : **com·pat·i·ble**
compateble : **com·pat·i·ble**
com·pat·i·ble
compeet : **com·pete**
compeit : **com·pete**
com·pel
compell : **com·pel**
compelsory : **com·pul·so·ry**
compencate : **com·pen·sate**
compendeum : **com·pen·di·um**
compendiom : **com·pen·di·um**
com·pen·di·um
com·pen·sate
compesition : **com·po·si·tion**
compess : **com·pass**
competator : **com·pet·i·tor**
com·pete
com·pe·tence
competense : **com·pe·tence**
competicion : **com·pe·ti·tion**
competince : **com·pe·tence**
competirer : **com·pet·i·tor**
competistion : **com·pe·ti·tion**
com·pe·ti·tion
com·pet·i·tor
compindium : **com·pen·di·um**
compinsate : **com·pen·sate**
compis : **com·pass**
compisition : **com·po·si·tion**
compitence : **com·pe·tence**
compitition : **com·pe·ti·tion**
com·pla·cen·cy
complacensy : **com·pla·cen·cy**
com·pla·cent (self-satisfied);
  com·plai·sant (eager to
  please)
complacincy : **com·pla·cen·cy**
complaicency : **com·pla·cen·cy**
complaicent : **com·pla·cent**
  (self-satisfied) *or*
  com·plai·sant (eager to
  please)

com·plain
com·plai·sant (eager to please);
  com·pla·cent (self-satisfied)
complaisency : **com·pla·cen·cy**
complane : **com·plain**
complasency : **com·pla·cen·cy**
complasent : **com·pla·cent**
  (self-satisfied) *or*
  com·plai·sant (eager to
  please)
compleat : **com·plete**
complection : **com·plex·ion**
compleet : **com·plete**
compleetion : **com·ple·tion**
com·ple·ment (that which
  completes); **com·pli·ment**
  (flattering remark)
complesion : **com·ple·tion**
com·plete
completian : **com·ple·tion**
com·ple·tion
complexian : **com·plex·ion**
com·plex·ion
com·pli·ance
complianse : **com·pli·ance**
com·pli·ant
complicitty : **com·plic·i·ty**
com·plic·i·ty
complience : **com·pli·ance**
compliense : **com·pli·ance**
complient : **com·pli·ant**
com·pli·ment (flattering
  remark); **com·ple·ment** (that
  which completes)
complisitty : **com·plic·i·ty**
complisity : **com·plic·i·ty**
complition : **com·ple·tion**
compoanent : **com·po·nent**
componant : **com·po·nent**
com·po·nent
composate : **com·pos·ite**
composet : **com·pos·ite**

composhure : **com·po·sure**
composicion : **com·po·si·tion**
composit : **com·pos·ite**
com·pos·ite
com·po·si·tion
compossite : **com·pos·ite**
com·po·sure
compozure : **com·po·sure**
comprahend : **com·pre·hend**
comprahensible :
  com·pre·hen·si·ble
compramise : **com·pro·mise**
compramize : **com·pro·mise**
comprehenceble :
  com·pre·hen·si·ble
comprehencible :
  com·pre·hen·si·ble
com·pre·hend
comprehensable :
  com·pre·hen·si·ble
comprehenseble :
  com·pre·hen·si·ble
com·pre·hen·si·ble
compremise : **com·pro·mise**
compremize : **com·pro·mise**
compreshion : **com·pres·sion**
compresible : **com·press·ible**
compresion : **com·pres·sion**
compresor : **com·pres·sor**
compressable : **com·press·ible**
compresser : **com·pres·sor**
com·press·ible
com·pres·sion
com·pres·sor
comprimise : **com·pro·mise**
comprimize : **com·pro·mise**
com·prise
comprize : **com·prise**
com·pro·mise
compromize : **com·pro·mise**
comp·trol·ler *or* **con·trol·ler**
compulcery : **com·pul·so·ry**

compulsery : **com·pul·so·ry**
com·pul·so·ry
compuss : **com·pass**
comraderie : **ca·ma·ra·de·rie**
comradry : **ca·ma·ra·de·rie**
comroderie : **ca·ma·ra·de·rie**
comune : **com·mune**
comunicable :
   com·mu·ni·ca·ble
comunicate : **com·mu·ni·cate**
comunion : **com·mu·nion**
comunism : **com·mu·nism**
comunity : **com·mu·ni·ty**
comute : **com·mute**
conafer : **co·ni·fer**
concard : **con·cord**
con·ceal
conceave : **con·ceive**
con·cede
conceed : **con·cede**
conceel : **con·ceal**
conceeve : **con·ceive**
conceil : **con·ceal**
con·ceit
con·ceiv·able
con·ceive
conceiveable : **con·ceiv·able**
concensus : **con·sen·sus**
concentrait : **con·cen·trate**
con·cen·trate
con·cen·tric
concentrick : **con·cen·tric**
con·cept
con·cep·tu·al
conceptuel : **con·cep·tu·al**
conceptule : **con·cep·tu·al**
con·cern
con·cert
con·ces·sion
conciderable : **con·sid·er·able**
conciel : **con·ceal**
conciet : **con·ceit**

concieve : **con·ceive**
con·cil·i·ate
conciliatorry : **con·cil·ia·to·ry**
con·cil·ia·to·ry
concillatory : **con·cil·ia·to·ry**
concilleate : **con·cil·i·ate**
concilliate : **con·cil·i·ate**
concilliatory : **con·cil·ia·to·ry**
concillitory : **con·cil·ia·to·ry**
concintrate : **con·cen·trate**
concirt : **con·cert**
con·cise
concomatant : **con·com·i·tant**
concometent : **con·com·i·tant**
con·com·i·tant
concomitent : **con·com·i·tant**
concommitant : **con·com·i·tant**
concommitent : **con·com·i·tant**
con·cord
concreet : **con·crete**
concreit : **con·crete**
con·crete
con·cur
concure : **con·cur**
concurent : **con·cur·rent**
concurn : **con·cern**
concurr : **con·cur**
concurrant : **con·cur·rent**
con·cur·rent
concushion : **con·cus·sion**
concusion : **con·cus·sion**
concussien : **con·cus·sion**
con·cus·sion
concution : **con·cus·sion**
condament : **con·di·ment**
condaminium :
   con·do·min·i·um
condamint : **con·di·ment**
condascend : **con·de·scend**
condascension :
   con·de·scen·sion
condement : **con·di·ment**

condeminium :
  con·do·min·i·um
condemm : **con·demn**
con·demn
condence : **con·dense**
con·dense
con·de·scend
con·de·scen·sion
condescinsion :
  con·de·scen·sion
condesend : **con·de·scend**
condesension : **con·de·scen·sion**
condessend : **con·de·scend**
condicion : **con·di·tion**
con·di·ment
condiscend : **con·de·scend**
condission : **con·di·tion**
con·di·tion
condolance : **con·do·lence**
condolanse : **con·do·lence**
con·do·lence
condolense : **con·do·lence**
condomenium :
  con·do·min·i·um
condominiem :
  con·do·min·i·um
con·do·min·i·um
condominnium :
  con·do·min·i·um
conduceve : **con·du·cive**
con·du·cive
conducter : **con·duc·tor**
con·duc·tor
conduet : **con·duit**
con·duit
condusive : **con·du·cive**
condute : **con·duit**
coneac : **co·gnac**
confadence : **con·fi·dence**
confadential : **con·fi·den·tial**
confedaracy : **con·fed·er·a·cy**
confedence : **con·fi·dence**

confedential : **con·fi·den·tial**
con·fed·er·a·cy
confederasy : **con·fed·er·a·cy**
con·fed·er·ate
confederet : **con·fed·er·ate**
confederissy : **con·fed·er·a·cy**
confederisy : **con·fed·er·a·cy**
confedirate : **con·fed·er·ate**
conferance : **con·fer·ence**
conferanse : **con·fer·ence**
confered : **con·ferred**
con·fer·ee
con·fer·ence
conferense : **con·fer·ence**
conferie : **con·fer·ee**
con·ferred
conferree : **con·fer·ee**
conferrence : **con·fer·ence**
confery : **con·fer·ee**
confesion : **con·fes·sion**
confessian : **con·fes·sion**
con·fes·sion
confeti : **con·fet·ti**
con·fet·ti
con·fi·dant or **con·fi·dante** (one
  confided in); **con·fi·dent**
  (assured)
con·fi·dante or **con·fi·dant** (one
  confided in); **con·fi·dent**
  (assured)
con·fi·dence
confidense : **con·fi·dence**
confidenshial : **con·fi·den·tial**
confidensial : **con·fi·den·tial**
con·fi·dent (assured);
  con·fi·dant (one confided in)
con·fi·den·tial
confidintial : **con·fi·den·tial**
configeration :
  con·fig·u·ra·tion
configguration :
  con·fig·u·ra·tion

con·fig·u·ra·tion
con·fla·gra·tion
conflagretion : **con·fla·gra·tion**
conflegration : **con·fla·gra·tion**
confligration : **con·fla·gra·tion**
confuree : **con·fer·ee**
confurred : **con·ferred**
con·fused
confuzed : **con·fused**
con·geal
congeel : **con·geal**
congeenial : **con·ge·nial**
congeil : **con·geal**
con·ge·nial
conginial : **con·ge·nial**
congizant : **cog·ni·zant**
congnac : **co·gnac**
congradulate : **con·grat·u·late**
congragate : **con·gre·gate**
congragration : **con·gre·ga·tion**
congratalate : **con·grat·u·late**
con·grat·u·late
congregacion : **con·gre·ga·tion**
con·gre·gate
con·gre·ga·tion
congres : **con·gress**
con·gress
congrigate : **con·gre·gate**
congrigation : **con·gre·ga·tion**
congriss : **con·gress**
congruance : **con·gru·ence**
congruanse : **con·gru·ence**
con·gru·ence
congruense : **con·gru·ence**
congugal : **con·ju·gal**
coniac : **co·gnac**
con·ic
con·i·fer
conivance : **con·niv·ance**
conjagle : **con·ju·gal**
conjigal : **con·ju·gal**
con·ju·gal

conker : **con·quer**
conkeror : **con·quer·or**
connatation : **con·no·ta·tion**
Connectacutt : **Con·nect·i·cut**
Connectecut : **Con·nect·i·cut**
Con·nect·i·cut
Connetacut : **Con·nect·i·cut**
Conneticut : **Con·nect·i·cut**
connic : **con·ic**
connifer : **co·ni·fer**
con·niv·ance
connivanse : **con·niv·ance**
connivence : **con·niv·ance**
con·nois·seur
connoser : **con·nois·seur**
connossure : **con·nois·seur**
con·no·ta·tion
con·note
conosseur : **con·nois·seur**
conotation : **con·no·ta·tion**
conote : **con·note**
conpare : **com·pare**
con·quer
conquerer : **con·quer·or**
con·quer·or
conquor : **con·quer**
conqur : **con·quer**
conqurer : **con·quer·or**
consacrate : **con·se·crate**
consalate : **con·sul·ate**
consalation : **con·so·la·tion**
consarn : **con·cern**
con·science (moral sense);
  con·scious (awake)
con·scious (awake);
  con·science (moral sense)
conseal : **con·ceal**
con·se·crate
consede : **con·cede**
conseed : **con·cede**
conseel : **con·ceal**
conseeve : **con·ceive**

conseil : **con·ceal**
conseit : **con·ceit**
conseive : **con·ceive**
consensis : **con·sen·sus**
con·sen·sus
consentrate : **con·cen·trate**
consentric : **con·cen·tric**
consept : **con·cept**
conseptual : **con·cep·tu·al**
con·se·quence
consequense : **con·se·quence**
consequince : **con·se·quence**
consern : **con·cern**
consert : **con·cert**
conservatian : **con·ser·va·tion**
con·ser·va·tion
con·ser·va·tive
conservatorry : **con·ser·va·to·ry**
con·ser·va·to·ry
conservetive : **con·ser·va·tive**
conservetory : **con·ser·va·to·ry**
conservitive : **con·ser·va·tive**
conseshion : **con·ces·sion**
consesion : **con·ces·sion**
consession : **con·ces·sion**
consice : **con·cise**
consicrate : **con·se·crate**
con·sid·er·able
considerible : **con·sid·er·able**
consieve : **con·ceive**
consilate : **con·sul·ate**
consilation : **con·so·la·tion**
consilatory : **con·cil·ia·to·ry**
consiliate : **con·cil·i·ate**
consiliatory : **con·cil·ia·to·ry**
consilitory : **con·cil·ia·to·ry**
consillatory : **con·cil·ia·to·ry**
consilliate : **con·cil·i·ate**
consilliatory : **con·cil·ia·to·ry**
consillitory : **con·cil·ia·to·ry**
consintrate : **con·cen·trate**
consise : **con·cise**

consistancy : **con·sis·ten·cy**
consistansy : **con·sis·ten·cy**
consistant : **con·sis·tent**
con·sis·ten·cy
consistensy : **con·sis·ten·cy**
con·sis·tent
consoladate : **con·sol·i·date**
con·so·la·tion
consoledate : **con·sol·i·date**
con·sol·i·date
consoomer : **con·sum·er**
conspeeracy : **con·spir·a·cy**
consperacy : **con·spir·a·cy**
con·spir·a·cy
conspirasy : **con·spir·a·cy**
conspirater : **con·spir·a·tor**
con·spir·a·tor
conspirisy : **con·spir·a·cy**
constabble : **con·sta·ble**
con·sta·ble
constallation : **con·stel·la·tion**
con·stan·cy
constapate : **con·sti·pate**
constatute : **con·sti·tute**
consteble : **con·sta·ble**
constelation : **con·stel·la·tion**
con·stel·la·tion
constency : **con·stan·cy**
constensy : **con·stan·cy**
constepate : **con·sti·pate**
constetue : **con·sti·tute**
con·sti·pate
constituancy : **con·stit·u·en·cy**
con·stit·u·en·cy
constituensy : **con·stit·u·en·cy**
con·sti·tute
con·sul (diplomat); **coun·cil**
  (assembly); **coun·sel** (advice;
  lawyer)
con·sul·ate
consulltane : con·**sul·tant**
con·sul·tant

consultent : **con·sul·tant**
con·sum·er
consumor : **con·sum·er**
consurn : **con·cern**
consurvation : **con·ser·va·tion**
contageous : **con·ta·gious**
con·ta·gious
containence : **con·ti·nence**
(self-restraint) *or*
coun·te·nance (face)
contajious : **con·ta·gious**
contamenate : **con·tam·i·nate**
con·tam·i·nate
contemperary :
con·tem·po·rary
contempirary : **con·tem·po·rary**
contemporarry :
con·tem·po·rary
con·tem·po·rary
contemporery :
con·tem·po·rary
contenence : **con·ti·nence**
(self-restraint) *or*
coun·te·nance (face)
contenent : **con·ti·nent**
contenentel : **con·ti·nen·tal**
contengent : **con·tin·gent**
con·tes·tant
contestent : **con·tes·tant**
contestint : **con·tes·tant**
contimporary :
con·tem·po·rary
continance : **con·ti·nence**
(self-restraint) *or*
coun·te·nance (face)
con·ti·nence (self-restraint);
coun·te·nance (face)
con·ti·nent
con·ti·nen·tal
continentle : **con·ti·nen·tal**
con·tin·gent
contingint : **con·tin·gent**

con·tin·u·al
continuel : **con·tin·u·al**
continule : **con·tin·u·al**
con·tour
con·tra·band
con·tra·cep·tive
contracter : **con·trac·tor**
con·trac·tor
con·tra·dict
contradictery : **con·tra·dic·to·ry**
contradictorry :
con·tra·dic·to·ry
con·tra·dic·to·ry
contrarry : **con·trary**
con·trary
contraseptive : **con·tra·cep·tive**
contravercial : **con·tro·ver·sial**
contravercy : **con·tro·ver·sy**
contraverseal : **con·tro·ver·sial**
contraversial : **con·tro·ver·sial**
contraversy : **con·tro·ver·sy**
contreband : **con·tra·band**
contreceptive : **con·tra·cep·tive**
contredict : **con·tra·dict**
contredictory : **con·tra·dic·to·ry**
contrery : **con·trary**
contreversial : **con·tro·ver·sial**
contreversy : **con·tro·ver·sy**
contriband : **con·tra·band**
contridict : **con·tra·dict**
contridictory : **con·tra·dic·to·ry**
con·triv·ance
contrivence : **con·triv·ance**
contrivense : **con·triv·ance**
con·trol
controll : **con·trol**
con·trol·ler *or* **comp·trol·ler**
con·tro·ver·sial
con·tro·ver·sy
contry : **coun·try**
contur : **con·tour**
conture : **con·tour**

convacation : **con·vo·ca·tion**
con·va·les·cence
convalescense : **con·va·les·cence**
convalesence : **con·va·les·cence**
convalessence : **con·va·les·cence**
convay : **con·vey**
convayance : **con·vey·ance**
convean : **con·vene**
conveen : **con·vene**
conveenience : **con·ve·nience**
convelescence : **con·va·les·cence**
con·vene
conveneance : **con·ve·nience**
con·ve·nience
conveniense : **con·ve·nience**
con·ve·nient
con·ver·gence
convergince : **con·ver·gence**
convertable : **con·vert·ible**
con·vert·er (one that converts);
  con·vert·or (electrical device)
con·vert·ible
con·vert·or (electrical device);
  con·vert·er (one that
  converts)
convexety : **con·vex·i·ty**
convexitty : **con·vex·i·ty**
con·vex·i·ty
con·vey
con·vey·ance
conveyence : **con·vey·ance**
convication : **con·vo·ca·tion**
convience : **con·ve·nience**
convient : **con·ve·nient**
convilescence : **con·va·les·cence**
convine : **con·vene**
convinience : **con·ve·nience**
convinient : **con·ve·nient**
con·vo·ca·tion
convurgence : **con·ver·gence**
conyac : **co·gnac**
coocumber : **cu·cum·ber**

coogar : **cou·gar**
cooger : **cou·gar**
cookoo : **cuck·oo**
coo·lie (laborer); **cool·ly** (in a
  cool manner)
cool·ly (in a cool manner);
  coo·lie (laborer)
co·op·er·ate
coopon : **cou·pon**
co·or·di·nate
corage : **cour·age**
corageous : **cou·ra·geous**
cor·al (reef); **cho·ral** (relating
  to a choir); **cho·rale** (hymn);
  cor·ral (horse pen)
corale : **cho·ral** (relating to a
  choir) or **cho·rale** (hymn) or
  cor·al (reef) or **cor·ral** (horse
  pen)
coralle : **cho·ral** (relating to a
  choir) or **cho·rale** (hymn) or
  cor·al (reef) or **cor·ral** (horse
  pen)
coranation : **cor·o·na·tion**
cord (rope); **chord** (music)
cordaroy : **cor·du·roy**
cordeal : **cor·dial**
cordeality : **cor·dial·i·ty**
corderoy : **cor·du·roy**
cordialety : **cor·dial·i·ty**
cor·dial·i·ty
cordiallity : **cor·dial·i·ty**
cordiroy : **cor·du·roy**
cor·du·roy
corect : **cor·rect**
corel : **cho·ral** (relating to a
  choir) or **cho·rale** (hymn) or
  cor·al (reef) or **cor·ral** (horse
  pen)
corelate : **cor·re·late**
coreographer :
  cho·re·og·ra·pher

corespondence :
  cor·re·spon·dence
corgeality : **cor·dial·i·ty**
corgial : **cor·dial**
coridor : **cor·ri·dor**
coriographer :
  cho·re·og·ra·pher
cornace : **cor·nice**
cornation : **cor·o·na·tion**
cor·nea
cornia : **cor·nea**
cor·nice
cornise : **cor·nice**
corobarate : **cor·rob·o·rate**
corode : **cor·rode**
corolary : **cor·ol·lary**
cor·ol·lary
cor·o·na·tion
cor·o·ner
cororoborate : **cor·rob·o·rate**
corparate : **cor·po·rate**
corperal : **cor·po·ral**
corperate : **cor·po·rate**
cor·po·ral
cor·po·rate
corporel : **cor·po·ral**
corps (military unit); **corpse**
  (dead body)
corpse (dead body); **corps**
  (military unit)
corrador : **cor·ri·dor**
corragation : **cor·ru·ga·tion**
cor·ral (horse pen); **cho·ral**
  (relating to a choir);
  cho·rale (hymn); **cor·al** (reef)
corralate : **cor·re·late**
corrallary : **cor·ol·lary**
cor·rect
correl : **cho·ral** (relating to a
  choir) *or* **cho·rale** (hymn) *or*
  cor·al (reef) *or* **cor·ral** (horse
  pen)

cor·re·late
corresponanse :
  cor·re·spon·dence
correspondance :
  cor·re·spon·dence
cor·re·spon·dence
corridoor : **cor·ri·dor**
cor·ri·dor
corrobborate : **cor·rob·o·rate**
corroberate : **cor·rob·o·rate**
cor·rob·o·rate
cor·rode
corroll : **cho·ral** (relating to a
  choir) *or* **cho·rale** (hymn) *or*
  cor·al (reef) *or* **cor·ral** (horse
  pen)
corrollary : **cor·ol·lary**
corrollery : **cor·ol·lary**
corroner : **cor·o·ner**
cor·ru·ga·tion
cor·rupt
corrus : **cho·rus**
corteous : **cour·te·ous**
cortesy : **cour·te·sy**
corugation : **cor·ru·ga·tion**
corupt : **cor·rupt**
corus : **cho·rus**
corvet : **cor·vette**
cor·vette
cosmapolitan :
  cos·mo·pol·i·tan
cosmepolitan : **cos·mo·pol·i·tan**
cos·met·ic
cosmettic : **cos·met·ic**
cos·mo·pol·i·tan
cosmopoliten :
  cos·mo·pol·i·tan
cosmopollitan :
  cos·mo·pol·i·tan
cotarie : **co·te·rie**
coteree : **co·te·rie**
co·te·rie

cotery : **co·te·rie**
cot·tage
cottege : **cot·tage**
cotten : **cot·ton**
cottige : **cot·tage**
cot·ton
cou·gar
couger : **cou·gar**
cough
coun·cil (assembly); **con·sul**
   (diplomat); **coun·sel** (advice;
   lawyer)
coun·sel (advice; lawyer);
   con·sul (diplomat); **coun·cil**
   (assembly)
counseler : **coun·sel·or**
counsellor : **coun·sel·or**
coun·sel·or
counsillor : **coun·sel·or**
coun·te·nance (face);
   con·ti·nence (self-restraint)
countenanse : **con·ti·nence**
   (self-restraint) or
   coun·te·nance (face)
countenence : **con·ti·nence**
   (self-restraint) or
   coun·te·nance (face)
coun·ter·feit
counterfet : **coun·ter·feit**
counterfiet : **coun·ter·feit**
counterfit : **coun·ter·feit**
count·ess
countinance : **con·ti·nence**
   (self-restraint) or
   coun·te·nance (face)
countiss : **count·ess**
coun·try
coupan : **cou·pon**
coupelet : **coup·let**
coupeling : **coup·ling**
coupleing : **coup·ling**
coup·let

coup·ling
cou·pon
couponn : **cou·pon**
cour·age
cou·ra·geous
couragious : **cou·ra·geous**
courege : **cour·age**
cou·ri·er
courige : **cour·age**
courrier : **cou·ri·er**
course (direction); **coarse**
   (rough)
courtasy : **cour·te·sy**
   (politeness) or **curt·sy** (bow)
cour·te·ous
courtessy : **cour·te·sy**
   (politeness) or **curt·sy** (bow)
cour·te·sy (politeness); **curt·sy**
   (bow)
courtious : **cour·te·ous**
courtisy : **cour·te·sy**
   (politeness) or **curt·sy** (bow)
courtmarshall : **court-mar·tial**
court-mar·tial
cousen : **cous·in**
cous·in
cov·e·nant
covenent : **cov·e·nant**
covennant : **cov·e·nant**
cov·er·age
coverege : **cov·er·age**
coverige : **cov·er·age**
covrage : **cov·er·age**
cowardace : **cow·ard·ice**
cow·ard·ice
cowardise : **cow·ard·ice**
cowardiss : **cow·ard·ice**
cowerdice : **cow·ard·ice**
coy·ote
coyotee : **coy·ote**
coyotie : **coy·ote**
crainium : **cra·ni·um**

cranbary : **cran•ber•ry**
cran•ber•ry
cranbery : **cran•ber•ry**
craniem : **cra•ni•um**
cra•ni•um
cra•ter
crator : **cra•ter**
cra•vat
cravatt : **cra•vat**
creak (noise); **creek** (stream)
creamary : **cream•ery**
creamerry : **cream•ery**
cream•ery
creamory : **cream•ery**
crease
creater : **cre•ator**
cre•ator
crea•ture
crecent : **cres•cent**
credability : **cred•i•bil•i•ty**
credable : **cred•i•ble**
cre•dence
credense : **cre•dence**
credibilety : **cred•i•bil•i•ty**
cred•i•bil•i•ty
credibillity : **cred•i•bil•i•ty**
cred•i•ble
credince : **cre•dence**
cre•do
creedence : **cre•dence**
creedo : **cre•do**
creek (stream); **creak** (noise);
  crick (pain in neck)
creemery : **cream•ery**
creep
creese : **crease**
creeture : **crea•ture**
cre•scen•do
cres•cent
creshendo : **cre•scen•do**
cressant : **cres•cent**
cressendo : **cre•scen•do**

cressent : **cres•cent**
creture : **crea•ture**
crev•asse (crack in ice);
  crev•ice (narrow crack)
crevat : **cra•vat**
crevatte : **cra•vat**
crev•ice (narrow crack);
  crev•asse (crack in ice)
crevisse : **crev•asse** (crack in
  ice) *or* **crev•ice** (narrow
  crack)
criator : **cre•ator**
crick (pain in neck); **creek**
  (stream)
crimenal : **crim•i•nal**
crim•i•nal
crimminal : **crim•i•nal**
crimsen : **crim•son**
crim•son
criptic : **cryp•tic**
crisanthamum :
  chry•san•the•mum
crisanthemum :
  chry•san•the•mum
cri•ses (*plur.*); **cri•sis** (*sing.*)
cri•sis (*sing.*); **cri•ses** (*plur.*)
crissis : **cri•sis**
cristal : **crys•tal**
Cristian : **Chris•tian**
Cristianity : **Chris•tian•i•ty**
critacism : **crit•i•cism**
critearia : **cri•te•ria**
critearion : **cri•te•ri•on**
criteek : **cri•tique**
criteeque : **cri•tique**
criteeria : **cri•te•ria**
criteerion : **cri•te•ri•on**
cri•te•ria (*plur.*); **cri•te•ri•on**
  (*sing.*)
cri•te•ri•on (*sing.*); **cri•te•ria**
  (*plur.*)
crit•ic

criticise (*Brit.*) : **crit·i·cize**
crit·i·cism
crit·i·cize
cri·tique
critiria : **cri·te·ria**
critirion : **cri·te·ri·on**
critisism : **crit·i·cism**
critisize : **crit·i·cize**
crittacize : **crit·i·cize**
crittic : **crit·ic**
critticism : **crit·i·cism**
critticize : **crit·i·cize**
crocadial : **croc·o·dile**
crocadile : **croc·o·dile**
crockodile : **croc·o·dile**
croc·o·dile
cromeum : **chro·mi·um**
cromiem : **chro·mi·um**
cromium : **chro·mi·um**
cronic : **chron·ic**
cronicle : **chron·i·cle**
cronollogy : **chro·nol·o·gy**
cronologgy : **chro·nol·o·gy**
cronology : **chro·nol·o·gy**
croose : **cruise**
croud : **crowd**
crowd
crucefy : **cru·ci·fy**
cru·cial
crucibal : **cru·ci·ble**
cru·ci·ble
cruciffy : **cru·ci·fy**
cru·ci·fy
cruise
cruse : **cruise**
crushall : **cru·cial**
crusial : **cru·cial**
crusible : **cru·ci·ble**
crusify : **cru·ci·fy**
crus·ta·cean
crustacion : **crus·ta·cean**
crustashean : **crus·ta·cean**

cruze : **cruise**
cryp·tic
cryptick : **cryp·tic**
crysanthamum :
    chry·san·the·mum
crysanthemum :
    chry·san·the·mum
crys·tal
crystall : **crys·tal**
crystell : **crys·tal**
csar : **czar**
cuadrant : **quad·rant**
cuarto : **quar·to**
cubbard : **cup·board**
cub·i·cal (cube-shaped);
    cub·i·cle (compartment)
cub·i·cle (compartment);
    cub·i·cal (cube-shaped)
cuck·oo
cucomber : **cu·cum·ber**
cucoo : **cuck·oo**
cu·cum·ber
cud·gel
cudgle : **cud·gel**
cue (signal; poolstick); **queue**
    (pigtail; line)
Cuebec : **Que·bec**
cujel : **cud·gel**
culenery : **cu·li·nary**
cu·li·nary
cullenery : **cu·li·nary**
cullinary : **cu·li·nary**
cullmination : **cul·mi·na·tion**
cullprit : **cul·prit**
culltivate : **cul·ti·vate**
culmanation : **cul·mi·na·tion**
culmenation : **cul·mi·na·tion**
cul·mi·na·tion
culpabal : **cul·pa·ble**
cul·pa·ble
culpible : **cul·pa·ble**
culpret : **cul·prit**

cul·prit
cultavate : **cul·ti·vate**
cul·ti·vate
cummercial : **com·mer·cial**
cumpass : **com·pass**
cup·board
cupbord : **cup·board**
cup·ful
cupfull : **cup·ful**
cuplet : **coup·let**
cupling : **coup·ling**
cupon : **cou·pon**
curafe : **ca·rafe**
curage : **cour·age**
curdal : **cur·dle**
curdel : **cur·dle**
cur·dle
cureo : **cu·rio**
curiculum : **cur·ric·u·lum**
cu·rio
curios : **cu·ri·ous**
curiosety : **cu·ri·os·i·ty**
cu·ri·os·i·ty
curiossity : **cu·ri·os·i·ty**
cu·ri·ous
curnel : **col·o·nel** (military
    officer) *or* **ker·nel** (seed)
cur·rant (berry); **cur·rent**
    (*noun,* flow; *adj.,*
    contemporary)
cur·rent (*noun,* flow; *adj.,*
    contemporary); **cur·rant**
    (berry)
cur·ric·u·lum
currier : **cou·ri·er**
cursary : **cur·so·ry**
curserry : **cur·so·ry**
cursery : **cur·so·ry**
cur·so·ry
curteous : **cour·te·ous**
curt·sey *or* **curt·sy** (bow);
    cour·te·sy (politeness)

curt·sy *or* **curt·sey** (bow);
    cour·te·sy (politeness)
cusin : **cous·in**
cus·tard
custerd : **cus·tard**
custodean : **cus·to·di·an**
cus·to·di·an
cus·tom·er
custommer : **cus·tom·er**
cut·lass
cutless : **cut·lass**
cutliss : **cut·lass**
cuzzin : **cous·in**
cwire : **choir**
cy·a·nide
cyanied : **cy·a·nide**
cy·ber·net·ics
cybernettics : **cy·ber·net·ics**
cycal : **cy·cle**
cy·cle (rotation); **sick·le** (knife)
cycloan : **cy·clone**
cy·clone
cyg·net (swan); **sig·net** (ring)
cyl·in·der
cyllinder : **cyl·in·der**
cym·bal (brass plate); **sym·bol**
    (meaningful image)
cymbol : **cym·bal** (brass plate)
    or **sym·bol** (meaningful
    image)
cyn·i·cism
cynisism : **cyn·i·cism**
cyote : **coy·ote**
cy·press
cypriss : **cy·press**
czar *or* **tsar**
Czechoslavokia :
    Czecho·slo·va·kia
Czecho·slo·va·kia
Czeckoslovakia :
    Czecho·slo·va·kia

D

dachshound : **dachs·hund**
dachs·hund
dackshund : **dachs·hund**
dad·dy
dady : **dad·dy**
daery : **dairy** (milk farm) *or*
  di·a·ry (daybook)
daffadil : **daf·fo·dil**
daffault : **de·fault**
daf·fo·dil
daffodill : **daf·fo·dil**
dafodil : **daf·fo·dil**
daggerotype : **da·guerre·o·type**
da·guerre·o·type
daguerrotype :
  da·guerre·o·type
dahl·ia
dai·ly
dai·qui·ri
daiquiry : **dai·qui·ri**
dairdevil : **dare·dev·il**
dairy (milk farm); **di·a·ry**
  (daybook)
Dalas : **Dal·las**
daley : **dai·ly**
dalinquent : **de·lin·quent**
Dal·las
Dalles : **Dal·las**
dallia : **dahl·ia**
dal·li·ance
dallianse : **dal·li·ance**
dallience : **dal·li·ance**
Dallis : **Dal·las**
Dallmatian : **Dal·ma·tian**
dallyance : **dal·li·ance**
Dalmashin : **Dal·ma·tian**
Dal·ma·tian
Dalmation : **Dal·ma·tian**
daly : **dai·ly**
damadge : **dam·age**

dam·age
damidge : **dam·age**
damige : **dam·age**
dammed (blocked); **damned**
  (condemned)
damned (condemned);
  dammed (blocked)
damozel : **dam·sel**
dam·sel
damsill : **dam·sel**
damsul : **dam·sel**
damzel : **dam·sel**
danc·er
dandalion : **dan·de·li·on**
dan·de·li·on
dandilion : **dan·de·li·on**
dandreff : **dan·druff**
dandriff : **dan·druff**
dan·druff
dandylion : **dan·de·li·on**
Danemark : **Den·mark**
Danesh : **Dan·ish**
dangeriss : **dan·ger·ous**
dan·ger·ous
Dan·ish
Dannish : **Dan·ish**
Dannube : **Dan·ube**
danser : **danc·er**
Dan·ube
dapravity : **de·prav·i·ty**
daquerri : **dai·qui·ri**
daquiri : **dai·qui·ri**
daralict : **der·e·lict**
daredevel : **dare·dev·il**
dare·dev·il
dary : **dairy** (milk farm) *or*
  di·a·ry (daybook)
da·ta (*plur.*); **da·tum** (*sing.*)
da·tum (*sing.*); **da·ta** (*plur.*)
daugh·ter

dauter : **daugh·ter**
dautter : **daugh·ter**
dazle : **daz·zle**
dazzal : **daz·zle**
dazzel : **daz·zle**
daz·zle
deacan : **dea·con**
dea·con
deadicate : **ded·i·cate**
dead·li·er
deadlyer : **dead·li·er**
deaf·en
deaf·ness
deafniss : **deaf·ness**
deakon : **dea·con**
dealt
deapth : **depth**
dear (precious); **deer** (animal)
dearth
death
deaty : **de·i·ty**
debachery : **de·bauch·ery**
de·ba·cle
debait : **de·bate**
debakle : **de·ba·cle**
debanair : **deb·o·nair**
de·bate
debauchary : **de·bauch·ery**
de·bauch·ery
debawchery : **de·bauch·ery**
debbacle : **de·ba·cle**
debbate : **de·bate**
debbonair : **deb·o·nair**
debbonare : **deb·o·nair**
debbris : **de·bris**
debecal : **de·ba·cle**
debinair : **deb·o·nair**
deb·o·nair
debonare : **deb·o·nair**
debree : **de·bris**
debres : **de·bris**

de·bris
debter : **debt·or**
debt·or (one who owes); **de·ter** (to prevent)
debue : **de·but**
de·but
decadance : **de·ca·dence**
decadanse : **de·ca·dence**
de·cade
de·ca·dence
decadense : **de·ca·dence**
decaid : **de·cade**
decapatate : **de·cap·i·tate**
decapetate : **de·cap·i·tate**
decapitait : **de·cap·i·tate**
de·cap·i·tate
decappitate : **de·cap·i·tate**
decarate : **dec·o·rate**
decathalon : **de·cath·lon**
decathelon : **de·cath·lon**
de·cath·lon
deccade : **de·cade**
deccadence : **de·ca·dence**
deccorate : **dec·o·rate**
de·ceased
deceatful : **de·ceit·ful**
deceave : **de·ceive**
decebel : **dec·i·bel**
deceble : **dec·i·bel**
decedence : **de·ca·dence**
deceesed : **de·ceased**
deceised : **de·ceased**
de·ceit·ful
deceitfull : **de·ceit·ful**
de·ceive
decemal : **dec·i·mal**
De·cem·ber
de·cen·cy
decendant : **de·scen·dant**
decendent : **de·scen·dant**
decensy : **de·cen·cy**

de·cent (respectable); **de·scent**
  (act of going down);
  dis·sent (disagreement)
decesed : **de·ceased**
decetful : **de·ceit·ful**
deceve : **de·ceive**
decibal : **dec·i·bel**
dec·i·bel
decibell : **dec·i·bel**
de·cide
decidewous : **de·cid·u·ous**
deciduiss : **de·cid·u·ous**
de·cid·u·ous
decietful : **de·ceit·ful**
decietfull : **de·ceit·ful**
decieve : **de·ceive**
decifer : **de·ci·pher**
dec·i·mal
decimel : **dec·i·mal**
decimmal : **dec·i·mal**
decincy : **de·cen·cy**
de·ci·pher
deciphur : **de·ci·pher**
deciple : **dis·ci·ple**
decisian : **de·ci·sion**
de·ci·sion
decission : **de·ci·sion**
decizion : **de·ci·sion**
deckade : **de·cade**
decklaration : **dec·la·ra·tion**
deckorate : **dec·o·rate**
declair : **de·clare**
declaratian : **dec·la·ra·tion**
dec·la·ra·tion
de·clare
decleration : **dec·la·ra·tion**
decliration : **dec·la·ra·tion**
decontamanate :
  de·con·tam·i·nate
decontamenate :
  de·con·tam·i·nate
de·con·tam·i·nate

decontamminate :
  de·con·tam·i·nate
de·cor
decoram : **de·co·rum**
dec·o·rate
decore : **de·cor**
decorem : **de·co·rum**
decorr : **de·cor**
decorrum : **de·co·rum**
de·co·rum
decreace : **de·crease**
de·crease
decreece : **de·crease**
decreese : **de·crease**
decreise : **de·crease**
decrepatude : **de·crep·i·tude**
decrepet : **de·crep·it**
decrepid : **de·crep·it**
de·crep·it
de·crep·i·tude
decreppit : **de·crep·it**
decreppitude : **de·crep·i·tude**
decrese : **de·crease**
dedacate : **ded·i·cate**
deddicate : **ded·i·cate**
dedduce : **de·duce**
dedduction : **de·duc·tion**
dedecate : **ded·i·cate**
ded·i·cate
dedlier : **dead·li·er**
dedoose : **de·duce**
de·duce
deducktion : **de·duc·tion**
de·duc·tion
deduse : **de·duce**
deecon : **dea·con**
deer (animal); **dear** (precious)
deesall : **die·sel**
deesel : **die·sel**
deeth : **death**
de·face
defacit : **def·i·cit**

defallt : **de·fault**
defalt : **de·fault**
def·a·ma·tion
defammation : **def·a·ma·tion**
defanitely : **def·i·nite·ly**
defanition : **def·i·ni·tion**
defase : **de·face**
defaullt : **de·fault**
de·fault
de·feat
defeet : **de·feat**
defeit : **de·feat**
defemation : **def·a·ma·tion**
defence (*Brit.*) : **de·fense**
defencible : **de·fen·si·ble**
de·fen·dant
defendent : **de·fen·dant**
defendint : **de·fen·dant**
defensable : **de·fen·si·ble**
de·fense
defenseble : **de·fen·si·ble**
defensibal : **de·fen·si·ble**
de·fen·si·ble
defered : **de·ferred**
de·ferred
defete : **de·feat**
defface : **de·face**
deffamation : **def·a·ma·tion**
deffeat : **de·feat**
deffen : **deaf·en**
deffenatly : **def·i·nite·ly**
deffendent : **de·fen·dant**
deffense : **de·fense**
deffered : **de·ferred**
defferred : **de·ferred**
defficit : **def·i·cit**
deffinitely : **def·i·nite·ly**
deffinition : **def·i·ni·tion**
deffness : **deaf·ness**
de·fi·ance
defianse : **de·fi·ance**
de·fi·cient

def·i·cit
defience : **de·fi·ance**
defiense : **de·fi·ance**
defimation : **def·a·ma·tion**
de·fin·able
definately : **def·i·nite·ly**
definatly : **def·i·nite·ly**
defineable : **de·fin·able**
defineble : **de·fin·able**
definetion : **def·i·ni·tion**
definetly : **def·i·nite·ly**
definibal : **de·fin·able**
definible : **de·fin·able**
def·i·nite·ly
def·i·ni·tion
definitly : **def·i·nite·ly**
defiset : **def·i·cit**
defisient : **de·fi·cient**
defisit : **def·i·cit**
defrad : **de·fraud**
de·fraud
defrod : **de·fraud**
defth : **depth**
defyance : **de·fi·ance**
degenarate : **de·gen·er·ate**
de·gen·er·ate
degennerate : **de·gen·er·ate**
deginerate : **de·gen·er·ate**
deginnerate : **de·gen·er·ate**
deg·ra·da·tion
degradeation : **deg·ra·da·tion**
degredation : **deg·ra·da·tion**
dehidrate : **de·hy·drate**
dehli : **Del·hi** (city) *or* **deli**
  (delicatessen)
dehydrait : **de·hy·drate**
de·hy·drate
deiffy : **de·i·fy**
de·i·fy
deisel : **die·sel**
deitary : **di·etary**
de·i·ty

dekathalon : **de·cath·lon**
dekathlon : **de·cath·lon**
delacacy : **del·i·ca·cy**
delacate : **del·i·cate**
delagate : **del·e·gate**
delaget : **del·e·gate**
delapidated : **di·lap·i·dat·ed**
delaterious : **del·e·te·ri·ous**
Delawair : **Del·a·ware**
Del·a·ware
Delawear : **Del·a·ware**
delearious : **de·lir·i·ous**
deleat : **de·lete**
delecacy : **del·i·ca·cy**
delecktable : **de·lec·ta·ble**
de·lec·ta·ble
delectibal : **de·lec·ta·ble**
delectible : **de·lec·ta·ble**
deleerious : **de·lir·i·ous**
deleet : **de·lete**
del·e·gate
delerious : **de·lir·i·ous**
de·lete
del·e·te·ri·ous
Deleware : **Del·a·ware**
Del·hi (city); **deli** (delicatessen)
deli (delicatessen); **Del·hi** (city)
delibberate : **de·lib·er·ate**
de·lib·er·ate
deliberet : **de·lib·er·ate**
del·i·ca·cy
delicasy : **del·i·ca·cy**
del·i·cate
delicatessan : **del·i·ca·tes·sen**
del·i·ca·tes·sen
deliceous : **de·li·cious**
delicet : **del·i·cate**
delicetessen : **del·i·ca·tes·sen**
de·li·cious
delinguent : **de·lin·quent**
delinquant : **de·lin·quent**
de·lin·quent

de·lir·i·ous
delishous : **de·li·cious**
deliterious : **del·e·te·ri·ous**
de·liv·er·ance
deliveranse : **de·liv·er·ance**
deliverence : **de·liv·er·ance**
dellaterious : **del·e·te·ri·ous**
dellegate : **del·e·gate**
Delleware : **Del·a·ware**
dellhi : **Del·hi** (city) *or* **deli**
  (delicatessen)
delli : **Del·hi** (city) *or* **deli**
  (delicatessen)
dellicacy : **del·i·ca·cy**
dellicate : **del·i·cate**
dellicatessen : **del·i·ca·tes·sen**
delliverence : **de·liv·er·ance**
delt : **dealt**
demacracy : **de·moc·ra·cy**
demagod : **demi·god**
dem·a·gog *or* **dem·a·gogue**
dem·a·gogue *or* **dem·a·gog**
demalition : **dem·o·li·tion**
demanstrate : **dem·on·strate**
de·mean
demeen : **de·mean**
demenshia : **de·men·tia**
demension : **di·men·sion**
de·men·tia
demeret : **de·mer·it**
de·mer·it
demerrit : **de·mer·it**
demi·god
demigogue : **dem·a·gogue**
demilition : **de·mo·li·tion**
de·mise
demize : **de·mise**
demmagogue : **dem·a·gogue**
demmigod : **demi·god**
demmise : **de·mise**
demmocracy : **de·moc·ra·cy**

demmolition : **de·mo·li·tion**
demmonstrate : **dem·on·strate**
de·moc·ra·cy
democrasy : **de·moc·ra·cy**
democricy : **de·moc·ra·cy**
democrisy : **de·moc·ra·cy**
demogod : **demi·god**
demogogue : **dem·a·gogue**
demolission : **de·mo·li·tion**
demolitian : **de·mo·li·tion**
de·mo·li·tion
demolizion : **de·mo·li·tion**
demonstrait : **dem·on·strate**
dem·on·strate
demuir : **de·mur** (to disagree)
   or **de·mure** (modest)
de·mur (to disagree); **de·mure**
   (modest)
de·mure (modest); **de·mur** (to
   disagree)
denam : **den·im**
denazen : **den·i·zen**
dence : **dense**
dencity : **den·si·ty**
denezen : **den·i·zen**
den·im
denisen : **den·i·zen**
den·i·zen
Denmarck : **Den·mark**
Den·mark
dennim : **den·im**
dennizen : **den·i·zen**
dennotation : **de·no·ta·tion**
dennote : **de·note**
dennounce : **de·nounce**
denntal : **den·tal**
dennum : **den·im**
denomanation :
   de·nom·i·na·tion
denomenation :
   de·nom·i·na·tion
de·nom·i·na·tion

denommination :
   de·nom·i·na·tion
de·no·ta·tion
de·note
denottation : **de·no·ta·tion**
de·nounce
denounciation :
   de·nun·ci·a·tion
denounse : **de·nounce**
denownce : **de·nounce**
densaty : **den·si·ty**
dense
densety : **den·si·ty**
densitty : **den·si·ty**
den·si·ty
den·tal
dentel : **den·tal**
dentestry : **den·tist·ry**
dentistery : **den·tist·ry**
den·tist·ry
denum : **den·im**
de·nun·ci·a·tion
denunsiation : **de·nun·ci·a·tion**
deodorant : **de·odor·ant**
deodirant : **de·odor·ant**
de·odor·ant
deodorent : **de·odor·ant**
depaty : **dep·u·ty**
dependabal : **de·pend·able**
de·pend·able
dependant : **de·pen·dent**
dependible : **de·pend·able**
depety : **dep·u·ty**
depewty : **dep·u·ty**
dephth : **depth**
de·plor·able
deploreble : **de·plor·able**
deplorible : **de·plor·able**
depopalate : **de·pop·u·late**
depoppulate : **de·pop·u·late**
de·pop·u·late
deposet : **de·pos·it**

de·pos·it
depossit : **de·pos·it**
depozit : **de·pos·it**
depposit : **de·pos·it**
depprivation : **de·pri·va·tion**
depravety : **de·prav·i·ty**
depravitty : **de·prav·i·ty**
de·prav·i·ty
depresent : **de·pres·sant**
de·pres·sant
depressent : **de·pres·sant**
deprevation : **de·pri·va·tion**
deprivatian : **de·pri·va·tion**
de·pri·va·tion
depth
deputty : **dep·u·ty**
dep·u·ty
deralict : **der·e·lict**
derelect : **der·e·lict**
derelick : **der·e·lict**
der·e·lict
derick : **der·rick**
derilict : **der·e·lict**
derishion : **de·ri·sion**
de·ri·sion
derission : **de·ri·sion**
derizion : **de·ri·sion**
dermatoligist : **der·ma·tol·o·gist**
dermatollogist :
   der·ma·tol·o·gist
der·ma·tol·o·gist
dermetologist :
   der·ma·tol·o·gist
dermitologist :
   der·ma·tol·o·gist
derreck : **der·rick**
derrelict : **der·e·lict**
der·rick
derrik : **der·rick**
derth : **dearth**
desacrate : **des·e·crate**
de·scen·dant or **de·scen·dent**

de·scen·dent or **de·scen·dant**
de·scent (act of going down);
   de·cent (respectable);
   dis·sent (disagreement)
describtion : **de·scrip·tion**
descriptian : **de·scrip·tion**
de·scrip·tion
deseased : **de·ceased**
des·e·crate
deseive : **de·ceive**
Desember : **De·cem·ber**
de·sert (arid land); **des·sert**
   (sweet dish)
desibel : **dec·i·bel**
desible : **dec·i·bel**
deside : **de·cide**
desiduous : **de·cid·u·ous**
desifer : **de·ci·pher**
de·sign
de·sign·er
designor : **de·sign·er**
desimal : **dec·i·mal**
desimel : **dec·i·mal**
desine : **de·sign**
desiner : **de·sign·er**
desipher : **de·ci·pher**
desirabal : **de·sir·able**
de·sir·able
desireble : **de·sir·able**
de·spair
desparado : **des·per·a·do**
desparate : **des·per·ate**
despare : **de·spair**
des·per·a·do
des·per·ate
desperato : **des·per·a·do**
despirate : **des·per·ate**
de·spise
despize : **de·spise**
des·pot
dessecrate : **des·e·crate**
dessect : **dis·sect**

dessendant : **de·scen·dant**

des·sert (sweet dish); **de·sert**
  (arid land)

dessign : **de·sign**

dessirable : **de·sir·able**

destanation : **des·ti·na·tion**

destany : **des·ti·ny**

destatute : **des·ti·tute**

desteny : **des·ti·ny**

destetute : **des·ti·tute**

des·ti·na·tion

destinct : **dis·tinct**

destinnation : **des·ti·na·tion**

destinny : **des·ti·ny**

des·ti·ny

des·ti·tute

destructable : **de·struc·ti·ble**

de·struc·ti·ble

de·tach

de·tain

detaintion : **de·ten·tion**

detanate : **det·o·nate**

detane : **de·tain**

detatch : **de·tach**

deteariorate : **de·te·ri·o·rate**

de·ten·tion

de·ter (to prevent); **debt·or** (one
  who owes)

deterent : **de·ter·rent**

detereorate : **de·te·ri·o·rate**

de·te·ri·o·rate

determen : **de·ter·mine**

determin : **de·ter·mine**

de·ter·mine

deterr : **debt·or** (one who owes)
  or **de·ter** (to prevent)

deterrant : **de·ter·rent**

de·test·able

detestible : **de·test·able**

deth : **death**

detinate : **det·o·nate**

detiriorate : **de·te·ri·o·rate**

det·o·nate

detramental : **det·ri·men·tal**

detremental : **det·ri·men·tal**

det·ri·men·tal

dettain : **de·tain**

detter : **debt·or** (one who owes)
  or **de·ter** (to prevent)

dettermine : **de·ter·mine**

dettonate : **det·o·nate**

dettor : **debt·or** (one who
  owes) or **de·ter** (to prevent)

devan : **di·van**

dev·as·tate

deveate : **de·vi·ate**

devel : **dev·il**

devellop : **de·vel·op**

de·vel·op

de·vel·oped

developped : **de·vel·oped**

deveous : **de·vi·ous**

devest : **di·vest**

devestate : **dev·as·tate**

de·vi·ate

de·vice (*noun*); **de·vise** (*verb*)

devide : **di·vide**

dev·il

devine : **di·vine**

devinity : **di·vin·i·ty**

de·vi·ous

de·vise (*verb*); **de·vice** (*noun*)

devision : **di·vi·sion**

devistate : **dev·as·tate**

devorce : **di·vorce**

devorse : **di·vorce**

dev·o·tee

devotie : **dev·o·tee**

devoty : **dev·o·tee**

de·vour

devowr : **de·vour**

devulge : **di·vulge**

devvil : **dev·il**

dexteriss : **dex·ter·ous**

dex·ter·ous
dexterus : **dex·ter·ous**
dextrous : **dex·ter·ous**
dezine : **de·sign**
diabalical : **di·a·bol·i·cal**
diabeates : **di·a·be·tes**
diabeetes : **di·a·be·tes**
di·a·be·tes
diabetese : **di·a·be·tes**
di·a·bet·ic
diabetis : **di·a·be·tes**
di·a·bol·i·cal
diabollical : **di·a·bol·i·cal**
di·ag·no·sis
di·a·gram
dialate : **di·late**
di·a·log or **di·a·logue**
di·a·logue or **di·a·log**
diamater : **di·am·e·ter**
diameater : **di·am·e·ter**
diameeter : **di·am·e·ter**
diameiter : **di·am·e·ter**
diamend : **di·a·mond**
di·am·e·ter
diamiter : **di·am·e·ter**
di·a·mond
diamund : **di·a·mond**
di·a·per
diarea : **di·ar·rhea**
diarhea : **di·ar·rhea**
di·ar·rhea
diarrhia : **di·ar·rhea**
di·a·ry (daybook); **dairy** (milk farm)
diaty : **de·i·ty**
dibetes : **di·a·be·tes**
dibetic : **di·a·bet·ic**
dibolical : **di·a·bol·i·cal**
Dicksie : **Dix·ie**
dicktator : **dic·ta·tor**
dictater : **dic·ta·tor**
dic·ta·tor

dic·tio·nary
dictionery : **dic·tio·nary**
die (perish); **dye** (color)
diefy : **de·i·fy**
diery : **dairy** (milk farm) or
    di·a·ry (daybook)
die·sel
diesell : **die·sel**
dietarry : **di·etary**
di·etary
dieterry : **di·etary**
dietery : **di·etary**
diety : **de·i·ty**
diferent : **dif·fer·ent**
diffacult : **dif·fi·cult**
diffecult : **dif·fi·cult**
differant : **dif·fer·ent**
dif·fer·ent
dif·fi·cult
diffrent : **dif·fer·ent**
dificult : **dif·fi·cult**
digestable : **di·gest·ible**
digesteble : **di·gest·ible**
di·gest·ible
dig·i·tal
digitel : **dig·i·tal**
digittal : **dig·i·tal**
dignafied : **dig·ni·fied**
dignatary : **dig·ni·tary**
dignaty : **dig·ni·ty**
dignefied : **dig·ni·fied**
dignetary : **dig·ni·tary**
dignety : **dig·ni·ty**
dig·ni·fied
dignifyed : **dig·ni·fied**
dignitarry : **dig·ni·tary**
dig·ni·tary
dignitery : **dig·ni·tary**
dignitty : **dig·ni·ty**
dig·ni·ty
dignosis : **di·ag·no·sis**
digram : **di·a·gram**

dijestible : **di·gest·ible**
dike
dilapedated : **di·lap·i·dat·ed**
di·lap·i·dat·ed
dilappidated : **di·lap·i·dat·ed**
di·late
dilectable : **de·lec·ta·ble**
dilema : **di·lem·ma**
di·lem·ma
dilemna : **di·lem·ma**
dil·i·gence
diligense : **dil·i·gence**
dilimma : **di·lem·ma**
dilirious : **de·lir·i·ous**
dilligence : **dil·i·gence**
dilogue : **di·a·logue**
dimend : **di·a·mond**
dimensian : **di·men·sion**
di·men·sion
dimond : **di·a·mond**
dinamic : **dy·nam·ic**
dinamite : **dy·na·mite**
dinasaur : **di·no·saur**
dinasty : **dy·nas·ty**
dinesaur : **di·no·saur**
di·no·saur
dinosore : **di·no·saur**
diodorant : **de·odor·ant**
diper : **di·a·per**
diplamat : **dip·lo·mat**
diplimat : **dip·lo·mat**
dip·lo·mat
directer : **di·rec·tor**
di·rec·tor
dirrea : **di·ar·rhea**
dirrhea : **di·ar·rhea**
dirth : **dearth**
diry : **di·a·ry**
disapearance : **dis·ap·pear·ance**
disapearence : **dis·ap·pear·ance**
disapoint : **dis·ap·point**
dis·ap·pear·ance

disappearanse :
  dis·ap·pear·ance
dis·ap·point
disasster : **dis·as·ter**
dis·as·ter
disasterous : **di·sas·trous**
di·sas·trous
disatisfy : **dis·sat·is·fy**
disberse : **dis·burse**
disbirse : **dis·burse**
disburce : **dis·burse**
dis·burse
disc or **disk**
discerage : **dis·cour·age**
dis·cern
discipal : **dis·ci·ple**
dis·ci·ple
dis·ci·pline
discloshure : **dis·clo·sure**
dis·clo·sure
dis·cour·age
discourige : **dis·cour·age**
dis·creet (prudent); **dis·crete**
  (separate)
dis·crep·an·cy
discrepency : **dis·crep·an·cy**
dis·crete (separate); **dis·creet**
  (prudent)
discurage : **dis·cour·age**
dis·ease
disect : **dis·sect**
diseese : **dis·ease**
disent : **de·cent** (respectable) or
  de·scent (act of going down)
  or **dis·sent** (disagreement)
disese : **dis·ease**
disgise : **dis·guise**
dis·guise
disguize : **dis·guise**
dis·in·fec·tant
disinfectent : **dis·in·fec·tant**
disintagrate : **dis·in·te·grate**

dis·in·te·grate
disipline : **dis·ci·pline**
disk *or* **disc**
dis·mal
dismel : **dis·mal**
disobediance : **dis·obe·di·ence**
dis·obe·di·ence
disobediense : **dis·obe·di·ence**
disobeedience : **dis·obe·di·ence**
dispair : **de·spair**
dis·par·age
dispare : **de·spair**
disparige : **dis·par·age**
disparrage : **dis·par·age**
dis·pel
dispell : **dis·pel**
dispence : **dis·pense**
dispencible : **dis·pen·sable**
dispensabal : **dis·pen·sable**
dis·pen·sable
dis·pense
dispensible : **dis·pen·sable**
dispise : **de·spise**
dis·pos·al
disposel : **dis·pos·al**
dispot : **des·pot**
dis·put·able
disputible : **dis·put·able**
disqualefy : **dis·qual·i·fy**
dis·qual·i·fy
disrubt : **dis·rupt**
dis·rupt
dis·sat·is·fy
dis·sect
dis·sent (disagreement);
   de·cent (respectable);
   de·scent (act of going down)
dissern : **dis·cern**
dissiple : **dis·ci·ple**
dis·tance
distanse : **dis·tance**
distence : **dis·tance**

distilary : **dis·till·ery**
distilery : **dis·till·ery**
distillary : **dis·till·ery**
dis·till·ery
dis·tinct
distributer : **dis·trib·u·tor**
dis·trib·u·tor
distructible : **de·struc·ti·ble**
diury : **di·a·ry**
di·van
divann : **di·van**
divedend : **div·i·dend**
divergance : **di·ver·gence**
di·ver·gence
divergense : **di·ver·gence**
di·vest
divet : **div·ot**
di·vide
div·i·dend
dividind : **div·i·dend**
divied : **di·vide**
di·vine
divinety : **di·vin·i·ty**
divinitty : **di·vin·i·ty**
di·vin·i·ty
divinnity : **di·vin·i·ty**
divishion : **di·vi·sion**
di·vi·sion
divission : **di·vi·sion**
divit : **div·ot**
divizion : **di·vi·sion**
di·vorce
divorse : **di·vorce**
div·ot
divour : **de·vour**
di·vulge
divurgence : **di·ver·gence**
divvest : **di·vest**
divvide : **di·vide**
divvot : **div·ot**
Dixee : **Dix·ie**
Dix·ie

Dixy : **Dix·ie**
diziness : **diz·zi·ness**
dizmal : **dis·mal**
diz·zi·ness
dizziniss : **diz·zi·ness**
dizzyness : **diz·zi·ness**
docell : **doc·ile**
dochshund : **dachs·hund**
doc·ile
docilitty : **do·cil·i·ty**
do·cil·i·ty
docill : **doc·ile**
docillety : **do·cil·i·ty**
docillity : **do·cil·i·ty**
docksology : **dox·ol·o·gy**
docter : **doc·tor**
docterate : **doc·tor·ate**
doc·tor
doc·tor·ate
doctoret : **doc·tor·ate**
doctorit : **doc·tor·ate**
doctren : **doc·trine**
doctrenaire : **doc·tri·naire**
doctrin : **doc·trine**
doc·tri·naire
doctrinare : **doc·tri·naire**
doc·trine
doctrinnaire : **doc·tri·naire**
documentarry :
  doc·u·men·ta·ry
doc·u·men·ta·ry
documentery : **doc·u·men·ta·ry**
documentry : **doc·u·men·ta·ry**
documintary : **doc·u·men·ta·ry**
dogerel : **dog·ger·el**
doggarel : **dog·ger·el**
doggeral : **dog·ger·el**
dog·ger·el
doggerle : **dog·ger·el**
doilie : **doi·ly**
doi·ly
dolar : **dol·lar**

doldrams : **dol·drums**
doldrems : **dol·drums**
dol·drums
doledrums : **dol·drums**
doler : **dol·lar**
dolfin : **dol·phin**
dol·lar
dolldrums : **dol·drums**
doller : **dol·lar**
dollphin : **dol·phin**
dolphen : **dol·phin**
dol·phin
do·main
domanant : **dom·i·nant**
domane : **do·main**
domaneering : **dom·i·neer·ing**
domenance : **dom·i·nance**
domeno : **dom·i·no**
domesstic : **do·mes·tic**
domessticity : **do·mes·tic·i·ty**
do·mes·tic
domesticety : **do·mes·tic·i·ty**
domesticitty : **do·mes·tic·i·ty**
do·mes·tic·i·ty
domestick : **do·mes·tic**
domestisity : **do·mes·tic·i·ty**
do·mi·cile
domicill : **do·mi·cile**
dom·i·nance
dominanse : **dom·i·nance**
dom·i·nant
dominearing : **dom·i·neer·ing**
dom·i·neer·ing
domineiring : **dom·i·neer·ing**
dominence : **dom·i·nance**
dominense : **dom·i·nance**
dominent : **dom·i·nant**
dom·i·no
dominoe : **dom·i·no**
domisile : **do·mi·cile**
domminance : **dom·i·nance**
domminant : **dom·i·nant**

dommino : **dom·i·no**
domocile : **do·mi·cile**
domosile : **do·mi·cile**
doner : **do·nor**
donkee : **don·key**
don·key
donkie : **don·key**
do·nor
doormouse : **dor·mouse**
dooty : **du·ty**
dor·mant
dormatory : **dor·mi·to·ry**
dorment : **dor·mant**
dormetory : **dor·mi·to·ry**
dormitorry : **dor·mi·to·ry**
dor·mi·to·ry
dor·mouse
dor·sal
dorsel : **dor·sal**
dorssal : **dor·sal**
dosadge : **dos·age**
dos·age
dosege : **dos·age**
dosier : **dos·sier**
dosige : **dos·age**
dosile : **doc·ile**
dosility : **do·cil·i·ty**
dosill : **doc·ile**
dossage : **dos·age**
dossiay : **dos·sier**
dos·sier
dossiey : **dos·sier**
dot·age
dotege : **dot·age**
dotige : **dot·age**
dottage : **dot·age**
doubal : **dou·ble**
doubel : **dou·ble**
doubious : **du·bi·ous**
dou·ble
doubley : **dou·bly**
dou·bloon

doublune : **dou·bloon**
dou·bly
doubt·ful
doubtfull : **doubt·ful**
doubt·less
doubtliss : **doubt·less**
doughter : **daugh·ter**
doul : **dow·el** (peg) *or* **du·al**
   (double) *or* **du·el** (fight)
douplex : **du·plex**
doutful : **doubt·ful**
doutless : **doubt·less**
dow·a·ger
dowajer : **dow·a·ger**
doweger : **dow·a·ger**
dow·el
dowell : **dow·el**
dowerry : **dow·ry**
dowery : **dow·ry**
dowger : **dow·a·ger**
dowiger : **dow·a·ger**
dowl : **dow·el**
downpore : **down·pour**
down·pour
down·ward
downwerd : **down·ward**
downword : **down·ward**
dow·ry
doxhund : **dachs·hund**
doxolagy : **dox·ol·o·gy**
doxoligy : **dox·ol·o·gy**
doxollogy : **dox·ol·o·gy**
dox·ol·o·gy
doyly : **doi·ly**
doz·en
dozin : **doz·en**
dozzen : **doz·en**
draft
dragen : **drag·on**
draggon : **drag·on**
dragin : **drag·on**
drag·on

dra·ma
dra·mat·i·cal·ly
dramaticaly : **dra·mat·i·cal·ly**
dramaticly : **dra·mat·i·cal·ly**
dramatise (*Brit.*) : **dra·ma·tize**
dra·ma·tize
dramattically : **dra·mat·i·cal·ly**
drametize : **dra·ma·tize**
dramitize : **dra·ma·tize**
dramma : **dra·ma**
drammatically : **dra·mat·i·cal·ly**
drammatize : **dra·ma·tize**
drapary : **drap·ery**
draperry : **drap·ery**
drap·ery
drapry : **drap·ery**
dras·ti·cal·ly
drasticaly : **dras·ti·cal·ly**
drastickally : **dras·ti·cal·ly**
drasticly : **dras·ti·cal·ly**
drastikally : **dras·ti·cal·ly**
draught (*Brit.*) : **draft**
dread·ful
dreadfull : **dread·ful**
dream
drearally : **drea·ri·ly**
drearely : **drea·ri·ly**
drea·ri·ly
drearly : **drea·ri·ly**
drea·ry
dredful : **dread·ful**
dreem : **dream**
dreerily : **drea·ri·ly**
dreery : **drea·ry**
dreiry : **drea·ry**
dreser : **dress·er**
dress·er
dressor : **dress·er**
dri·er (more dry); **dry·er**
  (device for drying)
drily : **dry·ly**
drinkabel : **drink·able**

drink·able
drinkeble : **drink·able**
drinkibal : **drink·able**
drinkible : **drink·able**
drival : **driv·el**
driv·el
drivle : **driv·el**
drivvel : **driv·el**
drizle : **driz·zle**
drizzal : **driz·zle**
driz·zle
drousiness : **drow·si·ness**
drow·si·ness
drowsiniss : **drow·si·ness**
drowsyness : **drow·si·ness**
drowziness : **drow·si·ness**
drudgerry : **drudg·ery**
drudg·ery
drudgiry : **drudg·ery**
drudgry : **drudg·ery**
drudjery : **drudg·ery**
drugery : **drudg·ery**
druggest : **drug·gist**
drug·gist
drugist : **drug·gist**
drunk·ard
drunkerd : **drunk·ard**
dry·er (device for drying);
  dri·er (more dry)
dry·ly
du·al (double); **du·el** (fight)
dubble : **dou·ble**
dubbloon : **dou·bloon**
dubblune : **dou·bloon**
dubbly : **dou·bly**
dubeous : **du·bi·ous**
du·bi·ous
dubloon : **dou·bloon**
dubly : **dou·bly**
Duch : **Dutch**
duch·ess
duchiss : **duch·ess**

duchuss : **duch•ess**
ducktile : **duc•tile**
ductel : **duc•tile**
duc•tile
ductill : **duc•tile**
ductle : **duc•tile**
du•el (fight); **du•al** (double)
dufel : **duf•fel**
duf•fel
duffle : **duf•fel**
dulard : **dull•ard**
dull•ard
dullerd : **dull•ard**
dullird : **dull•ard**
dul•ly (with dullness); **du•ly** (as is due)
du•ly (as is due); **dul•ly** (with dullness)
dumb•bell
dumbell : **dumb•bell**
dumb•found *or* **dum•found**
dumb•wait•er
dumbwaitor : **dumb•wait•er**
dumby : **dum•my**
dum•found *or* **dumb•found**
dummey : **dum•my**
dummie : **dum•my**
dum•my
dumwaiter : **dumb•wait•er**
dunce
dun•ga•ree
dungarey : **dun•ga•ree**
dungarie : **dun•ga•ree**
dungary : **dun•ga•ree**
dungean : **dun•geon**
dungen : **dun•geon**
dun•geon
dungeree : **dun•ga•ree**
dungin : **dun•geon**
dungiree : **dun•ga•ree**
dunjeon : **dun•geon**
dunse : **dunce**

duplacator : **du•pli•ca•tor**
duplecate : **du•pli•cate**
duplects : **du•plex**
du•plex
du•plic•ate
du•pli•ca•tor
duplicety : **du•plic•i•ty**
duplicitty : **du•plic•i•ty**
du•plic•i•ty
duplisity : **du•plic•i•ty**
durabal : **du•ra•ble**
durabilety : **du•ra•bil•i•ty**
du•ra•bil•i•ty
durabillity : **du•ra•bil•i•ty**
du•ra•ble
durebility : **du•ra•bil•i•ty**
dureble : **du•ra•ble**
du•ress
durible : **du•ra•ble**
durrable : **du•ra•ble**
durress : **du•ress**
durth : **dearth**
dutaful : **du•ti•ful**
Dutch
dutchess : **duch•ess**
du•te•ous
du•ti•ful
dutifull : **du•ti•ful**
dutious : **du•te•ous**
dutius : **du•te•ous**
dutty : **du•ty**
du•ty
dutyful : **du•ti•ful**
dutyous : **du•te•ous**
duzen : **doz•en**
duzzen : **doz•en**
dye (color); **die** (perish)
dye•ing (coloring); **dy•ing** (perishing)
dy•ing (perishing); **dye•ing** (coloring)
dyke : **dike**

dy·nam·ic
dynamick : **dy·nam·ic**
dynamight : **dy·na·mite**
dy·na·mite
dynammic : **dy·nam·ic**
dynassty : **dy·nas·ty**

dy·nas·ty
dynesty : **dy·nas·ty**
dynimite : **dy·na·mite**
dynisty : **dy·nas·ty**
dynomite : **dy·na·mite**
dyrea : **di·ar·rhea**

E

eagel : **ea·gle**
ea·ger
eagger : **ea·ger**
ea·gle
eaked : **eked**
eaking : **ek·ing**
ear·ache
earacke : **ear·ache**
earaik : **ear·ache**
earake : **ear·ache**
earie : **ae·rie** (nest) *or* **ee·rie** (weird) *or* **Erie** (lake and canal)
earing : **ear·ring** (jewelry) *or* **err·ing** (mistaking)
ear·li·er
ear·ly
earlyier : **ear·li·er**
earn (to work to gain); **urn** (vase)
ear·nest (sincere); **Er·nest** (name)
ear·ring (jewelry); **err·ing** (mistaking)
earth·en·ware
earthenwear : **earth·en·ware**
earth·ly
easal : **ea·sel**
ea·sel
easell : **ea·sel**
easill : **ea·sel**
eas·i·ly
easyly : **eas·i·ly**
eat·able
eather : **ei·ther** (one or the other) *or* **ether** (gas)
eatible : **eat·able**
eaves·drop·ping
ebbony : **eb·o·ny**
eboney : **eb·o·ny**

ebonie : **eb·o·ny**
ebonny : **eb·o·ny**
eb·o·ny
ebulient : **ebul·lient**
ebulliant : **ebul·lient**
ebul·lient
eccede : **ac·cede** (to give in) *or* **ex·ceed** (to surpass)
ecceed : **ac·cede** (to give in) *or* **ex·ceed** (to surpass)
ec·cen·tric
eccentrick : **ec·cen·tric**
eccept : **ac·cept** (to take) *or* **ex·cept** (to leave out)
eccerpt : **ex·cerpt**
eccert : **ex·cerpt** (to extract) *or* **ex·ert** (to put forth)
eccise : **ex·cise**
ecco : **echo**
eccology : **ecol·o·gy**
ecconomy : **econ·o·my**
Eccuador : **Ec·ua·dor**
Eccuadorian : **Ec·ua·do·re·an**
ecentric : **ec·cen·tric**
echalon : **ech·e·lon**
ech·e·lon
echilon : **ech·e·lon**
echo
echoe : **echo**
ecko : **echo**
eclec·tic
eclectick : **eclec·tic**
eclexic : **eclec·tic**
eclips : **eclipse**
eclipse
ecolagy : **ecol·o·gy**
ecollogy : **ecol·o·gy**
ecol·o·gy
econamy : **econ·o·my**
econimy : **econ·o·my**

econnomy : **econ·o·my**
econ·o·my
Ecquador : **Ec·ua·dor**
Ecquadorian : **Ec·ua·dor·ean**
ecsentric : **ec·cen·tric**
ecsort : **es·cort** (to accompany)
  or **ex·hort** (to urge)
ecstacy : **ec·sta·sy**
ecstassy : **ec·sta·sy**
ec·sta·sy
ec·stat·ic
ecstattic : **ec·stat·ic**
ecstesy : **ec·sta·sy**
ecstisy : **ec·sta·sy**
Ec·ua·dor
Ec·ua·dor·ean
Ecudor : **Ec·ua·dor**
Ecudore : **Ec·ua·dor**
Ecudorian : **Ec·ua·dor·ean**
ec·ze·ma
eczemma : **ec·ze·ma**
edable : **ed·i·ble**
edafy : **ed·i·fy**
Edanburgh : **Ed·in·burgh**
edator : **ed·i·tor**
eddible : **ed·i·ble**
eddify : **ed·i·fy**
Eddinburgh : **Ed·in·burgh**
eddit : **ed·it**
edditor : **ed·i·tor**
edditorial : **ed·it·or·i·al**
edducation : **ed·u·ca·tion**
edefy : **ed·i·fy**
ed·i·ble
ed·i·fy
Edinborough : **Ed·in·burgh**
Edinburg : **Ed·in·burgh**
Ed·in·burgh
Edinburo : **Ed·in·burgh**
edit
editer : **ed·i·tor**

edi·tion (book); **ad·di·tion**
  (adding)
ed·i·tor
editoreal : **ed·i·to·ri·al**
ed·i·to·ri·al
educatian : **ed·u·ca·tion**
ed·u·ca·tion
eegle : **ea·gle**
eeked : **eked**
eeking : **ek·ing**
ee·rie *or* **ee·ry** (weird);
  ae·rie (nest); **Erie** (lake and
  canal)
ee·ry *or* **ee·rie**
eesel : **ea·sel**
eevesdropping : **eaves·drop·ping**
Efel : **Eif·fel**
efemininate : **ef·fem·i·nate**
efervescent : **ef·fer·ves·cent**
efete : **ef·fete**
effeat : **ef·fete**
ef·fect (result); **af·fect** (to
  influence)
effegy : **ef·fi·gy**
effemanate : **ef·fem·i·nate**
ef·fem·i·nate
effeminent : **ef·fem·i·nate**
effemminate : **ef·fem·i·nate**
effervecent : **ef·fer·ves·cent**
effervesant : **ef·fer·ves·cent**
ef·fer·ves·cent
effervessent : **ef·fer·ves·cent**
ef·fete
efficency : **ef·fi·cien·cy**
efficiancy : **ef·fi·cien·cy**
ef·fi·cien·cy
efficiensy : **ef·fi·cien·cy**
ef·fi·gy
effiminant : **ef·fem·i·nate**
effinity : **af·fin·i·ty**
effishiency : **ef·fi·cien·cy**
effite : **ef·fete**

effrontary : **ef·fron·tery**
ef·fron·tery
effrontry : **ef·fron·tery**
eficiency : **ef·fi·cien·cy**
efigy : **ef·fi·gy**
efrontery : **ef·fron·tery**
eger : **ea·ger**
eggress : **egress** (exit) *or*
　ag·gress (to attack)
Egipt : **Egypt**
Egiptian : **Egyp·tian**
Egiypt : **Egypt**
Egiyptian : **Egyp·tian**
egle : **ea·gle**
egreegrious : **egre·grious**
egre·gious
egregous : **egre·grious**
egreigious : **egre·grious**
egrejious : **egre·grious**
egress (exit); **ag·gress** (to
　attack)
Eguador : **Ec·ua·dor**
Eguadorean : **Ec·ua·dor·ean**
eguana : **igua·na**
Egypt
Egyp·tian
Egyption : **Egyp·tian**
egzalt : **ex·alt** (to honor) *or*
　ex·ult (to rejoice)
egzema : **ec·ze·ma**
Eifel : **Eif·fel**
Eif·fel
Eiffle : **Eif·fel**
eightean : **eigh·teen**
eigh·teen
eightteen : **eigh·teen**
eiked : **eked**
eir : **err** (to mistake) *or* **heir**
　(inheritor)
eiress : **heir·ess**
eiriss : **heir·ess**
eirloom : **heir·loom**

eirlume : **heir·loom**
eisel : **ea·sel**
ei·ther (one or the other);
　ether (gas)
ejecktion : **ejec·tion**
ejec·tion
ekcentric : **ec·cen·tric**
eked
ekeing : **ek·ing**
ek·ing
eklectic : **eclec·tic**
ekstasy : **ec·sta·sy**
elabarate : **elab·o·rate**
elaberate : **elab·o·rate**
elab·o·rate
elaboret : **elab·o·rate**
elaborite : **elab·o·rate**
elagance : **el·e·gance**
elagy : **el·e·gy**
element : **el·e·ment**
elamental : **el·e·men·tal**
elaphant : **el·e·phant**
elaquence : **el·o·quence**
elasstic : **elas·tic**
elastec : **elas·tic**
elas·tic
elastick : **elas·tic**
elavate : **el·e·vate**
elavator : **el·e·va·tor**
El·ba (island); **El·be** (river)
El·be (river); **El·ba** (island)
elbo : **el·bow**
elboe : **el·bow**
el·bow
el·dest
eldist : **el·dest**
elead : **elide**
eleaven : **elev·en**
electefy : **elec·tri·fy**
electokute : **elec·tro·cute**
electracute : **elec·tro·cute**
electrafy : **elec·tri·fy**

electrecute : **elec·tro·cute**
elec·tric
electricety : **elec·tric·i·ty**
elec·tri·cian
electricion : **elec·tri·cian**
electricitty : **elec·tric·i·ty**
elec·tric·i·ty
electricute : **elec·tro·cute**
elec·tri·fy
electrision : **elec·tri·cian**
electrisity : **elec·tric·i·ty**
electrition : **elec·tri·cian**
elec·tro·cute
elede : **elide**
elefant : **el·e·phant**
el·e·gance
eleganse : **el·e·gance**
elegants : **el·e·gance**
elegence : **el·e·gance**
elegible : **el·i·gi·ble** (qualified)
  or **il·leg·i·ble** (unreadable)
el·e·gy
elejy : **el·e·gy**
elektric : **elec·tric**
el·e·ment
el·e·men·tal
elementel : **el·e·men·tal**
elementle : **el·e·men·tal**
elemintal : **el·e·men·tal**
el·e·phant
elephent : **el·e·phant**
elephunt : **el·e·phant**
elete : **elite**
elevait : **el·e·vate**
elevan : **elev·en**
el·e·vate
elevater : **el·e·va·tor**
el·e·va·tor
elev·en
elicet : **elic·it** (to draw out) *or*
  il·lic·it (unlawful)

elic·it (to draw out); **il·lic·it**
  (unlawful)
elickser : **elix·ir**
elide
eligance : **el·e·gance**
eligeble : **el·i·gi·ble** (qualified)
  or **il·leg·i·ble** (unreadable)
eli·gi·ble (qualified); **il·leg·i·ble**
  (unreadable)
eligy : **el·e·gy**
elijible : **el·i·gi·ble** (qualified)
  or **il·leg·i·ble** (unreadable)
elimental : **el·e·men·tal**
elim·i·nate
eliphant : **el·e·phant**
eliquence : **el·o·quence**
elisit : **elic·it** (to draw out) *or*
  il·lic·it (unlawful)
elite
elivate : **el·e·vate**
elivator : **el·e·va·tor**
elixer : **elix·ir**
elix·ir
elixor : **elix·ir**
ellagy : **el·e·gy**
ellbow : **el·bow**
ellectrify : **elec·tri·fy**
ellectrocute : **elec·tro·cute**
ellegance : **el·e·gance**
ellegy : **el·e·gy**
ellement : **el·e·ment**
ellemental : **el·e·men·tal**
ellephant : **el·e·phant**
ellevate : **el·e·vate**
ellevator : **el·e·va·tor**
elleven : **elev·en**
ellicit : **elic·it** (to draw out) *or*
  il·lic·it (unlawful)
ellide : **elide**
elligible : **el·i·gi·ble** (qualified)
  or **il·leg·i·ble** (unreadable)
ellite : **elite**

ellixir : **elix·ir**

elloquence : **el·o·quence**

ellucidate : **elu·ci·date**

ellusive : **elu·sive**

eloapment : **elope·ment**

elope·ment

elopment : **elope·ment**

el·o·quence

eloquense : **el·o·quence**

eloquince : **el·o·quence**

elucedate : **elu·ci·date**

elu·ci·date

elucive : **al·lu·sive** (making references) or **elu·sive** (avoiding) or **il·lu·sive** (deceptive)

elude (to escape); **al·lude** (to refer)

elusidate : **elu·ci·date**

elu·sion (evasion); **al·lu·sion** (reference); **il·lu·sion** (false idea or image)

elu·sive (avoiding); **al·lu·sive** (making references); **il·lu·sive** (deceptive)

emaceated : **ema·ci·at·ed**

ema·ci·at·ed

emagrant : **em·i·grant**

emancepate : **eman·ci·pate**

eman·ci·pate

emanent : **em·i·nent** (famous) or **im·ma·nent** (dwelling within) or **im·mi·nent** (impending)

emansipate : **eman·ci·pate**

emarald : **em·er·ald**

emasarry : **em·is·sary**

emas·cu·late

emasiate : **ema·ci·ate**

embacy : **em·bas·sy**

em·balm

embam : **em·balm**

em·bank·ment

embarass : **em·bar·rass**

embaress : **em·bar·rass**

em·bar·go

embariss : **em·bar·rass**

em·bark

em·bar·rass

embarriss : **em·bar·rass**

embasey : **em·bas·sy**

em·bas·sy

embasy : **em·bas·sy**

embelish : **em·bel·lish**

embellash : **em·bel·lish**

embellesh : **em·bel·lish**

em·bel·lish

embezel : **em·bez·zle**

embezle : **em·bez·zle**

embezzal : **em·bez·zle**

embezzel : **em·bez·zle**

em·bez·zle

embibe : **im·bibe**

emblam : **em·blem**

emblazen : **em·bla·zon**

em·bla·zon

em·blem

emblim : **em·blem**

emblum : **em·blem**

em·bodi·ment

embodimint : **em·bodi·ment**

embodyment : **em·bodi·ment**

embom : **em·balm**

embracable : **em·brace·able**

em·brace

em·brace·able

embracible : **em·brace·able**

embraice : **em·brace**

embrase : **em·brace**

embrasible : **em·brace·able**

embreo : **em·bryo**

embrio : **em·bryo**

embroidary : **em·broi·dery**

embroiderry : **em·broi·dery**

em·broi·dery
embroydery : **em·broi·dery**
em·bryo
embue : **im·bue**
emcumbrance : **en·cum·brance**
emegrant : **em·i·grant** (one
  leaving) *or* **im·mi·grant** (one
  coming in)
emend (to correct); **amend** (to
  change or add to)
em·er·ald
emeratus : **emer·i·tus**
emeretus : **emer·i·tus**
emer·gen·cy
emergensy : **emer·gen·cy**
emergincy : **emer·gen·cy**
emeritas : **emer·i·tus**
emeritis : **emer·i·tus**
emer·i·tus
emerold : **em·er·ald**
emerritus : **emer·i·tus**
emesarry : **em·is·sary**
emfeeble : **en·fee·ble**
emgagement : **en·gage·ment**
em·i·grant (one leaving);
  im·mi·grant (one coming in)
emind : **emend**
em·i·nent (famous);
  im·ma·nent (dwelling
  within); **im·mi·nent**
  (impending)
emisary : **em·is·sary**
emision : **emis·sion**
em·is·sary
emisserry : **em·is·sary**
emissery : **em·is·sary**
emissian : **emis·sion**
emis·sion
emition : **emis·sion**
emity : **en·mi·ty**
emmaculate : **im·mac·u·late**
emmancipate : **eman·ci·pate**

emmasculate : **emas·cu·late**
emmend : **emend**
emmerald : **em·er·ald**
emmergency : **emer·gen·cy**
emmeritus : **emer·i·tus**
emmigrant : **em·i·grant** (one
  leaving) *or* **im·mi·grant** (one
  coming in)
emminent : **em·i·nent** (famous)
  or **im·ma·nent** (dwelling
  within) *or* **im·mi·nent**
  (impending)
emmissary : **em·is·sary**
emmity : **en·mi·ty**
emmusion : **emul·sion**
emorald : **em·er·ald**
empact : **im·pact**
empair : **im·pair**
empale : **im·pale**
empanel : **im·pan·el**
empart : **im·part**
empassioned : **im·pas·sioned**
empeach : **im·peach**
empearian : **em·py·re·an**
empeccable : **im·pec·ca·ble**
empede : **im·pede**
empediment : **im·ped·i·ment**
emperial : **im·pe·ri·al**
emperil : **im·pe·ri·al** (relating
  to empire) *or* **im·per·il** (to
  endanger)
emphisema : **em·phy·se·ma**
emphisima : **em·phy·se·ma**
emphyseama : **em·phy·se·ma**
em·phy·se·ma
emphysima : **em·phy·se·ma**
emphyzema : **em·phy·se·ma**
empier : **em·pire**
empierian : **em·py·re·an**
em·pire
empirial : **im·pe·ri·al**
empirian : **em·py·re·an**

emplant : **im·plant**

emporeum : **em·po·ri·um**

emporiam : **em·po·ri·um**

em·po·ri·um

emposter : **im·pos·tor**

empouarium : **em·po·ri·um**

empound : **im·pound**

empoureum : **em·po·ri·um**

empoverish : **im·pov·er·ish**

empyre : **em·pire**

em·py·re·an

empyrian : **em·py·re·an**

emullsion : **emul·sion**

emulsian : **emul·sion**

emul·sion

emultion : **emul·sion**

emvironment : **en·vi·ron·ment**

emzyme : **en·zyme**

enamal : **enam·el**

enam·el

enamell : **enam·el**

enamerd : **enam·ored**

enamered : **enam·ored**

enamil : **enam·el**

enammel : **enam·el**

enammored : **enam·ored**

enam·ored

enamoured (*Brit.*) : **enam·ored**

enamy : **en·e·my**

enargy : **en·er·gy**

enbalm : **em·balm**

enbam : **em·balm**

enbankment : **em·bank·ment**

enbargo : **em·bar·go**

enbark : **em·bark**

enbarrass : **em·bar·rass**

enbassy : **em·bas·sy**

enbelish : **em·bel·lish**

enbellish : **em·bel·lish**

enbezzle : **em·bez·zle**

enblazon : **em·bla·zon**

enblem : **em·blem**

enbodiment : **em·bodi·ment**

enbrace : **em·brace**

enbraceable : **em·brace·able**

enbroidery : **em·broi·dery**

enbryo : **em·bryo**

encantation : **in·can·ta·tion**

encendiary : **in·cen·di·ary**

encercle : **en·cir·cle**

encessant : **in·ces·sant**

enciclopedia : **en·cyc·lo·pe·dia**

encinerate : **in·cin·er·ate**

encircel : **en·cir·cle**

en·cir·cle

encirkal : **en·cir·cle**

encirkle : **en·cir·cle**

encite : **in·cite** (to urge on) *or*
　in·sight (discernment)

encouradge : **en·cour·age**

en·cour·age

encourege : **en·cour·age**

encourige : **en·cour·age**

en·cum·brance

encumbranse : **en·cum·brance**

encumbrence : **en·cum·brance**

encumbrince : **en·cum·brance**

encurage : **en·cour·age**

encyclapedia : **en·cy·clo·pe·dia**

encyclepedia : **en·cy·clo·pe·dia**

encyclipedia : **en·cy·clo·pe·dia**

encyclopeadia :
　en·cy·clo·pe·dia

encyclopedea : **en·cy·clo·pe·dia**

en·cy·clo·pe·dia

encyclopeedia : **en·cy·clo·pe·dia**

endeaver : **en·deav·or**

en·deav·or

endevor : **en·deav·or**

endevvor : **en·deav·or**

endite : **in·dict** (to charge with
　a crime) *or* **in·dite** (to write)

endolent : **in·do·lent**

endomitable : **in·dom·i·ta·ble**

endoument : **en·dow·ment**
endowmate : **en·dow·ment**
endowmeant : **en·dow·ment**
en·dow·ment
endowmint : **en·dow·ment**
endulge : **in·dulge**
en·dur·ance
enduranse : **en·dur·ance**
endurence : **en·dur·ance**
endurrance : **en·dur·ance**
endurrence : **en·dur·ance**
endustrial : **in·dus·tri·al**
enebriate : **ine·bri·ate**
enemmy : **en·e·my**
en·e·my
en·er·gy
enerjy : **en·er·gy**
enerrgy : **en·er·gy**
enert : **in·ert**
enertia : **in·er·tia**
enfallible : **in·fal·li·ble**
enfatuate : **in·fat·u·ate**
enfeable : **en·fee·ble**
enfeebal : **en·fee·ble**
en·fee·ble
enfeible : **en·fee·ble**
enferior : **in·fe·ri·or**
enferno : **in·fer·no**
enfidel : **in·fi·del**
enfinite : **in·fi·nite**
enfirmary : **in·fir·ma·ry**
enfirmity : **in·fir·mi·ty**
enflammable : **in·flam·ma·ble**
enflexible : **in·flex·i·ble**
enfluence : **in·flu·ence**
enfuriate : **in·fu·ri·ate**
en·gage·ment
engagment : **en·gage·ment**
engeneer : **en·gi·neer**
engenious : **in·ge·nious**
engenue : **in·ge·nue**
engenuous : **in·gen·u·ous**

engest : **in·gest**
en·gi·neer
enginier : **en·gi·neer**
En·gland
englorious : **in·glo·ri·ous**
Englund : **En·gland**
engredient : **in·gre·di·ent**
enhabit : **in·hab·it**
enhale : **in·hale**
enhancemeant : **en·hance·ment**
en·hance·ment
enhancemint : **en·hance·ment**
enhansement : **en·hance·ment**
enherent : **in·her·ent**
enherit : **in·her·it**
enhibit : **in·hib·it**
eniggma : **enig·ma**
enig·ma
enimical : **in·im·i·cal**
enimy : **en·e·my**
enitial : **ini·tial**
enitiate : **ini·ti·ate**
enjineer : **en·gi·neer**
enmaty : **en·mi·ty**
enmety : **en·mi·ty**
enmitty : **en·mi·ty**
en·mi·ty
ennamel : **enam·el**
ennamored : **enam·ored**
ennate : **in·nate**
ennemy : **en·e·my**
ennigma : **enig·ma**
ennocence : **in·no·cence**
ennovate : **in·no·vate**
ennue : **en·nui**
ennuee : **en·nui**
en·nui
ennumerable : **in·nu·mer·a·ble**
ennumerate : **enu·mer·ate**
enoomerate : **enu·mer·ate**
enoui : **en·nui**
enouunciate : **enun·ci·ate**

enperil : **im·pe·ri·al** (relating to empire) *or* **im·per·il** (to endanger)

enphysema : **em·phy·se·ma**

enpire : **em·pire**

enpireal : **im·pe·ri·al**

enporium : **em·po·ri·um**

enpyrean : **em·py·re·an**

enscrutable : **in·scru·ta·ble**

ensiclopedia : **en·cy·clo·pe·dia**

en·sign

ensine : **en·sign**

ensipid : **in·sip·id**

ensircle : **en·cir·cle**

ensolence : **in·so·lence**

ensoluble : **in·sol·u·ble**

ensolvent : **in·sol·vent**

ensomnia : **in·som·nia**

ensouciant : **in·sou·ci·ant**

enstill : **in·still**

ensular : **in·su·lar**

ensulin : **in·su·lin**

ensurance : **in·sur·ance**

ensurgent : **in·sur·gent**

ensyclopedia : **en·cy·clo·pe·dia**

ensyme : **en·zyme**

entegrate : **in·te·grate**

entellect : **in·tel·lect**

entelligent : **in·tel·li·gent**

enteprise : **en·ter·prise**

enterance : **en·trance**

enterence : **en·trance**

enterpreneur : **en·tre·pre·neur**

enterpretation : **in·ter·pre·ta·tion**

en·ter·prise

enterprize : **en·ter·prise**

enterrogate : **in·ter·ro·gate**

en·ter·tain

entertane : **en·ter·tain**

enterval : **in·ter·val**

entervene : **in·ter·vene**

enterview : **in·ter·view**

entestine : **in·tes·tine**

entimacy : **in·ti·ma·cy**

entimate : **in·ti·mate**

entolerable : **in·tol·er·a·ble**

entolerance : **in·tol·er·ance**

entolerant : **in·tol·er·ant**

entouradge : **en·tou·rage**

en·tou·rage

entouraje : **en·tou·rage**

entouroge : **en·tou·rage**

entoxicate : **in·tox·i·cate**

en·trance

entranse : **en·trance**

entransigent : **in·tran·si·gent**

entrapreneur : **en·tre·pre·neur**

entraypreneur : **en·tre·pre·neur**

entrence : **en·trance**

entrense : **en·trance**

entrepeneur : **en·tre·pre·neur**

entrepid : **in·trep·id**

en·tre·pre·neur

entreprenoir : **en·tre·pre·neur**

entreprenoor : **en·tre·pre·neur**

entreprineur : **en·tre·pre·neur**

entricacy : **in·tri·ca·cy**

entricate : **in·tri·cate**

entrigue : **in·trigue**

entrince : **en·trance**

entrinse : **en·trance**

entroduce : **in·tro·duce**

entuition : **in·tu·ition**

enturage : **en·tou·rage**

enui : **en·nui**

enumarate : **enu·mer·ate**

enu·mer·ate

enunceate : **enun·ci·ate**

enun·ci·ate

enundate : **in·un·date**

enunsiate : **enun·ci·ate**

envade : **in·vade**

envalid : **in·va·lid** (sick or
  disabled) *or* **in·val·id** (not
  valid)
envalope : **en·ve·lope** (*noun*)
envellope : **en·ve·lope** (*noun*)
enveloap : **en·ve·lope** (*noun*)
en·vel·op (*verb*); **en·ve·lope**
  (*noun*)
en·ve·lope (*noun*); **en·vel·op**
  (*verb*)
enventory : **in·ven·to·ry**
enveous : **en·vi·ous**
envestigate : **in·ves·ti·gate**
enveterate : **in·vet·er·ate**
enviernment : **en·vi·ron·ment**
envigorate : **in·vig·o·rate**
envilope : **en·ve·lope** (*noun*)
envincible : **in·vin·ci·ble**
enviolable : **in·vi·o·la·ble**
enviolate : **in·vi·o·late**
enviornment : **en·vi·ron·ment**
enviorns : **en·vi·rons**
en·vi·ous
enviran : **en·vi·rons**
enviranment : **en·vi·ron·ment**
envirement : **en·vi·ron·ment**
envirens : **en·vi·rons**
envirnment : **en·vi·ron·ment**
envirns : **en·vi·rons**
en·vi·ron·ment
en·vi·rons
enviruns : **en·vi·rons**
en·vis·age
envisege : **en·vis·age**
envisible : **in·vis·i·ble**
envisige : **en·vis·age**
envissage : **en·vis·age**
envius : **en·vi·ous**
envizage : **en·vis·age**
en·voy
envyous : **en·vi·ous**
enwee : **en·nui**

enzime : **en·zyme**
en·zyme
epacurean : **ep·i·cu·re·an**
epasode : **ep·i·sode**
epataph : **ep·i·taph**
epathet : **ep·i·thet**
epecurean : **ep·i·cu·re·an**
epesode : **ep·i·sode**
ep·ic (narrative); **ep·och** (era)
epick : **ep·ic** (narrative) *or*
  ep·och (era)
ep·i·cu·re·an
epicurian : **ep·i·cu·re·an**
ep·i·gram
Episcapalian : **Epis·co·pa·lian**
Episcipalian : **Epis·co·pa·lian**
Epis·co·pa·lian
episoad : **ep·i·sode**
ep·i·sode
epissel : **epis·tle**
epissle : **epis·tle**
epis·tle
epistol : **epis·tle**
epitaff : **ep·i·taph**
ep·i·taph
ep·i·thet
ep·och (era); **ep·ic** (narrative)
eppic : **ep·ic** (narrative) *or*
  ep·och (era)
eppicurean : **ep·i·cu·re·an**
eppigram : **ep·i·gram**
Eppiscopalian : **Epis·co·pa·lian**
eppisode : **ep·i·sode**
eppistle : **epis·tle**
eppitaph : **ep·i·taph**
eppithet : **ep·i·thet**
eqal : **equal**
eqity : **eq·ui·ty**
Equador : **Ec·ua·dor**
Equadorian : **Ec·ua·dor·ean**
equal
equall : **equal**

equassion : **equa·tion**
equater : **equa·tor**
equatian : **equa·tion**
equa·tion
equa·tor
equaty : **eq·ui·ty**
equel : **equal**
equetty : **eq·ui·ty**
equety : **eq·ui·ty**
equil : **equal**
equitty : **eq·ui·ty**
eq·ui·ty
erand : **er·rand**
erase
eratic : **er·rat·ic**
eratick : **er·rat·ic**
erb : **herb**
erbage : **herb·age**
erbal : **herb·al**
erbege : **herb·age**
erbel : **herb·al**
erbige : **herb·age**
Erie (lake and canal); **ee·rie** (weird)
erlier : **ear·li·er**
erly : **ear·ly**
ermen : **er·mine**
ermin : **er·mine**
er·mine
ern : **earn** (to work to gain) *or* **urn** (vase)
Er·nest (name); **ear·nest** (sincere)
eroodite : **er·u·dite**
eror : **er·ror**
erosean : **ero·sion**
erosian : **ero·sion**
erosien : **ero·sion**
ero·sion
erossion : **ero·sion**
er·otic
erotick : **erot·ic**

erotion : **ero·sion**
erottic : **erot·ic**
err (to mistake); **heir** (inheritor)
er·rand
errase : **erase**
er·rat·ic
errattic : **er·rat·ic**
errend : **er·rand**
errer : **er·ror**
errind : **er·rand**
errir : **er·ror**
errlier : **ear·li·er**
er·ror
errosion : **ero·sion**
errotic : **erot·ic**
errudite : **er·u·dite**
erthenware : **earth·en·ware**
erthly : **earth·ly**
er·u·dite
esay : **es·say**
es·cape
eschoir : **es·quire**
es·cort
escuire : **es·quire**
esel : **ea·sel**
esence : **es·sence**
esential : **es·sen·tial**
eshelon : **ech·e·lon**
eshilon : **ech·e·lon**
Eskamo : **Es·ki·mo**
Eskemo : **Es·ki·mo**
Eskimmo : **Es·ki·mo**
Es·ki·mo
Eskimoe : **Es·ki·mo**
eskwire : **es·quire**
esofagus : **esoph·a·gus**
esophagas : **esoph·a·gus**
esophages : **esoph·a·gus**
esophagis : **esoph·a·gus**
esoph·a·gus
esophegus : **esoph·a·gus**
esophigus : **esoph·a·gus**

esophogus : **esoph·a·gus**
especialy : **es·pe·cial·ly**
es·pe·cial·ly
esquier : **es·quire**
es·quire
essance : **es·sence**
es·say
es·sence
essencial : **es·sen·tial**
essense : **es·sence**
essenshial : **es·sen·tial**
es·sen·tial
essintial : **es·sen·tial**
essophagus : **esoph·a·gus**
essquire : **es·quire**
estamate : **es·ti·mate**
estatic : **ec·stat·ic**
es·teem
estemate : **es·ti·mate**
esteme : **es·teem**
es·thet·ic or **aes·thet·ic**
estimant : **es·ti·mate**
es·ti·mate
estiment : **es·ti·mate**
etaquette : **et·i·quette**
etequette : **et·i·quette**
eter·nal
eternall : **eter·nal**
eternel : **eter·nal**
eternetty : **eter·ni·ty**
eternety : **eter·ni·ty**
eternitty : **eter·ni·ty**
eter·ni·ty
ethacal : **eth·i·cal**
etheareal : **ethe·re·al**
ethecal : **eth·i·cal**
etheerial : **ethe·re·al**
etheirial : **ethe·re·al**
Etheopia : **Ethi·o·pia**
ether (gas); **ei·ther** (one or the other)
ethe·re·al

etherial : **ethe·re·al**
eth·i·cal
ethicle : **eth·i·cal**
ethikal : **eth·i·cal**
Ethiopea : **Ethi·o·pia**
Ethi·o·pia
ethnec : **eth·nic**
eth·nic
ethnick : **eth·nic**
etikit : **et·i·quette**
etiquet : **et·i·quette**
et·i·quette
etiquit : **et·i·quette**
etiquitte : **et·i·quette**
etternal : **eter·nal**
ettiquette : **et·i·quette**
eturnal : **eter·nal**
Eucarist : **Eu·cha·rist**
Eu·cha·rist
Euchrist : **Eu·cha·rist**
eufemism : **eu·phe·mism**
eufonious : **eu·pho·ni·ous**
euforia : **eu·pho·ria**
eulagy : **eu·lo·gy**
eulegy : **eu·lo·gy**
euligy : **eu·lo·gy**
euloggy : **eu·lo·gy**
eu·lo·gy
eunach : **eu·nuch**
eunech : **eu·nuch**
euneck : **eu·nuch**
eunich : **eu·nuch**
eunick : **eu·nuch**
eu·nuch
euphamism : **eu·phe·mism**
euphemesm : **eu·phe·mism**
eu·phe·mism
euphimism : **eu·phe·mism**
euphoneous : **eu·pho·ni·ous**
eu·pho·ni·ous
euphonius : **eu·pho·ni·ous**
euphorea : **eu·pho·ria**

eu·pho·ria
euphorria : **eu·pho·ria**
eureaka : **eu·re·ka**
eureeka : **eu·re·ka**
eu·re·ka
eurika : **eu·re·ka**
Euroap : **Eu·rope**
Europ : **Eu·rope**
Eu·rope
euthanacia : **eu·tha·na·sia**
eu·tha·na·sia
euthanazia : **eu·tha·na·sia**
euthenasia : **eu·tha·na·sia**
euthinasia : **eu·tha·na·sia**
evacion : **eva·sion**
evacive : **eva·sive**
evacooate : **evac·u·ate**
evacuait : **evac·u·ate**
evac·u·ate
evadence : **ev·i·dence**
evakauate : **evac·u·ate**
evalution : **ev·o·lu·tion**
evalutionary : **ev·o·lu·tion·ary**
ev·a·nes·cence
evanescense : **ev·a·nes·cence**
evanesense : **ev·a·nes·cence**
evanessance : **ev·a·nes·cence**
evanessence : **ev·a·nes·cence**
evangelesm : **evan·ge·lism**
evan·ge·lism
evangellism : **evan·ge·lism**
evanjelism : **evan·ge·lism**
evaparate : **evap·o·rate**
evaperate : **evap·o·rate**
evapirate : **evap·o·rate**
evaporait : **evap·o·rate**
evap·o·rate
evapperate : **evap·o·rate**
evapporate : **evap·o·rate**
Evarest : **Ev·er·est**
Evarist : **Ev·er·est**
evaseve : **eva·sive**

eva·sion
eva·sive
evassion : **eva·sion**
evassive : **eva·sive**
evation : **eva·sion**
evazion : **eva·sion**
evedence : **ev·i·dence**
eveneng : **eve·ning**
evenescence : **ev·a·nes·cence**
eve·ning
event·ful
eventfull : **event·ful**
eventially : **even·tu·al·ly**
even·tu·al·ly
eventualy : **even·tu·al·ly**
eventuelly : **even·tu·al·ly**
eventuilly : **even·tu·al·ly**
eventuily : **even·tu·al·ly**
Ev·er·est
Everist : **Ev·er·est**
evesdropping : **eaves·drop·ping**
evidanse : **ev·i·dence**
ev·i·dence
evidense : **ev·i·dence**
evilution : **ev·o·lu·tion**
evilutionary : **ev·o·lu·tion·ary**
evinescence : **ev·a·nes·cence**
evintful : **event·ful**
Evirest : **Ev·er·est**
evning : **eve·ning**
evolusion : **ev·o·lu·tion**
evolusionary : **ev·o·lu·tion·ary**
evolutian : **ev·o·lu·tion**
evolutianary : **ev·o·lu·tion·ary**
ev·o·lu·tion
evolutionarry : **ev·o·lu·tion·ary**
ev·o·lu·tion·ary
evolutionerry : **ev·o·lu·tion·ary**
evolutionery : **ev·o·lu·tion·ary**
Evrist : **Ev·er·est**
ewe (female sheep); **yew** (tree);
  you (pron.)

exacution : **ex·e·cu·tion**

exacutive : **ex·ec·u·tive**

exadus : **ex·o·dus**

exagerate : **ex·ag·ger·ate**

exaggarate : **ex·ag·ger·ate**
ex·ag·ger·ate

exaggirate : **ex·ag·ger·ate**

exajerate : **ex·ag·ger·ate**

exale : **ex·hale**

ex·alt (to honor); **ex·ult** (to rejoice)

examplary : **ex·em·pla·ry**

exaqution : **ex·e·cu·tion**

exasparate : **ex·as·per·ate**

exasperait : **ex·as·per·ate**
ex·as·per·ate

exasperrate : **ex·as·per·ate**

exaspirate : **ex·as·per·ate**

exassperate : **ex·as·per·ate**

exaust : **ex·haust**

excape : **es·cape**

excasperate : **ex·as·per·ate**

excavatian : **ex·ca·va·tion**
ex·ca·va·tion

excede : **ac·cede** (to give in) *or* **ex·ceed** (to surpass)

ex·ceed (to surpass); **ac·cede** (to give in)

ex·cel

excelence : **ex·cel·lence**

excell : **ex·cel**

excellance : **ex·cel·lence**

excellanse : **ex·cel·lence**
ex·cel·lence

excellense : **ex·cel·lence**

exemplify : **ex·em·pli·fy**

excempt : **ex·empt**

ex·cept (to leave out); **ac·cept** (to take)

excercise : **ex·er·cise**

ex·cerpt

excersise : **ex·er·cise**

excert : **ex·cerpt** (extract) *or* **ex·ert** (to put forth)

excertion : **ex·er·tion**

excevation : **ex·ca·va·tion**

excibition : **ex·hi·bi·tion**

excilarate : **ex·hil·a·rate**

excilaration : **ex·hil·a·ra·tion**

excile : **ex·ile**

excirpt : **ex·cerpt**

ex·cise

excist : **ex·ist**

excistence : **ex·is·tence**

excistentialism : **ex·is·ten·tial·ism**

excitemeant : **ex·cite·ment**
ex·cite·ment

excitment : **ex·cite·ment**

excize : **ex·cise**

ex·claim

exclaimation : **ex·cla·ma·tion**

exclamasion : **ex·cla·ma·tion**

exclamatian : **ex·cla·ma·tion**
ex·cla·ma·tion

exclame : **ex·claim**

exclemation : **ex·cla·ma·tion**

exclimation : **ex·cla·ma·tion**

excloosive : **ex·clu·sive**

exclucive : **ex·clu·sive**

excluseve : **ex·clu·sive**
ex·clu·sive

excort : **es·cort** (to accompany) *or* **ex·hort** (to urge)

excrament : **ex·cre·ment**

excremant : **ex·cre·ment**
ex·cre·ment

excriment : **ex·cre·ment**

excroosiating : **ex·cru·ci·at·ing**

excruceating : **ex·cru·ci·at·ing**
ex·cru·ci·at·ing

excrusiating : **ex·cru·ci·at·ing**

excume : **ex·hume**

exebition : **ex·hi·bi·tion**

execkutive : **ex·ec·u·tive**
execusion : **ex·e·cu·tion**
executeve : **ex·ec·u·tive**
executian : **ex·e·cu·tion**
ex·e·cu·tion
ex·ec·u·tive
exedus : **ex·o·dus**
exeed : **ac·cede** (to give in) *or*
  ex·ceed (to surpass)
exel : **ax·le** (wheel shaft) *or*
  ex·cel (to be superior)
exelence : **ex·cel·lence**
exellence : **ex·cel·lence**
exema : **ec·ze·ma**
exemplafy : **ex·em·pli·fy**
exemplarry : **ex·em·pla·ry**
ex·em·pla·ry
exemplerry : **ex·em·pla·ry**
exemplery : **ex·em·pla·ry**
exempley : **ex·em·pli·fy**
ex·em·pli·fy
exemplury : **ex·em·pla·ry**
ex·empt
exept : **ac·cept** (to take) *or*
  ex·cept (to leave out)
exeqution : **ex·e·cu·tion**
exercion : **ex·er·tion**
ex·er·cise
exercize : **ex·er·cise**
exerpt : **ex·cerpt**
exersion : **ex·er·tion**
exersise : **ex·er·cise**
ex·ert (to put forth); **ex·cerpt**
  (extract)
exertian : **ex·er·tion**
ex·er·tion
exhail : **ex·hale**
exhailation : **ex·ha·la·tion**
ex·ha·la·tion
ex·hale
ex·haust
exhawst : **ex·haust**

exhibbit : **ex·hib·it**
exhibet : **ex·hib·it**
ex·hib·it
ex·hi·bi·tion
ex·hil·a·rate
ex·hil·a·ra·tion
exhile : **ex·ile**
exhilerate : **ex·hil·a·rate**
exhileration : **ex·hil·a·ra·tion**
exhilirate : **ex·hil·a·rate**
exhorbitant : **ex·or·bi·tant**
ex·hort
exhuberance : **ex·u·ber·ance**
ex·hume
exibbet : **ex·hib·it**
exibit : **ex·hib·it**
exibition : **ex·hi·bi·tion**
exicution : **ex·e·cu·tion**
exidus : **ex·o·dus**
exigancy : **ex·i·gen·cy**
ex·i·gen·cy
exigensy : **ex·i·gen·cy**
exilarait : **ex·hil·a·rate**
exilarate : **ex·hil·a·rate**
exilaration : **ex·hil·a·ra·tion**
ex·ile
exileration : **ex·hil·a·ra·tion**
exise : **ex·cise**
exishency : **ex·i·gen·cy**
ex·ist
existance : **ex·is·tence**
existanse : **ex·is·tence**
existantialism :
    ex·is·ten·tial·ism
ex·is·tence
existencialism :
    ex·is·ten·tial·ism
existense : **ex·is·tence**
existensialism :
    ex·is·ten·tial·ism
ex·is·ten·tial·ism

existentiallism :
  ex·is·ten·tial·ism
exitement : **ex·cite·ment**
exize : **ex·cise**
exodas : **ex·o·dus**
exodis : **ex·o·dus**
exodos : **ex·o·dus**
ex·o·dus
ex·or·bi·tant
exort : **ex·hort**
expance : **ex·panse**
ex·panse
expeadient : **ex·pe·di·ent**
expearience : **ex·pe·ri·ence**
expeariment : **ex·per·i·ment**
ex·pec·tant
expectent : **ex·pec·tant**
expeddition : **ex·pe·di·tion**
expediant : **ex·pe·di·ent**
ex·pe·di·ent
expedision : **ex·pe·di·tion**
ex·pe·di·tion
expedittion : **ex·pe·di·tion**
expeedient : **ex·pe·di·ent**
expeerience : **ex·pe·ri·ence**
expeeriment : **ex·per·i·ment**
expeirience : **ex·pe·ri·ence**
expeiriment : **ex·per·i·ment**
expence : **ex·pense**
expencive : **ex·pen·sive**
expendachure : **ex·pen·di·ture**
expendature : **ex·pen·di·ture**
expendeture : **ex·pen·di·ture**
ex·pen·di·ture
ex·pense
expenseve : **ex·pen·sive**
ex·pen·sive
experament : **ex·per·i·ment**
experement : **ex·per·i·ment**
experiance : **ex·pe·ri·ence**
experianse : **ex·pe·ri·ence**
ex·pe·ri·ence

experiense : **ex·pe·ri·ence**
ex·per·i·ment
ex·pert
expier : **ex·pire**
ex·plain
explaination : **ex·pla·na·tion**
ex·pla·na·tion
explane : **ex·plain**
explannation : **ex·pla·na·tion**
explenation : **ex·pla·na·tion**
explination : **ex·pla·na·tion**
expload : **ex·plode**
exploasion : **ex·plo·sion**
ex·plode
explosian : **ex·plo·sion**
ex·plo·sion
explotion : **ex·plo·sion**
explozion : **ex·plo·sion**
expurt : **ex·pert**
exquesite : **ex·qui·site**
exquisate : **ex·qui·site**
exquiset : **ex·qui·site**
ex·qui·site
exquizite : **ex·qui·site**
exsasperate : **ex·as·per·ate**
exsel : **ex·cel**
exsellanse : **ex·cel·lence**
exsellence : **ex·cel·lence**
exsercise : **ex·er·cise**
exsertion : **ex·er·tion**
exsibition : **ex·hi·bi·tion**
exsilaration : **ex·hil·a·ra·tion**
exsile : **ex·ile**
exsileration : **ex·hil·a·ra·tion**
exsise : **ex·cise**
exsist : **ex·ist**
exsistence : **ex·is·tence**
exsistentialism :
  ex·is·ten·tial·ism
exsitement : **ex·cite·ment**
exsize : **ex·cise**
exsort : **ex·hort**

exspire : **ex·pire**
exstol : **ex·tol**
exsume : **ex·hume**
extenguish : **ex·tin·guish**
extermanate : **ex·ter·mi·nate**
extermenate : **ex·ter·mi·nate**
exterminait : **ex·ter·mi·nate**
ex·ter·mi·nate
extinguesh : **ex·tin·guish**
ex·tin·guish
extinquish : **ex·tin·guish**
ex·tol
extoll : **ex·tol**
extraordenary :
  ex·traor·di·nary
extraordinarry :
  ex·traor·di·nary
ex·traor·di·nary
extraordinery : **ex·traor·di·nary**
ex·trav·a·gance
extravaganse : **ex·trav·a·gance**

extravagence : **ex·trav·a·gance**
extravegance : **ex·trav·a·gance**
extravert : **ex·tro·vert**
extravigance : **ex·trav·a·gance**
extravirt : **ex·tro·vert**
extream : **ex·treme**
extreem : **ex·treme**
ex·treme
extrivert : **ex·tro·vert**
extroardinary : **ex·traor·di·nary**
extrordinary : **ex·traor·di·nary**
ex·tro·vert
exubarance : **ex·u·ber·ance**
ex·u·ber·ance
exuberanse : **ex·u·ber·ance**
exuberence : **ex·u·ber·ance**
exuberense : **ex·u·ber·ance**
ex·ult (to rejoice); **ex·alt** (to
  honor)
exume : **ex·hume**
exurpt : **ex·cerpt**

F

fabble : **fa·ble**
fabbric : **fab·ric**
fabel : **fa·ble**
fa·ble
fabrec : **fab·ric**
fab·ric
fabrick : **fab·ric**
fa·cade
facaid : **fa·cade**
facalty : **fa·cil·i·ty** (aptitude;
  building) *or* **fac·ul·ty** (ability;
  teachers)
faceal : **fa·cial** (relating to the
  face) *or* **fac·ile** (superficial)
faceatious : **fa·ce·tious**
faceetious : **fa·ce·tious**
faceitious : **fa·ce·tious**
facelty : **fa·cil·i·ty** (aptitude;
  building) *or* **fac·ul·ty** (ability;
  teachers)
faceshious : **fa·ce·tious**
fac·et
fa·ce·tious
facetius : **fa·ce·tious**
fa·cial (relating to the face);
  fac·ile (superficial)
fac·ile (superficial); **fa·cial**
  (relating to the face)
facilety : **fa·cil·i·ty**
fa·cil·i·ty
facillity : **fa·cil·i·ty**
facimile : **fac·sim·i·le**
facination : **fas·ci·na·tion**
facism : **fas·cism**
facit : **fac·et**
facksimile : **fac·sim·i·le**
fackulty : **fac·ul·ty**
facsimely : **fac·sim·i·le**
fac·sim·i·le
facsimily : **fac·sim·i·le**

facsimmile : **fac·sim·i·le**
factary : **fac·to·ry**
factery : **fac·to·ry**
fac·to·ry
fac·ul·ty
faery : **fairy** (sprite) *or* **fer·ry**
  (boat)
Fahr·en·heit
Fahrenhiet : **Fahr·en·heit**
Fahrenhite : **Fahr·en·heit**
faign : **feign**
faimous : **fa·mous**
fair (equitable; bazaar); **fare**
  (fee)
Fairenheit : **Fahr·en·heit**
fairwell : **fare·well**
fairy (sprite); **fer·ry** (boat)
falacious : **fal·la·cious**
falacy : **fal·la·cy**
falcan : **fal·con**
falcify : **fal·si·fy**
fal·con
falible : **fal·li·ble**
falken : **fal·con**
falkon : **fal·con**
fallable : **fal·li·ble**
fal·la·cious
fallacius : **fal·la·cious**
fal·la·cy
fallashious : **fal·la·cious**
fallasy : **fal·la·cy**
fallatious : **fal·la·cious**
fallcon : **fal·con**
falleble : **fal·li·ble**
fallecy : **fal·la·cy**
fallesy : **fal·la·cy**
fallibal : **fal·li·ble**
fallibel : **fal·li·ble**
fal·li·ble
fallic : **phal·lic**

fallicy : **fal·la·cy**
fallisy : **fal·la·cy**
fallsify : **fal·si·fy**
fallty : **faulty**
falsafy : **fal·si·fy**
falsefy : **fal·si·fy**
falsety : **fal·si·ty**
fal·si·fy
falsitty : **fal·si·ty**
fal·si·ty
famaly : **fam·i·ly**
famely : **fam·i·ly**
famen : **fam·ine**
fameous : **fa·mous**
famesh : **fam·ish**
familar : **fa·mil·iar**
fa·mil·iar
familier : **fa·mil·iar**
familliar : **fa·mil·iar**
familly : **fam·i·ly**
fam·i·ly
famin : **fam·ine**
fam·ine
fam·ish
fammiliar : **fa·mil·iar**
fammily : **fam·i·ly**
fammine : **fam·ine**
fammish : **fam·ish**
fa·mous
fanatec : **fa·nat·ic**
fa·nat·ic
fanatick : **fa·nat·ic**
fanattic : **fa·nat·ic**
fan·ci·ful
fancifull : **fan·ci·ful**
fan·cy
fancyful : **fan·ci·ful**
fane : **feign**
fanfair : **.fan·fare**
fan·fare
fannatic : **fa·nat·ic**
fansiful : **fan·ci·ful**

fansy : **fan·cy**
fantasstic : **fan·tas·tic**
fantassy : **fan·ta·sy**
fantastec : **fan·tas·tic**
fan·tas·tic
fantastick : **fan·tas·tic**
fan·ta·sy or **phan·ta·sy**
fantesy : **fan·ta·sy**
fantissy : **fan·ta·sy**
fantisy : **fan·ta·sy**
fantom : **phan·tom**
farce
farcecal : **far·ci·cal**
far·ci·cal
farcicle : **far·ci·cal**
fare (fee); **fair** (equitable;
 bazaar)
fare·well
farmacy : **phar·ma·cy**
Farrenheit : **Fahr·en·heit**
farry : **fairy** (sprite) or **fer·ry**
 (boat)
farse : **farce**
farsecal : **far·ci·cal**
farsical : **far·ci·cal**
fasade : **fa·cade**
fascenation : **fas·ci·na·tion**
fascesm : **fas·cism**
fascinacion : **fas·ci·na·tion**
fascinatian : **fas·ci·na·tion**
fas·ci·na·tion
fas·cism
faset : **fac·et**
fasetious : **fa·ce·tious**
fashial : **fa·cial**
fashianable : **fash·ion·able**
fashienable : **fash·ion·able**
fash·ion·able
fashionibal : **fash·ion·able**
fashionible : **fash·ion·able**
fasility : **fa·cil·i·ty**
fasination : **fas·ci·na·tion**

fasit : **fac·et**
fasodd : **fa·cade**
fassetious : **fa·ce·tious**
fassination : **fas·ci·na·tion**
fassionable : **fash·ion·able**
fassism : **fas·cism**
fasteadious : **fas·tid·i·ous**
fasteedious : **fas·tid·i·ous**
fastideous : **fas·tid·i·ous**
fas·tid·i·ous
fastidius : **fas·tid·i·ous**
fat·al
fateague : **fa·tigue**
fategue : **fa·tigue**
fatel : **fa·tal**
fatham : **fa·thom**
fathem : **fa·thom**
fa·thom
fatige : **fa·tigue**
fa·tigue
fatique : **fa·tigue**
fatteague : **fa·tigue**
fattigue : **fa·tigue**
fau·cet
faucit : **fau·cet**
faul·ty
faun (mythical being); **fawn**
 (young deer)
fauset : **fau·cet**
favarable : **fa·vor·able**
faverable : **fa·vor·able**
faverite : **fa·vor·ite**
fa·vor·able
favorate : **fa·vor·ite**
favoret : **fa·vor·ite**
favorible : **fa·vor·able**
fa·vor·ite
fawn (young deer); **faun**
 (mythical being)
faze (to disturb); **phase** (step in
 a process)
feable : **fee·ble**

feacundity : **fe·cun·di·ty**
Feaji : **Fi·ji**
feance : **fi·an·cé** (*masc.*) *or*
 fi·an·cée (*fem.*)
fear·ful
fearfull : **fear·ful**
feasable : **fea·si·ble**
feasco : **fi·as·co**
feaseble : **fea·si·ble**
feasibal : **fea·si·ble**
fea·si·ble
feath·er
feazible : **fea·si·ble**
Feb·ru·ary
Februery : **Feb·ru·ary**
Febuarry : **Feb·ru·ary**
Febuery : **Feb·ru·ary**
fecundety : **fe·cun·di·ty**
fecunditty : **fe·cun·di·ty**
fe·cun·di·ty
fedaral : **fed·er·al**
fedderal : **fed·er·al**
fedelity : **fi·del·i·ty**
fed·er·al
federel : **fed·er·al**
federil : **fed·er·al**
fediral : **fed·er·al**
fedrel : **fed·er·al**
feebal : **fee·ble**
fee·ble
Feegee : **Fi·ji**
Feejee : **Fi·ji**
feerful : **fear·ful**
feesible : **fea·si·ble**
feetus : **fe·tus**
feign
feild : **field**
fein : **feign**
feirful : **fear·ful**
felan : **fel·on**
felany : **fel·o·ny**
felen : **fel·on**

feleny : **fel·o·ny**
felicety : **fe·lic·i·ty**
felicitty : **fe·lic·i·ty**
fe·lic·i·ty
felisity : **fe·lic·i·ty**
fellicity : **fe·lic·i·ty**
fellisity : **fe·lic·i·ty**
fellon : **fel·on**
fellony : **fel·o·ny**
fel·on
fel·o·ny
femail : **fe·male**
fe·male
femaminity : **fem·i·nin·i·ty**
femanine : **fem·i·nine**
femenine : **fem·i·nine**
feminen : **fem·i·nine**
feminenity : **fem·i·nin·i·ty**
feminin : **fem·i·nine**
fem·i·nine
femininety : **fem·i·nin·i·ty**
femininitty : **fem·i·nin·i·ty**
fem·i·nin·i·ty
feminity : **fem·i·nin·i·ty**
feminnine : **fem·i·nine**
femminine : **fem·i·nine**
femmininity : **fem·i·nin·i·ty**
fenagle : **fi·na·gle**
fence
Fenix : **Phoe·nix**
fennagle : **fi·na·gle**
fenomenal : **phe·nom·e·nal**
fenomenon : **phe·nom·e·non**
fense : **fence**
ferlough : **fur·lough**
ferlow : **fur·lough**
fernace : **fur·nace**
fe·ro·cious
feroshious : **fe·ro·cious**
ferotious : **fe·ro·cious**
ferrocious : **fe·ro·cious**
fer·ry (boat); **fairy** (sprite)

fertalizer : **fer·til·iz·er**
fer·tile
fertilety : **fer·til·i·ty**
fertiliser : **fer·til·iz·er**
fertilitty : **fer·til·i·ty**
fer·til·i·ty
fer·til·iz·er
fertill : **fer·tile**
fertillity : **fer·til·i·ty**
fertillizer : **fer·til·iz·er**
fervant : **fer·vent**
fer·vent
ferver : **fer·vor**
fer·vor
fesible : **fea·si·ble**
festaval : **fes·ti·val**
festeval : **fes·ti·val**
fes·ti·val
festivall : **fes·ti·val**
festivel : **fes·ti·val**
festivle : **fes·ti·val**
fether : **feath·er**
fetis : **fe·tus**
fetther : **feath·er**
fe·tus
feud
feu·dal (medieval social order);
   fu·tile (without success)
feudel : **feu·dal** (medieval social
   order) *or* **fu·tile** (without
   success)
feushia : **fuch·sia**
Fevrary : **Feb·ru·ary**
fewd : **feud**
fi·an·cé (*masc.*); **fi·an·cée**
   (*fem.*)
fi·an·cée (*fem.*); **fi·an·cé**
   (*masc.*)
fiancey : **fiancé** (*masc.*) *or*
   fi·an·cée (*fem.*)
fianse : **fi·an·cé** (*masc.*) *or*
   fi·an·cée (*fem.*)

fiansey : **fi·an·cé** (*masc.*) *or*
  fi·an·cée (*fem.*)
fiary : **fi·ery**
fi·as·co
fiasko : **fi·as·co**
fickal : **fick·le**
fickel : **fick·le**
fick·le
ficsion : **fis·sion**
fidelety : **fi·del·i·ty**
fidelitty : **fi·del·i·ty**
fi·del·i·ty
fidellity : **fi·del·i·ty**
field
fi·ery
fiftean : **fif·teen**
fif·teen
fiftene : **fif·teen**
fif·ti·eth
fif·ty
fiftyeth : **fif·ti·eth**
Figi : **Fi·ji**
Fi·ji
fikle : **fick·le**
filabuster : **fi·li·bus·ter**
fil·a·ment
filamete : **fil·a·ment**
Filapino : **Fil·i·pi·no**
filay : **fi·let** (filet mignon) *or*
  fil·let (boneless meat or fish)
fileal : **fil·ial**
filement : **fil·a·ment**
Filepino : **Fil·i·pi·no**
fi·let (filet mignon); **fil·let**
  (boneless meat or fish)
filey : **fi·let** (filet mignon) *or*
  fil·let (boneless meat or fish)
fil·ial
fi·li·bus·ter
filiel : **fil·ial**
filiment : **fil·a·ment**
Filipeno : **Fil·i·pi·no**

Fil·i·pi·no
fillabuster : **fi·li·bus·ter**
fillay : **fi·let** (filet mignon) *or*
  fil·let (boneless meat or fish)
fil·let (boneless meat or fish);
  fi·let (filet mignon)
filley : **fi·let** (filet mignon) *or*
  fil·let (boneless meat or fish)
fillial : **fil·ial**
fillibuster : **fi·li·bus·ter**
filliment : **fil·a·ment**
Fillipino : **Fil·i·pi·no**
fimale : **fe·male**
finagal : **fi·na·gle**
fi·na·gle
finaly : **fi·nal·ly**
fi·nal·ly
fi·nance
financeer : **fi·nan·cier**
financeir : **fi·nan·cier**
fi·nan·cial
fi·nan·cier
finanse : **fi·nance**
finanseir : **fi·nan·cier**
finanshial : **fi·nan·cial**
finansier : **fi·nan·cier**
finantial : **fi·nan·cial**
finesce : **fi·nesse**
finess : **fi·nesse**
fi·nesse
fin·icky
finicy : **fin·icky**
fin·ish (to complete); **Finn·ish**
  (from Finland)
Fin·land
finnagle : **fi·na·gle**
finnally : **fi·nal·ly**
finness : **fi·nesse**
finnicky : **fin·icky**
Finn·ish (from Finland);
  fin·ish (to complete)
Finnland : **Fin·land**

fiord or **fjord**
firey : **fi·ery**
firlough : **fur·lough**
firtile : **fer·tile**
firtility : **fer·til·i·ty**
firy : **fi·ery**
fishary : **fish·ery**
fisherry : **fish·ery**
fish·ery
fishion : **fis·sion**
fision : **fis·sion**
fis·sion
fistacuffs : **fist·i·cuffs**
fistecuffs : **fist·i·cuffs**
fist·i·cuffs
fitus : **fe·tus**
fivteen : **fif·teen**
fivtieth : **fif·ti·eth**
fivty : **fif·ty**
fixety : **fix·i·ty**
fixitty : **fix·i·ty**
fix·i·ty
fizion : **fis·sion**
fjord or **fiord**
flac·cid
flacid : **flac·cid**
flagan : **flag·on**
flagen : **flag·on**
flaggon : **flag·on**
flag·on
fla·grant
flagrent : **fla·grant**
flair (talent); **flare** (torch)
flamboiant : **flam·boy·ant**
flam·boy·ant
flamboyent : **flam·boy·ant**
flambuoyant : **flam·boy·ant**
flameboyant : **flam·boy·ant**
flanel : **flan·nel**
flannal : **flan·nel**
flan·nel
flare (torch); **flair** (talent)

flasid : **flac·cid**
flassid : **flac·cid**
flautest : **flut·ist**
flaut·ist or **flut·ist**
flaver : **fla·vor**
fla·vor
fleacy : **fleecy**
flecksible : **flex·i·ble**
fledgleng : **fledg·ling**
fledg·ling
fleecy
fleesy : **fleecy**
flertatious : **flir·ta·tious**
flexable : **flex·i·ble**
flexeble : **flex·i·ble**
flex·i·ble
flimsey : **flim·sy**
flim·si·ness
flimssness : **flim·si·ness**
flimziness : **flim·si·ness**
flimzy : **flim·sy**
flipant : **flip·pant**
flip·pant
flippent : **flip·pant**
flippint : **flip·pant**
flirtacious : **flir·ta·tious**
flirtashious : **flir·ta·tious**
flir·ta·tious
flirtatius : **flir·ta·tious**
floatsam : **flot·sam**
floora : **flo·ra**
Floorida : **Flor·i·da**
flo·ra
flored : **flor·id** (ornate; ruddy)
  or **flu·o·ride** (dental
  treatment)
Floreda : **Flor·i·da**
flo·res·cent (flowering);
  flu·o·res·cent (emitting light)
floresh : **flour·ish**
florest : **flo·rist**

flor·id (ornate; ruddy);
  flu·o·ride (dental treatment)
Flor·i·da
floridation : **flu·o·ri·da·tion**
floride : **flor·id** (ornate; ruddy)
  or **flu·o·ride** (dental
  treatment)
florish : **flour·ish**
flo·rist
florra : **flo·ra**
florrescent : **flo·res·cent**
  (flowering) *or* **flu·o·res·cent**
  (emitting light)
florressent : **flo·res·cent**
  (flowering) *or* **flu·o·res·cent**
  (emitting light)
florrid : **flor·id** (ornate; ruddy)
  or **flu·o·ride** (dental
  treatment)
Florrida : **Flor·i·da**
florridation : **flu·o·ri·da·tion**
florride : **flor·id** (ornate;
  ruddy) *or* **flu·o·ride** (dental
  treatment)
florrish : **flour·ish**
florrist : **flo·rist**
flot·sam
flotsem : **flot·sam**
flotsum : **flot·sam**
flottsam : **flot·sam**
floun·der
flour (grain meal); **flow·er**
  (plant)
flourescent : **flu·o·res·cent**
flouresh : **flour·ish**
flouridation : **flu·o·ri·da·tion**
flouride : **flor·id** (ornate;
  ruddy) *or* **flu·o·ride** (dental
  treatment)
flour·ish
flourrish : **flour·ish**
floutest : **flut·ist**

floutist : **flut·ist**
flow·er (plant); **flour** (grain
  meal)
flowera : **flo·ra**
flowerist : **flo·rist**
flownder : **floun·der**
fluancy : **flu·en·cy**
fluansy : **flu·en·cy**
fluant : **flu·ent**
flu·en·cy
fluensy : **flu·en·cy**
flu·ent
fluoradation : **flu·o·ri·da·tion**
fluoredation : **flu·o·ri·da·tion**
flu·o·res·cent (emitting light);
  flo·res·cent (flowering)
fluoresent : **flo·res·cent**
  (flowering) *or* **flu·o·res·cent**
  (emitting light)
fluoressent : **flo·res·cent**
  (flowering) *or* **flu·o·res·cent**
  (emitting light)
fluorid : **flor·id** (ornate; ruddy)
  or **flu·o·ride** (dental
  treatment)
flu·o·ri·da·tion
flu·o·ride (dental treatment);
  flor·id (ornate; ruddy)
fluoried : **flor·id** (ornate;
  ruddy) *or* **flu·o·ride** (dental
  treatment)
flutest : **flut·ist**
flut·ist *or* **flaut·ist**
fluttist : **flut·ist**
foacal : **fo·cal**
foacused : **fo·cused**
foam
fobia : **pho·bia**
fo·cal
focel : **fo·cal**
fo·cused

fo·cus·ing
focussed : **fo·cused**
focussing : **fo·cus·ing**
Foenix : **Phoe·nix**
foe·tus (*Brit.*) : **fe·tus**
fog·ey (old-fashioned person);
  fog·gy (misty) *or* **fo·gy**
  (old-fashioned person)
fog·gy (misty); **fo·gy**
  (old-fashioned person)
fo·gy *or* **fog·ey** (old-fashioned
  person); **fog·gy** (misty)
foibal : **foi·ble**
foibel : **foi·ble**
foi·ble
foilage : **fo·liage**
foilege : **fo·liage**
foilige : **fo·liage**
fokal : **fo·cal**
fokissed : **fo·cused**
fokle : **fo·cal**
fokused : **fo·cused**
folage : **fo·liage**
foleo : **fo·lio**
fo·liage
folicle : **fol·li·cle**
folige : **fo·liage**
fo·lio
follacle : **fol·li·cle**
follakle : **fol·li·cle**
follecle : **fol·li·cle**
follekle : **fol·li·cle**
folleo : **fo·lio**
follical : **fol·li·cle**
fol·li·cle
follikle : **fol·li·cle**
follio : **fo·lio**
folyage : **fo·liage**
fome : **foam**
fonetic : **pho·net·ic**
foram : **fo·rum**

forarm : **fore·arm**
forbare : **for·bear** (to restrain
  oneself) *or* **fore·bear**
  (ancestor)
forbarence : **for·bear·ance**
for·bear (to restrain oneself);
  fore·bear (ancestor)
for·bear·ance
forbearanse : **for·bear·ance**
forbearence : **for·bear·ance**
forbearense : **for·bear·ance**
forberance : **for·bear·ance**
for·bid
forbode : **fore·bode**
forcast : **fore·cast**
forcaster : **fore·cast·er**
forceble : **forc·ible**
force·ful
forcefull : **force·ful**
forcibal : **forc·ible**
forcibel : **forc·ible**
forc·ible
fore·arm
forebare : **for·bear** (to restrain
  oneself) *or* **fore·bear**
  (ancestor)
fore·bear (ancestor); **for·bear**
  (to restrain oneself)
forebearance : **for·bear·ance**
forebid : **for·bid**
foreboad : **fore·bode**
fore·bode
fore·cast
fore·cast·er
forecastor : **fore·cast·er**
fore·fa·ther
forefeit : **for·feit**
forefet : **for·feit**
forefit : **for·feit**
foregetful : **for·get·ful**
foregive : **for·give**
foregn : **for·eign**

foregner : **for•eign•er**
fore•go *or* **for•go**
fore•gone
foregotten : **for•got•ten**
fore•head
for•eign
for•eign•er
foreignor : **for•eign•er**
forelorn : **for•lorn**
forem : **fo•rum**
fore•man
foremat : **for•mat**
foremidable : **for•mi•da•ble**
foremula : **for•mu•la**
foren : **for•eign**
forencic : **fo•ren•sic**
forener : **for•eign•er**
forenicate : **for•ni•cate**
forensec : **fo•ren•sic**
fo•ren•sic
forensick : **fo•ren•sic**
fore•see
foreshadoe : **fore•shad•ow**
fore•shad•ow
for•est
fore•stall
forestary : **for•est•ry**
foresterry : **for•est•ry**
forestery : **for•est•ry**
for•est•ry
foreswear : **for•swear**
foresythia : **for•syth•ia**
foreteen : **four•teen**
fore•tell
foretification : **for•ti•fi•ca•tion**
foretress : **for•tress**
foretuitious : **for•tu•itous**
foretunate : **for•tu•nate**
foretune : **for•tune**
foreward : **fore•word** (preface)
  or **for•ward** (ahead)
fore•warn

fore•word (preface); **for•ward**
  (ahead)
forfather : **fore•fa•ther**
for•feit
forfet : **for•feit**
forfiet : **for•feit**
forfit : **for•feit**
forgary : **forg•ery**
forgerry : **forg•ery**
forg•ery
for•get•ful
forgetfull : **for•get•ful**
forgeting : **for•get•ting**
for•get•ting
forgitful : **for•get•ful**
forgiting : **for•get•ting**
forgitting : **for•get•ting**
for•give
for•go *or* **fore•go**
forgone : **fore•gone**
for•got•ten
forgry : **forg•ery**
forhead : **fore•head**
forign : **for•eign**
foriginer : **for•eign•er**
forim : **fo•rum**
forin : **for•eign**
foriner : **for•eign•er**
forinsic : **fo•ren•sic**
forist : **for•est**
foristry : **for•est•ry**
forjery : **forg•ery**
for•lorn
formadyhide : **form•al•de•hyde**
formaldehide : **form•al•de•hyde**
formaldehied : **form•al•de•hyde**
form•al•de•hyde
formaldihyde : **form•al•de•hyde**
formalldehyde :
  form•al•de•hyde
forman : **fore•man**
for•mat

formeldehyde : **form·al·de·hyde**
for·mi·da·ble
formiddable : **for·mi·da·ble**
formideble : **for·mi·da·ble**
formidibal : **for·mi·da·ble**
formidibel : **for·mi·da·ble**
formidible : **for·mi·da·ble**
formoola : **for·mu·la**
for·mu·la
formulah : **for·mu·la**
formulla : **for·mu·la**
fornacate : **for·ni·cate**
fornecate : **for·ni·cate**
fornicait : **for·ni·cate**
for·ni·cate
forram : **fo·rum**
forrem : **fo·rum**
forrensic : **fo·ren·sic**
forrest : **for·est**
forrestry : **for·est·ry**
forrim : **fo·rum**
forrist : **for·est**
forristry : **for·est·ry**
forrum : **fo·rum**
forsee : **fore·see**
forseful : **force·ful**
forshadow : **fore·shad·ow**
forsible : **forc·ible**
forsithea : **for·syth·ia**
forsithia : **for·syth·ia**
forstall : **fore·stall**
forsware : **for·swear**
for·swear
forsythea : **for·syth·ia**
for·syth·ia
fort (bulwark); **forte** (strong
  point)
fortafication : **for·ti·fi·ca·tion**
fortafy : **for·ti·fy**
fortatude : **for·ti·tude**
forte (strong point); **fort**
  (bulwark)

forteen : **four·teen**
fortefication : **for·ti·fi·ca·tion**
fortefy : **for·ti·fy**
fortell : **fore·tell**
fortetude : **for·ti·tude**
forth (forward); **fourth** (4th)
fortien : **for·tune**
for·ti·eth
fortifacation : **for·ti·fi·ca·tion**
for·ti·fi·ca·tion
fortifikation : **for·ti·fi·ca·tion**
for·ti·fy
fortifycation : **for·ti·fi·ca·tion**
fortine : **for·tune**
fortitood : **for·ti·tude**
for·ti·tude
fortooitous : **for·tu·itous**
fortoon : **for·tune**
fortoonate : **for·tu·nate**
fortres : **for·tress**
fortrese : **for·tress**
for·tress
fortriss : **for·tress**
fortruss : **for·tress**
fortuatous : **for·tu·itous**
fortuetous : **for·tu·itous**
fortuitious : **for·tu·itous**
for·tu·itous
fortuitus : **for·tu·itous**
for·tu·nate
for·tune
fortunet : **for·tu·nate**
fortunete : **for·tu·nate**
fortunit : **for·tu·nate**
for·ty
fortyeth : **for·ti·eth**
fortyith : **for·ti·eth**
fo·rum
forust : **for·est**
forustry : **for·est·ry**
for·ward (ahead); **fore·word**
  (preface)

forwarn : **fore·warn**
fosell : **fos·sil**
fosil : **fos·sil**
fosile : **fos·sil**
fossel : **fos·sil**
fossell : **fos·sil**
fos·sil
fossile : **fos·sil**
fossill : **fos·sil**
fotagrafy : **pho·tog·ra·phy**
foul (offensive); **fowl** (bird)
foundary : **found·ry**
founderry : **found·ry**
foundery : **found·ry**
foundiry : **found·ry**
found·ry
foun·tain
founten : **foun·tain**
fountian : **foun·tain**
fountin : **foun·tain**
fourarm : **fore·arm**
fourbid : **for·bid**
fourbode : **fore·bode**
fourcast : **fore·cast**
fourcaster : **fore·cast·er**
fourensic : **fo·ren·sic**
fourfather : **fore·fa·ther**
fourtean : **four·teen**
four·teen
fourtene : **four·teen**
fourth (4th); **forth** (forward)
fourtieth : **for·ti·eth**
fourtification : **for·ti·fi·ca·tion**
fourtify : **for·ti·fy**
fourtine : **four·teen**
fourtress : **for·tress**
fourtuitous : **for·tu·itous**
fourtunate : **for·tu·nate**
fourtune : **for·tune**
fourty : **for·ty**
fowl (bird); **foul** (offensive)
foyble : **foi·ble**

fra·cas
frachion : **frac·tion**
frachure : **frac·ture**
fracis : **fra·cas**
frackas : **fra·cas**
fracktion : **frac·tion**
frackture : **frac·ture**
frackus : **fra·cas**
fractian : **frac·tion**
frac·tion
frac·ture
fracus : **fra·cas**
fragell : **frag·ile**
fraggile : **frag·ile**
fragil : **frag·ile**
frag·ile
fragill : **frag·ile**
fra·grance
fragranse : **fra·grance**
fra·grant
fragrence : **fra·grance**
fragrense : **fra·grance**
fragrent : **fra·grant**
fragrince : **fra·grance**
fragrinse : **fra·grance**
fragrint : **fra·grant**
fragrunce : **fra·grance**
fragrunse : **fra·grance**
fragrunt : **fra·grant**
fraighter : **freight·er**
frail
fraiter : **freight·er**
frajile : **frag·ile**
frakas : **fra·cas**
frale : **frail**
franc (money); **frank** (honest)
fran·chise
franchize : **fran·chise**
franetic : **fre·net·ic**
frank (honest); **franc** (money)
franshise : **fran·chise**
frater : **freight·er**

fraternety : **fra·ter·ni·ty**
fraternitty : **fra·ter·ni·ty**
fra·ter·ni·ty
fraturnity : **fra·ter·ni·ty**
fraudulant : **fraud·u·lent**
fraud·u·lent
frawdulent : **fraud·u·lent**
fraxion : **frac·tion**
fraxure : **frac·ture**
freak
freckal : **freck·le**
freckel : **freck·le**
freck·le
freek : **freak**
freight·er
freightor : **freight·er**
freik : **freak**
freind : **friend**
freiter : **freight·er**
freke : **freak**
frekkle : **freck·le**
frend : **friend**
fre·net·ic
frenetick : **fre·net·ic**
frenettic : **fre·net·ic**
frennetic : **fre·net·ic**
frensy : **fren·zy**
fren·zy
frequancy : **fre·quen·cy**
frequansy : **fre·quen·cy**
fre·quen·cy
frequensy : **fre·quen·cy**
fri·ar (monk); **fry·er** (fried fowl)
frieghter : **freight·er**
friend
fri·er or **fry·er** (fried fowl); **fri·ar** (monk)
frigat : **frig·ate**
frig·ate
friged : **frig·id**
frigedity : **fri·gid·i·ty**

friget : **frig·ate**
friggate : **frig·ate**
frigget : **frig·ate**
friggid : **frig·id**
friggidity : **fri·gid·i·ty**
friggit : **frig·ate**
frig·id
frigidety : **fri·gid·i·ty**
frigiditty : **fri·gid·i·ty**
fri·gid·i·ty
frigit : **frig·ate** (ship) or **frig·id** (cold)
frinetic : **fre·net·ic**
friquency : **fre·quen·cy**
frivalous : **friv·o·lous**
frivalus : **friv·o·lous**
frivelous : **friv·o·lous**
frivilous : **friv·o·lous**
frivilus : **friv·o·lous**
frivolety : **fri·vol·i·ty**
frivolis : **friv·o·lous**
fri·vol·i·ty
frivollity : **fri·vol·i·ty**
friv·o·lous
frol·ic
frolick : **frol·ic**
frollic : **frol·ic**
frontadge : **front·age**
front·age
fron·tal
frontear : **fron·tier**
fronteer : **fron·tier**
frontege : **front·age**
fronteir : **fron·tier**
frontel : **fron·tal**
frontespiece : **fron·tis·piece**
frontidge : **front·age**
fron·tier
frontige : **front·age**
frontispeace : **fron·tis·piece**
frontispeice : **fron·tis·piece**
frontispice : **fron·tis·piece**

fron·tis·piece
frontspiece : **fron·tis·piece**
frovolitty : **fri·vol·i·ty**
fru·gal
frugel : **fru·gal**
fruit·ful
fruitfull : **fruit·ful**
frutful : **fruit·ful**
fry·er *or* **fri·er** (fried fowl);
  fri·ar (monk)
fuchea : **fuch·sia**
fuchia : **fuch·sia**
fuch·sia
fucilage : **fu·se·lage**
fuciloge : **fu·se·lage**
fudal : **feu·dal** (medieval social
  order) *or* **fu·tile** (without
  success)
fued : **feud**
fuedal : **feu·dal** (medieval
  social order) *or* **fu·tile**
  (without success)
fugative : **fu·gi·tive**
fugetive : **fu·gi·tive**
fugiteve : **fu·gi·tive**
fu·gi·tive
fujitive : **fu·gi·tive**
fulcram : **ful·crum**
fulcrem : **ful·crum**
fulcrim : **ful·crum**
ful·crum
ful·fil *or* **ful·fill**
ful·fill *or* **ful·fil**
fullcrem : **ful·crum**
fullcrum : **ful·crum**
fullfil : **ful·fill**
fullfill : **ful·fill**
fullsome : **ful·some**
ful·some
fumagate : **fum·i·gate**
fumegate : **fum·i·gate**
fumigait : **fum·i·gate**

fum·i·gate
fun·da·men·tal
fundamintal : **fun·da·men·tal**
fundemental : **fun·da·men·tal**
fundimental : **fun·da·men·tal**
funel : **fun·nel**
funell : **fun·nel**
funil : **fun·nel**
funill : **fun·nel**
funnal : **fun·nel**
fun·nel
funnell : **fun·nel**
funnil : **fun·nel**
furer : **fu·ror**
fur·lough
furlowe : **fur·lough**
fur·nace
furnature : **fur·ni·ture**
furnece : **fur·nace**
furness : **fur·nace**
furneture : **fur·ni·ture**
furnice : **fur·nace**
furniss : **fur·nace**
fur·ni·ture
furoar : **fu·ror**
fu·ror
furrer : **fu·ror**
furror : **fu·ror**
fusalage : **fu·se·lage**
fu·se·lage
fuselodge : **fu·se·lage**
fuseloge : **fu·se·lage**
fushea : **fuch·sia**
fushia : **fuch·sia**
fusilage : **fu·se·lage**
fusiloge : **fu·se·lage**
fu·sion
fussion : **fu·sion**
futele : **feu·dal** (medieval social
  order) *or* **fu·tile** (without
  success)

futell : **feu·dal** (medieval social order) *or* **fu·tile** (without success)
fu·tile (without success); **feu·dal** (medieval social order)
futilety : **fu·til·i·ty**

futilitty : **fu·til·i·ty**
fu·til·i·ty
futill : **fu·tile**
futillity : **fu·til·i·ty**
fuzion : **fu·sion**
fyord : **fjord**

G

gabardeen : **gab·ar·dine**
gabardene : **gab·ar·dine**
gab·ar·dine *or* **gab·er·dine**
gabbardine : **gab·ar·dine**
gabberdine : **gab·ar·dine**
gab·ble (to babble); **ga·ble** (roof feature)
gabel : **gab·ble** (to babble) *or* **ga·ble** (roof feature)
gab·er·dine *or* **gab·ar·dine**
ga·ble (roof feature); **gab·ble** (to babble)
gache : **gauche**
gad·get
gadgit : **gad·get**
gadjet : **gad·get**
Gaelec : **Gael·ic**
Gael·ic
gaget : **gad·get**
gai·ety *or* **gay·ety**
Gailic : **Gael·ic**
gai·ly *or* **gay·ly**
gait (way of walking); **gate** (door)
ga·la
galactec : **ga·lac·tic**
ga·lac·tic
galary : **gal·lery**
gal·axy
galen : **gal·lon**
galery : **gal·lery**
Galic : **Gael·ic**
galion : **gal·le·on** (ship) *or* **gal·lon** (measure)
galip : **gal·lop**
galla : **ga·la**
gallacksy : **gal·axy**
gallactic : **ga·lac·tic**
gallantery : **gal·lant·ry**
gal·lant·ry

gallap : **gal·lop**
gallary : **gal·lery**
gallaxy : **gal·axy**
gallen : **gal·le·on** (ship) *or* **gal·lon** (measure)
gallentry : **gal·lant·ry**
gal·le·on (ship); **gal·lon** (measure)
gallep : **gal·lop**
gal·lery
gallexy : **gal·axy**
gal·ley
gallin : **gal·le·on** (ship) *or* **gal·lon** (measure)
gallintry : **gal·lant·ry**
gallion : **gal·le·on** (ship) *or* **gal·lon** (measure)
gallip : **gal·lop**
gallixy : **gal·axy**
gal·lon (measure); **gal·le·on** (ship)
gal·lop (canter); **Gal·lup** (poll)
gallosh : **ga·losh** (footwear) *or* **gou·lash** (stew)
galluntry : **gal·lant·ry**
Gal·lup (poll); **gal·lop** (canter)
gally : **gal·ley**
galon : **gal·le·on** (ship) *or* **gal·lon** (measure)
galop : **gal·lop**
ga·losh (footwear); **gou·lash** (stew)
galvanise : **gal·va·nize**
gal·va·nize
galvenize : **gal·va·nize**
galvinize : **gal·va·nize**
gambet : **gam·bit**
gam·bit
gam·ble (to risk or bet); **gam·bol** (to frolic)

129

gam·bol (to frolic); **gam·ble** (to risk or bet)

gamet : **gam·ut**

gamit : **gam·ut**

gammet : **gam·ut**

gammit : **gam·ut**

gammut : **gam·ut**

gam·ut

gandola : **gon·do·la**

gangrean : **gan·grene**

gangreen : **gan·grene**

gan·grene

gangrine : **gan·grene**

gaol (*Brit.*) : **jail**

ga·rage

garantee : **guar·an·tee**

garason : **gar·ri·son**

gardeenia : **gar·de·nia**

gar·den

gar·de·nia

gardian : **guard·ian**

gardin : **gar·den**

gardinia : **gar·de·nia**

garentee : **guar·an·tee**

garesh : **gar·ish**

garet : **gar·ret**

gargoil : **gar·goyle**

gargoyl : **gar·goyle**

gar·goyle

garintee : **guar·an·tee**

gar·ish

garison : **gar·ri·son**

garit : **gar·ret**

gar·land

garlec : **gar·lic**

garlend : **gar·land**

gar·lic

garlick : **gar·lic**

garlind : **gar·land**

garlund : **gar·land**

garmant : **gar·ment**

gar·ment

garmet : **gar·ment**

garmint : **gar·ment**

gar·net

garnit : **gar·net**

garodge : **ga·rage**

garoge : **ga·rage**

garrage : **ga·rage**

garrentee : **guar·an·tee**

garreson : **gar·ri·son**

gar·ret

garrisen : **gar·ri·son**

garrish : **gar·ish**

gar·ri·son

garrit : **gar·ret**

gar·ru·lous

garulous : **gar·ru·lous**

gasaleen : **gas·o·line**

gasalene : **gas·o·line**

gasaline : **gas·o·line**

gas·e·ous

gasiline : **gas·o·line**

gasious : **gas·e·ous**

gas·ket

gaskit : **gas·ket**

gasolean : **gas·o·line**

gasoleen : **gas·o·line**

gasolene : **gas·o·line**

gas·o·line

gasseous : **gas·e·ous**

gassoline : **gas·o·line**

gastly : **ghast·ly**

gate (door); **gait** (way of walking)

gauche

gaudy

gauge

gauky : **gawky**

gaurantee : **guar·an·tee**

gaurd : **guard**

gaurdian : **guard·ian**

gause : **gauze**

gauze

gaval : **gav·el**
gav·el
gavell : **gav·el**
gavil : **gav·el**
gavvel : **gav·el**
gavvil : **gav·el**
gawdy : **gaudy**
gawky
gawze : **gauze**
gay·ety *or* **gai·ety**
gay·ly *or* **gai·ly**
gazet : **ga·zette**
gazett : **ga·zette**
ga·zette
gazzette : **ga·zette**
geagraphy : **ge·og·ra·phy**
Gealic : **Gael·ic**
gealogy : **ge·ol·o·gy**
geametry : **ge·om·e·try**
geanology : **ge·ne·al·o·gy**
gear
gearth : **girth**
geer : **gear**
gehad : **ji·had**
geir : **gear**
geiser : **gey·ser**
gel *or* jell
gelaten : **gel·a·tin**
gel·a·tin
gelitin : **gel·a·tin**
gellatin : **gel·a·tin**
Gem·i·ni
Geminie : **Gem·i·ni**
Geminni : **Gem·i·ni**
gemnasium : **gym·na·si·um**
gemnasstics : **gym·nas·tics**
gemnast : **gym·nast**
gemnastecs : **gym·nas·tics**
gemnasticks : **gym·nas·tics**
gemnest : **gym·nast**
gemnist : **gym·nast**
genarator : **gen·er·a·tor**

ge·ne·al·o·gy
Geneava : **Ge·ne·va**
Geneeva : **Ge·ne·va**
geneology : **ge·ne·al·o·gy**
gen·era (*plur.,* class or kind);
   genre (class of literature)
gen·er·al
generater : **gen·er·a·tor**
gen·er·a·tor
generel : **gen·er·al**
ge·ner·ic
generick : **ge·ner·ic**
generil : **gen·er·al**
gen·er·ous
generric : **gen·er·ic**
generus : **gen·er·ous**
gen·e·sis
geneticks : **ge·net·ics**
ge·net·ics
genettics : **ge·net·ics**
Ge·ne·va
Genieva : **Ge·ne·va**
genious : **gen·ius**
geniral : **gen·er·al**
genirator : **gen·er·a·tor**
genirous : **gen·er·ous**
genisis : **gen·e·sis**
gen·ius (intellectual power);
   ge·nus (*sing.,* class or kind)
Geniva : **Ge·ne·va**
gennerate : **gen·er·ate**
gennerator : **gen·er·a·tor**
genneric : **ge·ner·ic**
gennerous : **gen·er·ous**
gennesis : **gen·e·sis**
gennetics : **ge·net·ics**
gennirate : **gen·er·ate**
genooine : **gen·u·ine**
genre (class of literature);
   gen·era (*plur.,* class or kind)
genteal : **gen·teel**

gen·teel (polite); gen·tile (not
  Jewish)

gentele : gen·teel (polite) or
  gen·tile (not Jewish)

gen·tile (not Jewish); gen·teel
  (polite)

genuin : gen·u·ine

gen·u·ine

ge·nus (sing., class or kind);
  gen·ius (intellectual power)

genuwine : gen·u·ine

geoggrapy : ge·og·ra·phy

geografy : ge·og·ra·phy

ge·og·ra·phy

geogrefy : ge·og·ra·phy

geogrephy : ge·og·ra·phy

geogriphy : ge·og·ra·phy

geolegy : ge·ol·o·gy

geollogy : ge·ol·o·gy

geologgy : ge·ol·o·gy

ge·ol·o·gy

ge·om·e·try

geomettry : ge·om·e·try

geommetry : ge·om·e·try

geonoligy : ge·ne·al·o·gy

geonollogy : ge·ne·al·o·gy

geonre : genre

Georga : Geor·gia

Geor·gia

gerage : ga·rage

gerand : ger·und

geraneum : ge·ra·ni·um

geraniam : ge·ra·ni·um

geraniem : ge·ra·ni·um

ge·ra·ni·um

gerantology : ger·on·tol·o·gy

gerder : gird·er

gerdle : gir·dle

gerend : ger·und

gerkin : gher·kin

Germanny : Ger·ma·ny

Ger·ma·ny

Germeny : Ger·ma·ny

gerontolegy : ger·on·tol·o·gy

gerontoligy : ger·on·tol·o·gy

gerontollogy : ger·on·tol·o·gy

ger·on·tol·o·gy

gerranium : ge·ra·ni·um

gerrund : ger·und

gerth : girth

ger·und

gess : guess

gessture : ges·ture

gest : gist (essence) or jest
  (joke)

gester : ges·ture (movement) or
  jest·er (joker)

ges·ture (movement); jest·er
  (joker)

gesyr : gey·ser

gettho : ghet·to

Gettisburg : Get·tys·burg

getto : ghet·to

Gettysberg : Get·tys·burg

Get·tys·burg

Gettysburgh : Get·tys·burg

geuss : guess

gey·ser

ghast·ly

gherken : gher·kin

gher·kin

ghet·to

ghoul·ish

ghulish : ghoul·ish

ghurkin : gher·kin

gi·ant

gibe (to taunt); jibe (to change
  course in boat; to agree)

Gibralltar : Gi·bral·tar

Gi·bral·tar

Gibralter : Gi·bral·tar

gidance : guid·ance

gient : gi·ant

gier : gear

gieser : **gey·ser**

gihad : **ji·had**

gild (to cover with gold); **gilled** (having gills); **guild** (union)

gillatine : **guil·lo·tine**

gilled (having gills); **gild** (to cover with gold); **guild** (union)

gilliteen : **guil·lo·tine**

gillotine : **guil·lo·tine**

gilt (covered with gold); **guilt** (shame)

gimick : **gim·mick**

Gimini : **Gem·i·ni**

gimmeck : **gim·mick**

gimmic : **gim·mick**

gim·mick

gimnasium : **gym·na·si·um**

gimnasstics : **gym·nas·tics**

gimnast : **gym·nast**

gimnastecs : **gym·nas·tics**

gimnasticks : **gym·nas·tics**

gimnest : **gym·nast**

gimnist : **gym·nast**

ginacology : **gy·ne·col·o·gy**

ginasis : **gen·e·sis**

gincolijy : **gy·ne·col·o·gy**

ginecolligy : **gy·ne·col·o·gy**

ginecollogy : **gy·ne·col·o·gy**

gingam : **ging·ham**

ging·ham

ginghem : **ging·ham**

gingum : **ging·ham**

ginicology : **gy·ne·col·o·gy**

ginocology : **gy·ne·col·o·gy**

gipcem : **gyp·sum**

gipcim : **gyp·sum**

gipsam : **gyp·sum**

gipsem : **gyp·sum**

gipsey : **gyp·sy**

gipsim : **gyp·sum**

gipsy : **gyp·sy**

girafe : **gi·raffe**

gi·raffe

girage : **ga·rage**

giraph : **gi·raffe**

girascope : **gy·ro·scope**

girate : **gy·rate**

gird·er

gir·dle

girgle : **gur·gle**

girocompass : **gy·ro·com·pass**

girocompess : **gy·ro·com·pass**

girrate : **gy·rate**

girth

giser : **gey·ser**

gist (essence); **jest** (joke)

gister : **ges·ture** (movement) *or* **jest·er** (joker)

gitar : **gui·tar**

gittar : **gui·tar**

giullotine : **guil·lo·tine**

giutar : **gui·tar**

glaceir : **gla·cier**

glacher : **gla·cier**

gla·cier

gladdiator : **glad·i·a·tor**

gladeator : **glad·i·a·tor**

gladiater : **glad·i·a·tor**

glad·i·a·tor

glamarous : **glam·or·ous**

glamerous : **glam·or·ous**

glammorous : **glam·or·ous**

glam·or *or* **glam·our**

glam·or·ous

glamorus : **glam·or·ous**

glam·our *or* **glam·or**

glamourous : **glam·or·ous**

glance

glanse : **glance**

Glasco : **Glas·gow**

Glascoe : **Glas·gow**

Glascow : **Glas·gow**

Glas·gow

glasher : **gla·cier**
Glasscow : **Glas·gow**
glass·ware
glasswear : **glass·ware**
glasware : **glass·ware**
gleam
gleem : **gleam**
gleim : **gleam**
glemmer : **glim·mer**
glimer : **glim·mer**
glim·mer
glimpce : **glimpse**
glimpse
glimse : **glimpse**
glissen : **glis·ten**
glissten : **glis·ten**
glis·ten
gloabal : **glob·al**
gloat
glob·al
globall : **glob·al**
globel : **glob·al**
glorafication : **glo·ri·fi·ca·tion**
glorafy : **glo·ri·fy**
glorefication : **glo·ri·fi·ca·tion**
glorefy : **glo·ri·fy**
gloreous : **glo·ri·ous**
glorifacation : **glo·ri·fi·ca·tion**
glorifecation : **glo·ri·fi·ca·tion**
glo·ri·fi·ca·tion
glo·ri·fy
glo·ri·ous
glorius : **glo·ri·ous**
glorrification : **glo·ri·fi·ca·tion**
glorrify : **glo·ri·fy**
glorrious : **glo·ri·ous**
glorry : **glo·ry**
glo·ry
glosary : **glos·sa·ry**
glosery : **glos·sa·ry**
glos·sa·ry
glossery : **glos·sa·ry**

glote : **gloat**
gluton : **glut·ton**
glutonny : **glut·tony**
gluttan : **glut·ton**
glutten : **glut·ton**
gluttenny : **glut·tony**
glutteny : **glut·tony**
gluttin : **glut·ton**
gluttiny : **glut·tony**
glut·ton
glut·tony
gnarled
gnarreled : **gnarled**
gnarrled : **gnarled**
gnash
gnat
gnaw
gnoam : **gnome**
gnome (dwarf); **Nome** (city)
gnu (antelope); **knew** (was aware); **new** (not old)
goache : **gauche**
goal
goard : **gourd**
goashe : **gauche**
goa·tee
goatey : **goa·tee**
goatie : **goa·tee**
gobblen : **gob·lin**
gobblet : **gob·let**
gobblin : **gob·lin**
gobblit : **gob·let**
goblen : **gob·lin**
gob·let
gob·lin
goblit : **gob·let**
goche : **gauche**
goddes : **god·dess**
god·dess
goddiss : **god·dess**
godess : **god·dess**
god·li·ness

godlyness : **god·li·ness**
gofer : **go·pher**
gole : **goal**
gon·do·la
gondolla : **gon·do·la**
gooce : **goose**
good-by or **good-bye**
good-bye or **good-by**
goose
go·pher
gophur : **go·pher**
gord : **gourd**
gorey : **gory**
gor·geous
Gorgia : **Geor·gia**
gorgious : **gor·geous**
gorgius : **gor·geous**
gorila : **go·ril·la** (ape) or
  guer·ril·la (warrior)
go·ril·la (ape); **guer·ril·la**
  (warrior)
gorjeous : **gor·geous**
gormay : **gour·met**
gormet : **gour·met**
gorry : **gory**
gory
gosamer : **gos·sa·mer**
gosemer : **gos·sa·mer**
gosimer : **gos·sa·mer**
gosip : **gos·sip**
gos·pel
gospell : **gos·pel**
gospil : **gos·pel**
gospul : **gos·pel**
gos·sa·mer
gossamere : **gos·sa·mer**
gossamir : **gos·sa·mer**
gossemer : **gos·sa·mer**
gossep : **gos·sip**
gossimer : **gos·sa·mer**
gos·sip
gosspel : **gos·pel**

gossup : **gos·sip**
gosup : **gos·sip**
gotee : **goa·tee**
gothec : **goth·ic**
goth·ic
gothick : **goth·ic**
gou·lash (stew); **ga·losh**
  (footwear)
goulosh : **ga·losh** (footwear) or
  gou·lash (stew)
goun : **gown**
gourd
gourmay : **gour·met**
gour·met
gourmey : **gour·met**
govanor : **gov·er·nor**
govenor : **gov·er·nor**
goverment : **gov·ern·ment**
gov·ern
gov·er·nance
governanse : **gov·er·nance**
governence : **gov·er·nance**
governense : **gov·er·nance**
governer : **gov·er·nor**
governince : **gov·er·nance**
governmant : **gov·ern·ment**
gov·ern·ment
gov·er·nor
govirn : **gov·ern**
govirnance : **gov·er·nance**
govner : **gov·er·nor**
govurn : **gov·ern**
govurnor : **gov·er·nor**
govvern : **gov·ern**
govvernance : **gov·er·nance**
govvernment : **gov·ern·ment**
govvernnor : **gov·er·nor**
gown
grace·ful
gracefull : **grace·ful**
graceous : **gra·cious**
gra·cious

gracius : **gra·cious**
graddual : **grad·u·al**
gradduate : **grad·u·ate**
gradeant : **gra·di·ent**
gradiant : **gra·di·ent**
gra·di·ent
graduait : **grad·u·ate**
grad·u·al
grad·u·ate
graduel : **grad·u·al**
graduill : **grad·u·al**
graduwel : **grad·u·al**
graffec : **graph·ic**
graffete : **graf·fi·ti** (writing) *or*
    graph·ite (carbon)
graffic : **graph·ic**
graffically : **graph·i·cal·ly**
graf·fi·ti (writing); **graph·ite**
    (carbon)
graffitti : **graf·fi·ti**
grafitti : **graf·fi·ti**
gragarious : **gre·gar·i·ous**
graiceful : **grace·ful**
grainarry : **gra·na·ry**
grainary : **gra·na·ry**
grainerry : **gra·na·ry**
grainery : **gra·na·ry**
grainular : **gran·u·lar**
grainule : **gran·ule**
graitful : **grate·ful**
graiven : **grav·en**
graize : **graze**
gramar : **gram·mar**
gramer : **gram·mar**
gram·mar
grammer : **gram·mar**
grammir : **gram·mar**
granade : **gre·nade**
granaid : **gre·nade**
gra·na·ry
grandelaquence :
    gran·dil·o·quence

grandelloquence :
    gran·dil·o·quence
grandeloquance :
    gran·dil·o·quence
grandeloquence :
    gran·dil·o·quence
grandeoce : **gran·di·ose**
grandeose : **gran·di·ose**
gran·deur
grandilaquence :
    gran·dil·o·quence
gran·dil·o·quence
grandiloquense :
    gran·dil·o·quence
grandiloquince :
    gran·dil·o·quence
grandioce : **gran·di·ose**
gran·di·ose
grandoor : **gran·deur**
grandur : **gran·deur**
grandure : **gran·deur**
granerry : **gra·na·ry**
granery : **gra·na·ry**
grannule : **gran·ule**
granool : **gran·ule**
granoolar : **gran·u·lar**
gran·u·lar
gran·ule
granuler : **gran·u·lar**
granulir : **gran·u·lar**
graphec : **graph·ic**
graphecally : **graph·i·cal·ly**
grapheit : **graph·ite**
graph·ic
graph·i·cal·ly
graphick : **graph·ic**
graphickelly : **graph·i·cal·ly**
graphicly : **graph·i·cal·ly**
graph·ite (carbon); **graf·fi·ti**
    (writing)
graple : **grap·ple**
grappal : **grap·ple**

grappel : **grap·ple**
grap·ple
graseful : **grace·ful**
grasious : **grac·ious**
gratafication : **grat·i·fi·ca·tion**
gratafy : **grat·i·fy**
gratatude : **grat·i·tude**
grate (framework); **great** (large)
grate·ful
gratefull : **grate·ful**
gratefy : **grat·i·fy**
gratetude : **grat·i·tude**
gratful : **grate·ful**
gratiffication : **grat·i·fi·ca·tion**
grat·i·fi·ca·tion
grat·i·fy
grat·is
gratitood : **grat·i·tude**
grat·i·tude
gratitued : **grat·i·tude**
gratiutous : **gra·tu·itous**
grattafication : **grat·i·fi·ca·tion**
grattatude : **grat·i·tude**
grattifacation : **grat·i·fi·ca·tion**
grattiffication : **grat·i·fi·ca·tion**
grattify : **grat·i·fy**
grattis : **grat·is**
grattitude : **grat·i·tude**
grattuitous : **gra·tu·itous**
grattus : **grat·is**
gratuetous : **gra·tu·itous**
gratuitious : **gra·tu·itous**
gra·tu·itous
gratus : **grat·is**
gravatate : **grav·i·tate**
grav·el
gravell : **grav·el**
grav·en
gravetate : **grav·i·tate**
gravety : **grav·i·ty**
gravil : **grav·el**
grav·i·tate

gravitty : **grav·i·ty**
grav·i·ty
gravvel : **grav·el**
gravvitate : **grav·i·tate**
gravvity : **grav·i·ty**
gray or **grey**
grayhound : **grey·hound**
graze
gready : **greedy**
greanery : **green·ery**
Greasian : **Gre·cian**
greasy
great (large); **grate** (framework)
greatful : **grate·ful**
greating : **greet·ing**
greavance : **griev·ance**
greave (armored legging);
   grieve (to mourn)
Gre·cian
Greecian : **Gre·cian**
greedy
greenary : **green·ery**
greenerry : **green·ery**
green·ery
Greenich : **Green·wich**
Green·wich
Greenwitch : **Green·wich**
Greesian : **Gre·cian**
greesy : **greasy**
greet·ing
greevance : **griev·ance**
grefitti : **graf·fi·ti**
gregairious : **gre·gar·i·ous**
gregareous : **gre·gar·i·ous**
gre·gar·i·ous
gregarius : **gre·gar·i·ous**
greggarious : **gre·gar·i·ous**
greif : **grief**
greisy : **greasy**
greivance : **griev·ance**
greive : **greave** (armored
   legging) or **grieve** (to mourn)

greivence : **griev·ance**
gremlan : **grem·lin**
gremlen : **grem·lin**
grem·lin
gremlun : **grem·lin**
gre·nade
grenaid : **gre·nade**
Grennich : **Green·wich**
Grenwich : **Green·wich**
Grenwitch : **Green·wich**
greve : **greave** (armored
    legging) *or* **grieve** (to mourn)
grey *or* **gray**
grey·hound
gridiern : **grid·iron**
gridiren : **grid·iron**
gridirn : **grid·iron**
grid·iron
grief
griefance : **griev·ance**
griefitti : **graf·fi·ti**
griev·ance
grievanse : **griev·ance**
grieve (to mourn); **greave**
    (armored legging)
grievense : **griev·ance**
grif·fin *or* **grif·fon** *or* **gryph·on**
griffiti : **graf·fi·ti**
grif·fon *or* **grif·fin** *or* **gryph·on**
grigarious : **gre·gar·i·ous**
grill (to broil); **grille** (screen)
grille (screen); **grill** (to broil)
gri·mace
grimece : **gri·mace**
grimice : **gri·mace**
grimise : **gri·mace**
grimlin : **grem·lin**
grimmace : **gri·mace**
grisled : **griz·zled**
gris·ly (gruesome); **griz·zly**
    (grayish, as the bear)
grissel : **gris·tle**

grissle : **gris·tle**
gris·tle
grivance : **griev·ance**
griz·zled
griz·zly (grayish, as the bear);
    gris·ly (gruesome)
groacer : **gro·cer**
groacery : **gro·cery**
groaned
groap : **grope**
groape : **grope**
groatesque : **gro·tesque**
gro·cer
grocerry : **gro·cery**
gro·cery
grociary : **gro·cery**
grociery : **gro·cery**
groned : **groaned**
grooling : **gru·el·ing**
grope
groser : **gro·cer**
grotesk : **gro·tesque**
groteske : **gro·tesque**
gro·tesque
grouchy
grov·eled *or* **grov·elled**
grov·el·ing *or* **grov·el·ling**
grov·elled *or* **grov·eled**
grov·el·ling *or* **grov·el·ing**
groviled : **grov·eled**
grovilling : **grov·el·ing**
grovveled : **grov·eled**
growchy : **grouchy**
gru·el·ing
gruesom : **grue·some**
grue·some
gruling : **gru·el·ing**
grulling : **gru·el·ing**
grusome : **grue·some**
grusum : **grue·some**
gryph·on *or* **grif·fin** *or* **grif·fon**
guage : **gauge**

guar•an•tee
guard
guard•ian
guardien : **guard•ian**
guarintie : **guar•an•tee**
Guatamala : **Gua•te•ma•la**
Gua•te•ma•la
Guatemalla : **Gua•te•ma•la**
Guattemala : **Gua•te•ma•la**
guerila : **go•ril•la** (ape) or **guer•ril•la** (warrior)
guer•ril•la (warrior); **go•ril•la** (ape)
guess
guetar : **gui•tar**
guid•ance
guidanse : **guid•ance**
guiddance : **guid•ance**
guidence : **guid•ance**
guidense : **guid•ance**
guild (union); **gild** (to cover with gold); **gilled** (having gills)
guillatine : **guil•lo•tine**
guilletine : **guil•lo•tine**
guillotene : **guil•lo•tine**
guil•lo•tine
guilt (shame); **gilt** (covered with gold)
gui•tar
gulash : **ga•losh** (footwear) or **gou•lash** (stew)
gulet : **gul•let**
gulible : **gul•li•ble**
gullable : **gul•li•ble**
gullat : **gul•let**
gulleble : **gul•li•ble**
gul•let
gullibal : **gul•li•ble**
gul•li•ble
gullit : **gul•let**

gulosh : **ga•losh** (footwear) or **gou•lash** (stew)
gunery : **gun•nery**
gunnary : **gun•nery**
gun•nel or **gun•wale**
gunnerry : **gun•nery**
gun•nery
gun•wale or **gun•nel**
guord : **gourd**
guormet : **gour•met**
gurgal : **gur•gle**
gurgel : **gur•gle**
gur•gle
gurilla : **go•ril•la** (ape) or **guer•ril•la** (warrior)
gurkin : **gher•kin**
gurth : **girth**
guse : **goose**
Gwatemala : **Gua•te•ma•la**
gymnaisium : **gym•na•si•um**
gymnaseum : **gym•na•si•um**
gymnasiem : **gym•na•si•um**
gym•na•si•um
gymnasstics : **gym•nas•tics**
gym•nast
gymnastecs : **gym•nas•tics**
gymnasticks : **gym•nas•tics**
gym•nas•tics
gymnest : **gym•nast**
gymnist : **gym•nast**
gynacology : **gy•ne•col•o•gy**
gyncolijy : **gy•ne•col•o•gy**
gynecolligy : **gy•ne•col•o•gy**
gynecollogy : **gy•ne•col•o•gy**
gy•ne•col•o•gy
gynicology : **gy•ne•col•o•gy**
gynocology : **gy•ne•col•o•gy**
gyp
gypcem : **gyp•sum**
gypcim : **gyp•sum**
gyped : **gypped**
gypped

gypsam : **gyp·sum**
gypsem : **gyp·sum**
gypsey : **gyp·sy**
gypsie : **gyp·sy**
gypsim : **gyp·sum**
gyp·sum
gyp·sy
gyracompass : **gy·ro·com·pass**
gyrait : **gy·rate**
gyrascope : **gy·ro·scope**

gy·rate
gyricompass : **gy·ro·com·pass**
gyriscope : **gy·ro·scope**
gy·ro·com·pass
gyrocompess : **gy·ro·com·pass**
gyrocompiss : **gy·ro·com·pass**
gyroscoap : **gy·ro·scope**
gy·ro·scope
gyrrate : **gy·rate**
gyser : **gey·ser**

H

habbet : **hab·it**
habbit : **hab·it**
habbitable : **hab·it·able**
habetable : **hab·it·able**
hab·it
habitabel : **hab·it·able**
hab·it·able
habitibal : **hab·it·able**
habitible : **hab·it·able**
haceinda : **ha·ci·en·da**
hachery : **hatch·ery**
hachet : **hatch·et**
hachit : **hatch·et**
ha·ci·en·da
haciendah : **ha·ci·en·da**
hack·neyed
hacknied : **hack·neyed**
hackny : **hack·neyed**
haddeck : **had·dock**
haddoc : **had·dock**
had·dock
hadj *or* hajj (pilgrimage); **hag**
  (witch); **Hague** (city)
hadock : **had·dock**
Haeti : **Hai·ti**
haf : **half**
hafhazard : **hap·haz·ard**
hag (witch); **Hague** (city); **hajj**
  (pilgrimage)
hagard : **hag·gard**
haggal : **hag·gle**
hag·gard
haggel : **hag·gle**
haggerd : **hag·gard**
haggird : **hag·gard**
hag·gle
Hague (city); **hag** (witch); **hajj**
  (pilgrimage)
hailo : **ha·lo**
hailstoan : **hail·stone**

hail·stone
hair (on head); **heir** (inheritor)
hairbrained : **hare·brained**
hairbraned : **hare·brained**
hairlip : **hare·lip**
haissen : **has·ten**
haisten : **has·ten**
Haitee : **Hai·ti**
Hai·ti
Haity : **Hai·ti**
hajj *or* **hadj** (pilgrimage); **hag**
  (witch); **Hague** (city)
halabut : **hal·i·but**
halatosis : **hal·i·to·sis**
halceon : **hal·cy·on**
halcion : **hal·cy·on**
hal·cy·on
halebut : **hal·i·but**
halestone : **hail·stone**
haletosis : **hal·i·to·sis**
half (*sing.*); **halve** (*verb*);
  halves (*plur.*)
halfhazard : **hap·haz·ard**
halfs : **halves**
haliard : **hal·yard**
halibet : **hal·i·but**
hal·i·but
halitoses : **hal·i·to·sis**
hal·i·to·sis
hallabet : **hal·i·but**
hallalujah : **hal·le·lu·jah**
Hallaween : **Hal·low·een**
hallcyon : **hal·cy·on**
halleloojah : **hal·le·lu·jah**
hal·le·lu·jah
halleluyah : **hal·le·lu·jah**
hal·liard *or* **hal·yard**
hallibut : **hal·i·but**
hallierd : **hal·yard**
hallilujah : **hal·le·lu·jah**

141

hallitosis : **hal·i·to·sis**
Halloeen : **Hal·low·een**
halloocination :
   hal·lu·ci·na·tion
Hallowean : **Hal·low·een**
Hal·low·een
Hallowene : **Hal·low·een**
hallucenation : **hal·lu·ci·na·tion**
hal·lu·ci·na·tion
hallusination : **hal·lu·ci·na·tion**
hallyard : **hal·yard**
ha·lo
Haloween : **Hal·low·een**
halseon : **hal·cy·on**
halsion : **hal·cy·on**
halucination : **hal·lu·ci·na·tion**
halve (*verb*); **half** (*sing.*);
   halves (*plur.*)
halves (*plur.*); **half** (*sing.*);
   halve (*verb*)
hal·yard *or* **hal·liard**
hamberger : **ham·burg·er**
hambirger : **ham·burg·er**
ham·burg·er
hamburgur : **ham·burg·er**
hamer : **ham·mer**
hammack : **ham·mock**
hammar : **ham·mer**
hammeck : **ham·mock**
ham·mer
ham·mock
hamock : **ham·mock**
handal : **han·dle**
handecap : **hand·i·cap**
handecraft : **hand·i·craft**
Han·del (composer); **han·dle**
   (part for grasping)
handework : **hand·i·work**
hand·ful
handfull : **hand·ful**
hand·i·cap
hand·i·craft

handikraft : **hand·i·craft**
handil : **han·dle**
handiwerk : **hand·i·work**
hand·i·work
handiwurk : **hand·i·work**
handkercheif : **hand·ker·chief**
hand·ker·chief
handkerchiff : **hand·ker·chief**
handkirchief : **hand·ker·chief**
handkurchief : **hand·ker·chief**
han·dle (part for grasping);
   Han·del (composer)
hand·made (made by hand);
   hand·maid (female servant)
hand·maid (female servant);
   hand·made (made by hand)
hand·some (good-looking);
   han·som (cab)
handycap : **hand·i·cap**
handycraft : **hand·i·craft**
handywork : **hand·i·work**
han·gar (airplane shed);
   hang·er (device for hanging)
hang·er (device for hanging);
   han·gar (airplane shed)
hankercheif : **hand·ker·chief**
hankerchief : **hand·ker·chief**
hankerchiff : **hand·ker·chief**
hanndle : **han·dle**
han·som (cab); **hand·some**
   (good-looking)
hant : **haunt**
hanted : **haun·ted**
hap·haz·ard
haphazerd : **hap·haz·ard**
haphazzard : **hap·haz·ard**
haphazzerd : **hap·haz·ard**
hapiness : **hap·pi·ness**
hap·less
hapliss : **hap·less**
hap·pi·ness
happiniss : **hap·pi·ness**

happless : **hap·less**
happyness : **hap·pi·ness**
haram : **har·em**
harasment : **ha·rass·ment**
ha·rass
ha·rass·ment
harbar : **har·bor**
harbenger : **har·bin·ger**
harber : **har·bor**
har·bin·ger
harbinjer : **har·bin·ger**
harboar : **har·bor**
har·bor
har·di·ness
hardiniss : **har·di·ness**
hard·ware
hardwear : **hard·ware**
hardwere : **hard·ware**
hardwhere : **hard·ware**
hardyness : **har·di·ness**
hare·brained
harebraned : **hare·brained**
hare·lip
har·em
haress : **ha·rass** (to annoy) *or*
  heir·ess (inheritor)
haretic : **her·e·tic**
harim : **har·em**
Harlam : **Har·lem**
harlaquin : **har·le·quin**
Har·lem
harlequen : **har·le·quin**
har·le·quin
harlequine : **har·le·quin**
harlet : **har·lot**
harliquin : **har·le·quin**
harlit : **har·lot**
har·lot
Harlum : **Har·lem**
harmoanious : **har·mo·ni·ous**
harmoneous : **har·mo·ni·ous**
har·mon·i·ca

harmonicka : **har·mon·i·ca**
harmonika : **har·mon·i·ca**
har·mo·ni·ous
harmonius : **har·mo·ni·ous**
harmonnica : **har·mon·i·ca**
harnass : **har·ness**
harnes : **har·ness**
har·ness
harniss : **har·ness**
harnuss : **har·ness**
Har·old (name); her·ald
  (messenger)
har·poon
harpsachord : **harp·si·chord**
harpsechord : **harp·si·chord**
harp·si·chord
harpsicord : **harp·si·chord**
harpune : **har·poon**
harram : **har·em**
harrasment : **ha·rass·ment**
harrass : **ha·rass** (to annoy) *or*
  heir·ess (inheritor)
harrassment : **ha·rass·ment**
harrbinger : **har·bin·ger**
harrbor : **har·bor**
harrem : **har·em**
harress : **ha·rass** (to annoy) *or*
  heir·ess (inheritor)
harrim : **har·em**
harring : **her·ring**
Harrlem : **Har·lem**
harrlequin : **har·le·quin**
harrlot : **har·lot**
harrum : **har·em**
hart (male deer); **heart** (body
  organ)
hartbeat : **heart·beat**
hartbroken : **heart·bro·ken**
hartburn : **heart·burn**
harten : **heart·en**
harth : **hearth**
harty : **hearty**

harum : **har•em**
har•vest
harvist : **har•vest**
harvust : **har•vest**
hasard : **haz•ard**
hasienda : **ha•ci•en•da**
hasle : **has•sle**
hassal : **has•sle**
hassel : **has•sle**
hassen : **has•ten**
hassienda : **ha•ci•en•da**
has•sle
has•ten
hatchary : **hatch•ery**
hatcherry : **hatch•ery**
hatch•ery
hatch•et
hatchit : **hatch•et**
Hati : **Hai•ti**
haugh•ty
haunt•ed
havec : **hav•oc**
haveck : **hav•oc**
havic : **hav•oc**
havick : **hav•oc**
hav•oc
havock : **hav•oc**
havvoc : **hav•oc**
Hawahi : **Ha•waii**
Hawai : **Ha•waii**
Ha•waii
Hawiei : **Ha•waii**
Hawii : **Ha•waii**
hawnt : **haunt**
haw•thorn (shrub);
   Haw•thorne (author)
Haw•thorne (author);
   haw•thorn (shrub)
hawtty : **haugh•ty**
Hawyii : **Ha•waii**
hayday : **hey•day**
haz•ard

hazellnut : **ha•zel•nut**
ha•zel•nut
hazerd : **haz•ard**
hazilnut : **ha•zel•nut**
hazird : **haz•ard**
hazzard : **haz•ard**
hazzerd : **haz•ard**
heackle : **heck•le**
head•ache
headacke : **head•ache**
headake : **head•ache**
head•dress
head•line
headonism : **he•do•nism**
headress : **head•dress**
heafer : **heif•er**
heal (to cure); **heel** (back of the
   foot)
healix : **he•lix**
healpful : **help•ful**
health
heanous : **hei•nous**
heap
hearce : **hearse**
heard (*past of* to hear); **herd**
   (group of animals)
hear•ing
hear•say (rumor); **her•e•sy**
   (dissent)
hearse (funeral car); **hers**
   (belonging to her)
heart (body organ); **hart** (male
   deer)
heart•beat
heart•bro•ken
heart•burn
hearth
hearty
heath
hea•then
heath•er
heave

heav·en

heavi·ly

heaviweight : **heavy·weight**

heaviwieght : **heavy·weight**

heavy

heavyly : **heavi·ly**

heavywaight : **heavy·weight**

heavy·weight

heccle : **heck·le**

heckal : **heck·le**

heckel : **heck·le**

heck·le

hecktic : **hec·tic**

hectec : **hec·tic**

hec·tic

hectick : **hec·tic**

hedache : **head·ache**

heddonism : **he·do·nism**

hedline : **head·line**

hedonesm : **he·do·nism**

he·do·nism

heed·ful

heedfull : **heed·ful**

heel (back of the foot); **heal** (to cure)

heep : **heap**

heering : **hear·ing**

heeth : **heath**

heethen : **hea·then**

heffer : **heif·er**

hegeminny : **he·ge·mo·ny**

hegemone : **he·ge·mo·ny**

he·ge·mo·ny

hegimony : **he·ge·mo·ny**

heif·er

height

hei·nous

heir (inheritor); **hair** (on head)

heir·ess (inheritor); **ha·rass** (to annoy)

heiriss : **heir·ess**

heir·loom

heirlume : **heir·loom**

heirse : **hearse**

heithen : **hea·then**

heive : **heave**

hejemony : **he·ge·mo·ny**

hejiminy : **he·ge·mo·ny**

helacopter : **hel·i·cop·ter**

helecopter : **hel·i·cop·ter**

heleum : **he·li·um**

helicks : **he·lix**

hel·i·cop·ter

heliem : **he·li·um**

helikopter : **hel·i·cop·ter**

he·li·um

he·lix

hellacopter : **hel·i·cop·ter**

hellecopter : **hel·i·cop·ter**

hellicopter : **hel·i·cop·ter**

hellium : **he·li·um**

hellix : **he·lix**

hellmet : **hel·met**

hellth : **health**

hel·met

helmit : **hel·met**

helmut : **hel·met**

help·ful

helpfull : **help·ful**

helth : **health**

hemasphere : **hemi·sphere**

hemesphere : **hemi·sphere**

hemisfere : **hemi·sphere**

hemispear : **hemi·sphere**

hemispfere : **hemi·sphere**

hemisphear : **hemi·sphere**

hemispheir : **hemi·sphere**

hemi·sphere

hemmisphere : **hemi·sphere**

hemmophilia : **he·mo·phil·ia**

hemmorrhage : **hem·or·rhage**

hemmorroid : **hem·or·rhoid**

hemofilia : **he·mo·phil·ia**

hemophealia : **he·mo·phil·ia**

hemophelea : **he·mo·phil·ia**

hemophelia : **he·mo·phil·ia**

he·mo·phil·ia

hemophillia : **he·mo·phil·ia**

hemorhoid : **hem·or·rhoid**

hemoridge : **hem·or·rhage**

hemorige : **hem·or·rhage**

hemoroid : **hem·or·rhoid**

hemorredge : **hem·or·rhage**

hemorrege : **hem·or·rhage**

hem·or·rhage

hemorrhige : **hem·or·rhage**

hem·or·rhoid

hemorrige : **hem·or·rhage**

hemorroid : **hem·or·rhoid**

hencefoarth : **hence·forth**

hence·forth

hencefourth : **hence·forth**

henseforth : **hence·forth**

her·ald (messenger); **Har·old** (name)

heraldery : **her·ald·ry**

her·ald·ry

herass : **ha·rass** (to annoy) or **heir·ess** (inheritor)

herassment : **ha·rass·ment**

herasy : **her·e·sy**

heratage : **her·i·tage**

heratic : **her·e·tic**

herb·age

herb·al

herbedge : **herb·age**

herbege : **herb·age**

herbel : **herb·al**

herbiage : **herb·age**

herbige : **herb·age**

herd (group of animals); **heard** (past *of* to hear)

herdle : **hur·dle** (to leap a barrier) or **hur·tle** (to dash)

heredditary : **he·red·i·tary**

heredetery : **he·red·i·tary**

heredety : **he·red·i·ty**

he·red·i·tary

herediterry : **he·red·i·tary**

hereditery : **he·red·i·tary**

hereditty : **he·red·i·ty**

he·red·i·ty

heresay : **hear·say** (rumor) *or* **her·e·sy** (dissent)

heresey : **hear·say** (rumor) *or* **her·e·sy** (dissent)

her·e·sy (dissent); **hear·say** (rumor)

heretage : **her·i·tage**

her·e·tic

heretick : **her·e·tic**

hering : **her·ring**

herissy : **her·e·sy**

her·i·tage

heritedge : **her·i·tage**

heritege : **her·i·tage**

heritige : **her·i·tage**

hermat : **her·mit**

hermatige : **her·mit·age**

hermet : **her·mit**

hermetage : **her·mit·age**

hermett : **her·mit**

her·mit

her·mit·age

hermut : **her·mit**

hernea : **her·nia**

her·nia

hernya : **her·nia**

her·o·in (drug); **her·o·ine** (great woman)

her·o·ine (great woman); **her·o·in** (drug)

heroldery : **her·ald·ry**

heroldry : **her·ald·ry**

her·on

Heroshima : **Hi·ro·shi·ma**

herrald : **her·ald**

herraldry : **her·ald·ry**

herreditary : **he·red·i·tary**
herredity : **he·red·i·ty**
herress : **ha·rass** (to annoy) *or*
   heir·ess (inheritor)
herressy : **her·e·sy**
herresy : **her·e·sy**
herretic : **her·e·tic**
herrin : **her·on**
her·ring
herritage : **her·i·tage**
herron : **her·on**
herrse : **hearse**
hers (belonging to her); **hearse**
   (funeral car)
her's : **hers**
herse : **hearse**
herth : **hearth**
hertle : **hur·dle** (to leap a
   barrier) *or* **hur·tle** (to dash)
he's (he is); **his** (belonging to
   him)
hesatant : **hes·i·tant**
hesatate : **hes·i·tate**
hes·i·tant
hes·i·tate
hesitent : **hes·i·tant**
hessitant : **hes·i·tant**
hessitate : **hes·i·tate**
het·er·o·ge·neous *or*
   het·er·og·e·nous
heterogenius :
   het·er·o·ge·neous
het·er·og·e·nous *or*
   het·er·o·ge·neous
hether : **heath·er**
heve : **heave**
heven : **heav·en**
hevven : **heav·en**
hevvy : **heavy**
hevvyweight : **heavy·weight**
hevy : **heavy**
hevywait : **heavy·weight**

hey·day
hezitant : **hes·i·tant**
hiacenth : **hy·a·cinth**
hiacinth : **hy·a·cinth**
hiararchy : **hi·er·ar·chy**
hiasenth : **hy·a·cinth**
hiasinth : **hy·a·cinth**
hiatis : **hi·a·tus**
hi·a·tus
hibernait : **hi·ber·nate**
hi·ber·nate
hibred : **hy·brid**
hibryd : **hy·brid**
hiburnate : **hi·ber·nate**
hiccough (*Brit.*) : **hic·cup**
hic·cup
hickarry : **hick·o·ry**
hickary : **hick·o·ry**
hickerry : **hick·o·ry**
hickery : **hick·o·ry**
hick·o·ry
hiddeous : **hid·eous**
hiddious : **hid·eous**
hid·eous
hidious : **hid·eous**
hidius : **hid·eous**
hidrant : **hy·drant**
hidraulic : **hy·draul·ic**
hidrent : **hy·drant**
hidrint : **hy·drant**
hidrogen : **hy·dro·gen**
hieana : **hy·e·na**
hiefer : **heif·er**
hieght : **height**
hiena : **hy·e·na**
hienous : **hei·nous**
hi·er·ar·chy
hierarky : **hi·er·ar·chy**
hieress : **heir·ess**
hierloom : **heir·loom**
hifen : **hy·phen**
higene : **hy·giene**

highjack : **hi·jack**
high·ness
highniss : **high·ness**
hight : **height**
higiene : **hy·giene**
hi·jack
hilairious : **hi·lar·i·ous**
hilareous : **hi·lar·i·ous**
hi·lar·i·ous
hillarious : **hi·lar·i·ous**
him (that man); **hymn** (song)
himmorroid : **hem·or··rhoid**
himn : **hymn**
himnal : **hym·nal**
himnel : **hym·nal**
himorhoid : **hem·or·rhoid**
himoroid : **hem·or·rhoid**
himorrhage : **hem·or·rhage**
himorroid : **hem·or·rhoid**
hinderance : **hin·drance**
hinderense : **hin·drance**
hin·drance
hindranse : **hin·drance**
hindrence : **hin·drance**
hindrense : **hin·drance**
hiness : **high·ness**
hinotism : **hyp·no·tism**
hipadermic : **hy·po·der·mic**
hiphen : **hy·phen**
hipnatism : **hyp·no·tism**
hipnetism : **hyp·no·tism**
hipnosis : **hyp·no·sis**
hipnotism : **hyp·no·tism**
hipocrisy : **hy·poc·ri·sy**
hipocrite : **hyp·o·crite**
hipodermic : **hy·po·der·mic**
hipothesis : **hy·poth·e·sis**
hirarchy : **hi·er·ar·chy**
Hiroshema : **Hi·ro·shi·ma**
Hi·ro·shi·ma
his (belonging to him); **he's** (he is)

hisstory : **his·to·ry**
histarical : **hys·ter·i·cal**
histeria : **hys·te·ria**
histerical : **hys·ter·i·cal**
histericle : **hys·ter·i·cal**
histerikal : **hys·ter·i·cal**
histery : **his·to·ry**
historey : **his·to·ry**
historry : **his·to·ry**
his·to·ry
histry : **his·to·ry**
hite : **height**
hoard (cache); **horde** (multitude)
hoarmone : **hor·mone**
hoarse (rough-voiced); **horse** (animal)
hoary
hoastess : **hos·tess**
holacaust : **hol·o·caust**
ho·li·ness
hollacaust : **hol·o·caust**
hollocaust : **hol·o·caust**
hollocost : **hol·o·caust**
Holloween : **Hal·low·een**
hol·ly (tree); **ho·ly** (sacred); **whol·ly** (completely)
hol·o·caust
holocost : **hol·o·caust**
ho·ly (sacred); **hol·ly** (tree); **whol·ly** (completely)
holyness : **ho·li·ness**
homacidal : **ho·mi·cid·al**
homacide : **ho·mi·cide**
homadge : **hom·age**
hom·age
homage : **hom·age**
homagenious : **ho·mo·ge·neous**
homaly : **hom·i·ly**
homasidal : **ho·mi·cid·al**
homaside : **ho·mi·cide**
homasidel : **ho·mi·cid·al**

homege : **hom•age**
home•ly (plain); **hom•i•ly**
  (sermon)
homesidal : **ho•mi•cid•al**
homeside : **ho•mi•cide**
home•stead
homested : **home•stead**
ho•mi•cid•al
ho•mi•cide
homidge : **hom•age**
homige : **hom•age**
hom•i•ly (sermon); **home•ly**
  (plain)
hommage : **hom•age**
hommige : **hom•age**
hommily : **hom•i•ly**
hommonim : **hom•onym**
hommonym : **hom•onym**
homocidal : **ho•mi•cid•al**
homocide : **hom•i•cide**
ho•mo•ge•neous or
  ho•mog•e•nous
homogenious : **ho•mo•ge•neous**
homogenius : **ho•mo•ge•neous**
ho•mog•e•nize
ho•mog•e•nous or
  ho•mo•ge•neous
homogonize : **ho•mog•e•nize**
homonim : **hom•onym**
hom•onym
homosidal : **ho•mi•cid•al**
homoside : **ho•mi•cide**
homosidel : **ho•mi•cid•al**
Honalulu : **Ho•no•lu•lu**
honarary : **hon•or•ary**
honasty : **hon•es•ty**
Honelulu : **Ho•no•lu•lu**
honer : **hon•or**
honerary : **hon•or•ary**
hon•est
hon•esty
hon•ey

honie : **hon•ey**
honist : **hon•est**
Honnelulu : **Ho•no•lu•lu**
honnest : **hon•est**
honnesty : **hon•es•ty**
honney : **hon•ey**
honnist : **hon•est**
Honnolulu : **Ho•no•lu•lu**
honnor : **hon•or**
honnorable : **hon•or•able**
honnorary : **hon•or•ary**
Ho•no•lu•lu
hon•or
hon•or•able
hon•or•ary
honorery : **hon•or•ary**
honorible : **hon•or•able**
hoodlam : **hood•lum**
hoodlem : **hood•lum**
hoodlim : **hood•lum**
hood•lum
hoolagan : **hoo•li•gan**
hoolegan : **hoo•li•gan**
hoo•li•gan
horascope : **horo•scope**
horde (multitude); **hoard**
  (cache)
horey : **hoary**
horible : **hor•ri•ble**
horify : **hor•ri•fy**
horizen : **ho•ri•zon**
ho•ri•zon
horizun : **ho•ri•zon**
hormoan : **hor•mone**
hor•mone
hor•net
hornit : **hor•net**
hornut : **hor•net**
horo•scope
horrable : **hor•ri•ble**
horrafy : **hor•ri•fy**
horreble : **hor•ri•ble**

horred : **hor·rid**
horrefy : **hor·ri·fy**
horribal : **hor·ri·ble**
hor·ri·ble
hor·rid
hor·ri·fy
horrizon : **ho·ri·zon**
horroscope : **horo·scope**
horry : **hoary**
horse (animal); **hoarse**
   (rough-voiced)
hortaculture : **hor·ti·cul·ture**
horteculture : **hor·ti·cul·ture**
hor·ti·cul·ture
hosary : **ho·siery**
hoserry : **ho·siery**
hosery : **ho·siery**
ho·siery
hospece : **hos·pice**
hospetal : **hos·pi·tal**
hos·pice
hospise : **hos·pice**
hos·pi·ta·ble
hos·pi·tal
hospiteble : **hos·pi·ta·ble**
hospitibal : **hos·pi·ta·ble**
hospitible : **hos·pi·ta·ble**
hospitle : **hos·pi·tal**
hospittable : **hos·pi·ta·ble**
hospittal : **hos·pi·tal**
hospittle : **hos·pi·tal**
hos·tage
hostege : **hos·tage**
hos·tel (lodging house);
   hos·tile (antagonistic)
hostes : **host·ess**
host·ess
hostige : **hos·tage**
hostil : **hos·tel** (lodging house)
   or **hos·tile** (antagonistic)
hos·tile (antagonistic); **hos·tel**
   (lodging house)

hostilety : **hos·til·i·ty**
hostilitty : **hos·til·i·ty**
hos·til·i·ty
hostill : **hos·tel** (lodging house)
   or **hos·tile** (antagonistic)
hostillity : **hos·til·i·ty**
hostiss : **host·ess**
houghty : **haugh·ty**
hour (60 minutes); **our**
   (belonging to us)
Housten : **Hous·ton**
Hous·ton
hoval : **hov·el**
hov·el
hovil : **hov·el**
hovvel : **hov·el**
huligan : **hoo·li·gan**
humain : **hu·mane**
hu·man (human being);
   hu·mane (compassionate)
hu·mane (compassionate);
   hu·man (human being)
humanety : **hu·man·i·ty**
humanitty : **hu·man·i·ty**
hu·man·i·ty
humannity : **hu·man·i·ty**
humed : **hu·mid**
humer : **hu·mor**
humerous : **hu·mer·us** (arm
   bone) *or* **hu·mor·ous** (funny)
hu·mer·us (arm bone);
   hu·mor·ous (funny)
humess : **hu·mus**
hu·mid
humiddity : **hu·mid·i·ty**
humidefy : **hu·mid·i·fy**
humidetty : **hu·mid·i·ty**
humidety : **hu·mid·i·ty**
humidiffy : **hu·mid·i·fy**
hu·mid·i·fy
humiditty : **hu·mid·i·ty**
hu·mid·i·ty

humileate : **hu·mil·i·ate**
humilety : **hu·mil·i·ty**
hu·mil·i·ate
humilitty : **hu·mil·i·ty**
hu·mil·i·ty
humilliate : **hu·mil·i·ate**
humillity : **hu·mil·i·ty**
humis : **hu·mus**
hummid : **hu·mid**
hummidify : **hu·mid·i·fy**
hummor : **hu·mor**
hu·mor
hu·mor·ous (funny);
  hu·mer·us (arm bone)
humorous : **hu·mer·us** (arm
  bone) *or* **hu·mor·ous** (funny)
humous : **hu·mus**
hu·mus
Hun·ga·ry (nation); **hun·gry**
  (having hunger)
hungery : **Hun·ga·ry** (nation)
  or **hun·gry** (having hunger)
hun·gry (having hunger);
  Hun·ga·ry (nation)
hunta : **jun·ta**
hurdel : **hur·dle** (to leap a
  barrier) *or* **hur·tle** (to dash)
hurdil : **hur·dle** (to leap a
  barrier) *or* **hur·tle** (to dash)
hurdill : **hur·dle** (to leap a
  barrier) *or* **hur·tle** (to dash)
hur·dle (to leap a barrier);
  hur·tle (to dash)
hurecane : **hur·ri·cane**
huricane : **hur·ri·cane**
hurracane : **hur·ri·cane**
hurrecane : **hur·ri·cane**
hurricain : **hur·ri·cane**
hur·ri·cane
hur·tle (to dash); **hur·dle** (to
  leap a barrier)
hus·band

husbandery : **hus·band·ry**
hus·band·ry
husbend : **hus·band**
husbendry : **hus·band·ry**
husbind : **hus·band**
husbindry : **hus·band·ry**
hussband : **hus·band**
hussel : **hus·tle**
hussle : **hus·tle**
husstle : **hus·tle**
Husston : **Hous·ton**
hustal : **hus·tle**
hustel : **hus·tle**
hus·tle
Huston : **Hous·ton**
hy·a·cinth
hyatus : **hi·a·tus**
hybred : **hy·brid**
hy·brid
hydragen : **hy·dro·gen**
hydrallic : **hy·drau·lic**
hy·drant
hydraulec : **hy·drau·lic**
hy·drau·lic
hydraulick : **hy·drau·lic**
hydrawlic : **hy·drau·lic**
hydregen : **hy·dro·gen**
hydrent : **hy·drant**
hydrigen : **hy·dro·gen**
hydrint : **hy·drant**
hy·dro·gen
hydrojen : **hy·dro·gen**
hydrojin : **hy·dro·gen**
hydrollic : **hy·drau·lic**
hyeana : **hy·e·na**
hyeena : **hy·e·na**
hy·e·na
hyfen : **hy·phen**
hyfin : **hy·phen**
hygeine : **hy·giene**
hygene : **hy·giene**
hy·giene

hyicinth : **hy·a·cinth**

hyina : **hy·e·na**

hymn (song); **him** (that man)

hym·nal

hymnel : **hym·nal**

hymnul : **hym·nal**

hypacrite : **hyp·o·crite**

hypedermic : **hy·po·der·mic**

hy·per·bo·la (curved line);
   hy·per·bo·le (exaggeration)

hy·per·bo·le (exaggeration);
   hy·per·bo·la (curved line)

hy·phen

hyphin : **hy·phen**

hypnetism : **hyp·no·tism**

hypnitism : **hyp·no·tism**

hypnoasis : **hyp·no·sis**

hyp·no·sis

hyp·no·tism

hypockrisy : **hy·poc·ri·sy**

hypocracy : **hy·poc·ri·sy**

hypocrassy : **hy·poc·ri·sy**

hypocrasy : **hy·poc·ri·sy**

hypocresy : **hy·poc·ri·sy**

hypocrete : **hyp·o·crite**

hypocricy : **hy·poc·ri·sy**

hy·poc·ri·sy

hypocrit : **hyp·o·crite**

hyp·o·crite

hy·po·der·mic

hypodermick : **hy·po·der·mic**

hypodirmic : **hy·po·der·mic**

hypothasis : **hy·poth·e·sis**

hy·poth·e·ses (*plur.*);
   hy·poth·e·sis (*sing.*)

hy·poth·e·sis (*sing.*);
   hy·poth·e·ses (*plur.*)

hystaria : **hys·te·ria**

hystarical : **hys·ter·i·cal**

hysterea : **hys·te·ria**

hys·te·ria

hys·ter·i·cal

hystericle : **hys·ter·i·cal**

hysterikal : **hys·ter·i·cal**

hysterria : **hys·te·ria**

I

iadine : **io·dine**
Iawa : **Io·wa**
icecle : **ici·cle**
icecycle : **ici·cle**
icical : **ici·cle**
ici·cle
ic·ing
icon *or* **ikon**
iconaclast : **icon·o·clast**
iconiclast : **icon·o·clast**
iconnoclast : **icon·o·clast**
icon·o·clast
iconoklast : **icon·o·clast**
icycle : **ici·cle**
Ida·ho
iddiocy : **id·i·o·cy**
iddiom : **id·i·om**
iddiosyncrasy : **id·io·syn·cra·sy**
iddiot : **id·i·ot**
ide·al
idealise (*Brit.*) : **ide·al·ize**
idealogy : **ide·ol·o·gy**
ideel : **ide·al**
ideelize : **ide·al·ize**
Ideho : **Ida·ho**
idele : **ide·al**
idelize : **ide·al·ize**
ideloigy : **ide·ol·o·gy**
identacal : **iden·ti·cal**
identecal : **iden·ti·cal**
identety : **iden·ti·ty**
iden·ti·cal
identicle : **iden·ti·cal**
identidy : **iden·ti·ty**
identikal : **iden·ti·cal**
identikle : **iden·ti·cal**
identitty : **iden·ti·ty**
iden·ti·ty
ideocy : **id·i·o·cy**
ideolijy : **ide·ol·o·gy**

ideollogy : **ide·ol·o·gy**
ide·ol·o·gy
ideom : **id·i·om**
ideosyncrasy : **id·io·syn·cra·sy**
idiacy : **id·i·o·cy**
idiam : **id·i·om**
idiasy : **id·i·o·cy**
idiasyncrasy : **id·io·syn·cra·sy**
idiel : **ide·al**
idielize : **ide·al·ize**
Idiho : **Ida·ho**
idine : **io·dine**
id·i·o·cy
idiology : **ide·ol·o·gy**
id·i·om
idiosincrasy : **id·io·syn·cra·sy**
idiosincresy : **id·io·syn·cra·sy**
idiosy : **id·i·o·cy**
idiosyncrassy : **id·io·syn·cra·sy**
id·io·syn·cra·sy
idiosyncrissy : **id·io·syn·cra·sy**
id·i·ot
idium : **id·i·om**
idle (inactive); **idol** (image);
   idyll (pastoral)
idol (image); **idle** (inactive);
   idyll (pastoral)
idol·a·ter
idolator : **idol·a·ter**
idoliter : **idol·a·ter**
idyl *or* **idyll** (pastoral); **idle**
   (inactive); **idol** (image)
idyll *or* **idyl** (pastoral); **idle**
   (inactive); **idol** (image)
Ifel : **Eif·fel**
iffete : **ef·fete**
Iffle : **Eif·fel**
ig·loo
iglu : **ig·loo**
ig·ne·ous

153

ignetion : **ig·ni·tion**
ignight : **ig·nite**
ignious : **ig·ne·ous**
ignishion : **ig·ni·tion**
ignission : **ig·ni·tion**
ig·nite
ignitian : **ig·ni·tion**
ig·ni·tion
ignittion : **ig·ni·tion**
ignius : **ig·ne·ous**
ignobal : **ig·no·ble**
ignobel : **ig·no·ble**
ig·no·ble
ignomenious : **ig·no·min·i·ous**
ignomineous : **ig·no·min·i·ous**
ig·no·min·i·ous
ignominius : **ig·no·min·i·ous**
ignominnious : **ig·no·min·i·ous**
ignoraimus : **ig·no·ra·mus**
ignorammis : **ig·no·ra·mus**
ignorammus : **ig·no·ra·mus**
ig·no·ra·mus
ig·no·rance
ignoranse : **ig·no·rance**
ignoremus : **ig·no·ra·mus**
ignorence : **ig·no·rance**
ignorense : **ig·no·rance**
igua·na
iguanna : igua·na
igwana : igua·na
ikon or **icon**
ikonoclast : **icon·o·clast**
iland : **is·land**
ilastic : **elas·tic**
ilectefy : **elec·tri·fy**
ilectracute : **elec·tro·cute**
ilectrafy : **elec·tri·fy**
ilectrecute : **elec·tro·cute**
ilectric : **elec·tric**
ilectricety : **elec·tric·i·ty**
ilectricion : **elec·tri·cian**
ilectricitty : **elec·tric·i·ty**

ilectricity : **elec·tric·i·ty**
ilectricute : **elec·tro·cute**
ilectrify : **elec·tri·fy**
ilectrision : **elec·tri·cian**
ilectrisity : **elec·tric·i·ty**
ilectrition : **elec·tri·cian**
ilectrocute : **elec·tro·cute**
ilectrokute : **elec·tro·cute**
ilegible : **el·i·gi·ble** (qualified)
   or **il·leg·i·ble** (unreadable)
ilektric : **elec·tric**
ilicit : **elic·it** (to draw out) *or*
   il·lic·it (unlawful)
ilickser : **elix·ir**
iliminate : **elim·i·nate**
Ilinois : **Il·li·nois**
iliterate : **il·lit·er·ate**
ilixer : **elix·ir**
ilixir : **elix·ir**
ilixor : **elix·ir**
Illanois : **Il·li·nois**
illastic : **elas·tic**
illastrate : **il·lus·trate**
illeagal : **il·le·gal**
illectrify : **elec·tri·fy**
illectrocute : **elec·tro·cute**
illeegal : **il·le·gal**
il·le·gal
illegeble : **el·i·gi·ble** (qualified)
   or **il·leg·i·ble** (unreadable)
illegel : **il·le·gal**
illegibal : **el·i·gi·ble** (qualified)
   or **il·leg·i·ble** (unreadable)
il·leg·i·ble (unreadable);
   el·i·gi·ble (qualified)
illegitemant : **il·le·git·i·mate**
illegitemate : **il·le·git·i·mate**
il·le·git·i·mate
illegitimet : **il·le·git·i·mate**
illegle : **il·le·gal**
illejitimate : **il·le·git·i·mate**
illestrate : **il·lus·trate**

il·lic·it (unlawful); **elic·it** (to draw out)

Il·li·nois

Illinoy : **Il·li·nois**

illistrate : **il·lus·trate**

il·lit·er·ate

illixir : **elix·ir**

illude : **elude** (to escape) *or* **al·lude** (to refer)

illumanate : **il·lu·mi·nate**

illumenate : **il·lu·mi·nate**

il·lu·mi·nate

Illunois : **Il·li·nois**

illusary : **il·lu·so·ry**

illusery : **il·lu·so·ry**

il·lu·sion (false idea or image); **al·lu·sion** (reference); **elu·sion** (evasion)

il·lu·sive (deceptive); **al·lu·sive** (making references); **elu·sive** (avoiding)

il·lu·so·ry

illusry : **il·lu·so·ry**

illustrait : **il·lus·trate**

il·lus·trate

iloapment : **elope·ment**

ilopement : **elope·ment**

ilopment : **elope·ment**

ilude : **elude** (to escape) *or* **al·lude** (to refer)

iluminate : **il·lu·mi·nate**

ilusion : **al·lu·sion** (reference) *or* **elu·sion** (evasion) *or* **il·lu·sion** (false idea or image)

ilusive : **al·lu·sive** (making references) *or* **elu·sive** (avoiding) *or* **il·lu·sive** (deceptive)

ilusory : **il·lu·so·ry**

imaculate : **im·mac·u·late**

imaculet : **im·mac·u·late**

imagary : **im·ag·ery**

im·age

imagenation : **imag·i·na·tion**

imagene : **imag·ine**

im·ag·ery

imagin : **imag·ine**

imag·i·na·tion

imagry : **im·ag·ery**

imancepate : **eman·ci·pate**

imancipate : **eman·ci·pate**

imanent : **em·i·nent** (famous) *or* **im·ma·nent** (dwelling within) *or* **im·mi·nent** (impending)

imansipate : **eman·ci·pate**

imarald : **em·er·ald**

imasarry : **em·is·sary**

imatate : **im·i·tate**

imbacile : **im·be·cile**

imbacy : **em·bas·sy**

imbalm : **em·balm**

imbam : **em·balm**

imbankment : **em·bank·ment**

imbargo : **em·bar·go**

imbark : **em·bark**

imbasey : **em·bas·sy**

imbassy : **em·bas·sy**

imbasy : **em·bas·sy**

im·be·cile

imbecill : **im·be·cile**

imbelish : **em·bel·lish**

imbellash : **em·bel·lish**

imbellesh : **em·bel·lish**

imbellish : **em·bel·lish**

imbesill : **im·be·cile**

imbezel : **em·bez·zle**

imbezle : **em·bez·zle**

imbezzal : **em·bez·zle**

imbezzel : **em·bez·zle**

imbezzle : **em·bez·zle**

im·bibe

imbicile : **im·be·cile**

imblam : **em·blem**
imblazen : **em·bla·zon**
imblazon : **em·bla·zon**
imblem : **em·blem**
imblim : **em·blem**
imblum : **em·blem**
imbodiment : **em·bod·i·ment**
imbodimint : **em·bod·i·ment**
imbodyment : **em·bod·i·ment**
imbom : **em·balm**
imbrace : **em·brace**
imbrase : **em·brace**
imbreo : **em·bryo**
imbrio : **em·bryo**
imbroidary : **em·broi·dery**
imbroiderry : **em·broi·dery**
imbroidery : **em·broi·dery**
imbryo : **em·bryo**
im·bue
imediate : **im·me·di·ate**
imege : **im·age**
imerald : **em·er·ald**
imeratus : **emer·i·tus**
imeritus : **emer·i·tus**
imerold : **em·er·ald**
imerritus : **emer·i·tus**
imesarry : **em·is·sary**
imige : **im·age**
imigery : **im·ag·ery**
iminent : **em·i·nent** (famous) *or*
   im·ma·nent (dwelling within)
   or **im·mi·nent** (impending)
imisary : **em·is·sary**
imissary : **em·is·sary**
im·i·tate
imity : **en·mi·ty**
im·mac·u·late
immaculet : **im·mac·u·late**
immage : **im·age**
immagery : **im·ag·ery**
immagination : **imag·i·na·tion**
immakulate : **im·mac·u·late**

immancipate : **eman·ci·pate**
im·ma·nent (dwelling within);
   em·i·nent (famous);
   im·mi·nent (impending)
immeadiate : **im·me·di·ate**
immedeate : **im·me·di·ate**
im·me·di·ate
immediet : **im·me·di·ate**
immeediate : **im·me·di·ate**
immerald : **em·er·ald**
im·mi·grant (one coming in);
   em·i·grant (one leaving)
im·mi·nent (impending);
   em·i·nent (famous);
   im·ma·nent (dwelling within)
immissary : **em·is·sary**
immitate : **im·i·tate**
immity : **en·mi·ty**
im·mor·al
immorel : **im·mor·al**
im·mor·tal
immortel : **im·mor·tal**
im·mov·able
immovibal : **im·mov·able**
immovible : **im·mov·able**
im·mune
imoral : **im·mor·al**
imorald : **em·er·ald**
imortal : **im·mor·tal**
imovable : **im·mov·able**
impacient : **im·pa·tient**
impail : **im·pale**
im·pair
impairious : **im·pe·ri·ous**
impairitive : **im·per·a·tive**
impaitient : **im·pa·tient**
im·pale
im·pal·pa·ble
impalpeble : **im·pal·pa·ble**
impalpibal : **im·pal·pa·ble**
impalpible : **im·pal·pa·ble**
imparative : **im·per·a·tive**

imparcial : **im·par·tial**
impare : **im·pair**
imparil : **im·per·il**
imparious : **im·pe·ri·ous**
imparshial : **im·par·tial**
im·part
im·par·tial
impashient : **im·pa·tient**
impashioned : **im·pas·sioned**
impass : **im·passe**
im·passe
im·pas·sioned
impatiant : **im·pa·tient**
im·pa·tient
impatus : **im·pe·tus**
im·peach
impead : **im·pede**
impearian : **em·py·re·an**
impecable : **im·pec·ca·ble**
im·pec·ca·ble
impeccibal : **im·pec·ca·ble**
impeccible : **im·pec·ca·ble**
impeckable : **im·pec·ca·ble**
impeckible : **im·pec·ca·ble**
impeddament : **im·ped·i·ment**
impeddement : **im·ped·i·ment**
impeddiment : **im·ped·i·ment**
im·pede
impedimant : **im·ped·i·ment**
im·ped·i·ment
impeech : **im·peach**
impeerial : **im·pe·ri·al**
impeid : **im·pede**
impeirial : **im·pe·ri·al**
impenatant : **im·pen·i·tent**
impenitant : **im·pen·i·tent**
im·pen·i·tent
im·per·a·tive
impereal : **im·pe·ri·al**
imperel : **im·per·il**
im·pe·ri·al
im·per·il

imperill : **im·per·il**
im·pe·ri·ous
imperitive : **im·per·a·tive**
imperril : **im·per·il**
impertenent : **im·per·ti·nent**
impertinant : **im·per·ti·nent**
im·per·ti·nent
imperveous : **im·per·vi·ous**
im·per·vi·ous
impervius : **im·per·vi·ous**
impetis : **im·pe·tus**
impettis : **im·pe·tus**
im·pe·tus
imphisema : **em·phy·se·ma**
imphisima : **em·phy·se·ma**
imphyseama : **em·phy·se·ma**
imphysema : **em·phy·se·ma**
imphysima : **em·phy·se·ma**
impiatty : **im·pi·e·ty**
impier : **em·pire**
impierian : **em·py·re·an**
impietty : **im·pi·e·ty**
im·pi·e·ty
impinitent : **im·pen·i·tent**
impire : **em·pire**
impirian : **em·py·re·an**
impitus : **im·pe·tus**
implament : **im·ple·ment**
im·plant
im·ple·ment
impliment : **im·ple·ment**
imporeum : **em·po·ri·um**
imporiam : **em·po·ri·um**
imporium : **em·po·ri·um**
im·por·tant
importent : **im·por·tant**
im·pos·ter or **im·pos·tor**
im·pos·tor or **im·pos·ter**
impotance : **im·po·tence**
im·po·tence
impotense : **im·po·tence**
impouarium : **em·po·ri·um**

impoureum : **em·po·ri·um**
impoveresh : **im·pov·er·ish**
im·pov·er·ish
impovrish : **im·pov·er·ish**
impracate : **im·pre·cate**
impractacle : **im·prac·ti·cal**
impractecle : **im·prac·ti·cal**
im·prac·ti·cal
impracticle : **im·prac·ti·cal**
impravise : **im·pro·vise**
im·pre·cate
impreshion : **im·pres·sion**
impresion : **im·pres·sion**
impressian : **im·pres·sion**
im·pres·sion
impricate : **im·pre·cate**
imprisen : **im·pris·on**
im·pris·on
imprisson : **im·pris·on**
imprivise : **im·pro·vise**
imprizen : **im·pris·on**
imprizon : **im·pris·on**
impromptoo : **im·promp·tu**
im·promp·tu
impromptue : **im·promp·tu**
impromtu : **im·promp·tu**
im·pro·vise
improvize : **im·pro·vise**
im·pugn
impune : **im·pugn**
impunety : **im·pu·ni·ty**
impunitty : **im·pu·ni·ty**
im·pu·ni·ty
impurvious : **im·per·vi·ous**
impyre : **em·pire**
impyrean : **em·py·re·an**
inagurate : **in·au·gu·rate**
inain : **inane**
inamerd : **en·am·ored**
inamered : **en·am·ored**
inammored : **en·am·ored**
inamored : **en·am·ored**

inamoured : **en·am·ored**
inamy : **en·e·my**
inane
in·apt (not apt); **in·ept** (unskilled)
inargy : **en·er·gy**
inate : **in·nate**
inaugarate : **in·au·gu·rate**
inaugerate : **in·au·gu·rate**
inaugurait : **in·au·gu·rate**
in·au·gu·rate
inawgurate : **in·au·gu·rate**
inbalm : **en·balm**
inbankment : **em·bank·ment**
inbargo : **em·bar·go**
inbark : **em·bark**
inbassy : **em·bas·sy**
inbelish : **em·bel·lish**
inbellish : **em·bel·lish**
inbezzle : **em·bez·zle**
inbibe : **im·bibe**
inblazon : **em·bla·zon**
inblem : **em·blem**
inbodiment : **em·bodi·ment**
inbrace : **em·brace**
inbroidery : **em·broi·dery**
inbryo : **em·bryo**
incandecent : **in·can·des·cent**
incandescant : **in·can·des·cent**
in·can·des·cent
incandessent : **in·can·des·cent**
incapabal : **in·ca·pa·ble**
in·ca·pa·ble
incapeble : **in·ca·pa·ble**
incapibal : **in·ca·pa·ble**
incapible : **in·ca·pa·ble**
in·car·cer·ate
incarcirate : **in·car·cer·ate**
incarserate : **in·car·cer·ate**
in·cen·di·ary
incendierry : **in·cen·di·ary**
incendiery : **in·cen·di·ary**

incenerate : **in·cin·er·ate**
incercle : **en·cir·cle**
incert : **in·sert**
incesant : **in·ces·sant**
in·ces·sant
incessent : **in·ces·sant**
incessint : **in·ces·sant**
in·cest
inciclopedia : **en·cy·clo·pe·dia**
in·ci·dent
incinarate : **in·cin·er·ate**
in·cin·er·ate
incinnerate : **in·cin·er·ate**
incinuate : **in·sin·u·ate**
incipiant : **in·cip·i·ent**
in·cip·i·ent
incippient : **in·cip·i·ent**
incircel : **en·cir·cle**
incircle : **en·cir·cle**
incirkal : **en·cir·cle**
incirkle : **en·cir·cle**
inciser : **in·ci·sor**
in·ci·sion
in·ci·sor
incission : **in·ci·sion**
in·cite (to urge on); **in·sight**
  (discernment)
incizion : **in·ci·sion**
incizor : **in·ci·sor**
inclament : **in·cle·ment**
inclemant : **in·cle·ment**
in·cle·ment
incliment : **in·cle·ment**
incohairent : **in·co·her·ent**
incohearent : **in·co·her·ent**
incoherant : **in·co·her·ent**
in·co·her·ent
incredable : **in·cred·i·ble**
in·cred·i·ble
incumbrance : **en·cum·brance**
incumbranse : **en·cum·brance**
incumbrence : **en·cum·brance**

incumbrince : **en·cum·brance**
incyclapedia : **en·cy·clo·pe·dia**
incyclepedia : **en·cy·clo·pe·dia**
incyclipedia : **en·cy·clo·pe·dia**
incyclopeadia : **en·cy·clo·pe·dia**
incyclopedea : **en·cy·clo·pe·dia**
incyclopedia : **en·cy·clo·pe·dia**
incyclopeedia : **en·cy·clo·pe·dia**
indago : **in·di·go**
indalent : **in·do·lent**
indavidual : **in·di·vid·u·al**
Indeana : **In·di·ana**
indeaver : **en·deav·or**
indeavor : **en·deav·or**
indegent : **in·di·gent**
indego : **in·di·go**
indelable : **in·del·i·ble**
indeleble : **in·del·i·ble**
indelent : **in·do·lent**
in·del·i·ble
indellible : **in·del·i·ble**
independance : **in·de·pen·dence**
independanse : **in·de·pen·dence**
in·de·pen·dence
independense : **in·de·pen·dence**
indepindence : **in·de·pen·dence**
indevidual : **in·di·vid·u·al**
indevor : **en·deav·or**
indevvor : **en·deav·or**
in·dex
in·dex·es or **in·di·ces**
In·di·ana
Indianaplis : **In·di·a·nap·o·lis**
In·di·a·nap·o·lis
Indianappolis :
  In·di·a·nap·o·lis
Indianna : **In·di·ana**
Indiannapolis :
  In·di·a·nap·o·lis
in·di·ces or **in·dex·es**
in·dict (to charge with a
  crime); **in·dite** (to write)

in·dict·ment
in·di·gent
indiggo : **in·di·go**
indigint : **in·di·gent**
in·dig·nant
indignate : **in·dig·nant**
indignent : **in·dig·nant**
indignety : **in·dig·ni·ty**
indignint : **in·dig·nant**
indignitty : **in·dig·ni·ty**
in·dig·ni·ty
in·di·go
in·dis·pens·able
indispensible : **in·dis·pens·able**
in·dite (to write); **in·dict** (to charge with a crime)
iditement : **in·dict·ment**
iditment : **in·dict·ment**
in·di·vid·u·al
individuel : **in·di·vid·u·al**
individule : **in·di·vid·u·al**
indivvidual : **in·di·vid·u·al**
indolant : **in·do·lent**
in·do·lent
indolint : **in·do·lent**
indomatable : **in·dom·i·ta·ble**
indometable : **in·dom·i·ta·ble**
in·dom·i·ta·ble
indomitibal : **in·dom·i·ta·ble**
indomitible : **in·dom·i·ta·ble**
indommitable : **in·dom·i·ta·ble**
indoument : **en·dow·ment**
indowmate : **en·dow·ment**
indowmeant : **en·dow·ment**
indowment : **en·dow·ment**
indowmint : **en·dow·ment**
in·dulge
indurance : **en·dur·ance**
induranse : **en·dur·ance**
indurence : **en·dur·ance**
indurrance : **en·dur·ance**
indurrence : **en·dur·ance**

industreal : **in·dus·tri·al**
in·dus·tri·al
industriel : **in·dus·tri·al**
ineabriate : **ine·bri·ate**
inebreate : **ine·bri·ate**
ine·bri·ate
inecksorable : **in·ex·o·ra·ble**
inedable : **in·ed·i·ble**
ineddible : **in·ed·i·ble**
inedeble : **in·ed·i·ble**
inedibal : **in·ed·i·ble**
in·ed·i·ble
inefable : **in·ef·fa·ble**
in·ef·fa·ble
ineffeble : **in·ef·fa·ble**
ineffibal : **in·ef·fa·ble**
ineffible : **in·ef·fa·ble**
inemmy : **en·e·my**
inemy : **en·e·my**
in·ept (unskilled); **in·apt** (not apt)
inercia : **in·er·tia**
inergy : **en·er·gy**
inerjy : **en·er·gy**
inerrgy : **en·er·gy**
inershia : **in·er·tia**
in·ert
inertea : **in·er·tia**
in·er·tia
inetible : **in·ed·i·ble**
inettible : **in·ed·i·ble**
inevatable : **in·ev·i·ta·ble**
in·ev·i·ta·ble
ineviteble : **in·ev·i·ta·ble**
inevitibal : **in·ev·i·ta·ble**
inevitible : **in·ev·i·ta·ble**
inexerable : **in·ex·o·ra·ble**
in·ex·o·ra·ble
inexorible : **in·ex·o·ra·ble**
infadel : **in·fi·del**
infalible : **in·fal·li·ble**
infallable : **in·fal·li·ble**

infalleble : **in·fal·li·ble**
infallibal : **in·fal·li·ble**
in·fal·li·ble
infammous : **in·fa·mous**
infammus : **in·fa·mous**
in·fa·mous
infamus : **in·fa·mous**
in·fan·cy
infansy : **in·fan·cy**
infantary : **in·fan·try**
infantcy : **in·fan·cy**
infantery : **in·fan·try**
in·fan·try
infantsy : **in·fan·cy**
infattuate : **in·fat·u·ate**
in·fat·u·ate
infeable : **en·fee·ble**
infearior : **in·fe·ri·or**
infechion : **in·fec·tion**
infectian : **in·fec·tion**
in·fec·tion
infedel : **in·fi·del**
infeebal : **en·fee·ble**
infeeble : **en·fee·ble**
infeerior : **in·fe·ri·or**
infeible : **en·fee·ble**
infemous : **in·fa·mous**
infency : **in·fan·cy**
infensy : **in·fan·cy**
infentry : **in·fan·try**
infereor : **in·fe·ri·or**
inferier : **in·fe·ri·or**
in·fe·ri·or
infermary : **in·fir·ma·ry**
infermity : **in·fir·mi·ty**
in·fer·nal
infernel : **in·fer·nal**
in·fer·no
infexion : **in·fec·tion**
in·fi·del
infidelety : **in·fi·del·i·ty**
infidelitty : **in·fi·del·i·ty**

in·fi·del·i·ty
infidell : **in·fi·del**
infidellity : **in·fi·del·i·ty**
infinate : **in·fi·nite**
infincy : **in·fan·cy**
infinet : **in·fi·nite**
infinete : **in·fi·nite**
infinety : **in·fin·i·ty**
in·fi·nite
in·fin·i·ty
infinnite : **in·fi·nite**
infinnity : **in·fin·i·ty**
infinsy : **in·fan·cy**
infintry : **in·fan·try**
in·fir·ma·ry
infirmery : **in·fir·ma·ry**
infirmety : **in·fir·mi·ty**
infirmitty : **in·fir·mi·ty**
in·fir·mi·ty
infirmry : **in·fir·ma·ry**
infirory : **in·fir·ma·ry**
inflaimable : **in·flam·ma·ble**
inflamable : **in·flam·ma·ble**
inflamatory : **in·flam·ma·to·ry**
inflameble : **in·flam·ma·ble**
inflametory : **in·flam·ma·to·ry**
in·flam·ma·ble
inflammatorry :
    in·flam·ma·to·ry
in·flam·ma·to·ry
inflammetory :
    in·flam·ma·to·ry
inflammibal : **in·flam·ma·ble**
inflammible : **in·flam·ma·ble**
inflammitory :
    in·flam·ma·to·ry
inflecksible : **in·flex·i·ble**
inflexable : **in·flex·i·ble**
inflexeble : **in·flex·i·ble**
inflexibal : **in·flex·i·ble**
in·flex·i·ble
inflooence : **in·flu·ence**

influance : **in·flu·ence**
influanse : **in·flu·ence**
in·flu·ence
influense : **in·flu·ence**
infureate : **in·fu·ri·ate**
in·fu·ri·ate
infurnal : **in·fer·nal**
infurno : **in·fer·no**
infurriate : **in·fu·ri·ate**
ingagement : **en·gage·ment**
ingagment : **en·gage·ment**
ingat : **in·got**
ingeanious : **in·ge·nious**
ingeenious : **in·ge·nious**
ingeneer : **en·gi·neer**
ingeneous : **in·ge·nious**
ingenew : **in·ge·nue**
in·ge·nious (intelligent);
  in·gen·u·ous (simple-minded)
ingenius : **in·ge·nious**
ingenoo : **in·ge·nue**
in·ge·nue
in·gen·u·ous (simple-minded);
  in·ge·nious (intelligent)
in·gest
inget : **in·got**
ingineer : **en·gi·neer**
inginier : **en·gi·neer**
inginue : **in·ge·nue**
ingloreous : **in·glo·ri·ous**
in·glo·ri·ous
inglorius : **in·glo·ri·ous**
Inglund : **En·gland**
in·got
ingott : **in·got**
ingreadient : **in·gre·di·ent**
ingredeant : **in·gre·di·ent**
ingrediant : **in·gre·di·ent**
in·gre·di·ent
ingreedient : **in·gre·di·ent**
ingridient : **in·gre·di·ent**
ingure : **in·jure**

inhabbet : **in·hab·it**
inhabbit : **in·hab·it**
inhabet : **in·hab·it**
in·hab·it
inhail : **in·hale**
in·hale
inhancement : **en·hance·ment**
inhancemint : **en·hance·ment**
inhansement : **en·hance·ment**
inharent : **in·her·ent**
inharit : **in·her·it**
inharitance : **in·her·i·tance**
inharrit : **in·her·it**
inharritance : **in·her·i·tance**
inhear : **in·here**
inhearent : **in·her·ent**
inherant : **in·her·ent**
in·here
in·her·ent
inheret : **in·her·it**
inheretance : **in·her·i·tance**
inherint : **in·her·ent**
in·her·it
in·her·i·tance
inheritanse : **in·her·i·tance**
inheritence : **in·her·i·tance**
inheritense : **in·her·i·tance**
inherrit : **in·her·it**
inherritance : **in·her·i·tance**
inhibbet : **in·hib·it**
inhibbit : **in·hib·it**
inhibet : **in·hib·it**
in·hib·it
inhirent : **in·her·ent**
inibit : **in·hib·it**
inicial : **ini·tial**
iniciate : **ini·tiate**
iniggma : **enig·ma**
inigma : **enig·ma**
inimacal : **in·im·i·cal**
inimecal : **in·im·i·cal**
in·im·i·cal

inimicle : **in·im·i·cal**
inimikal : **in·im·i·cal**
inimmical : **in·im·i·cal**
inimy : **en·e·my**
inindate : **in·un·date**
iniqiety : **in·iq·ui·ty**
iniquitty : **in·iq·ui·ty**
in·iq·ui·ty
inishall : **ini·tial**
inishiate : **ini·tiate**
initeate : **ini·tiate**
ini·tial
ini·tiate
injere : **in·jure**
injery : **in·ju·ry**
injest : **in·gest**
injineer : **en·gi·neer**
injur : **in·jure**
in·jure
injurry : **in·ju·ry**
in·ju·ry
inmaty : **en·mi·ty**
inmety : **en·mi·ty**
inmitty : **en·mi·ty**
inmity : **en·mi·ty**
innacence : **in·no·cence**
innait : **in·nate**
innamored : **enam·ored**
in·nate
innavate : **in·no·vate**
innemy : **en·e·my**
innert : **in·ert**
innervene : **in·ter·vene**
innerview : **in·ter·view**
innigma : **enig·ma**
innitial : **ini·tial**
innitiate : **ini·tiate**
innivate : **in·no·vate**
in·no·cence
innocense : **in·no·cence**
innocince : **in·no·cence**
innocinse : **in·no·cence**

innovait : **in·no·vate**
in·no·vate
in·nu·en·do
innuindo: **in·nu·en·do**
in·nu·mer·a·ble
innumerible : **in·nu·mer·a·ble**
innumirable : **in·nu·mer·a·ble**
inocence : **in·no·cence**
inovate : **in·no·vate**
inphysema : **em·phy·se·ma**
inpire : **em·pire**
inporium : **em·po·ri·um**
inquisator : **in·quis·i·tor**
inquisiter : **in·quis·i·tor**
in·quis·i·tor
inquissitor : **in·quis·i·tor**
inquizitor : **in·quis·i·tor**
in·road
inrode : **in·road**
insain : **in·sane**
in·sane
in·scru·ta·ble
inscruteble : **in·scru·ta·ble**
inscrutibal : **in·scru·ta·ble**
inscrutible : **in·scru·ta·ble**
inseart : **in·sert**
insectacide : **in·sec·ti·cide**
in·sec·ti·cide
insectiside : **in·sec·ti·cide**
insendiary : **in·cen·di·ary**
insenerate : **in·cin·er·ate**
insenuate : **in·sin·u·ate**
insergent : **in·sur·gent**
in·sert
insessant : **in·ces·sant**
insessent : **in·ces·sant**
insest : **in·cest**
inshurance : **in·sur·ance**
insiclopedia : **en·cy·clo·pe·dia**
insiddious : **in·sid·i·ous**
insident : **in·ci·dent**
insideous : **in·sid·i·ous**

in·sid·i·ous
insidius : **in·sid·i·ous**
in·sight (discernment); **in·cite**
  (to urge on)
insign : **en·sign**
insinarate : **in·cin·er·ate**
insine : **en·sign**
insinerate : **in·cin·er·ate**
insinnuate : **in·sin·u·ate**
in·sin·u·ate
insiped : **in·sip·id**
insipiant : **in·cip·i·ent**
in·sip·id
insipient : **in·cip·i·ent**
insippid : **in·sip·id**
insippient : **in·cip·i·ent**
insircle : **en·cir·cle**
insision : **in·ci·sion**
insisor : **in·ci·sor**
insistance : **in·sis·tence**
in·sis·tence
insistense : **in·sis·tence**
insizor : **in·ci·sor**
insoalence : **in·so·lence**
in·so·lence
insolense : **in·so·lence**
insollance : **in·so·lence**
insollence : **in·so·lence**
insolluble : **in·sol·u·ble**
insoluable : **in·sol·u·ble**
insolubal : **in·sol·u·ble**
in·sol·u·ble
insolvant : **in·sol·vent**
in·sol·vent
insomnea : **in·som·nia**
in·som·nia
insouceant : **in·sou·ci·ant**
in·sou·ci·ant
insoucient : **in·sou·ci·ant**
inspecter : **in·spec·tor**
in·spec·tor
instagate : **in·sti·gate**

in·stance
instanse : **in·stance**
instantaineous :
  in·stan·ta·neous
in·stan·ta·neous
instantanious : **in·stan·ta·neous**
instantanius : **in·stan·ta·neous**
instatute : **in·sti·tute**
in·stead
insted : **in·stead**
instegate : **in·sti·gate**
instence : **in·stance**
instetute : **in·sti·tute**
instigait : **in·sti·gate**
in·sti·gate
instil : **in·still**
in·still
in·sti·tute
instructer : **in·struc·tor**
in·struc·tor
insuciant : **in·sou·ci·ant**
in·su·lar
insulen : **in·su·lin**
insuler : **in·su·lar**
in·su·lin
insullin : **in·su·lin**
in·sur·ance
insuranse : **in·sur·ance**
insurence : **in·sur·ance**
insurense : **in·sur·ance**
in·sur·gent
insurgient : **in·sur·gent**
insyclopedia : **en·cy·clo·pe·dia**
intagrate : **in·te·grate**
intallect : **in·tel·lect**
intarogate : **in·ter·ro·gate**
intarrogate : **in·ter·ro·gate**
intarrupt : **in·ter·rupt**
intearior : **in·te·ri·or**
inteerior : **in·te·ri·or**
integrait : **in·te·grate**
in·te·grate

intelect : **in·tel·lect**
inteligent : **in·tel·li·gent**
intellagent : **in·tel·li·gent**
in·tel·lect
intellegent : **in·tel·li·gent**
in·tel·li·gent
intence : **in·tense**
in·tense
inteprise : **en·ter·prise**
interagate : **in·ter·ro·gate**
interance : **en·trance**
in·ter·cede
interceed : **in·ter·cede**
in·ter·cept
interduce : **in·tro·duce**
interem : **in·ter·im**
interence : **en·trance**
in·ter·est
interfear : **in·ter·fere**
interfearence : **in·ter·fer·ence**
interfeer : **in·ter·fere**
interfeerence : **in·ter·fer·ence**
interferance : **in·ter·fer·ence**
interferanse : **in·ter·fer·ence**
in·ter·fere
in·ter·fer·ence
interferense : **in·ter·fer·ence**
interier : **in·te·ri·or**
in·ter·im
in·te·ri·or
interist : **in·ter·est**
interogate : **in·ter·ro·gate**
interpratation :
 in·ter·pre·ta·tion
in·ter·pre·ta·tion
interprise : **en·ter·prise**
interpritation :
 in·ter·pre·ta·tion
interprize : **en·ter·prise**
interragate : **in·ter·ro·gate**
interrigate : **in·ter·ro·gate**
interrim : **in·ter·im**

interrogait : **in·ter·ro·gate**
in·ter·ro·gate
interrum : **in·ter·im**
in·ter·rupt
intersede : **in·ter·cede**
interseed : **in·ter·cede**
intersept : **in·ter·cept**
in·ter·state (between states);
 in·tra·state (within a state)
intertain : **en·ter·tain**
intertane : **en·ter·tain**
interum : **in·ter·im**
interupt : **in·ter·rupt**
in·ter·val
intervean : **in·ter·vene**
interveen : **in·ter·vene**
interveiw : **in·ter·view**
intervel : **in·ter·val**
in·ter·vene
intervenous : **in·tra·ve·nous**
in·ter·view
intervil : **in·ter·val**
intesten : **in·tes·tine**
intestin : **in·tes·tine**
in·tes·tine
intigrate : **in·te·grate**
intillect : **in·tel·lect**
in·ti·ma·cy
intimant : **in·ti·mate**
intimassy : **in·ti·ma·cy**
intimasy : **in·ti·ma·cy**
in·ti·mate
intiment : **in·ti·mate**
intimet : **in·ti·mate**
intimissy : **in·ti·ma·cy**
intimisy : **in·ti·ma·cy**
intimit : **in·ti·mate**
intimmacy : **in·ti·ma·cy**
intirval : **in·ter·val**
intuition : **in·tu·ition**
intocksicate : **in·tox·i·cate**
in·tol·er·a·ble

in·tol·er·ance
intoleranse : **in·tol·er·ance**
in·tol·er·ant
intolerence : **in·tol·er·ance**
intolerent : **in·tol·er·ant**
intolerible : **in·tol·er·a·ble**
intolirable : **in·tol·er·a·ble**
intollarent : **in·tol·er·ant**
intollerable : **in·tol·er·a·ble**
intollerance : **in·tol·er·ance**
intollerant : **in·tol·er·ant**
intoxacate : **in·tox·i·cate**
intoxecate : **in·tox·i·cate**
in·tox·i·cate
intracacy : **in·tri·ca·cy**
intracate : **in·tri·cate**
intraduce : **in·tro·duce**
intrance : **en·trance**
intrancigent : **in·tran·si·gent**
intransagent : **in·tran·si·gent**
intranse : **en·trance**
intransegent : **in·tran·si·gent**
in·tran·si·gent
in·tra·state (within a state);
    in·ter·state (between states)
intravainous : **in·tra·ve·nous**
intravanous : **in·tra·ve·nous**
intraveinous : **in·tra·ve·nous**
intravenious : **in·tra·ve·nous**
in·tra·ve·nous
intravienous : **in·tra·ve·nous**
intreague : **in·trigue**
intrecacy : **in·tri·ca·cy**
intreeg : **in·trigue**
intrence : **en·trance**
intrense : **en·trance**
intrensic : **in·trin·sic**
intreped : **in·trep·id**
in·trep·id
intreppid : **in·trep·id**
intrest : **in·ter·est**
intrevenous : **in·tra·ve·nous**

in·tri·ca·cy
intricait : **in·tri·cate**
intricassy : **in·tri·ca·cy**
intricasy : **in·tri·ca·cy**
intricat : **in·tri·cate**
in·tri·cate
intricet : **in·tri·cate**
intricisy : **in·tri·ca·cy**
in·trigue
intrince : **en·trance**
intrinse : **en·trance**
in·trin·sic
intrinsick : **in·trin·sic**
in·tro·duce
introduse : **in·tro·duce**
intrupt : **in·ter·rupt**
intuishion : **in·tu·ition**
intuission : **in·tu·ition**
in·tu·ition
inuendo : **in·nu·en·do**
inumerable : **in·nu·mer·a·ble**
inunciate : **enun·ci·ate**
in·un·date
in·vade
invaid : **in·vade**
invaigh : **in·veigh**
invaled : **in·va·lid** (sick or
    disabled) *or* **in·val·id** (not
    valid)
in·va·lid (sick or disabled);
    in·val·id (not valid)
invallid : **in·va·lid** (sick or
    disabled) *or* **in·val·id** (not
    valid)
invalope : **en·vel·op** (*verb*) *or*
    en·ve·lope (*noun*)
in·va·sion
invassion : **in·va·sion**
invation : **in·va·sion**
invay : **in·veigh**
invazion : **in·va·sion**
in·veigh

invelid : **in·va·lid** (sick or disabled) *or* **in·val·id** (not valid)

invellope : **en·vel·op** (*verb*) *or* **en·ve·lope** (*noun*)

inveloap : **en·vel·op** (*verb*) *or* **en·ve·lope** (*noun*)

invelop : **en·vel·op** (*verb*) *or* **en·ve·lope** (*noun*)

invelope : **en·vel·op** (*verb*) *or* **en·ve·lope** (*noun*)

invencible : **in·vin·ci·ble**

inventorry : **in·ven·to·ry**
in·ven·to·ry

inveous : **en·vi·ous**

investagate : **in·ves·ti·gate**

investegate : **in·ves·ti·gate**

investigait : **in·ves·ti·gate**
in·ves·ti·gate

invetarate : **in·vet·er·ate**

inveterat : **in·vet·er·ate**
in·vet·er·ate

inveteret : **in·vet·er·ate**

invetterate : **in·vet·er·ate**

invey : **in·veigh**

invialable : **in·vi·o·la·ble**

invialate : **in·vi·o·late**

inviernment : **en·vi·ron·ment**

invigarate : **in·vig·o·rate**

invigerate : **in·vig·o·rate**

inviggorate : **in·vig·o·rate**
in·vig·o·rate

invilable : **in·vi·o·la·ble**

invilate : **in·vi·o·late**

invilope : **en·vel·op** (*verb*) *or* **en·ve·lope** (*noun*)

invinceble : **in·vin·ci·ble**
in·vin·ci·ble

invinsible : **in·vin·ci·ble**

invintory : **in·ven·to·ry**
in·vi·o·la·ble
in·vi·o·late

inviolible : **in·vi·o·la·ble**

inviornment : **en·vi·ron·ment**

invious : **en·vi·ous**

inviranment : **en·vi·ron·ment**

invirenment : **en·vi·ron·ment**

invirirnment : **en·vi·ron·ment**

invirnment : **en·vi·ron·ment**

invironment : **en·vi·ron·ment**

invisable : **in·vis·i·ble**
in·vis·i·ble

invissible : **in·vis·i·ble**

invius : **en·vi·ous**

invizible : **in·vis·i·ble**

invyous : **en·vi·ous**

io·dine

Io·wa

Ioway : **Io·wa**

iracible : **iras·ci·ble**

iragate : **ir·ri·gate**

irasceble : **iras·ci·ble**
iras·ci·ble

irassible : **iras·ci·ble**

iratate : **ir·ri·tate**

irelevant : **ir·rel·e·vant**

irevocable : **ir·re·vo·ca·ble**

irie : **ae·rie** (nest) *or* **ee·rie** (weird) *or* **Erie** (lake and canal)

irigate : **ir·ri·gate**

iritate : **ir·ri·tate**

irn : **earn** (to work to gain) *or* **urn** (vase)

irragate : **ir·ri·gate**
ir·rel·e·vant

irrelevent : **ir·rel·e·vant**

irretate : **ir·ri·tate**
ir·re·vo·ca·ble

irrevokable : **ir·re·vo·ca·ble**
ir·ri·gate
ir·ri·tate

isalation : **iso·la·tion**

isicle : **ici·cle**

ising : **ic·ing**
is·land
ismis : **isth·mus**
ismiss : **isth·mus**
ismus : **isth·mus**
iso·la·tion
iso·mer
isomere : **iso·mer**
isoscelees : **isos·ce·les**
isos·ce·les
isoseles : **isos·ce·les**
isoselles : **isos·ce·les**
isosseles : **isos·ce·les**
iso·tope
Is·ra·el
Israle : **Is·ra·el**
Isreal : **Is·ra·el**
issotope : **iso·tope**
isthmas : **isth·mus**
isthmis : **isth·mus**
isthmiss : **isth·mus**
isth·mus
italacize : **ital·i·cize**
italasize : **ital·i·cize**
italecize : **ital·i·cize**
ital·ic

italicise : **ital·i·cize**
ital·i·cize
italick : **ital·ic**
italisize : **ital·i·cize**
itallic : **ital·ic**
itallicize : **ital·i·cize**
itemise : **item·ize**
item·ize
itenerant : **itin·er·ant**
itenerent : **itin·er·ant**
ither : **ei·ther** (one or the
    other) *or* **ether** (gas)
ithsmis : **isth·mus**
itimize : **item·ize**
itinarant : **itin·er·ant**
itin·er·ant
itinerent : **itin·er·ant**
itomize : **item·ize**
its (belonging to it); **it's** (it is)
it's (it is); **its** (belonging to it)
itumize : **item·ize**
ivary : **ivo·ry**
ivery : **ivo·ry**
ivesdropping : **eaves·drop·ping**
ivo·ry
ivvory : **ivo·ry**

J

jack•al
jackel : **jack•al**
jackle : **jack•al**
jagaur : **jag•uar**
jaged : **jag•ged**
jag•ged
jaggid : **jag•ged**
jag•uar
jaguarr : **jag•uar**
jaguire : **jag•uar**
jagwar : **jag•uar**
jagwer : **jag•uar**
jail
jail•er *or* **jail•or**
jail•or *or* **jail•er**
jale : **jail**
jaler : **jail•er**
jallopy : **ja•lopy**
jaloppe : **ja•lopy**
ja•lopy
Jamaca : **Ja•mai•ca**
Jamaeca : **Ja•mai•ca**
Ja•mai•ca
Jamaika : **Ja•mai•ca**
Jamayka : **Ja•mai•ca**
jambaree : **jam•bo•ree**
jambiree : **jam•bo•ree**
jam•bo•ree
jamborie : **jam•bo•ree**
jambory : **jam•bo•ree**
janator : **jan•i•tor**
janatorial : **jan•i•to•ri•al**
jandice : **jaun•dice**
janetor : **jan•i•tor**
janetorial : **jan•i•to•ri•al**
jangal : **jan•gle** (harsh ringing sound) *or* **jin•gle** (pleasant ringing sound)

jangel : **jan•gle** (harsh ringing sound) *or* **jin•gle** (pleasant ringing sound)
jan•gle (harsh ringing sound); **jin•gle** (pleasant ringing sound)
janiter : **jan•i•tor**
janiterial : **jan•i•to•ri•al**
jan•i•tor
janitoreal : **jan•i•to•ri•al**
jan•i•to•ri•al
jannitor : **jan•i•tor**
jannitorial : **jan•i•to•ri•al**
Jannuary : **Jan•u•ary**
janquil : **jon•quil**
Januarry : **Jan•u•ary**
Jan•u•ary
Januerry : **Jan•u•ary**
Januery : **Jan•u•ary**
Januwary : **Jan•u•ary**
Januwery : **Jan•u•ary**
Ja•pan
Japaneese : **Jap•a•nese**
Jap•a•nese
Japaneze : **Jap•a•nese**
Japannese : **Jap•a•nese**
Jappan : **Ja•pan**
Jappanese : **Jap•a•nese**
jargan : **jar•gon**
jargen : **jar•gon**
jargin : **jar•gon**
jar•gon
jasmen : **jas•mine**
jasmin : **jas•mine**
jas•mine *or* **jes•sa•mine**
jassmine : **jas•mine**
jaudiss : **jaun•dice**
jaundace : **jaun•dice**
jaundase : **jaun•dice**
jaun•dice

jaundish : **jaun·dice**
javalen : **jav·e·lin**
javalin : **jav·e·lin**
javaline : **jav·e·lin**
javelen : **jav·e·lin**
jav·e·lin
javlen : **jav·e·lin**
javlin : **jav·e·lin**
jazmine : **jas·mine**
jazzmine : **jas·mine**
jealis : **jeal·ous**
jeallous : **jeal·ous**
jeal·ous
jealus : **jeal·ous**
jehad : **ji·had**
jejoon : **je·june**
je·june
jell or **gel**
jellitan : **gel·a·tin**
jellous : **jeal·ous**
jelopy : **ja·lopy**
jelous : **jeal·ous**
Jemaica : **Ja·mai·ca**
jemnasium : **gym·na·si·um**
jemnasstics : **gym·nas·tics**
jemnast : **gym·nast**
jemnastecs : **gym·nas·tics**
jemnasticks : **gym·nas·tics**
jemnest : **gym·nast**
jemnist : **gym·nast**
jengle : **jan·gle** (harsh ringing
    sound) or **jin·gle** (pleasant
    ringing sound)
jenre : **genre**
jeop·ar·dy
jeoprady : **jeop·ar·dy**
jeoprody : **jeop·ar·dy**
jepardy : **jeop·ar·dy**
jepordy : **jeop·ar·dy**
jepperdy : **jeop·ar·dy**
jepprady : **jeop·ar·dy**
jepprody : **jeop·ar·dy**

jeramiad : **jer·e·mi·ad**
jeremaid : **jer·e·mi·ad**
jer·e·mi·ad
jerimiad : **jer·e·mi·ad**
jernalism : **jour·nal·ism**
jerrand : **ger·und**
jerremiad : **jer·e·mi·ad**
jerrund : **ger·und**
Jerrusalem : **Je·ru·sa·lem**
jerrybilt : **jer·ry-built**
jer·ry-built
jersee : **jer·sey**
jer·sey
jersie : **jer·sey**
jerssey : **jer·sey**
jersy : **jer·sey**
jerund : **ger·und**
Je·ru·sa·lem
Jeruselem : **Je·ru·sa·lem**
Jerushalom : **Je·ru·sa·lem**
jerybuilt : **jer·ry-built**
jesamine : **jas·mine**
jessamen : **jas·mine**
jessamin : **jas·mine**
jes·sa·mine or **jas·mine**
jesster : **ges·ture** (movement) or
    jest·er (joker)
jessymine : **jas·mine**
jest (joke); **gist** (essence)
jest·er (joker); **ges·ture**
    (movement)
jestor : **jest·er** (joker) or
    ges·ture (movement)
jesture : **jest·er** (joker) or
    ges·ture (movement)
jetison : **jet·ti·son**
jet·sam
jetsem : **jet·sam**
jetsim : **jet·sam**
jetsum : **jet·sam**
jettason : **jet·ti·son**
jettisen : **jet·ti·son**

jet·ti·son
jettsam : **jet·sam**
jeuel : **jew·el**
jeueled : **jew·eled**
jeueler : **jew·el·er**
jeuelry : **jew·el·ry**
jewal : **jew·el**
jewaled : **jew·eled**
jewaler : **jew·el·er**
jewalry : **jew·el·ry**
jewbilee : **ju·bi·lee**
Jewdism : **Ju·da·ism**
Jewdyism : **Ju·da·ism**
jew·el
jew·eled *or* **jew·elled**
jew·el·er *or* **jew·el·ler**
jewelery : **jew·el·ry**
jew·elled *or* **jew·eled**
jew·el·ler *or* **jew·el·er**
jewellery (*Brit.*) : **jew·el·ry**
jewl : **jew·el**
jewled : **jew·eled**
jewler : **jew·el·er**
jewlry : **jew·el·ry**
jibe (to change course in boat; to agree); **gibe** (to taunt)
ji·had
jijune : **je·june**
jilopy : **ja·lopy**
Jimaica : **Ja·mai·ca**
Jimaka : **Ja·mai·ca**
jimnasium : **gym·na·si·um**
jimnasstics : **gym·nas·tics**
jimnast : **gym·nast**
jimnastecs : **gym·nas·tics**
jimnasticks : **gym·nas·tics**
jimnest : **gym·nast**
jimnist : **gym·nast**
jingal : **jan·gle** (harsh ringing sound) *or* **jin·gle** (pleasant ringing sound)

jingel : **jan·gle** (harsh ringing sound) *or* **jin·gle** (pleasant ringing sound)
jin·gle (pleasant ringing sound); **jan·gle** (harsh ringing sound)
jip : **gyp**
jipcem : **gyp·sum**
jipcim : **gyp·sum**
jipped : **gypped**
jipsam : **gyp·sum**
jipsem : **gyp·sum**
jipsey : **gyp·sy**
jipsim : **gyp·sum**
jipsy : **gyp·sy**
jirascope : **gy·ro·scope**
jirate : **gy·rate**
jirocompass : **gy·ro·com·pass**
jirocompess : **gy·ro·com·pass**
jirrate : **gy·rate**
jirsey : **jer·sey**
jist : **gist** (essence) *or* **jest** (joke)
jockee : **jock·ey**
jock·ey
jocky : **jock·ey**
jo·cose
joc·u·lar
joculer : **joc·u·lar**
joddper : **jodh·pur**
jodhper : **jodh·pur**
jodh·pur
jodper : **jodh·pur**
jodpur : **jodh·pur**
johdpur : **jodh·pur**
johnquil : **jon·quil**
joiful : **joy·ful**
joious : **joy·ous**
joist
jokose : **jo·cose**
jokular : **joc·u·lar**
jolity : **jol·li·ty**
jollety : **jol·li·ty**

jollitty : **jol·li·ty**
jol·li·ty
joncuil : **jon·quil**
jon·quil
jonquill : **jon·quil**
jonra : **genre**
joocy : **juicy**
joonta : **jun·ta**
jornalism : **jour·nal·ism**
jorneyman : **jour·ney·man**
jossel : **jos·tle**
jostel : **jos·tle**
jos·tle
jour·nal·ism
journelism : **jour·nal·ism**
jour·ney·man
jouryman : **jour·ney·man**
joveal : **jo·vial**
jo·vial
joy·ful
joyfull : **joy·ful**
joy·ous
joyst : **joist**
joyus : **joy·ous**
jubalant : **ju·bi·lant**
jubalee : **ju·bi·lee**
jubalint : **ju·bi·lant**
jubelant : **ju·bi·lant**
ju·bi·lant
ju·bi·lee
jubilent : **ju·bi·lant**
jubillee : **ju·bi·lee**
jubilly : **ju·bi·lee**
jucstapose : **jux·ta·pose**
jucy : **juicy**
Judahism : **Ju·da·ism**
Ju·da·ism
judeciary : **ju·di·cia·ry**
judge
judgement (*Brit.*) : **judg·ment**
judgerry : **ju·di·cia·ry**
judg·ment

judiceal : **ju·di·cial**
ju·di·cial
judiciarry : **ju·di·cia·ry**
ju·di·cia·ry
ju·di·cious
judishall : **ju·di·cial**
judishious : **ju·di·cious**
judisial : **ju·di·cial**
Judism : **Ju·da·ism**
judissiary : **ju·di·ci·ary**
judissious : **ju·di·cious**
juditial : **ju·di·cial**
juditiary : **ju·di·ci·ary**
juditious : **ju·di·cious**
juge : **judge**
jugement : **judg·ment**
jugernaut : **jug·ger·naut**
juggal : **jug·gle**
juggerknot : **jug·ger·naut**
jug·ger·naut
juggernot : **jug·ger·naut**
jugglar : **jug·gler** (one who
  juggles) *or* **jug·u·lar** (vein)
jug·gle
jug·gler (one who juggles);
  jug·u·lar (vein)
juggular : **jug·gler** (one who
  juggles) *or* **jug·u·lar** (vein)
jugguler : **jug·gler** (one who
  juggles) *or* **jug·u·lar** (vein)
jugler : **jug·gler** (one who
  juggles) *or* **jug·u·lar** (vein)
Ju·go·sla·via *or* **Yu·go·sla·via**
jugoular : **jug·gler** (one who
  juggles) *or* **jug·u·lar** (vein)
jug·u·lar (vein); **jug·gler** (one
  who juggles)
juguler : **jug·gler** (one who
  juggles) *or* **jug·u·lar** (vein)
jugulir : **jug·gler** (one who
  juggles) *or* **jug·u·lar** (vein)
juicy

ju·lep
julip : **ju·lep**
jullip : **ju·lep**
junaper : **ju·ni·per**
junchure : **junc·ture**
juncion : **junc·tion**
juncshion : **junc·tion**
juncshure : **junc·ture**
junc·tion
junc·ture
juncure : **junc·ture**
Ju·neau (city); **Ju·no** (goddess)
Juneoh : **Ju·neau**
juneper : **ju·ni·per**
jungal : **jun·gle**
jungel : **jun·gle**
jun·gle
junier : **jun·ior**
Junieu : **Ju·neau**
jun·ior
ju·ni·per
junipper : **ju·ni·per**
jun·ket
junkit : **jun·ket**
junktion : **junc·tion**
junkture : **junc·ture**
junnior : **ju·nior**
Ju·no (goddess); **Ju·neau** (city)
Junoe : **Ju·neau**
junquet : **jun·ket**
jun·ta
juntah : **jun·ta**
juntion : **junc·tion**
jurer : **ju·ror**
juresdiction : **ju·ris·dic·tion**
juressdiction : **ju·ris·dic·tion**
jurisdicion : **ju·ris·dic·tion**
jurisdicktion : **ju·ris·dic·tion**
ju·ris·dic·tion
jurissdiction : **ju·ris·dic·tion**
jurnalism : **jour·nal·ism**
jurneyman : **jour·ney·man**

ju·ror
jurrer : **ju·ror**
jurybuilt : **jer·ry-built**
justace : **jus·tice**
justafiable : **jus·ti·fi·able**
justefiable : **jus·ti·fi·able**
justefy : **jus·ti·fy**
jus·tice
justiffy : **jus·ti·fy**
justifiabel : **jus·ti·fi·able**
jus·ti·fi·able
jus·ti·fy
justifyable : **jus·ti·fi·able**
justis : **jus·tice**
justise : **jus·tice**
justiss : **jus·tice**
juvanile : **ju·ve·nile**
juvenial : **ju·ve·nile**
ju·ve·nile
juvinile : **ju·ve·nile**
jux·ta·pose
jymnaisium : **gym·na·si·um**
jymnaseum : **gym·na·si·um**
jymnasiem : **gym·na·si·um**
jymnasstics : **gym·nas·tics**
jymnastecs : **gym·nas·tics**
jymnasticks : **gym·nas·tics**
jymnest : **gym·nast**
jymnist : **gym·nast**
jyp : **gyp**
jypcem : **gyp·sum**
jypcim : **gyp·sum**
jyped : **gypped**
jypped : **gypped**
jypsam : **gyp·sum**
jypsem : **gyp·sum**
jypsey : **gyp·sy**
jypsie : **gyp·sy**
jypsim : **gyp·sum**
jyracompass : **gy·ro·com·pass**
jyrait : **gy·rate**
jyrascope : **gy·ro·scope**

jyricompass : **gy·ro·com·pass**
jyriscope : **gy·ro·scope**
jyrocompess : **gy·ro·com·pass**

jyrocompiss : **gy·ro·com·pass**
jyroscoap : **gy·ro·scope**
jyrrate : **gy·rate**

K

kacki : **kha·ki**
kactis : **cac·tus**
kactus : **cac·tus**
kadet : **ca·det**
kaffee : **cof·fee**
kahki : **kha·ki**
Kairo : **Cai·ro**
kakhi : **kha·ki**
kaki : **kha·ki**
kakki : **kha·ki**
kakky : **kha·ki**
kaky : **kha·ki**
kaleidascope : **ka·lei·do·scope**
kaleidescope : **ka·lei·do·scope**
ka·lei·do·scope
kalico : **cal·i·co**
kalidoscope : **ka·lei·do·scope**
kaliedoscope : **ka·lei·do·scope**
kalipso : **ca·lyp·so**
kalisthenics : **cal·is·then·ics**
kalisthinics : **cal·is·then·ics**
kalleidoscope : **ka·lei·do·scope**
kallisthenics : **cal·is·then·ics**
kalypso : **ca·lyp·so**
kan·ga·roo
kangarue : **kan·ga·roo**
kangeroo : **kan·ga·roo**
kangiroo : **kan·ga·roo**
kangroo : **kan·ga·roo**
kanguru : **kan·ga·roo**
kanine : **ca·nine**
kaos : **cha·os**
Kan·sas
Kansus : **Kan·sas**
kar·at or **car·at** (weight of
   gems); **car·et** (^); **car·rot**
   (vegetable)
karet : **kar·at** (weight of gems)
   or **car·et** (^) or **car·rot**
   (vegetable)

karisma : **char·is·ma**
karosene : **ker·o·sene**
karrat : **kar·at** (weight of gems)
   or **car·et** (^) or **car·rot**
   (vegetable)
karret : **kar·at** (weight of gems)
   or **car·et** (^) or **car·rot**
   (vegetable)
kataclism : **cat·a·clysm**
kataclysm : **cat·a·clysm**
katsup : **cat·sup**
kayac : **kay·ak**
kayack : **kay·ak**
kay·ak
keanness : **keen·ness**
keeness : **keen·ness**
keen·ness
keesh : **quiche**
kelogram : **ki·lo·gram**
Keltic : **Celt·ic**
kemono : **ki·mo·no**
ken (to know); **kin** (relatives)
kendal : **kin·dle**
kendengarten : **kin·der·gar·ten**
kendle : **kin·dle**
kendling : **kin·dling**
kendred : **kin·dred**
kenel : **ken·nel**
kenetic : **ki·net·ic**
kennal : **ken·nel**
ken·nel
kennle : **ken·nel**
Kentuckey : **Ken·tucky**
Ken·tucky
Kentuky : **Ken·tucky**
keosk : **ki·osk**
kerasene : **ker·o·sene**
kernal : **col·o·nel** (military
   officer) or **ker·nel** (seed)

ker·nel (seed); **col·o·nel**
  (military officer)
kernele : **col·o·nel** (military
  officer) *or* **ker·nel** (seed)
keroseen : **ker·o·sene**
ker·o·sene
kerosine : **ker·o·sene**
kerrosene : **ker·o·sene**
ketchap : **cat·sup**
ketchep : **cat·sup**
ketch·up *or* **cat·sup**
ketle : **ket·tle**
ketsup : **cat·sup**
kettal : **ket·tle**
kettel : **ket·tle**
ket·tle
keyosk : **ki·osk**
kha·ki
khaky : **kha·ki**
kiask : **ki·osk**
kibbits : **kib·butz** (collective
  farm) *or* **ki·bitz** (to offer
  advice)
kibbitz : **kib·butz** (collective
  farm) *or* **ki·bitz** (to offer
  advice)
kib·butz (collective farm);
  ki·bitz (to offer advice)
kibetz : **kib·butz** (collective
  farm) *or* **ki·bitz** (to offer
  advice)
kibits : **kib·butz** (collective
  farm) *or* **ki·bitz** (to offer
  advice)
kibetz : **kib·butz** (collective
  farm) *or* **ki·bitz** (to offer
  advice)
ki·bitz (to offer advice);
  kib·butz (collective farm)
kiche : **quiche**
kichen : **kitch·en**
kichin : **kitch·en**
kiddergarden : **kin·der·gar·ten**
kiddney : **kid·ney**
kid·nap·er *or* **kid·nap·per**

kid·nap·ing *or* **kid·nap·ping**
kid·nap·per *or* **kid·nap·er**
kid·nap·ping *or* **kid·nap·ing**
kid·ney
kidnie : **kid·ney**
kidny : **kid·ney**
kilagram : **ki·lo·gram**
Kilamanjaro : **Kil·i·man·ja·ro**
kilameter : **ki·lo·me·ter**
kilegram : **ki·lo·gram**
Kilemanjaro : **Kil·i·man·ja·ro**
kiligram : **ki·lo·gram**
Kil·i·man·ja·ro
killogram : **ki·lo·gram**
killometer : **ki·lo·me·ter**
ki·lo·gram
kilomeater : **ki·lo·me·ter**
kilomeeter : **ki·lo·me·ter**
ki·lo·me·ter
kilometre (*Brit.*) : **ki·lo·me·ter**
kimmono : **ki·mo·no**
ki·mo·no
kin (relatives); **ken** (to know)
kindal : **kin·dle**
kindel : **kin·dle**
kindergarden : **kin·der·gar·ten**
kindergardin : **kin·der·gar·ten**
kin·der·gar·ten
kinderguarden : **kin·der·gar·ten**
kin·dle
kindleing : **kin·dling**
kin·dling
kindread : **kin·dred**
kin·dred
kindrid : **kin·dred**
kindrud : **kin·dred**
ki·net·ic
kinetick : **ki·net·ic**
kinettic : **ki·net·ic**
kingdam : **king·dom**
kingdem : **king·dom**
king·dom

kingdum : **king·dom**

kinnetic : **ki·net·ic**

kintergarden : **kin·der·gar·ten**

kintergarten : **kin·der·gar·ten**

Kintucky : **Ken·tucky**

ki·osk

kishe : **quiche**

kis·met

kismit : **kis·met**

kiss·able

kissible : **kiss·able**

kissmet : **kis·met**

kitch·en

kitchin : **kitch·en**

kitchun : **kitch·en**

kiten : **kit·ten**

kitshen : **kitch·en**

kit·ten

kittin : **kit·ten**

kiyak : **kay·ak**

kizmet : **kis·met**

klepptomaniac :
   klep·to·ma·ni·ac

kleptamaniac : **klep·to·ma·ni·ac**

kleptemaniac : **klep·to·ma·ni·ac**

kleptomainiac :
   klep·to·ma·ni·ac

kleptomaneac :
   klep·to·ma·ni·ac

klep·to·ma·ni·ac

kliptomaniac : **klep·to·ma·ni·ac**

knap·sack

knew (was aware); **gnu**
   (antelope); **new** (not old)

knicht : **knight**

knick·knack

knicknack : **knick·knack**

knife

knifes (verb); **knives** (*plur.*)

knight (medieval soldier);
   night (not day)

knigt : **knight**

knikknak : **knick·knack**

knite : **knight**

knives (*plur.*); **knifes** (*verb*)

knoal : **knoll**

knole : **knoll**

knoll

knolledge : **knowl·edge**

knollege : **knowl·edge**

knollegible : **knowl·edge·able**

knot (in rope; one nautical
   mile); **not** (negative)

knot·hole

know (to be aware of); **no**
   (negative); **now** (at this time)

knowledgable :
   knowl·edge·able

knowl·edge

knowl·edge·able

knowledgible : **knowl·edge·able**

knowlege : **knowl·edge**

knowlegeable : **knowl·edge·able**

knowlegible : **knowl·edge·able**

knowlidge : **knowl·edge**

knowlige : **knowl·edge**

knuckal : **knuck·le**

knuckel : **knuck·le**

knuck·le

knukkle : **knuck·le**

ko·ala

koalla : **ko·ala**

koff : **cough**

koffee : **cof·fee**

kohlrabbi : **kohl·ra·bi**

kohl·ra·bi

kohlrobbi : **kohl·ra·bi**

kohlrobi : **kohl·ra·bi**

kohlroby : **kohl·ra·bi**

koleidoscope : **ka·lei·do·scope**

kollidoscope : **ka·lei·do·scope**

kollrabi : **kohl·ra·bi**

kolrabi : **kohl·ra·bi**

komquat : **kum·quat**

Ko·rea
Koria : **Ko·rea**
Korrea : **Ko·rea**
kough : **cough**
kowala : **ko·ala**
kowalla : **ko·ala**
kremlen : **krem·lin**
krem·lin
krimlin : **krem·lin**
krimmlin : **krem·lin**
kripton : **kryp·ton**
kryppton : **kryp·ton**

kryp·ton
kumkwat : **kum·quat**
kum·quat
kumquot : **kum·quat**
kurnel : **col·o·nel** (military
    officer) *or* **ker·nel** (seed)
kwagmire : **quag·mire**
kwick : **quick**
kyack : **kay·ak**
kymono : **ki·mo·no**
kyosk : **ki·osk**

L

labal : **la·bel**
laballed : **la·beled**
labarinth : **lab·y·rinth**
labbel : **la·bel**
labbor : **la·bor**
labbored : **la·bored**
labborious : **la·bo·ri·ous**
la·bel
la·beled *or* **la·belled**
la·belled *or* **la·beled**
laber : **la·bor**
labered : **la·bored**
laberinth : **lab·y·rinth**
laberynth : **lab·y·rinth**
labil : **la·bel**
labirinth : **lab·y·rinth**
labirynth : **lab·y·rinth**
lable : **la·bel**
labled : **la·beled**
la·bor
laboratorry : **lab·o·ra·to·ry**
lab·o·ra·to·ry
la·bored
laboreous : **la·bo·ri·ous**
la·bo·ri·ous
laborratory : **lab·o·ra·to·ry**
laborred : **la·bored**
laborrious : **la·bo·ri·ous**
labortory : **lab·o·ra·to·ry**
Labradoor : **Lab·ra·dor**
Lab·ra·dor
Labradore : **Lab·ra·dor**
labratory : **lab·o·ra·to·ry**
Labredor : **Lab·ra·dor**
labretory : **lab·o·ra·to·ry**
Labridor : **Lab·ra·dor**
labrinth : **lab·y·rinth**
labritory : **lab·o·ra·to·ry**
labrotory : **lab·o·ra·to·ry**
labrynth : **lab·y·rinth**

labul : **la·bel**
lab·y·rinth
lacadaisical : **lack·a·dai·si·cal**
lacerait : **lac·er·ate**
lac·er·ate
lacey : **lacy**
lacivious : **las·civ·i·ous**
lack·a·dai·si·cal
lackadasical : **lack·a·dai·si·cal**
lacker : **lac·quer**
lacksitive : **lax·a·tive**
lacksity : **lax·i·ty**
lackydaisical : **lack·a·dai·si·cal**
lac·quer
lacuer : **lac·quer**
lacy
ladal : **la·dle**
ladel : **la·dle**
ladill : **la·dle**
laditude : **lat·i·tude**
la·dle
laff : **laugh**
laffable : **laugh·able**
laffible : **laugh·able**
laffter : **laugh·ter**
lagard : **lag·gard**
la·ger (beer); **log·ger** (tree cutter)
lag·gard
lagger : **la·ger** (beer) *or* **log·ger** (tree cutter)
laggerd : **lag·gard**
laggoon : **la·goon**
la·goon
lagune : **la·goon**
lair (nest, burrow); **lay·er** (one that lays; one thickness)
laith : **lath** (board) *or* **lathe** (machine)

laithe : **lath** (board) *or* **lathe**
  (machine)
lamanate : **lam·i·nate**
lamenate : **lam·i·nate**
lam·i·nate
laminnate : **lam·i·nate**
lamminate : **lam·i·nate**
lam·poon
lampune : **lam·poon**
lanalen : **lan·o·lin**
lanalin : **lan·o·lin**
lance
lan·cet
lanch : **launch**
lancit : **lan·cet**
landlover : **land·lub·ber**
land·lub·ber
landluvver : **land·lub·ber**
landscaip : **land·scape**
land·scape
landskape : **land·scape**
lannolin : **lan·o·lin**
lanolen : **lan·o·lin**
lan·o·lin
lanse : **lance**
lanset : **lan·cet**
lansit : **lan·cet**
lapal : **la·pel**
la·pel
lapell : **la·pel**
lappel : **la·pel**
laquer : **lac·quer**
lar·ce·ny
larciny : **lar·ce·ny**
larengitis : **lar·yn·gi·tis**
larenx : **lar·ynx**
lar·gess *or* **lar·gesse**
lar·gesse *or* **lar·gess**
lar·i·at
lariet : **lar·i·at**
laringitis : **lar·yn·gi·tis**
larinks : **lar·ynx**

larinx : **lar·ynx**
larrangitis : **lar·yn·gi·tis**
larrengitus : **lar·yn·gi·tis**
larriat : **lar·i·at**
larriet : **lar·i·at**
larrinks : **lar·ynx**
larrinx : **lar·ynx**
larseny : **lar·ce·ny**
larsinny : **lar·ce·ny**
larsiny : **lar·ce·ny**
lar·va (*sing.*); **lar·vae** (*plur.*)
lar·vae (*plur.*); **lar·va** (*sing.*)
lar·yn·gi·tis
laryngitus : **lar·yn·gi·tis**
larynjitis : **lar·yn·gi·tis**
lar·ynx
lasarate : **lac·er·ate**
lasciveous : **las·civ·i·ous**
las·civ·i·ous
laserate : **lac·er·ate**
lasserate : **lac·er·ate**
lassivious : **las·civ·i·ous**
Latan : **Lat·in**
latancy : **la·ten·cy**
latansy : **la·ten·cy**
latant : **la·tent**
latarel : **lat·er·al**
latatude : **lat·i·tude**
Laten : **Lat·in**
la·ten·cy
latensy : **la·ten·cy**
la·tent
lat·er·al
laterel : **lat·er·al**
latetude : **lat·i·tude**
lath (board); **lathe** (machine)
lathe (machine); **lath** (board)
latice : **lat·tice**
Lat·in
latise : **lat·tice**
latiss : **lat·tice**
lat·i·tude

lattece : **lat·tice**

latteral : **lat·er·al**

lat·tice

Lattin : **Lat·in**

lattise : **lat·tice**

lattiss : **lat·tice**

lattiude : **lat·i·tude**

laud·able

laudible : **laud·able**

laugh

laugh·able

laughible : **laugh·able**

laugh·ter

launch

laundary : **laun·dry**

launderry : **laun·dry**

laundery : **laun·dry**

laun·dry

lavalear : **lav·a·liere**

lavaleer : **lav·a·liere**

lav·a·liere

lavander : **lav·en·der**

laveleer : **lav·a·liere**

lavelier : **lav·a·liere**

laveliere : **lav·a·liere**

lavendar : **lav·en·der**

lav·en·der

lavesh : **lav·ish**

lavinder : **lav·en·der**

lav·ish

lavvish : **lav·ish**

lawdable : **laud·able**

lawdible : **laud·able**

law·ful

lawfull : **law·ful**

lawnch : **launch**

lawndry : **laun·dry**

lax·a·tive

laxety : **lax·i·ty**

laxitive : **lax·a·tive**

laxitty : **lax·i·ty**

lax·i·ty

lay (to put down; *past of* to lie); **lie** (to recline)

lay·er (one that lays; one thickness); **lair** (nest, burrow)

lay·ing (act of putting down); **ly·ing** (act of reclining)

leace : **lease**

leach (to dissolve); **leech** (bloodsucker)

lead (to guide; a metal); **led** (*past of* to lead)

lead·en

leaf

leafs : **leaves**

leag : **league**

leagal : **le·gal**

leagality : **le·gal·i·ty**

leagion : **le·gion**

leagle : **le·gal**

league

leak (to let out); **leek** (vegetable)

lean (to incline); **lien** (legal claim)

leanient : **le·nient**

lean-to

leap

leapard : **leop·ard**

leaperd : **leop·ard**

leaque : **league**

learn

lear·y *or* **leer·y**

lease

leasure : **lei·sure**

leater : **li·ter**

leathal : **le·thal**

leath·er

leavel : **lev·el**

leaveled : **lev·eled**

leav·en

leaverage : **lev·er·age**

leaves

leavity : **lev·i·ty**

leaward : **lee·ward**

Lebannon : **Leb·a·non**

Leb·a·non

Lebbanon : **Leb·a·non**

Lebenon : **Leb·a·non**

Lebinon : **Leb·a·non**

lechary : **lech·ery**

lech·ery

led (*past of* to lead); **lead** (to guide; a metal)

ledden : **lead·en**

led·ger

leece : **lease**

leech (bloodsucker); **leach** (to dissolve)

leef : **leaf**

leefs : **leaves**

leegue : **league**

leek (vegetable); **leak** (to let out)

leen : **lean** (to incline) *or* **lien** (legal claim)

leento : **lean-to**

leep : **leap**

leer·y *or* **lear·y**

leese : **lease**

leesure : **lei·sure**

leeter : **li·ter**

leethal : **le·thal**

leeves : **leaves**

lee·ward

leewerd : **lee·ward**

leeword : **lee·ward**

leftenant : **lieu·ten·ant**

legability : **leg·i·bil·i·ty**

leg·a·cy

le·gal

legalety : **le·gal·i·ty**

legalitty : **le·gal·i·ty**

le·gal·i·ty

legallity : **le·gal·i·ty**

legassy : **leg·a·cy**

legasy : **leg·a·cy**

legebility : **leg·i·bil·i·ty**

legeble : **leg·i·ble**

legel : **le·gal**

leg·end

legendarry : **leg·end·ary**

leg·end·ary

legenderry : **leg·end·ary**

legendery : **leg·end·ary**

legeon : **le·gion**

leger : **led·ger**

legeslator : **leg·is·la·tor**

leggend : **leg·end**

leggendery : **leg·end·ary**

legger : **led·ger**

leggion : **le·gion**

leggislator : **leg·is·la·tor**

leggitimate : **le·git·i·mate**

legian : **le·gion**

legibal : **leg·i·ble**

legibel : **leg·i·ble**

legibilety : **leg·i·bil·i·ty**

legibilitty : **leg·i·bil·i·ty**

leg·i·bil·i·ty

legibillity : **leg·i·bil·i·ty**

leg·i·ble

legicy : **leg·a·cy**

legind : **leg·end**

le·gion

legislater : **leg·is·la·tor**

leg·is·la·tor

legissy : **leg·a·cy**

legitamacy : **le·git·i·ma·cy**

legitamet : **le·git·i·mate**

legitemacy : **le·git·i·ma·cy**

legitemate : **le·git·i·mate**

le·git·i·ma·cy

legitimassy : **le·git·i·ma·cy**

legitimasy : **le·git·i·ma·cy**

le·git·i·mate

legitimet : **le·git·i·mate**

legitimisy : **le·git·i·ma·cy**
legittimacy : **le·git·i·ma·cy**
legle : **le·gal**
leip : **leap**
leishure : **lei·sure**
lei·sure
lejend : **leg·end**
lejendary : **leg·end·ary**
lemen : **lem·on**
lemenade : **lem·on·ade**
lemin : **lem·on**
leminade : **lem·on·ade**
lemmon : **lem·on**
lemmonade : **lem·on·ade**
lemmur : **le·mur**
lem·on
lem·on·ade
lemonaid : **lem·on·ade**
le·mur
lemure : **le·mur**
lenghth : **length**
length
leniant : **le·nient**
le·nient
lental : **len·til** (legume) or
   lin·tel (door beam)
lenth : **length**
len·til (legume); **lin·tel** (door
   beam)
lentle : **lentil** (legume) or
   lin·tel (door beam)
leop·ard
leoperd : **leop·ard**
lepard : **leop·ard**
lep·er
leperd : **leop·ard**
leppard : **leop·ard**
lepper : **lep·er**
lepperd : **leop·ard**
lerch : **lurch**
lerk : **lurk**
lern : **learn**

les·sen (to decrease); **les·son**
   (thing studied)
les·son (thing studied); **les·sen**
   (to decrease)
letchery : **lech·ery**
leter : **li·ter**
le·thal
lethel : **le·thal**
lether : **leath·er**
lettisse : **let·tuce**
lettiss : **let·tuce**
let·tuce
lettus : **let·tuce**
lettuse : **let·tuce**
leucimia : **leu·ke·mia**
leukeamia : **leu·ke·mia**
leukemea : **leu·ke·mia**
leu·ke·mia
leukimia : **leu·ke·mia**
leval : **lev·el**
levaled : **lev·eled**
levarage : **lev·er·age**
lev·el
lev·eled
levelled : **lev·eled**
leven : **leav·en**
lev·er·age
leverege : **lev·er·age**
leverige : **lev·er·age**
levety : **lev·i·ty**
le·vi·a·than
leviathen : **le·vi·a·than**
leviethan : **le·vi·a·than**
levirige : **lev·er·age**
levitty : **lev·i·ty**
lev·i·ty
levven : **leav·en**
levvity : **lev·i·ty**
lewdicrous : **lu·di·crous**
liabilety : **li·a·bil·i·ty**
li·a·bil·i·ty
liabillity : **li·a·bil·i·ty**

li·a·ble (responsible or susceptible); li·bel (damaging printed statements)

li·ai·son

li·ar (teller of lies); lyre (stringed instrument)

liason : li·ai·son

libaral : lib·er·al

libartine : lib·er·tine

libary : li·brary

libberal : lib·er·al

libbertine : lib·er·tine

libberty : lib·er·ty

libedo : li·bi·do

li·bel (damaging printed statements); li·a·ble (responsible or susceptible)

libelity : li·a·bil·i·ty

lib·er·al

liberall : lib·er·al

liberel : lib·er·al

libertean : lib·er·tine

liberteen : lib·er·tine

libertene : lib·er·tine

lib·er·tine

lib·er·ty

li·bi·do

librarry : li·brary

li·brary

librery : li·brary

licarish : lic·o·rice

licence : li·cense

li·cense

licenze : li·cense

licerice : lic·o·rice

li·chen (fungus); lik·en (to compare)

licken : li·chen (fungus) or lik·en (to compare)

lickerish : lic·o·rice

lic·o·rice

licorish : lic·o·rice

lie (to recline); lay (to put down)

lieing : lay·ing (act of putting down) or ly·ing (act of reclining)

lien (legal claim); lean (to incline)

lietenent : lieu·ten·ant

lieu·ten·ant

lieutennant : lieu·ten·ant

lifegard : life·guard

lifegaurd : life·guard

life·guard

lik·en (to compare); li·chen (fungus)

li·lac

lilack : li·lac

lilly : lily

lily

limarick : lim·er·ick

lim·er·ick

limet : lim·it

lim·it

limmerick : lim·er·ick

limmit : lim·it

limosine : lim·ou·sine

limouseen : lim·ou·sine

limousene : lim·ou·sine

lim·ou·sine

limozene : lim·ou·sine

limozine : lim·ou·sine

limph : lymph

limrick : lim·er·ick

limur : le·mur

linament : lin·ea·ment (outline) or lin·i·ment (painkiller)

Lin·coln

Lincon : Lin·coln

Linconn : Lin·coln

lin·ea·ment (outline); lin·i·ment (painkiller)

lin·ear

linement : **lin·ea·ment** (outline)
  or lin·i·ment (painkiller)
lin·en
lingeray : **lin·ge·rie**
lingerey : **lin·ge·rie**
lin·ge·rie
linght : **length**
liniar : **lin·ear**
linient : **le·nient**
lin·i·ment (painkiller);
  lin·ea·ment (outline)
linnament : **lin·e·a·ment**
  (outline) or **lin·i·ment**
  (painkiller)
linnear : **lin·ear**
linnen : **lin·en**
linniar : **lin·ear**
linnoleum : **li·no·leum**
li·no·leum
linoliem : **li·no·leum**
linolium : **li·no·leum**
linon : **lin·en**
linsherie : **lin·ge·rie**
lintal : **len·til** (legume) or
  lin·tel (door beam)
lin·tel (door beam); **len·til**
  (legume)
lintle : **len·til** (*legume*)or lin·tel
  (door beam)
linx : **lynx**
li·on·ess
lionness : **li·on·ess**
liquaffy : **liq·ue·fy**
liquafy : **liq·ue·fy**
liqued : **li·quid**
liq·ue·fy
liq·uid
liquiffy : **liq·ue·fy**
liquify : **liq·ue·fy**
liquorice (*Brit*.) : **lic·o·rice**
liquorish : **lic·o·rice**
lirk : **lurk**

lisense : **li·cense**
lissener : **lis·ten·er**
lis·ten·er
lit·a·ny
litaracy : **lit·er·a·cy**
litegate : **lit·i·gate**
liteny : **lit·a·ny**
li·ter
literachure : **lit·er·a·ture**
lit·er·a·cy
literassy : **lit·er·a·cy**
lit·er·a·ture
litergy : **lit·ur·gy**
litericy : **lit·er·a·cy**
literissy : **lit·er·a·cy**
literisy : **lit·er·a·cy**
literture : **lit·er·a·ture**
lit·i·gate
litiny : **lit·a·ny**
litrature : **lit·er·a·ture**
litre (*Brit*.) : **li·ter**
littany : **lit·a·ny**
littature : **lit·er·a·ture**
littature : **lit·er·a·ture**
litteracy : **lit·er·a·cy**
litterature : **lit·er·a·ture**
littigate : **lit·i·gate**
litturgy : **lit·ur·gy**
lit·ur·gy
liturjy : **lit·ur·gy**
live·li·hood
livelyhood : **live·li·hood**
livlihood : **live·li·hood**
liz·ard
lizerd : **liz·ard**
lizzard : **liz·ard**
lizzerd : **liz·ard**
loathesome : **loath·some**
loath·some
lo·cal (regional); **lo·cale**
  (region, setting)
lo·cale (region, setting); **lo·cal**
  (regional)

locamotion : **lo·co·mo·tion**
lo·co·mo·tion
logarhythm : **log·a·rithm**
logarithem : **log·a·rithm**
log·a·rithm
logarythm : **log·a·rithm**
loggarithm : **log·a·rithm**
log·ger (tree cutter); **la·ger**
  (beer)
logorithm : **log·a·rithm**
loial : **loy·al**
Londen : **Lon·don**
Londin : **Lon·don**
Lon·don
lone·li·ness
lone·ly
longatude : **lon·gi·tude**
longerie : **lin·ge·rie**
longetude : **lon·gi·tude**
longevety : **lon·gev·i·ty**
longevitty : **lon·gev·i·ty**
lon·gev·i·ty
longitood : **lon·gi·tude**
lon·gi·tude
longitued : **lon·gi·tude**
longivity : **lon·gev·i·ty**
longue : **lounge**
lonliness : **lone·li·ness**
lonly : **lone·ly**
loobricant : **lu·bri·cant**
loodricrous : **lu·di·crous**
lookemia : **leu·ke·mia**
loominary : **lu·mi·nary**
loonacy : **lu·na·cy**
loonasy : **lu·na·cy**
loonatic : **lu·na·tic**
loose (not attached); **lose** (to
  misplace)
Loosiana : **Lou·i·si·ana**
lootenent : **lieu·ten·ant**
loquaceous : **lo·qua·cious**

lo·qua·cious
loquaicious : **lo·qua·cious**
loquasious : **lo·qua·cious**
loquatious : **lo·qua·cious**
loquecious : **lo·qua·cious**
lose (to misplace); **loose** (not
  attached)
losinge : **loz·enge**
lossinge : **loz·enge**
lotery : **lot·tery**
lothesome : **loath·some**
lothsome : **loath·some**
lotis : **lo·tus**
lottary : **lot·tery**
lotterry : **lot·tery**
lot·tery
lo·tus
Loueesiana : **Lou·i·si·ana**
Louiseana : **Lou·i·si·ana**
Lou·i·si·ana
Louiziana : **Lou·i·si·ana**
Lousiana : **Lou·i·si·ana**
lounge
loungue : **lounge**
lov·able
loveable : **lov·able**
love·li·er
loveloarn : **love·lorn**
love·lorn
lovelyer : **love·li·er**
lovible : **lov·able**
lovlier : **love·li·er**
lovlorn : **love·lorn**
lowngue : **lounge**
loy·al
loyel : **loy·al**
loyil : **loy·al**
loyl : **loy·al**
loz·enge
lozinge : **loz·enge**
lozzinge : **loz·enge**

lubracant : **lu·bri·cant**
lubrecant : **lu·bri·cant**
lu·bri·cant
lubricent : **lu·bri·cant**
luced : **lu·cid**
lucer : **lu·cre**
luchre : **lu·cre**
lu·cid
lucksuriant : **lux·u·ri·ant**
lucksury : **lux·u·ry**
lu·cra·tive
lu·cre
lucretive : **lu·cra·tive**
ludacrous : **lu·di·crous**
ludecrous : **lu·di·crous**
ludicrace : **lu·di·crous**
ludicrass : **lu·di·crous**
ludicris : **lu·di·crous**
lu·di·crous
ludicrus : **lu·di·crous**
luekemia : **leu·ke·mia**
luetenant : **lieu·ten·ant**
lugage : **lug·gage**
lugege : **lug·gage**
lug·gage
luggege : **lug·gage**
luggidge : **lug·gage**
luggige : **lug·gage**
lugguage : **lug·gage**
lugige : **lug·gage**
Luisiana : **Lou·i·si·ana**
lukemia : **leu·ke·mia**
luker : **lu·cre**
lukre : **lu·cre**
lulaby : **lul·la·by**
luliby : **lul·la·by**
lul·la·by
lulleby : **lul·la·by**
lulliby : **lul·la·by**
lum·bar (of the loins); **lum·ber** (timber)

lum·ber (timber); **lum·bar** (of the loins)
lumenary : **lu·mi·nary**
lumenescent : **lu·mi·nes·cent**
luminarry : **lu·mi·nary**
lu·mi·nary
luminecent : **lu·mi·nes·cent**
luminery : **lu·mi·nary**
lu·mi·nes·cent
luminescint : **lu·mi·nes·cent**
luminessent : **lu·mi·nes·cent**
lu·na·cy
lunasy : **lu·na·cy**
lu·na·tic
lunatick : **lu·na·tic**
lun·cheon
lunchin : **lun·cheon**
lunchion : **lun·cheon**
lunesy : **lu·na·cy**
lunetic : **lu·na·tic**
lunissy : **lu·na·cy**
lunisy : **lu·na·cy**
lunitic : **lu·na·tic**
lurch
lu·rid
lurk
lurn : **learn**
lurrid : **lu·rid**
lurtch : **lurch**
lused : **lu·cid**
lusid : **lu·cid**
lus·ter
lustre (*Brit.*) : **lus·ter**
lutenant : **lieu·ten·ant**
luxeriant : **lux·u·ri·ant**
luxerry : **lux·u·ry**
luxery : **lux·u·ry**
luxiry : **lux·u·ry**
luxureant : **lux·u·ri·ant**
lux·u·ri·ant
luxurient : **lux·u·ri·ant**

lux·u·ry
lying (act of reclining); **lay·ing** (act of putting down)
lymph

lynx
lyre (stringed instrument); **li·ar** (teller of lies)

M

macab : **ma•ca•bre**
macaber : **ma•ca•bre**
ma•ca•bre
macah : **ma•caw**
macanic : **me•chan•ic**
macanical : **me•chan•i•cal**
macannic : **me•chan•ic**
macannical : **me•chan•i•cal**
macaroney : **mac•a•ro•ni**
mac•a•ro•ni
macarony : **mac•a•ro•ni**
ma•caw
maccaroni : **mac•a•ro•ni**
machanic : **me•chan•ic**
machanical : **me•chan•i•cal**
macharel : **mack•er•el**
macharell : **mack•er•el**
macharil : **mack•er•el**
ma•chete
machetey : **ma•chete**
machetie : **ma•chete**
machette : **ma•chete**
machettie : **ma•chete**
machinary : **ma•chin•ery**
ma•chine
machinerry : **ma•chin•ery**
ma•chin•ery
macironi : **mac•a•ro•ni**
mackarel : **mack•er•el**
mackaroni : **mac•a•ro•ni**
mackeral : **mack•er•el**
mack•er•el
mackiral : **mack•er•el**
macob : **ma•ca•bre**
Mad•a•gas•car
Madagascer : **Mad•a•gas•car**
Madagaskar : **Mad•a•gas•car**
madamoiselle : **mad•e•moi•selle**
madamozel : **mad•e•moi•selle**
Maddagascar : **Mad•a•gas•car**

mademaselle : **ma•de•moi•selle**
mademoisell : **ma•de•moi•selle**
ma•de•moi•selle
mademoizelle : **ma•de•moi•selle**
mademoselle : **ma•de•moi•selle**
madragal : **mad•ri•gal**
madregal : **mad•ri•gal**
mad•ri•gal
madrigall : **mad•ri•gal**
madrigle : **mad•ri•gal**
maelstorm : **mael•strom**
mael•strom
maelstrum : **mael•strom**
mae•stro
magasine : **mag•a•zine**
magazean : **mag•a•zine**
magazene : **mag•a•zine**
mag•a•zine
magec : **mag•ic**
ma•gen•ta
magesstic : **ma•jes•tic**
magestic : **ma•jes•tic**
magestrate : **mag•is•trate**
magesty : **maj•es•ty**
magezine : **mag•a•zine**
maggazine : **mag•a•zine**
magget : **mag•got**
maggistrate : **mag•is•trate**
maggit : **mag•got**
mag•got
maggut : **mag•got**
mag•ic
magichian : **ma•gi•cian**
ma•gi•cian
magicion : **ma•gi•cian**
magick : **mag•ic**
maginta : **ma•gen•ta**
mag•is•trate
magizine : **mag•a•zine**
magnafy : **mag•ni•fy**

189

magnanamous :
   mag·nan·i·mous
magnanemous :
   mag·nan·i·mous
mag·nan·i·mous
magnanimus : **mag·nan·i·mous**
magnannimous :
   mag·nan·i·mous
mag·nate (important person);
   mag·net (something with
   attractive force)
magnatude : **mag·ni·tude**
magnefy : **mag·ni·fy**
mag·net (something with
   attractive force); **mag·nate**
   (important person)
mag·net·ic
magnettic : **mag·net·ic**
magnetude : **mag·ni·tude**
magnify : **mag·ni·fy**
mag·ni·fy
magnitood : **mag·ni·tude**
mag·ni·tude
magnoalia : **mag·no·lia**
mag·no·lia
magnollia : **mag·no·lia**
magnolya : **mag·no·lia**
magot : **mag·got**
ma·ha·ra·ja *or* **ma·ha·ra·jah**
ma·ha·ra·jah *or* **ma·ha·ra·ja**
maharasha : **ma·ha·ra·ja**
maharoja : **ma·ha·ra·ja**
mahoganie : **ma·hog·a·ny**
ma·hog·a·ny
mahogeny : **ma·hog·a·ny**
mahoggany : **ma·hog·a·ny**
mahogginy : **ma·hog·a·ny**
mahoginy : **ma·hog·a·ny**
mailstrom : **mael·strom**
main (primary); **Maine** (state);
   mane (hair)

Maine (state); **main** (primary);
   mane (hair)
mainia : **ma·nia**
maintainence : **main·te·nance**
main·te·nance
maintenanse : **main·te·nance**
maintenence : **main·te·nance**
maintenense : **main·te·nance**
maintennance : **main·te·nance**
maintinance : **main·te·nance**
maintinence : **main·te·nance**
maistro : **mae·stro**
maitenance : **main·te·nance**
maize (corn); **maze** (labyrinth)
majaraja : **ma·ha·ra·ja**
majenta : **ma·gen·ta**
majessty : **maj·es·ty**
ma·jes·tic
majestick : **ma·jes·tic**
maj·es·ty
majorety : **ma·jor·i·ty**
majoritty : **ma·jor·i·ty**
ma·jor·i·ty
majorrity : **ma·jor·i·ty**
mal·a·dy
mal·aise
malaize : **mal·aise**
malard : **mal·lard**
malarea : **ma·lar·ia**
ma·lar·ia
malase : **mal·aise**
malaze : **mal·aise**
maleable : **mal·lea·ble**
maledy : **mal·a·dy**
malerd : **mal·lard**
maleria : **ma·lar·ia**
malestrom : **mael·strom**
malet : **mal·let**
malevalent : **ma·lev·o·lent**
malevelent : **ma·lev·o·lent**
ma·lev·o·lent
malevolint : **ma·lev·o·lent**

mal·fea·sance
malfeasanse : **mal·fea·sance**
malfeasence : **mal·fea·sance**
malfeasense : **mal·fea·sance**
malfeasince : **mal·fea·sance**
malfeazance : **mal·fea·sance**
malfeesance : **mal·fea·sance**
malfisance : **mal·fea·sance**
mal·ice
malidy : **mal·a·dy**
ma·lign
ma·lig·nant
malignent : **ma·lig·nant**
malignint : **ma·lig·nant**
malird : **mal·lard**
malise : **mal·ice**
maliss : **mal·ice**
mallady : **mal·a·dy**
mallaise : **mal·aise**
mal·lard
mallaria : **ma·lar·ia**
mallarria : **ma·lar·ia**
mallat : **mal·let**
malleabal : **mal·lea·ble**
mal·lea·ble
mallerd : **mal·lard**
malleria : **ma·lar·ia**
mal·let
malliable : **mal·lea·ble**
mallible : **mal·lea·ble**
mallice : **mal·ice**
mallign : **ma·lign**
mallignant : **ma·lig·nant**
mallird : **mal·lard**
mallit : **mal·let**
mallovolent : **ma·lev·o·lent**
mallyable : **mal·lea·ble**
malody : **mal·a·dy**
malstrom : **mael·strom**
mamal : **mam·mal**
mamel : **mam·mal**

mameth : **mam·moth**
mamil : **mam·mal**
mamith : **mam·moth**
mam·mal
mammel : **mam·mal**
mammeth : **mam·moth**
mammil : **mam·mal**
mammith : **mam·moth**
mam·moth
mamoth : **mam·moth**
man·a·cle
manacure : **man·i·cure**
manafest : **man·i·fest**
manafesto : **man·i·fes·to**
manafold : **man·i·fold**
man·age
manageabal : **man·age·able**
man·age·able
managible : **man·age·able**
manakin : **man·i·kin** (little
    man) *or* **man·ne·quin**
    (model)
mandalen : **man·do·lin**
mandalin : **man·do·lin**
mandatorry : **man·da·to·ry**
man·da·to·ry
mandelin : **man·do·lin**
mandetory : **man·da·to·ry**
mandilin : **man·do·lin**
manditory : **man·da·to·ry**
man·do·lin
mane (hair); **main** (primary);
    Maine (state)
manea : **ma·nia**
maneac : **ma·ni·ac**
manecle : **man·a·cle**
manecure : **man·i·cure**
manefest : **man·i·fest**
manefesto : **man·i·fes·to**
manefold : **man·i·fold**
manege : **man·age**

manekin : **man·i·kin** (little man) or **man·ne·quin** (model)

manequin : **man·i·kin** (little man) or **man·ne·quin** (model)

ma·neu·ver

Manhatan : **Man·hat·tan**

Manhaten : **Man·hat·tan**

Man·hat·tan

Manhatten : **Man·hat·tan**

Manhattin : **Man·hat·tan**

ma·nia

ma·ni·ac

maniack : **ma·ni·ac**

manicle : **man·a·cle**

man·i·cure

man·i·fest

man·i·fes·to

man·i·fold

manige : **man·age**

man·i·kin or **man·ni·kin** (little man); **man·ne·quin** (model)

Ma·nila

Manilla : **Ma·nila**

man·li·ness

manlynes : **man·li·ness**

mannacle : **man·a·cle**

mannafest : **man·i·fest**

mannafesto : **man·i·fes·to**

mannage : **man·age**

mannageable : **man·age·able**

mannaquin : **man·i·kin** (little man) or **man·ne·quin** (model)

mannefest : **man·i·fest**

mannefesto : **man·i·fes·to**

mannekin : **man·i·kin** (little man) or **man·ne·quin** (model)

man·ne·quin (model); **man·i·kin** (little man)

man·ner (a way of doing); **man·or** (estate)

manneuver : **ma·neu·ver**

mannia : **ma·nia**

manniac : **ma·ni·ac**

mannical : **man·a·cle**

mannicure : **man·i·cure**

mannifest : **man·i·fest**

mannifesto : **man·i·fes·to**

man·ni·kin or **man·i·kin** (little man); **man·ne·quin** (model)

Mannila : **Ma·nila**

mannual : **man·u·al**

mannure : **ma·nure**

manny : **many**

manoor : **ma·nure**

manoor : **ma·nure**

manoover : **ma·neu·ver**

man·or (estate); **man·ner** (a way of doing)

mantal : **man·tel** (shelf) or **man·tle** (cape)

man·tel (shelf); **man·tle** (cape)

mantil : **man·tel** (shelf) or **man·tle** (cape)

mantill : **man·tel** (shelf) or **man·tle** (cape)

man·tis

man·tle (cape); **man·tel** (shelf)

mantus : **man·tis**

man·u·al

manuer : **ma·nure**

manuever : **ma·neu·ver**

manule : **man·u·al**

ma·nure

manuver : **ma·neu·ver**

many

manyfold : **man·i·fold**

maraner : **mar·i·ner**

maratal : **mar·i·tal**

mar·a·thon

ma·raud·er

marawder : **ma·raud·er**
marbal : **mar·ble**
marbel : **mar·ble**
marbil : **mar·ble**
marbile : **mar·ble**
mar·ble
mareen : **ma·rine**
marene : **ma·rine**
marener : **mar·i·ner**
maretal : **mar·i·tal**
marethon : **mar·a·thon**
margaren : **mar·ga·rine**
margarene : **mar·ga·rine**
margarin : **mar·ga·rine**
mar·ga·rine
margenal : **mar·gin·al**
margeren : **mar·ga·rine**
margerene : **mar·ga·rine**
margerin : **mar·ga·rine**
margerine : **mar·ga·rine**
mar·gin·al
marginel : **mar·gin·al**
marginnal : **mar·gin·al**
mariage : **mar·riage**
marige : **mar·riage**
mari·gold
Mariland : **Mary·land**
ma·rine
mar·i·ner
marinner : **mar·i·ner**
mar·i·tal
maritel : **mar·i·tal**
marithon : **mar·a·thon**
mar·ket·able
marketibal : **mar·ket·able**
marketible : **mar·ket·able**
markitable : **mar·ket·able**
mar·lin (fish); **mar·line** (cord)
mar·line (cord); **mar·lin** (fish)
mar·ma·lade
marmalaid : **mar·ma·lade**
marmelade : **mar·ma·lade**

marmelaid : **mar·ma·lade**
marmilade : **mar·ma·lade**
marmolade : **mar·ma·lade**
marmolaid : **mar·ma·lade**
marodder : **ma·raud·er**
ma·roon
marrage : **mar·riage**
marratal : **mar·i·tal**
marrathon : **mar·a·thon**
marrauder : **ma·raud·er**
marrege : **mar·riage**
mar·riage
marrige : **mar·riage**
marrine : **ma·rine**
marriner : **mar·i·ner**
marrital : **mar·i·tal**
marroon : **ma·roon**
marrune : **ma·roon**
marryage : **mar·riage**
Marryland : **Mary·land**
marrytal : **mar·i·tal**
Marsailles : **Mar·seilles**
Marsay : **Mar·seilles**
Mar·seilles
Marselles : **Mar·seilles**
Marsey : **Mar·seilles**
mar·shal (leader of military or
    police force); **mar·tial**
    (pertaining to war or
    combat)
marshall : **mar·shal** (leader of
    military or police force) *or*
    mar·tial (pertaining to war
    or combat)
marsh·mal·low
marshmellow : **marsh·mal·low**
marsoopial : **mar·su·pi·al**
marsupeal : **mar·su·pi·al**
mar·su·pi·al
martar : **mar·tyr**
marteeni : **mar·ti·ni**
marter : **mar·tyr**

mar·tial (pertaining to war or combat); **mar·shal** (leader of military or police force)
mar·ti·ni
martiny : **mar·ti·ni**
martir : **mar·tyr**
martor : **mar·tyr**
mar·tyr
marune : **ma·roon**
marvalous : **mar·vel·ous**
mar·vel
marvell : **mar·vel**
mar·vel·lous *or* **mar·vel·ous**
mar·vel·ous *or* **mar·vel·lous**
marvelus : **mar·vel·ous**
marvle : **mar·vel**
marygold : **mari·gold**
Mary·land
marytal : **mar·i·tal**
Masachusetts : **Mas·sa·chu·setts**
masacre : **mas·sa·cre**
mascaline : **mas·cu·line**
mas·cara
mascarra : **mas·cara**
masceline : **mas·cu·line**
mas·cot
mascott : **mas·cot**
masculen : **mas·cu·line**
masculin : **mas·cu·line**
mas·cu·line
mashean : **ma·chine**
masheenery : **ma·chin·ery**
mashete : **ma·chete**
mashette : **ma·chete**
mashine : **ma·chine**
mashinery : **ma·chin·ery**
maskara : **mas·cara**
maskarade : **mas·quer·ade**
maskarra : **mas·cara**
maskerade : **mas·quer·ade**
maskott : **mas·cot**

maskulen : **mas·cu·line**
maskuline : **mas·cu·line**
mas·och·ism
masokism : **mas·och·ism**
ma·son
mas·quer·ade
masquirade : **mas·quer·ade**
massacer : **mas·sa·cre**
Massachoosetts : **Mas·sa·chu·setts**
Mas·sa·chu·setts
Massachusitts : **Mas·sa·chu·setts**
mas·sa·cre
massecre : **mas·sa·cre**
Massichusetts : **Mas·sa·chu·setts**
massochism : **mas·och·ism**
masson : **ma·son**
masstoddon : **mast·odon**
mastadon : **mast·odon**
mastedon : **mast·odon**
masterpeace : **mas·ter·piece**
masterpeece : **mas·ter·piece**
masterpeice : **mas·ter·piece**
mas·ter·piece
mas·tery
mastidon : **mast·odon**
mast·odon
mastodont : **mast·odon**
mastry : **mas·tery**
matadoor : **mat·a·dor**
mat·a·dor
matanee : **mat·i·nee**
matearial : **ma·te·ri·al** (matter) *or* **ma·té·ri·el** (military equipment)
matedor : **mat·a·dor**
mateirial : **ma·te·ri·al** (matter) *or* **ma·té·ri·el** (military equipment)
matenance : **main·te·nance**

matenee : **mat·i·nee**
ma·te·ri·al (matter);
   ma·té·ri·el (military
   equipment)
ma·té·ri·el or **ma·te·ri·el**
   (military equipment);
   ma·te·ri·al (matter)
ma·ter·nal
maternel : **ma·ter·nal**
maternety : **ma·ter·ni·ty**
maternity : **ma·ter·ni·ty**
ma·ter·ni·ty
mathamatics : **math·e·mat·ics**
mathematicks : **math·e·mat·ics**
math·e·mat·ics
mathemattics : **math·e·mat·ics**
mathimathics : **math·e·mat·ics**
mathmatics : **math·e·mat·ics**
matidor : **mat·a·dor**
matinay : **mat·i·nee**
mat·i·nee or **mat·i·née**
matiney : **mat·i·nee**
matramony : **mat·ri·mo·ny**
matremony : **mat·ri·mo·ny**
matress : **mat·tress**
matriarc : **ma·tri·arch**
ma·tri·arch
matrimoney : **mat·ri·mo·ny**
mat·ri·mo·ny
matriss : **mat·tress**
mattador : **mat·a·dor**
matterial : **ma·te·ri·al** (matter)
   or **ma·té·ri·el** (military
   equipment)
matternal : **ma·ter·nal**
mattinee : **mat·i·nee**
mat·tress
mattriss : **mat·tress**
maturety : **ma·tu·ri·ty**
maturitty : **ma·tu·ri·ty**
ma·tu·ri·ty
maturnal : **ma·ter·nal**

maturnity : **ma·ter·ni·ty**
maudlen : **maud·lin**
maud·lin
mausaleum : **mau·so·le·um**
mau·so·le·um
mausoliem : **mau·so·le·um**
mausolium : **mau·so·le·um**
mauzoleum : **mau·so·le·um**
mavarick : **mav·er·ick**
mav·er·ick
mawdlin : **maud·lin**
maxamum : **max·i·mum**
maxem : **max·im**
maxemum : **max·i·mum**
max·im
maximem : **max·i·mum**
max·i·mum
maxum : **max·im**
mayennaise : **may·on·naise**
mayer : **may·or**
may·hem
mayhim : **may·hem**
mayinnaise : **may·on·naise**
maynaise : **may·on·naise**
mayonaise : **may·on·naise**
mayonaize : **may·on·naise**
may·on·naise
mayonnase : **may·on·naise**
may·or
maze (labyrinth); **maize** (corn)
mazerka : **ma·zur·ka**
mazochism : **mas·och·ism**
ma·zur·ka
meadian : **me·di·an**
meadiate : **me·di·ate**
meadiocre : **me·di·o·cre**
mead·ow
mea·ger
meagre : **mea·ger**
meanial : **me·nial**
meant
measels : **mea·sles**

mea·sles
measley : **mea·sly**
mea·sly
meastro : **mae·stro**
mea·sure
meazels : **mea·sles**
meazles : **mea·sles**
mecabre : **ma·ca·bre**
me·chan·ic
mechanick : **me·chan·ic**
mechannic : **me·chan·ic**
mechannical : **me·chan·i·cal**
medacal : **med·i·cal**
medacate : **med·i·cate**
medaeval : **me·di·eval**
medal (decoration); **med·dle** (to interfere); **met·tle** (spirit)
medalion : **me·dal·lion**
medallian : **me·dal·lion**
me·dal·lion
medatate : **med·i·tate**
medatation : **med·i·ta·tion**
meddeval : **me·di·eval**
meddevil : **me·di·eval**
meddic : **med·ic**
meddical : **med·i·cal**
meddicate : **med·i·cate**
meddicinal : **me·dic·i·nal**
medditate : **med·i·tate**
medditation : **med·i·ta·tion**
Meddditerranean : **Med·i·ter·ra·nean**
med·dle (to interfere); **med·al** (decoration); **met·tle** (spirit)
med·dler (one who meddles); **med·lar** (tree)
meddley : **med·ley**
meddow : **mead·ow**
medeate : **me·di·ate**
medecate : **med·i·cate**
medeival : **me·di·eval**
medetate : **med·i·tate**

medetation : **med·i·ta·tion**
Medeterranean : **Med·i·ter·ra·nean**
medeval : **me·di·eval**
mediacrity : **me·di·oc·ri·ty**
me·di·ae·val or **me·di·eval**
mediam : **me·di·um**
me·di·an
me·di·ate
med·ic
med·i·cal
med·i·cate
medicen : **med·i·cine**
medicenal : **me·dic·i·nal**
medicin : **med·i·cine**
me·dic·i·nal
med·i·cine
medicinel : **me·dic·i·nal**
medick : **med·ic**
medicle : **med·i·cal**
mediem : **me·di·um**
medien : **me·di·an**
me·di·eval or **me·di·ae·val**
medievel : **me·di·eval**
mediocer : **me·di·o·cre**
mediocraty : **me·di·oc·ri·ty**
me·di·o·cre
mediocrety : **me·di·oc·ri·ty**
mediocritty : **me·di·oc·ri·ty**
me·di·oc·ri·ty
medioker : **me·di·o·cre**
medisinal : **me·dic·i·nal**
medissinal : **me·dic·i·nal**
meditacion : **med·i·ta·tion**
meditait : **med·i·tate**
meditashion : **med·i·ta·tion**
med·i·tate
meditatian : **med·i·ta·tion**
Mediteranean : **Med·i·ter·ra·nean**
Mediterrainian : **Med·i·ter·ra·nean**

Med·i·ter·ra·nean
Mediterranian :
   Med·i·ter·ra·nean
me·di·um
medival : **me·di·eval**
med·lar (tree); **med·dler** (one
  who meddles)
med·ley
medlie : **med·ley**
medly : **med·ley**
medow : **mead·ow**
meedian : **me·di·an**
meediate : **me·di·ate**
meediocre : **me·di·o·cre**
meedium : **me·di·um**
meeger : **mea·ger**
meer : **mere** (nothing more
  than) *or* **mir·ror** (glass)
meesles : **mea·sles**
meesly : **mea·sly**
meger : **mea·ger**
meidian : **me·di·an**
meiger : **mea·ger**
meinial : **me·nial**
meladrama : **melo·dra·ma**
melady : **mel·o·dy**
melaise : **mal·aise**
melan : **mel·on**
melanchaly : **mel·an·choly**
mel·an·choly
melancolly : **mel·an·choly**
melancoly : **mel·an·choly**
mé·lange
melay : **me·lee**
me·lee
melencholy : **mel·an·choly**
melidy : **mel·o·dy**
melincholy : **mel·an·choly**
mellady : **mel·o·dy**
mellan : **mel·on**
mellancholy : **mel·an·choly**
mellange : **mé·lange**

mellencholy : **mel·an·choly**
mellidy : **mel·o·dy**
mellincholy : **mel·an·choly**
mellodrama : **melo·dra·ma**
mellody : **mel·o·dy**
mellon : **mel·on**
mel·low
mellowdrama : **melo·dra·ma**
melo·dra·ma
melodramma : **melo·dra·ma**
mel·o·dy
mel·on
melonge : **mé·lange**
melow : **mel·low**
memarabilia : **mem·o·ra·bil·ia**
memarable : **mem·o·ra·ble**
memarize : **mem·o·rize**
memary : **mem·o·ry**
membrain : **mem·brane**
mem·brane
me·men·to
Memfis : **Mem·phis**
meminto : **me·men·to**
memior : **mem·oir**
memiry : **mem·o·ry**
memmento : **me·men·to**
memmoir : **mem·oir**
memmorabilia :
  mem·o·ra·bil·ia
memmorable : **mem·o·ra·ble**
memmorial : **me·mo·ri·al**
memmorize : **mem·o·rize**
memmory : **mem·o·ry**
mem·oir
memorabeelia : **mem·o·ra·bil·ia**
mem·o·ra·bil·ia
memorabillia : **mem·o·ra·bil·ia**
mem·o·ra·ble
memoreal : **me·mo·ri·al**
memoreble : **mem·o·ra·ble**
me·mo·ri·al
memoribal : **mem·o·ra·ble**

memoribilia : **mem·o·ra·bil·ia**
memorible : **mem·o·ra·ble**
memorise (*Brit.*) : **mem·o·rize**
mem·o·rize
memorrial : **me·mo·ri·al**
mem·o·ry
memorybilia : **mem·o·ra·bil·ia**
Mem·phis
Memphiss : **Mem·phis**
Memphus : **Mem·phis**
men·ace
me·nag·er·ie
menagerrie : **me·nag·er·ie**
menagery : **me·nag·er·ie**
menagirie : **me·nag·er·ie**
menajerie : **me·nag·er·ie**
menapause : **men·o·pause**
mendacety : **men·dac·i·ty**
mendacitty : **men·dac·i·ty**
men·dac·i·ty
mendasity : **men·dac·i·ty**
mendassity : **men·dac·i·ty**
meneal : **me·nial**
meneral : **min·er·al**
meneret : **min·a·ret**
me·nial
menice : **men·ace**
meniss : **men·ace**
menistrone : **min·e·stro·ne**
mennace : **men·ace**
mennagerie : **me·nag·er·ie**
menneret : **min·a·ret**
mennice : **men·ace**
mennopause : **men·o·pause**
mennow : **min·now**
men·o·pause
Menphis : **Mem·phis**
ment : **meant**
men·tal
mentalety : **men·tal·i·ty**
mentalitty : **men·tal·i·ty**
men·tal·i·ty

mentallity : **men·tal·i·ty**
mentel : **men·tal**
menter : **men·tor**
menthal : **men·thol**
menthall : **men·thol**
men·thol
mentholl : **men·thol**
men·tor
merage : **mi·rage**
merangue : **me·ringue**
mercary : **mer·cu·ry**
mer·ce·nary
mercenery : **mer·ce·nary**
mercerial : **mer·cu·ri·al**
merchandice : **mer·chan·dise**
mer·chan·dise
mer·chant
merchantdise : **mer·chan·dise**
merchendise : **mer·chan·dise**
merchent : **mer·chant**
merchindise : **mer·chan·dise**
merchint : **mer·chant**
mer·ci·ful
mercifull : **mer·ci·ful**
mercinary : **mer·ce·nary**
mercureal : **mer·cu·ri·al**
mer·cu·ri·al
mer·cu·ry
mer·cy
mercyful : **mer·ci·ful**
mere (nothing more than);
    mir·ror (glass)
merecle : **mir·a·cle**
meremaid : **mer·maid**
meret : **mer·it**
merg·er
meriad : **myr·i·ad**
meriddian : **me·rid·i·an**
me·rid·i·an
meridien : **me·rid·i·an**
meringe : **me·ringue**
me·ringue

mer·it
merky : **murky**
mermade : **mer·maid**
mer·maid
mermer : **mur·mur**
mermur : **mur·mur**
merrangue : **me·ringue**
merridian : **me·rid·i·an**
mer·ri·ly
mer·ri·ment
merringue : **me·ringue**
merrit : **mer·it**
merryment : **mer·ri·ment**
mersenary : **mer·ce·nary**
mersiful : **mer·ci·ful**
mersinary : **mer·ce·nary**
mersy : **mer·cy**
merth : **mirth**
me·sa
mesage : **mes·sage**
mesiah : **mes·si·ah**
meskeet : **mes·quite**
mes·mer·ism
mesmirism : **mes·mer·ism**
mesmurism : **mes·mer·ism**
mesquete : **mes·quite**
mes·quite
messa : **me·sa**
mes·sage
messege : **mes·sage**
messia : **mes·si·ah**
mes·si·ah
messige : **mes·sage**
messmerism : **mes·mer·ism**
messquite : **mes·quite**
messure : **mea·sure**
mesure : **mea·sure**
metabalism : **me·tab·o·lism**
metabelism : **me·tab·o·lism**
metablism : **me·tab·o·lism**
me·tab·o·lism
metafor : **met·a·phor**

metallergy : **me·tal·lur·gy**
me·tal·lur·gy
metalurgy : **me·tal·lur·gy**
metamorfosis :
    meta·mor·pho·sis
metamorphasis :
    meta·mor·pho·sis
metamorphisis :
    meta·mor·pho·sis
meta·mor·pho·sis
met·a·phor
metaphore : **met·a·phor**
me·te·or
meteorallogy : **me·te·o·rol·o·gy**
meteoralogy : **me·te·o·rol·o·gy**
meteorollogy : **me·te·o·rol·o·gy**
me·te·o·rol·o·gy
me·ter
methain : **meth·ane**
methal : **meth·yl**
meth·ane
methel : **meth·yl**
methil : **meth·yl**
meth·yl
metickulous : **me·tic·u·lous**
me·tic·u·lous
meticulus : **me·tic·u·lous**
metifor : **met·a·phor**
metior : **me·te·or**
metiorology : **me·te·o·rol·o·gy**
metiphor : **met·a·phor**
metir : **me·ter**
metre (*Brit.*) : **me·ter**
met·ric
metrick : **met·ric**
metropalis : **me·trop·o·lis**
metropolice : **me·trop·o·lis**
me·trop·o·lis
metropoliss : **me·trop·o·lis**
mettabolism : **me·tab·o·lism**
mettaphor : **met·a·phor**
metticulous : **me·tic·u·lous**

met·tle (spirit); med·al (decoration); med·dle (to interfere)

mettric : met·ric

mettropolis : me·trop·o·lis

Mexaco : Mex·i·co

Mex·i·co

mezmerism : mes·mer·ism

Mi·ami

Miammi : Mi·ami

Miamy : Mi·ami

Michagan : Mich·i·gan

Michegan : Mich·i·gan

Mich·i·gan

micraphone : mi·cro·phone

microcosem : mi·cro·cosm

microcosim : mi·cro·cosm

mi·cro·cosm

microcossm : mi·cro·cosm

microcozm : mi·cro·cosm

mi·cro·phone

midaeval : me·di·eval

middal : mid·dle

middel : mid·dle

mid·dle

midg·et

midgit : midg·et

midieval : me·di·eval

Miditerranean : Med·i·ter·ra·nean

midle : mid·dle

miestro : mae·stro

mighty

migrain : mi·graine

mi·graine

migrane : mi·graine

mi·grant

migratery : mi·gra·to·ry

migratorry : mi·gra·to·ry

mi·gra·to·ry

migrent : mi·grant

migretory : mi·gra·to·ry

migritory : mi·gra·to·ry

milage : mile·age

milameter : mil·li·met·er

milatant : mil·i·tant

milatary : mil·i·tary

mile·age

mileau : mi·lieu

milege : mile·age

milenium : mil·len·ni·um

milennium : mil·len·ni·um

miletant : mil·i·tant

miletary : mil·i·tary

miliage : mile·age

milicia : mi·li·tia

mi·lieu

milimeter : mil·li·me·ter

milionaire : mil·lion·aire

miliou : mi·lieu

milisha : mi·li·tia

mil·i·tant

militarry : mil·i·tary

mil·i·tary

militent : mil·i·tant

militery : mil·i·tary

mi·li·tia

milleniem : mil·len·ni·um

mil·len·ni·um

millieu : mi·lieu

mil·li·me·ter

millimetre (Brit.) : mil·li·me·ter

millinnium : mil·len·ni·um

millionair : mil·lion·aire

mil·lion·aire

millionare : mil·lion·aire

millionnaire : mil·lion·aire

millitant : mil·i·tant

millitary : mil·i·tary

millitia : mi·li·tia

Millwaukee : Mil·wau·kee

Millwauky : Mil·wau·kee

Milwakee : Mil·wau·kee

Mil·wau·kee

Milwuakee : **Mil·wau·kee**
mim·ic
mimick : **mim·ic**
mimickery : **mim·ic·ry**
mim·ic·ry
mimmic : **mim·ic**
mimmicry : **mim·ic·ry**
mimmosa : **mi·mo·sa**
mi·mo·sa
minace : **men·ace**
minagerie : **me·nag·er·ie**
minamum : **min·i·mum**
minarel : **min·er·al**
min·a·ret
minarette : **min·a·ret**
Minasota : **Min·ne·so·ta**
minastrone : **min·e·stro·ne**
minature : **min·ia·ture**
Mineapolis : **Min·ne·ap·o·lis**
minemum : **min·i·mum**
min·er (mine worker); **min·or**
    (not major)
min·er·al
min·er·al·o·gy
minerel : **min·er·al**
mineret : **min·a·ret**
minerollogy : **min·er·al·o·gy**
minerology : **min·er·al·o·gy**
Minesota : **Min·ne·so·ta**
minester : **min·is·ter**
min·e·stro·ne
minestroni : **min·e·stro·ne**
minestrony : **min·e·stro·ne**
min·ia·ture
minimem : **min·i·mum**
min·i·mum
miniret : **min·a·ret**
min·is·ter
ministrone : **min·e·stro·ne**
miniture : **min·ia·ture**
minnace : **men·ace**
minnaret : **min·a·ret**

Minnasota : **Min·ne·so·ta**
Min·ne·ap·o·lis
Minneapolus : **Min·ne·ap·o·lis**
minneral : **min·er·al**
minneret : **min·a·ret**
Minnesoda : **Min·ne·so·ta**
Min·ne·so·ta
Minniapolis : **Min·ne·ap·o·lis**
minniature : **min·ia·ture**
minnimum : **min·i·mum**
Minnisota : **Min·ne·so·ta**
minnister : **min·is·ter**
min·now
min·or (not major); **min·er**
    (mine worker)
minstral : **min·strel**
min·strel
minstrell : **min·strel**
minstril : **min·strel**
minthol : **men·thol**
miopic : **my·o·pic**
mioppic : **my·o·pic**
mir·a·cle
mir·age
mircenary : **mer·ce·nary**
mirchandise : **mer·chan·dise**
mirchant : **mer·chant**
mirciful : **mer·ci·ful**
mircurial : **mer·cu·ri·al**
mircury : **mer·cu·ry**
mirecle : **mir·a·cle**
mirger : **merg·er**
miriad : **myr·i·ad**
mirical : **mir·a·cle**
miricle : **mir·a·cle**
mirky : **murky**
mirmaid : **mer·maid**
mirmur : **mur·mur**
miror : **mir·ror**
mirracle : **mir·a·cle**
mirrage : **mi·rage**
mirrer : **mir·ror**

mirrh : **mir·ror** (glass) *or*
  myrrh (perfume)
mir·ror
mirth
misanthroape : **mis·an·thrope**
mis·an·thrope
misarable : **mis·er·a·ble**
misary : **mis·ery**
miscelaneous : **mis·cel·la·neous**
mis·cel·la·neous
miscellanious : **mis·cel·la·neous**
mischeff : **mis·chief**
mischeif : **mis·chief**
mischeivous : **mis·chie·vous**
mis·chief
mischiefous : **mis·chie·vous**
mischievious : **mis·chie·vous**
mis·chie·vous
mischiff : **mis·chief**
mischiffous : **mis·chie·vous**
misdameanor : **mis·de·mean·or**
misdemeaner : **mis·de·mean·or**
mis·de·mean·or
misdemeenor : **mis·de·mean·or**
misdemenor : **mis·de·mean·or**
misdimeanor : **mis·de·mean·or**
miselanious : **mis·cel·la·neous**
misellaneous : **mis·cel·la·neous**
misenthrope : **mis·an·thrope**
mis·er·a·ble
miserble : **mis·er·a·ble**
miserible : **mis·er·a·ble**
mis·ery
Mishigan : **Mich·i·gan**
misinanthrope : **mis·an·thrope**
misionary : **mis·sion·ary**
Misissippi : **Mis·sis·sip·pi**
misle : **mis·sal** (prayerbook) *or*
  mis·sile (projectile)
misogenist : **mi·sog·y·nist**
misoginist : **mi·sog·y·nist**
mi·sog·y·nist

misogynnist : **mi·sog·y·nist**
misojinist : **mi·sog·y·nist**
Misouri : **Mis·sou·ri**
mispell : **mis·spell**
mis·sal (prayerbook); **mis·sile**
  (projectile)
missel : **mis·sal** (prayerbook) *or*
  mis·sile (projectile)
misseltoe : **mis·tle·toe**
misserable : **mis·er·a·ble**
missery : **mis·ery**
missiah : **mes·si·ah**
mis·sile (projectile); **mis·sal**
  (prayerbook)
mis·sion·ary
missionery : **mis·sion·ary**
Missisipi : **Mis·sis·sip·pi**
Mississipi : **Mis·sis·sip·pi**
Mis·sis·sip·pi
missle : **mis·sal** (prayerbook) *or*
  mis·sile (projectile)
missletoe : **mis·tle·toe**
mis·spell
Mis·sou·ri
misstress : **mis·tress**
Missuri : **Mis·sou·ri**
mistery : **mys·tery**
mistic : **mys·tic**
misticism : **mys·ti·cism**
mis·tle·toe
mistletow : **mis·tle·toe**
mis·tress
mithical : **myth·i·cal**
mithology : **my·thol·o·gy**
mity : **mighty**
mizery : **mis·ery**
mne·mon·ic
mnemonnic : **mne·mon·ic**
mneumonic : **mne·mon·ic**
mnimonic : **mne·mon·ic**
moaring : **moor·ing**
mobil : **mo·bile**

mo·bile
mobilety : **mo·bil·i·ty**
mo·bil·i·ty
mobillity : **mo·bil·i·ty**
moble : **mo·bile**
moccasen : **moc·ca·sin**
moc·ca·sin
moccason : **moc·ca·sin**
mockasin : **moc·ca·sin**
modafy : **mod·i·fy**
modarate : **mod·er·ate**
moddel : **mod·el**
modderate : **mod·er·ate**
moddern : **mod·ern**
moddest : **mod·est**
moddify : **mod·i·fy**
moddist : **mod·est**
moddle : **mod·el**
modefy : **mod·i·fy**
mod·el
mod·er·ate
moderet : **mod·er·ate**
mod·ern
mod·est
modiffy : **mod·i·fy**
mod·i·fy
modirn : **mod·ern**
modist : **mod·est**
modle : **mod·el**
mogal : **mo·gul**
mogel : **mo·gul**
mogle : **mo·gul**
mo·gul
mogule : **mo·gul**
molacule : **mol·e·cule**
molaculer : **mo·lec·u·lar**
mo·lar
mo·lec·u·lar
mol·e·cule
molequle : **mol·e·cule**
moler : **mo·lar**
molify : **mol·li·fy**

mollafy : **mol·li·fy**
mollecular : **mo·lec·u·lar**
mollecule : **mol·e·cule**
mollefy : **mol·li·fy**
mollesk : **mol·lusk**
mol·li·fy
mol·lusk
molusk : **mol·lusk**
momento : **me·men·to**
monalog : **mon·o·logue**
monapoly : **mo·nop·o·ly**
mon·ar·chy
monarky : **mon·ar·chy**
monastary : **mon·as·tery**
monasterry : **mon·as·tery**
mon·as·tery
monater : **mon·i·tor**
monatery : **mon·e·tary**
Mon·day
monestery : **mon·as·tery**
mon·e·tary
monetery : **mon·e·tary**
mon·ey
mon·eys *or* **mon·ies**
mon·ies *or* **mon·eys**
monitary : **mon·e·tary**
moniter : **mon·i·tor**
mon·i·tor
monnastery : **mon·as·tery**
monnitor : **mon·i·tor**
monnogamy : **mo·nog·a·my**
monnolith : **mon·o·lith**
monnolog : **mon·o·logue**
monnopoly : **mo·nop·o·ly**
Monntana : **Mon·tana**
monnument : **mon·u·ment**
monogammy : **mo·nog·a·my**
mo·nog·a·my
monogemy : **mo·nog·a·my**
monoleth : **mon·o·lith**
mon·o·lith
monolog : **mon·o·logue**

mon·o·logue
monopaly : **mo·nop·o·ly**
monoply : **mo·nop·o·ly**
mo·nop·o·ly
monsterous : **mon·strous**
monstrocity : **mon·stros·i·ty**
mon·stros·i·ty
monstrossity : **mon·stros·i·ty**
mon·strous
monstrousity : **mon·stros·i·ty**
mon·tage
Mon·tana
Montanna : **Mon·tana**
montoge : **mon·tage**
Mon·tre·al
Montreall : **Mon·tre·al**
Montrial : **Mon·tre·al**
montrosety : **mon·stros·i·ty**
mon·u·ment
mony : **mon·ey**
moor·ing
moose (elk); **mousse** (dessert)
morabund : **mor·i·bund**
mor·al (ethical; lesson);
  mo·rale (emotional state)
mo·rale (emotional state);
  mor·al (ethical; lesson)
moralety : **mo·ral·i·ty**
mo·ral·i·ty
morallity : **mo·ral·i·ty**
mo·rass
morcel : **mor·sel**
mor·dant (biting); **mor·dent**
  (Musical)
mor·dent *(Musical)*; **mor·dant**
  (biting)
morfeen : **mor·phine**
morfine : **mor·phine**
morgage : **mort·gage**
morgege : **mort·gage**
mor·i·bund
morings : **moor·ing**

Morman : **Mor·mon**
Mormen : **Mor·mon**
Mor·mon
mornful : **mourn·ful**
Mo·roc·co
Morocko : **Mo·roc·co**
Moroco : **Mo·roc·co**
morpheen : **mor·phine**
morphene : **mor·phine**
mor·phine
morrality : **mo·ral·i·ty**
morrass : **mo·rass**
morribund : **mor·i·bund**
mor·sel
morsil : **mor·sel**
morsle : **mor·sel**
mortafy : **mor·ti·fy**
mor·tal
mor·tar
mortefy : **mor·ti·fy**
mortel : **mor·tal**
morter : **mor·tar**
mort·gage
mortiffy : **mor·ti·fy**
mor·ti·fy
mortor : **mor·tar**
mor·tu·ary
mortuery : **mor·tu·ary**
mosk : **mosque**
moskeeto : **mos·qui·to**
moskito : **mos·qui·to**
Mos·lem *or* **Mus·lim**
Moslim : **Mus·lim**
mosque
mos·qui·to
mossoleum : **mau·so·le·um**
motavate : **mo·ti·vate**
moter : **mo·tor**
mo·ti·vate
mot·ley
mo·tor
mottley : **mot·ley**

moun·tain
mountan : **moun·tain**
Mountana : **Mon·ta·na**
mountian : **moun·tain**
mountin : **moun·tain**
mourn·ful
mournfull : **mourn·ful**
mouse (rodent); **mousse**
  (dessert)
mousse (dessert); **moose** (elk);
  mouse (rodent)
mov·able *or* **move·able**
move·able *or* **mov·able**
movible : **mov·able**
Mozlem : **Mus·lim**
mu·cous (*adj.*); **mu·cus** (*noun*)
mu·cus (*noun*); **mu·cous** (*adj.*)
muffen : **muf·fin**
muf·fin
multaple : **mul·ti·ple**
multaply : **mul·ti·ply**
multeple : **mul·ti·ple**
multeply : **mul·ti·ply**
multipal : **mul·ti·ple**
mul·ti·ple
mul·ti·ply
multipple : **mul·ti·ple**
mundain : **mun·dane**
mun·dane
Munday : **Mon·day**
municions : **mu·ni·tions**
mu·nic·i·pal
municiple : **mu·nic·i·pal**
munisipal : **mu·nic·i·pal**
mu·ni·tions
mu·ral
murcenary : **mer·ce·nary**
murchandise : **mer·chan·dise**
murchant : **mer·chant**
murcury : **mer·cu·ry**
murger : **merg·er**
murky

murmaid : **mer·maid**
murmer : **mur·mur**
mur·mur
murral : **mu·ral**
murrel : **mu·ral**
mursenary : **mer·ce·nary**
murth : **mirth**
mus·cle (body tissue); **mus·sel**
  (bivalve mollusk)
musecal : **mu·si·cal**
mu·se·um
mu·si·cal
mu·si·cian
musicion : **mu·si·cian**
musicle : **mu·si·cal**
musiem : **mu·se·um**
musium : **mu·se·um**
mus·ket
mus·ke·teer
musketere : **mus·ke·teer**
musketier : **mus·ke·teer**
muskit : **mus·ket**
muskiteer : **mus·ke·teer**
muslen : **mus·lin**
Mus·lim *or* **Mos·lem**
mus·lin
mus·sel (bivalve mollusk);
  mus·cle (body tissue)
mussle : **mus·cle** (body tissue)
  or **mus·sel** (bivalve mollusk)
musstard : **mus·tard**
mus·tard
musterd : **mus·tard**
mustird : **mus·tard**
mu·ta·bil·i·ty
mutabillity : **mu·ta·bil·i·ty**
mutalate : **mu·ti·late**
mutaneer : **mu·ti·neer**
mu·tant
mutany : **mu·ti·ny**
muteneer : **mu·ti·neer**
mutent : **mu·tant**

muteny : **mu·ti·ny**
mutibility : **mu·ta·bil·i·ty**
mu·ti·late
mutillate : **mu·ti·late**
mu·ti·neer
mutinere : **mu·ti·neer**
mutinier : **mu·ti·neer**
mu·ti·ny
mutten : **mut·ton**
muttin : **mut·ton**
mut·ton
muzel : **muz·zle**
muzeum : **mu·se·um**
Muzlim : **Mus·lim**
muzlin : **mus·lin**
muzzel : **muz·zle**
muz·zle
Myami: Mi·**ami**
mygraine : mi·graine

myistisism : **mys·ti·cism**
my·o·pic
myopick : **my·o·pic**
myoppic : **my·o·pic**
myr·i·ad
myrrh
mysterry : **mys·tery**
mys·tery
mys·tic
mys·ti·cism
mystick : **mys·tic**
mythacal : **myth·i·cal**
mythalogy : **my·thol·o·gy**
mythecal : **myth·i·cal**
myth·i·cal
mythicle : **myth·i·cal**
mythollogy : **my·thol·o·gy**
my·thol·o·gy

N

na·bob
nacent : na·scent
nadar : na·dir
nadeer : na·dir
nader : na·dir
na·dir
naevete : na·ive·te
naevety : na·ive·te
naibob : na·bob
naife : na·ive
naighbor : neigh·bor
naipalm : na·palm
naipam : na·palm
naipom : na·palm
Nai·ro·bi
nai·ve or na·ïve
naivetay : na·ive·te
na·ive·te or na·ive·té
naivety (Brit.) : na·ive·te
naivity : na·ive·te
na·ked
nakid : na·ked
nakked : na·ked
na·palm
napken : nap·kin
nap·kin
napom : na·palm
napsack : knap·sack
narate : nar·rate
naration : nar·ra·tion
narator : nar·ra·tor
narcisism : nar·cis·sism
nar·cis·sism
nar·cot·ic
narcotick : nar·cot·ic
narcottic : nar·cot·ic
narled : gnarled
nar·rate
narrater : nar·ra·tor
nar·ra·tion

nar·ra·tor
narrled : gnarled
narsisism : nar·cis·sism
na·sal
nasall : na·sal
na·scent
nascint : na·scent
nasea : nau·sea
nasel : na·sal
nasell : na·sal
nasent : na·scent
nash : gnash
nat : gnat
natiral : nat·u·ral
nativety : na·tiv·i·ty
nativitty : na·tiv·i·ty
na·tiv·i·ty
nattural : nat·u·ral
nat·u·ral
naturel : nat·u·ral
naturral : nat·u·ral
nau·sea
nau·se·ate
nausha : nau·sea
nausheate : nau·se·ate
naushia : nau·sea
nausia : nau·sea
nausiate : nau·se·ate
naut : knot (rope; one nautical
   mile); not (negative); nought
   (zero)
nau·ti·cal
nauticle : nau·ti·cal
nautilis : nau·ti·lus
nautillus : nau·ti·lus
nau·ti·lus
navagator : nav·i·ga·tor
Nav·a·ho or Nav·a·jo
Nav·a·jo or Nav·a·ho

na·val (of the navy); **na·vel**
   (belly button)
navegator : **nav·i·ga·tor**
Naveho : **Nav·a·ho**
na·vel (belly button); **na·val** (of
   the navy)
navigater : **nav·i·ga·tor**
nav·i·ga·tor
Naviho : **Nav·a·ho**
navil : **na·val** (of the navy) *or*
   na·vel (belly button)
navvigator : **nav·i·ga·tor**
naw : **gnaw**
nawsea : **nau·sea**
nawseate : **nau·se·ate**
nawsia : **nau·sea**
nawtical : **nau·ti·cal**
nawtilus : **nau·ti·lus**
naybob : **na·bob**
nay (no); **neigh** (whinny)
naypalm : **na·palm**
naypam : **na·palm**
naypom : **na·palm**
nealithic : **neo·lith·ic**
neap
neaphyte : **neo·phyte**
near
nearvous : **ner·vous**
neat
Nebbraska : **Ne·bras·ka**
nebbula : **neb·u·la** (*sing.*)
nebbulous : **neb·u·lous**
Ne·bras·ka
Nebrasska : **Ne·bras·ka**
neb·u·la (*sing.*)
neb·u·lae *or* neb·u·las (*plur.*)
neb·u·las *or* neb·u·lae (*plur.*)
nebulla : **neb·u·la** (*sing.*)
nebullous : **neb·u·lous**
neb·u·lous
nebulus : **neb·u·lous**
necesary : **ne·ces·sary**

necesity : **ne·ces·si·ty**
nec·es·sary
necessery : **nec·es·sary**
necessety : **ne·ces·si·ty**
necessitty : **ne·ces·si·ty**
ne·ces·si·ty
necissary : **nec·es·sary**
neck·lace
necklase : **neck·lace**
necklise : **neck·lace**
neckliss : **neck·lace**
necktar : **nec·tar**
necktarine : **nec·tar·ine**
nec·tar
nectarean : **nec·tar·ine**
nectareen : **nec·tar·ine**
nectarene : **nec·tar·ine**
nec·tar·ine
necter : **nec·tar**
necterine : **nec·tar·ine**
nectir : **nec·tar**
nectirine : **nec·tar·ine**
neece : **niece**
needal : **nee·dle**
needel : **nee·dle**
nee·dle
neep : **neap**
neer : **near**
neese : **niece**
neet : **neat**
nefew : **neph·ew**
neffew : **neph·ew**
neg·a·tive
negetive : **neg·a·tive**
neggative : **neg·a·tive**
neghbor : **neigh·bor**
negitive : **neg·a·tive**
neglagee : **neg·li·gee**
neglagence : **neg·li·gence**
neglegee : **neg·li·gee**
neglegence : **neg·li·gence**
neglegible : **neg·li·gi·ble**

negligeble : **neg·li·gi·ble**
negligibal : **neg·li·gi·ble**
neg·li·gee
neg·li·gence
negligense : **neg·li·gence**
negligibel : **neg·li·gi·ble**
neg·li·gi·ble
negligince : **neg·li·gence**
neglishay : **neg·li·gee**
neglishee : **neg·li·gee**
negociate : **ne·go·ti·ate**
negoshiate : **ne·go·ti·ate**
negoteate : **ne·go·ti·ate**
ne·go·ti·ate
neice : **niece**
neigh (whinny); **nay** (no)
neighber : **neigh·bor**
neigh·bor
neise : **niece**
nei·ther
nemesees : **nem·e·ses** (*plur.*)
nem·e·ses (*plur.*)
nem·e·sis (*sing.*)
nemesus : **nem·e·sis** (*sing.*)
nemises : **nem·e·ses** (*plur.*)
nemisis : **nem·e·sis** (*sing.*)
nemmises : **nem·e·ses** (*plur.*)
nemmisis : **nem·e·sis** (*sing.*)
nemonic : **mne·mon·ic**
nemonnic : **mne·mon·ic**
neofite : **neo·phyte**
neofyte : **neo·phyte**
neo·lith·ic
neolithick : **neo·lith·ic**
neolythic : **neo·lith·ic**
neo·phyte
neph·ew
nephiw : **neph·ew**
nephue : **neph·ew**
nervana : **nir·va·na**
nerviss : **ner·vous**
ner·vous

nervus : **ner·vous**
nesessary : **nec·es·sary**
nesessity : **ne·ces·si·ty**
nesissary : **nec·es·sary**
neugat : **nou·gat** (candy) *or*
  nug·get (lump)
neu·ral
neuralogy : **neu·rol·o·gy**
neurel : **neu·ral**
neuroligy : **neu·rol·o·gy**
neurollogy : **neu·rol·o·gy**
neu·rol·o·gy
neu·ron
neurosees : **neu·ro·ses** (*plur.*)
neu·ro·ses (*plur.*)
neu·ro·sis (*sing.*)
neurosus : **neu·ro·sis** (*sing.*)
neu·ter
neuteral : **neu·tral**
neu·tral
neutrel : **neu·tral**
neu·tron
Nev·a·da
Nevadda : **Nev·a·da**
new (not old); **gnu** (antelope);
  knew (was aware)
New·found·land
Newfundland : **New·found·land**
newget : **nou·gat** (candy) *or*
  nug·get (lump)
New Hampshir : **New**
  Hamp·shire
New Hamp·shire
New Hampsure : **New**
  Hamp·shire
New Hamshire : **New**
  Hamp·shire
New Jer·sey
New Jersy : **New Jer·sey**
New Mex·i·co
New Or·leans
New Orlines : **New Or·leans**

newrosis : **neu·ro·sis** (*sing.*)
newsreal : **news·reel**
news·reel
news·stand
newstand : **news·stand**
newter : **neu·ter**
newtron : **neu·tron**
New York
Newyork : **New York**
New Zea·land
New Zealund : **New Zea·land**
New Zeeland : **New Zea·land**
New Zeland : **New Zea·land**
Ni·ag·a·ra
Niagera : **Ni·ag·a·ra**
Niaggara : **Ni·ag·a·ra**
Niagra : **Ni·ag·a·ra**
nialism : **ni·hil·ism**
Niarobi : **Nai·ro·bi**
niave : **na·ive**
niavete : **na·ive·te**
Nibraska : **Ne·bras·ka**
nicatine : **nic·o·tine**
niccotine : **nic·o·tine**
nice·ty
nich : **niche**
niche
nicitty : **nice·ty**
nicity : **nice·ty**
nickal : **nick·el**
nickalodeon : **nick·el·ode·on**
nick·el
nick·el·ode·on
nickelodion : **nick·el·ode·on**
nickle : **nick·el**
nickleodeon : **nick·el·ode·on**
nicknack : **knick·knack**
nickotine : **nic·o·tine**
nicoteen : **nic·o·tine**
nicotene : **nic·o·tine**
nic·o·tine
niece

nieghbor : **neigh·bor**
niese : **niece**
niether : **nei·ther**
nieve : **na·ive**
nievete : **na·ive·te**
nife : **knife**
nifes : **knifes** (stabs) *or* **knives**
   (*plur.*)
nigardly : **nig·gard·ly**
Nigeeria : **Ni·ge·ria**
Nigerea : **Ni·ge·ria**
Ni·ge·ria
nig·gard·ly
niggerdly : **nig·gard·ly**
night (not day); **knight**
   (medieval soldier)
nihalism : **ni·hil·ism**
nihelism : **ni·hil·ism**
ni·hil·ism
Nijeria : **Ni·ge·ria**
nilism : **ni·hil·ism**
nilon : **ny·lon**
nimf : **nymph**
nimises : **nem·e·ses** (*plur.*)
nimisis : **nem·e·sis** (*sing.*)
nimmises : **nem·e·ses** (*plur.*)
nimmisis : **nem·e·sis** (*sing.*)
nimmonic : **mne·mon·ic**
nimonic : **mne·mon·ic**
nimph : **nymph**
ninetean : **nine·teen**
nine·teen
ninetene : **nine·teen**
nineth : **ninth**
nine·ti·eth
nine·ty
ninetyeth : **nine·ti·eth**
ninetyith : **nine·ti·eth**
ninteen : **nine·teen**
ninth
nintieth : **nine·ti·eth**
ninty : **nine·ty**

niophyte : **neo•phyte**
Nirobi : **Nai•ro•bi**
nir•va•na
nirvanna : **nir•va•na**
nitch : **niche**
nite : **knight** (medieval soldier)
    or **night** (not day)
nitragen : **ni•tro•gen**
nitregen : **ni•tro•gen**
ni•tro•gen
nitrogin : **ni•tro•gen**
nives : **knives**
no (negative); **know** (to be
    aware of); **now** (at this time)
noam : **gnome** (dwarf) *or*
    Nome (city)
nobilety : **no•bil•i•ty**
no•bil•i•ty
nobillity : **no•bil•i•ty**
noboddy : **no•body**
no•body
nockturnal : **noc•tur•nal**
nocternal : **noc•tur•nal**
noc•tur•nal
nocturnall : **noc•tur•nal**
nocturnel : **noc•tur•nal**
noddule : **nod•ule**
noduel : **nod•ule**
nod•ule
noledge : **knowl•edge**
noll : **knoll**
no•mad
Nome (city); **gnome** (dwarf)
nomenal : **nom•i•nal**
nomenate : **nom•i•nate**
nomenee : **nom•i•nee**
nom•i•nal
nom•i•nate
nom•i•nee
nominy : **nom•i•nee**
nommad : **no•mad**
nomminal : **nom•i•nal**

nomminate : **nom•i•nate**
nomminee : **nom•i•nee**
non•cha•lant
nonchalont : **non•cha•lant**
nonchelant : **non•cha•lant**
nonchilant : **non•cha•lant**
non•de•script
nondiscript : **non•de•script**
nonsence : **non•sense**
non•sense
nonshalant : **non•cha•lant**
nonshillant : **non•cha•lant**
nonsince : **non•sense**
nor•mal
nor•mal•cy
normalsy : **nor•mal•cy**
Normandee : **Nor•man•dy**
Nor•man•dy
normel : **nor•mal**
normelcy : **nor•mal•cy**
Normendy : **Nor•man•dy**
Normindy : **Nor•man•dy**
North Caralina : **North
    Car•o•li•na**
North Carlina : **North
    Car•o•li•na**
North Car•o•li•na
North Carrolina : **North
    Car•o•li•na**
North Dahkota : **North
    Da•ko•ta**
North Da•ko•ta
North Dakotah : **North
    Da•ko•ta**
Norwaygian : **Nor•we•gian**
Norweegian : **Nor•we•gian**
Norwegean : **Nor•we•gian**
Nor•we•gian
Norwejian : **Nor•we•gian**
nosetril : **nos•tril**
nostalgea : **nos•tal•gia**
nos•tal•gia

nostallgia : **nos·tal·gia**

nos·tril

nostrill : **nos·tril**

not (negative); **knot** (rope; one nautical mile); **nought** (zero)

not·a·ble

notafy : **not·i·fy**

notariety : **no·to·ri·ety**

noteble : **no·ta·ble**

notefy : **no·ti·fy**

noteriety : **no·to·ri·ety**

nothole : **knot·hole**

notible : **no·ta·ble**

noticable : **no·tice·able**

no·tice

no·tice·able

noticible : **no·tice·able**

notiffy : **no·ti·fy**

no·ti·fy

notiriety : **no·to·ri·ety**

notise : **no·tice**

notiseable : **no·tice·able**

notiss : **no·tice**

notoreous : **no·to·ri·ous**

notorietty : **no·to·ri·ety**

no·to·ri·ety

no·to·ri·ous

notorrious : **no·to·ri·ous**

notoryity : **no·to·ri·ety**

nottice : **no·tice**

nou·gat (candy); **nug·get** (lump)

nought (zero); **knot** (rope; one nautical mile); **not** (negative)

nour·ish

Nova Scocia : **No·va Sco·tia**

Nova Scosha : **No·va Sco·tia**

No·va Sco·tia

Nova Scotshia : **No·va Sco·tia**

novacaine : **no·vo·caine**

novacane : **no·vo·caine**

nov·ice

novise : **nov·ice**

noviss : **nov·ice**

no·vo·caine

novocane : **no·vo·caine**

novvice : **nov·ice**

now (at this time); **know** (to be aware of); **no** (negative)

now·a·days

nowdays : **now·a·days**

nowledge : **knowl·edge**

nozal : **noz·zle**

nozle : **noz·zle**

nozzal : **noz·zle**

noz·zle

nu : **gnu**

nu·ance

nuanse : **nu·ance**

nuckle : **knuck·le**

nu·cle·ar

nucleer : **nu·cle·ar**

nuclere : **nu·cle·ar**

nu·cle·us

nuclius : **nu·cle·us**

nucular : **nu·cle·ar**

nuculer : **nu·cle·ar**

nuculis : **nu·cle·us**

nuculus : **nu·cle·us**

nudaty : **nu·di·ty**

nudety : **nu·di·ty**

nuditty : **nu·di·ty**

nu·di·ty

nuematic : **pneu·mat·ic**

nuemonia : **pneu·mo·nia**

nueral : **neu·ral**

nuerology : **neu·rol·o·gy**

nueron : **neu·ron**

nueroses : **neu·ro·ses** (*plur.*)

nuerosis : **neu·ro·sis** (*sing.*)

nueter : **neu·ter**

nuetral : **neu·tral**

nuetron : **neu·tron**

nuget : **nougat** (candy) *or*
  nug·get (lump)
nugget (lump); **nou·gat** (candy)
nuggit : **nougat** (candy) *or*
  nug·get (lump)
nui·sance
nuisanse : **nui·sance**
nuisence : **nui·sance**
nuisense : **nui·sance**
nulify : **nul·li·fy**
nullafy : **nul·li·fy**
nullefy : **nul·li·fy**
nul·li·fy
num : **numb**
numaral : **nu·mer·al**
numarical : **nu·mer·i·cal**
numatic : **pneu·mat·ic**
numb
numb·ly
numbskull : **num·skull**
nu·mer·al
numerel : **nu·mer·al**
nu·mer·i·cal
numericle : **nu·mer·i·cal**
numiral : **nu·mer·al**
numly : **numb·ly**
numonia : **pneu·mo·nia**
num·skull
nunery : **nun·nery**
nunnary : **nun·nery**
nun·nery
nup·tial
nuptual : **nup·tial**
nuptuel : **nup·tial**
nuptule : **nup·tial**

nural : **neu·ral**
nurcery : **nurs·ery**
nurish : **nour·ish**
nurology : **neu·rol·o·gy**
nuron : **neu·ron**
nuroses : **neu·ro·ses** (*plur.*)
nurosis : **neu·ro·sis** (*sing.*)
nurral : **neu·ral**
nurralolgy : **neu·rol·o·gy**
nurrish : **nour·ish**
nurron : **neu·ron**
nursary : **nurs·ery**
nurserry : **nurs·ery**
nurs·ery
nursury : **nurs·ery**
nusance : **nui·sance**
nutral : **neu·tral**
nutrative : **nu·tri·tive**
nutreant : **nu·tri·ent**
nutretive : **nu·tri·tive**
nutriant : **nu·tri·ent**
nu·tri·ent
nu·tri·tion
nu·tri·tive
nutrittion : **nu·tri·tion**
nutron : **neu·tron**
nuzle : **nuz·zle**
nuzzal : **nuz·zle**
nuz·zle
nyeve : **na·ive**
nyevete : **na·ive·te**
ny·lon
nymf : **nymph**
nymph
Nyrobi : **Nai·ro·bi**

O

Oahoo : **Oa·hu**
Oa·hu
Oaklahoma : **Okla·ho·ma**
oa·ses (*plur.*)
oa·sis (*sing.*)
obaisance : **obei·sance**
obalisk : **obe·lisk**
obbelisk : **obe·lisk**
obcess : **ab·scess**
  (inflammation) *or* **ob·sess** (to
  preoccupy)
obcession : **ob·ses·sion**
obderate : **ob·du·rate**
ob·du·rate
obdurrate : **ob·du·rate**
obeadience : **obe·di·ence**
obeadient : **obe·di·ent**
obease : **obese**
obeasity : **obe·si·ty**
obecity : **obe·si·ty**
obedeance : **obe·di·ence**
obedianse : **obe·di·ence**
obediant : **obe·di·ent**
obe·di·ence
obediense : **obe·di·ence**
obe·di·ent
obeedience : **obe·di·ence**
obeedient : **obe·di·ent**
obeesity : **obe·si·ty**
obei·sance
obeisence : **obei·sance**
obeisense : **obei·sance**
obelesk : **obe·lisk**
obe·lisk
obellisk : **obe·lisk**
obese
obesety : **obe·si·ty**
obesitty : **obe·si·ty**
obe·si·ty
obeysance : **obei·sance**

obeysense : **obei·sance**
obittuary : **obit·u·ary**
obit·u·ary
obituery : **obit·u·ary**
objectafy : **ob·jec·ti·fy**
objectefy : **ob·jec·ti·fy**
objectiffy : **ob·jec·ti·fy**
ob·jec·ti·fy
obleek : **oblique**
obleeque : **oblique**
oblique
oblivian : **obliv·i·on**
oblivien : **obliv·i·on**
obliv·i·on
obnocksious : **ob·nox·ious**
ob·nox·ious
obo : **oboe**
oboe
obsalescent : **ob·so·les·cent**
ob·scene
obscerity : **ob·scu·ri·ty**
obscurety : **ob·scu·ri·ty**
ob·scu·ri·ty
obsean : **ob·scene**
obsene : **ob·scene**
obsequeous : **ob·se·qui·ous**
ob·se·qui·ous
ob·ser·vance
observanse : **ob·ser·vance**
observence : **ob·ser·vance**
observince : **ob·ser·vance**
obsesion : **ob·ses·sion**
ob·sess (to preoccupy);
  ab·scess (inflammation)
ob·ses·sion
obsiquious : **ob·se·qui·ous**
obsoleat : **ob·so·lete**
obsoleet : **ob·so·lete**
ob·so·les·cent
obsolessant : **ob·so·les·cent**

214

obsolessent : **ob·so·les·cent**
ob·so·lete
obstacal : **ob·sta·cle**
ob·sta·cle
obstecle : **ob·sta·cle**
obsticle : **ob·sta·cle**
ob·sti·nate
obstinet : **ob·sti·nate**
ob·tain
obtane : **ob·tain**
obthamalogy :
  oph·thal·mol·o·gy
obtical : **op·ti·cal**
obtimal : **op·ti·mal**
obtimism : **op·ti·mism**
obtimist : **op·ti·mist**
obtometrist : **op·tom·e·trist**
obtuce : **ob·tuse**
ob·tuse
obveate : **ob·vi·ate**
ob·vi·ate
obviaus : **ob·vi·ous**
ocaen : **ocean**
ocasion : **oc·ca·sion**
oc·ca·sion
occassion : **oc·ca·sion**
oc·cult
oc·cu·pant
occupent : **oc·cu·pant**
occupint : **oc·cu·pant**
oc·cur
occured : **oc·curred**
occurence : **oc·cur·rence**
occurrance : **oc·cur·rence**
occurranse : **oc·cur·rence**
oc·curred
oc·cur·rence
ocean
ocien : **ocean**
oc·ta·gon
octain : **oc·tane**
oc·tane

octapus : **oc·to·pus**
octegon : **oc·ta·gon**
octigon : **oc·ta·gon**
'oc·to·pus
octopuss : **oc·to·pus**
ocult : **oc·cult**
ocupant : **oc·cu·pant**
ocupent : **oc·cu·pant**
ocupint : **oc·cu·pant**
ocur : **oc·cur**
ocured : **oc·curred**
ocurence : **oc·cur·rence**
ocurrance : **oc·cur·rence**
ocurrence : **oc·cur·rence**
oddety : **odd·i·ty**
oddissey : **od·ys·sey**
odd·i·ty
oddysey : **od·ys·sey**
oder : **odor**
odissey : **od·ys·sey**
odor
odysey : **od·ys·sey**
od·ys·sey
odyssie : **od·ys·sey**
ofense : **of·fense**
offacer : **of·fi·cer**
offecer : **of·fi·cer**
offen : **of·ten**
of·fence *or* **of·fense**
of·fense *or* **of·fence**
offeratory : **of·fer·to·ry**
offeritory : **of·fer·to·ry**
of·fer·to·ry
of·fi·cer
of·ten
oftin : **of·ten**
oger : **ogre**
ogre
Ohio
Okla·ho·ma
Oklihoma : **Okla·ho·ma**
ole·an·der

olfactary : **ol·fac·to·ry**
olfactery : **ol·fac·to·ry**
ol·fac·to·ry
oliander : **ole·an·der**
Olimpic : **Olym·pic**
Olym·pic
Olympick : **Olym·pic**
omaga : **ome·ga**
omage : **hom·age**
ome·ga
om·elet *or* **om·elette**
om·elette *or* **om·elet**
omen
omenous : **om·i·nous**
omilet : **om·elet**
omin : **omen**
om·i·nous
omision : **omis·sion**
omis·sion
omit
omlet : **om·elet**
omlette : **om·elet**
ommage : **hom·age**
ommelet : **om·elet**
ommit : **omit**
ommlet : **om·elet**
omnipotance : **om·nip·o·tence**
om·nip·o·tence
omnipotense : **om·nip·o·tence**
onamatopoeia :
    on·o·mato·poe·ia
onarous : **oner·ous**
oner·ous
one·self
onesself : **one·self**
onest : **hon·est**
onix : **on·yx**
onnest : **hon·est**
onnist : **hon·est**
onnix : **on·yx**
onnomatopoeia :
    on·o·mato·poe·ia

onnor : **hon·or**
onnorable : **hon·or·able**
onnorible : **hon·or·able**
onnui : **en·nui**
onnyx : **on·yx**
onomatopia : **on·o·mato·poe·ia**
on·o·mato·poe·ia
onomotapoeia :
    on·o·mato·poe·ia
onor : **hon·or**
onorable : **hon·or·able**
onorarium : **hon·o·rar·i·um**
onoreble : **hon·or·able**
onorible : **hon·or·able**
Ontareo : **On·tar·io**
On·tar·io
Ontarrio : **On·tar·io**
Onterio : **On·tar·io**
ontourage : **en·tou·rage**
ontrepreneur : **en·tre·pre·neur**
on·ward
onwerd : **on·ward**
onword : **on·ward**
on·yx
opacety : **opac·i·ty**
opacitty : **opac·i·ty**
opac·i·ty
opal
opassity : **opac·i·ty**
opel : **opal**
openess : **open·ness**
open·ness
op·era
op·er·a·ble
operible : **op·er·a·ble**
opeum : **opi·um**
oph·thal·mol·o·gy
ophthemalogy :
    oph·thal·mol·o·gy
ophthmalligy :
    oph·thal·mol·o·gy

ophthmallogy :
  oph·thal·mol·o·gy
ophthmollogy :
  oph·thal·mol·o·gy
opiem : **opi·um**
opi·um
oponant : **op·po·nent**
oponent : **op·po·nent**
oportunity : **op·por·tu·ni·ty**
oposite : **op·po·site**
oppal : **opal**
oppasite : **op·po·site**
oppera : **op·era**
opperable : **op·er·a·ble**
oppertunity : **op·por·tu·ni·ty**
oppiset : **op·po·site**
oppisite : **op·po·site**
opponant : **op·po·nent**
op·po·nent
opponint : **op·po·nent**
opportunety : **op·por·tu·ni·ty**
opportunitty : **op·por·tu·ni·ty**
op·por·tu·ni·ty
opposate : **op·po·site**
opposet : **op·po·site**
op·po·site
oppresion : **op·pres·sion**
oppresor : **op·pres·sor**
op·press
oppresser : **op·pres·sor**
op·pres·sion
op·pres·sor
oppulence : **op·u·lence**
opress : **op·press**
opression : **op·pres·sion**
opressor : **op·pres·sor**
optamism : **op·ti·mism**
optemal : **op·ti·mal**
optemism : **op·ti·mism**
opthalmology :
  oph·thal·mol·o·gy

opthamology :
  oph·thal·mol·o·gy
opthemology :
  oph·thal·mol·o·gy
op·tic
optick : **op·tic**
optickal : **op·ti·cal**
opticle : **op·ti·cal**
op·ti·mal
optimel : **op·ti·mal**
optimest : **op·ti·mist**
op·ti·mism
op·ti·mist
optimizm : **op·ti·mism**
optimmism : **op·ti·mism**
optimmist : **op·ti·mist**
optomatrist : **op·tom·e·trist**
op·tom·e·trist
optomitrist : **op·tom·e·trist**
optommetrist : **op·tom·e·trist**
opulance : **op·u·lence**
opulanse : **op·u·lence**
op·u·lence
opulense : **op·u·lence**
opullence : **op·u·lence**
oracion : **ora·tion**
or·a·cle
orafice : **or·i·fice**
oragin : **or·i·gin**
Oragon : **Or·e·gon**
oral
orangatang : **orang·utan**
or·ange
orangootan : **orang·utan**
orang·utan
orashion : **ora·tion**
orater : **or·a·tor**
ora·tion
or·a·tor
orbet : **or·bit**
or·bit
orcestra : **or·ches·tra**

or•chard
orched : **or•chid**
orcherd : **or•chard**
or•ches•tra
or•chid
orchird : **or•chard**
orchistra : **or•ches•tra**
or•dain
ordanary : **or•di•nary**
ordane : **or•dain**
or•deal
ordeel : **or•deal**
ordenance : **or•di•nance** (rule,
   law) *or* **ord•nance**
   (weaponry)
ordenary : **or•di•nary**
ordenince : **or•di•nance** (rule,
   law) *or* **ord•nance**
   (weaponry)
or•di•nance (rule, law);
   ord•nance (weaponry)
ordinarry : **or•di•nary**
or•di•nary
ordinense : **or•di•nance** (rule,
   law) *or* **ord•nance**
   (weaponry)
ordinerry : **or•di•nary**
ordinery : **or•di•nary**
ordnance (weaponry);
   ordinance (rule, law)
ordnanse : **or•di•nance** (rule,
   law) *or* **ord•nance**
   (weaponry)
orecle : **or•a•cle**
orefice : **or•i•fice**
Or•e•gon (state); **or•i•gin**
   (beginning)
Oregone : **Or•e•gon**
orel : **oral**
orenge : **or•ange**
oreole : **ori•ole**
oretor : **or•a•tor**

orfan : **or•phan**
orfanage : **or•phan•age**
orfin : **or•phan**
orfinage : **or•phan•age**
orfun : **or•phan**
orfunage : **or•phan•age**
or•gan•dy
organesm : **or•gan•ism**
or•gan•ic
organick : **or•gan•ic**
or•gan•ism
organnic : **or•gan•ic**
orgendy : **or•gan•dy**
orgenism : **or•gan•ism**
orgindy : **or•gan•dy**
oriant : **ori•ent**
orical : **or•a•cle**
oricle : **or•a•cle**
ori•ent
ori•en•tal
orientall : **ori•en•tal**
orientel : **ori•en•tal**
or•i•fice
orifise : **or•i•fice**
orifiss : **or•i•fice**
orifrice : **or•i•fice**
origen : **Or•e•gon** (state) *or*
   or•i•gin (beginning)
origenal : **orig•i•nal**
origenate : **orig•i•nate**
or•i•gin (beginning); **Or•e•gon**
   (state)
originait : **orig•i•nate**
orig•i•nal
orig•i•nate
originel : **orig•i•nal**
originnate : **orig•i•nate**
Origon : **Or•e•gon**
orijen : **or•i•gin**
oringe : **or•ange**
oriol : **ori•ole**
ori•ole

orioll : **ori•ole**
oritor : **or•a•tor**
orkestra : **or•ches•tra**
orkid : **or•chid**
orkistra : **or•ches•tra**
ornait : **or•nate**
ornameant : **or•na•ment**
or•na•ment
ornamint : **or•na•ment**
ornamment : **or•na•ment**
ornary : **or•nery**
or•nate
ornathology : **or•ni•thol•o•gy**
ornement : **or•na•ment**
ornerry : **or•nery**
or•nery
ornethology : **or•ni•thol•o•gy**
orniment : **or•na•ment**
ornithalogy : **or•ni•thol•o•gy**
ornitholigy : **or•ni•thol•o•gy**
ornithollogy : **or•ni•thol•o•gy**
or•ni•thol•o•gy
ornory : **or•nery**
or•phan
or•phan•age
orphanege : **or•phan•age**
orphanige : **or•phan•age**
orphen : **or•phan**
orphenage : **or•phan•age**
orphin : **or•phan**
orphinage : **or•phan•age**
orphun : **or•phan**
orphunage : **or•phan•age**
orral : **oral**
orrange : **or•ange**
orrangutang : **orang•utan**
orrator : **or•a•tor**
orrattion : **ora•tion**
Orregon : **Or•e•gon**
orrient : **ori•ent**
orrifice : **or•i•fice**
orrigin : **or•i•gin**

orriginal : **orig•i•nal**
orringe : **or•ange**
orriole : **ori•ole**
orthadontist : **or•tho•don•tist**
orthadox : **or•tho•dox**
orthedontist : **or•tho•don•tist**
orthedox : **or•tho•dox**
orthodontest : **or•tho•don•tist**
or•tho•don•tist
or•tho•dox
oscellate : **os•cil•late**
oscilate : **os•cil•late**
os•cil•late
osify : **os•si•fy**
osillate : **os•cil•late**
osmoasis : **os•mo•sis**
os•mo•sis
osmossis : **os•mo•sis**
ospray : **os•prey**
ospree : **os•prey**
os•prey
osprie : **os•prey**
ospry : **os•prey**
ossafy : **os•si•fy**
ossefy : **os•si•fy**
ossiffy : **os•si•fy**
os•si•fy
ossillate : **os•cil•late**
ostencible : **os•ten•si•ble**
ostensable : **os•ten•si•ble**
ostensibal : **os•ten•si•ble**
os•ten•si•ble
ostentacious : **os•ten•ta•tious**
ostentashious : **os•ten•ta•tious**
os•ten•ta•tious
os•teo•path
ostinsible : **os•ten•si•ble**
ostintatious : **os•ten•ta•tious**
ostiopath : **os•teo•path**
ostracesm : **os•tra•cism**
ostracise : **os•tra•cize**
os•tra•cism

os·tra·cize
ostrage : os·trich
ostrasism : os·tra·cism
ostrasize : os·tra·cize
ostrech : os·trich
ostrecism : os·tra·cism
ostrecize : os·tra·cize
ostrege : os·trich
ostretch : os·trich
os·trich
ostricism : os·tra·cism
ostricize : os·tra·cize
ostrige : os·trich
ostritch : os·trich
Otawa : Ot·ta·wa
otoman : ot·to·man
Ot·ta·wa
Ottiwa : Ot·ta·wa
Ottoa : Ot·ta·wa
ot·to·man
ottomin : ot·to·man
Ottowa : Ot·ta·wa
ounce
ounse : ounce
our (belonging to us); hour (60 minutes)
outrageious : out·ra·geous
out·ra·geous
outrageus : out·ra·geous
outragious : out·ra·geous
ova (*plur.*); ovum (*sing.*)
ovar·i·an
ovarrian : ovar·i·an

ova·ry
ovaryan : ovar·i·an
overian : ovar·i·an
overrian : ovar·i·an
overry : ova·ry
overwelm : over·whelm
over·whelm
overy : ova·ry
overyan : ovar·i·an
ovum (*sing.*); ova (*plur.*)
ovvary : ova·ry
Owahu : Oa·hu
ownce : ounce
ownerous : on·er·ous
oxadation : ox·i·da·tion
oxagen : ox·y·gen
oxedation : ox·i·da·tion
oxegen : ox·y·gen
oxegin : ox·y·gen
Oxferd : Ox·ford
Ox·ford
ox·i·da·tion
oxigen : ox·y·gen
oxigin : ox·y·gen
oxsidation : ox·i·da·tion
ox·y·gen
oys·ter
oystir : oys·ter
Ozark
ozmosis : os·mo·sis
ozoan : ozone
ozone
Ozzark : Ozark
ozzone : ozone

P

pablem : **pab·u·lum**
pablum : **pab·u·lum**
pabulem : **pab·u·lum**
pab·u·lum
pacefy : **pac·i·fy**
pacifec : **pa·cif·ic**
paciffy : **pac·i·fy**
pa·cif·ic
pac·i·fi·er
pac·i·fist
pac·i·fy
pacivist : **pac·i·fist**
pac·ket
Packistan : **Pa·ki·stan**
packit : **pack·et**
pagamas : **pa·ja·mas**
pa·gan
pag·eant
pagen : **pa·gan**
pagent : **pag·eant**
paggan : **pa·gan**
pagiant : **pag·eant**
pagin : **pa·gan**
pagint : **pag·eant**
pa·go·da
pagota : **pa·go·da**
paid
pain (ache); **pane** (glass)
pain·ful
painfull : **pain·ful**
pair (two things); **pare** (to cut away); **pear** (fruit)
pais·ley
paizley : **pais·ley**
pa·ja·mas
pajammas : **pa·ja·mas**
Pakastan : **Pa·ki·stan**
paket : **pack·et**
Pa·ki·stan
palacade : **pal·i·sade**

pal·ace
palacial : **pa·la·tial**
palasade : **pal·i·sade**
palasaid : **pal·i·sade**
palase : **pal·ace**
palashial : **pa·la·tial**
pal·at·able
pa·la·tial
palatible : **pal·at·able**
Pal·es·tine
palice : **pal·ace**
palid : **pal·lid**
pal·i·sade
paliss : **pal·ace**
Palistine : **Pal·es·tine**
pallace : **pal·ace**
pallatable : **pal·at·able**
Pallestine : **Pal·es·tine**
pal·lid
pallisade : **pal·i·sade**
pal·lor
palm (tree; hand); **Pam** (name)
palor : **pal·lor**
pal·pa·ble
palpibal : **pal·pa·ble**
palpible : **pal·pa·ble**
Pam (name); **palm** (tree; hand)
pamflet : **pam·phlet**
pam·phlet
pamphlit : **pam·phlet**
pamplet : **pam·phlet**
pan·a·cea
panacia : **pan·a·cea**
Pa·na·ma
Panamma : **Pa·na·ma**
panaply : **pan·o·ply**
panarama : **pan·ora·ma**
panasia : **pan·a·cea**
pan·cre·as
pancreus : **pan·cre·as**

221

pandamonium :
   pan·de·mo·ni·um
pandemoniem :
   pan·de·mo·ni·um
pan·de·mo·ni·um
pandimonium :
   pan·de·mo·ni·um
pane (glass); **pain** (ache)
paneful : **pain·ful**
pan·el
pan·eled *or* **pan·elled**
panell : **pan·el**
pan·elled *or* **pan·eled**
panerama : **pan·ora·ma**
pan·ic
paniced : **pan·icked**
panick : **pan·ic**
pan·icked
pan·icky
panicy : **pan·icky**
paniked : **pan·icked**
panil : **pan·el**
paniled : **pan·eled**
panisea : **pan·a·cea**
pankreas : **pan·cre·as**
pankrius : **pan·cre·as**
pannacea : **pan·a·cea**
Pannama : **Pa·na·ma**
pannel : **pan·el**
panneled : **pan·eled**
panneply : **pan·o·ply**
pannic : **pan·ic**
panniply : **pan·o·ply**
pannoply : **pan·o·ply**
pan·o·ply
pan·ora·ma
panoramma : **pan·ora·ma**
panphlet : **pam·phlet**
pan·sy
panzy : **pan·sy**
pa·pa·cy
papasy : **pa·pa·cy**

paper mache : **pa·pier-mâ·ché**
papicy : **pa·pa·cy**
pa·pier-mâ·ché
papirus : **pa·py·rus**
papisy : **pa·pa·cy**
pappyrus : **pa·py·rus**
papreeka : **pa·pri·ka**
pa·pri·ka
papyris : **pa·py·rus**
pa·py·rus
paraboala: **pa·rab·o·la**
pa·rab·o·la
parabula : **pa·rab·o·la**
para·chute
paracite : **par·a·site**
pa·rade
paradice : **par·a·dise**
par·a·digm
paradime : **par·a·digm**
par·a·dise
par·a·dox
parafenalia : **par·a·pher·na·lia**
par·af·fin
par·a·gon
para·graph
paraid : **pa·rade**
par·a·keet
paralel : **par·al·lel**
paralesis : **pa·ral·y·sis**
paralisis : **pa·ral·y·sis**
par·al·lel
pa·ral·y·sis
para·noia
paranoya : **para·noia**
paraphenalia :
   par·a·pher·na·lia
par·a·pher·na·lia
paraphinalia : **par·a·pher·na·lia**
paraphrenalia :
   par·a·pher·na·lia
parashute : **para·chute**
par·a·site

para·sol
par·cel
parcell : **par·cel**
parcely : **pars·ley**
parden : **par·don**
pardin : **par·don**
par·don
pare (to cut away); **pair** (two
   things); **pear** (fruit)
paredigm : **par·a·digm**
paredime : **par·a·digm**
paredise : **par·a·dise**
paregon : **par·a·gon**
paret : **par·rot**
parety : **par·i·ty**
parichute : **para·chute**
paridigm : **par·a·digm**
paridise : **par·a·dise**
paridox : **par·a·dox**
paridy : **par·o·dy**
pariffin : **par·af·fin**
parifin : **par·af·fin**
parigraph : **para·graph**
parikeet : **par·a·keet**
par·ish (church community);
   per·ish (to cease to exist)
parisite : **par·a·site**
parisol : **para·sol**
paritty : **par·i·ty**
par·i·ty
parlament : **par·lia·ment**
par·lance
parlanse : **par·lance**
parlence : **par·lance**
parlense : **par·lance**
parler : **par·lor**
parleyment : **par·lia·ment**
par·lia·ment
parliment : **par·lia·ment**
par·lor
pa·ro·chi·al
par·o·dy

parot : **par·rot**
parrabola : **pa·rab·o·la**
parrade : **pa·rade**
parradise : **par·a·dise**
parradox : **par·a·dox**
parrafin : **par·af·fin**
parralel : **par·al·lel**
parralysis : **pa·ral·y·sis**
parret : **par·rot**
parridy : **par·o·dy**
parrifin : **par·af·fin**
parriket : **par·a·keet**
parrish : **par·ish** (church
   community) *or* **per·ish** (to
   cease to exist)
parrit : **par·rot**
parrity : **par·i·ty**
parrochial : **pa·ro·chi·al**
parrody : **par·o·dy**
parrokeet : **par·a·keet**
par·rot
parsel : **par·cel**
parsell : **par·cel**
pars·ley
parsly : **pars·ley**
partacle : **par·ti·cle**
partasan : **par·ti·san**
partesan : **par·ti·san**
partical : **par·ti·cle**
particepant : **par·tic·i·pant**
par·tic·i·pant
particlar : **par·tic·u·lar**
par·ti·cle
particlear : **par·tic·u·lar**
par·tic·u·lar
partikle : **par·ti·cle**
par·ti·san
partisen : **par·ti·san**
partisipant : **par·tic·i·pant**
partredge : **par·tridge**
partrege : **par·tridge**
par·tridge

partrige : **par·tridge**
Pas·a·de·na
Pasadina : **Pas·a·de·na**
pasafier : **pac·i·fi·er**
pasage : **pas·sage**
pashion : **pas·sion**
pasific : **pa·cif·ic**
pasifier : **pac·i·fi·er**
pasifist : **pac·i·fist**
pasify : **pac·i·fy**
pasion : **pas·sion**
pasley : **pais·ley**
Passadena : **Pas·a·de·na**
pas·sage
passege : **pas·sage**
passifier : **pac·i·fi·er**
passige : **pas·sage**
pas·sion
passtime : **pas·time**
pastary : **past·ry**
pas·tel
pastell : **pas·tel**
past·er (one that pastes);
  pas·tor (clergy)
pastery : **past·ry**
pasterize : **pas·teur·ize**
pas·teur·ize
pas·time
pas·tor (clergy); **past·er** (one
  that pastes)
pastorize : **pas·teur·ize**
past·ry
pasttime : **pas·time**
pasturize : **pas·teur·ize**
patchy
pateo : **pa·tio**
paternety : **pa·ter·ni·ty**
paternitty : **pa·ter·ni·ty**
pa·ter·ni·ty
pathalogy : **path·ol·o·gy**
pa·thet·ic
pathetick : **pa·thet·ic**

pathettic : **pa·thet·ic**
patholigy : **path·ol·o·gy**
pathollogy : **path·ol·o·gy**
path·ol·o·gy
pa·tio
patreot : **pa·tri·ot**
pa·tri·ot
pa·trol
patroll : **pa·trol**
pa·tron·age
patronige : **pa·tron·age**
pattio : **pa·tio**
paturnity : **pa·ter·ni·ty**
paucety : **pau·ci·ty**
pau·ci·ty
pause (to hesitate); **paws**
  (animal feet)
pausity : **pau·ci·ty**
pavilian : **pa·vil·ion**
pa·vil·ion
pavillion : **pa·vil·ion**
pawm : **palm**
paws (animal feet); **pause** (to
  hesitate)
payed : **paid**
peace (absence of conflict);
  piece (portion)
peace·ful
peacefull : **peace·ful**
peachy
peal (to ring); **peel** (to strip)
pea·nut
peany : **pe·o·ny**
pear (fruit); **pair** (two things);
  pare (to cut away)
pearl (gem); **purl** (knitting
  stitch)
peas·ant
peaseful : **peace·ful**
peasent : **peas·ant**
peasint : **peas·ant**
peavish : **pee·vish**

pebbal : **peb·ble**
pebbel : **peb·ble**
peb·ble
peble : **peb·ble**
pe·can
peccan : **pe·can**
pe·cu·liar
peculier : **pe·cu·liar**
pedagree : **ped·i·gree**
ped·al (foot lever); **ped·dle** (to sell); **pet·al** (flower part)
ped·ant
peddant : **ped·ant**
peddestal : **ped·es·tal**
peddigree : **ped·i·gree**
ped·dle (to sell); **ped·al** (foot lever); **pet·al** (flower part)
pedent : **ped·ant**
ped·es·tal
pedestill : **ped·es·tal**
ped·i·gree
pedistal : **ped·es·tal**
peeceful : **peace·ful**
peechy : **peachy**
peel (to strip); **peal** (to ring)
peenut : **pea·nut**
peeple : **peo·ple**
peeriod : **pe·ri·od**
pee·vish
peice : **peace** (absence of conflict) *or* **piece** (portion)
peirce : **pierce**
peise : **peace** (absence of conflict) *or* **piece** (portion)
pekan : **pe·can**
pelecan : **pel·i·can**
pelet : **pel·let**
pel·i·can
pelikan : **pel·i·can**
pel·let
pellican : **pel·i·can**
pellit : **pel·let**

pelvice : **pel·vis**
pel·vis
pelviss : **pel·vis**
penacillin : **pen·i·cil·lin**
pe·nal
pen·al·ty
pen·ance
penanse : **pen·ance**
penatrate : **pen·e·trate**
pencel : **pen·cil**
pen·chant
penchent : **pen·chant**
penchint : **pen·chant**
pen·cil
pen·dant (*noun or adj.*); **pen·dent** (*adj. only*)
pen·dent (*adj. only*); **pen·dant** (*noun or adj.*)
pendulam : **pen·du·lum**
pendulem : **pen·du·lum**
pen·du·lum
pen·e·trate
pen·guin
penicilin : **pen·i·cil·lin**
penicillan : **pen·i·cil·lin**
pen·i·cil·lin
penil : **pe·nal**
penilty : **pen·al·ty**
penince : **pen·ance**
penisillin : **pen·i·cil·lin**
pennacle : **pin·na·cle**
pennal : **pe·nal**
pennalty : **pen·al·ty**
pennance : **pen·ance**
pennetrate : **pen·e·trate**
pennicillin : **pen·i·cil·lin**
Pennsilvania : **Penn·syl·va·nia**
Pennsylvanea : **Penn·syl·va·nia**
Penn·syl·va·nia
pensil : **pen·cil**
pentaggon : **pen·ta·gon**
pen·ta·gon

pentegon : **pen·ta·gon**
penulty : **pen·al·ty**
penut : **pea·nut**
peonny : **pe·o·ny**
pe·o·ny
peo·ple
percarious : **pre·car·i·ous**
per·ceive
per·cent·age
percentege : **per·cent·age**
percentige : **per·cent·age**
perceve : **per·ceive**
percieve : **per·ceive**
percintage : **per·cent·age**
percipitation : **pre·cip·i·ta·tion**
peremptary : **pe·remp·to·ry**
peremptery : **pe·remp·to·ry**
pe·remp·to·ry
perfarate : **per·fo·rate**
perfectable : **per·fect·ible**
perfectibal : **per·fect·ible**
per·fect·ible
perfirate : **per·fo·rate**
per·fo·rate
per·for·mance
performanse : **per·for·mance**
performence : **per·for·mance**
performince : **per·for·mance**
perfunctary : **per·func·to·ry**
per·func·to·ry
perfunctry : **per·func·to·ry**
perfunktory : **per·func·to·ry**
perichute : **para·chute**
periferal : **pe·riph·er·al**
perigon : **par·a·gon**
per·il
pe·ri·od
peripharel : **pe·riph·er·al**
pe·riph·er·al
peri·scope
per·ish (to cease to exist);
    par·ish (church community)

perity : **par·i·ty**
perjery : **per·ju·ry**
per·ju·ry
perl : **pearl** (gem) *or* **purl**
    (knitting stitch)
per·ma·nent
per·me·able
per·me·ate
permeible : **per·me·able**
permenant : **per·ma·nent**
permiabel : **per·me·able**
permiable : **per·me·able**
permiate : **per·me·ate**
perminent : **per·ma·nent**
permisible : **per·mis·si·ble**
permissable : **per·mis·si·ble**
per·mis·si·ble
peroose : **pe·ruse**
perouette : **pir·ou·ette**
per·pe·trate
perpettual : **per·pet·u·al**
per·pet·u·al
perpetuel : **per·pet·u·al**
perpitrate : **per·pe·trate**
perril : **per·il**
perriod : **pe·ri·od**
perriscope : **peri·scope**
perruse : **pe·ruse**
persacute : **per·se·cute**
perscription : **pre·scrip·tion**
perseccute : **per·se·cute**
per·se·cute
persentage : **per·cent·age**
perserve : **pre·serve**
perserverance : **per·se·ver·ance**
perseveirance : **per·se·ver·ance**
per·se·ver·ance
perseveranse : **per·se·ver·ance**
perseverence : **per·se·ver·ance**
persicute : **per·se·cute**
per·son·age

per·son·al (private);
  per·son·nel (employees)
personege : per·son·age
personige : per·son·age
per·son·nel (employees);
  per·son·al (private)
per·suade
persuaid : per·suade
persue : pur·sue
persume : pre·sume
perswade : per·suade
pertanent : per·ti·nent
pertenant : per·ti·nent
perterb : per·turb
pertinant : per·ti·nent
per·ti·nent
pertinnent : per·ti·nent
per·turb
pe·ruse
peruze : pe·ruse
pervacive : per·va·sive
pervaseve : per·va·sive
per·va·sive
pervassive : per·va·sive
per·vert
pesimism : pes·si·mism
pesimist : pes·si·mist
pessamism : pes·si·mism
pessamist : pes·si·mist
pessant : peas·ant
pessemism : pes·si·mism
pessemist : pes·si·mist
pessent : peas·ant
pessimest : pes·si·mist
pes·si·mism
pes·si·mist
pessimizm : pes·si·mism
pessint : peas·ant
pestalence : pes·ti·lence
pestelence : pes·ti·lence
pestilance : pes·ti·lence
pes·ti·lence

pestilense : pes·ti·lence
pet·al (flower part); ped·al
  (foot lever); ped·dle (to sell)
peteet : pe·tite
petete : pe·tite
pe·tite
petoonia : pe·tu·nia
petrafy : pet·ri·fy
petrefy : pet·ri·fy
petriffy : pet·ri·fy
pet·ri·fy
pe·tro·leum
petroliam : pe·tro·leum
petrolium : pe·tro·leum
petrollium : pe·tro·leum
pettete : pe·tite
pettite : pe·tite
pettrify : pet·ri·fy
pettroleum : pe·tro·leum
pettulant : pet·u·lant
pettunia : pe·tu·nia
pet·u·lant
petulent : pet·u·lant
pe·tu·nia
petunya : pe·tu·nia
peuter : pew·ter
pew·ter
phalic : phal·lic
phal·lic
phantastic : fan·tas·tic
phan·ta·sy or fan·ta·sy
phan·tom
phar·ma·cy
pharmicy : phar·ma·cy
pharmissy : phar·ma·cy
pheas·ant
pheasco : fi·as·co
pheasent : pheas·ant
pheasint : pheas·ant
pheeble : fee·ble
Phenix : Phoe·nix
phe·nom·e·nal

phe·nom·e·non
phenominal : **phe·nom·e·nal**
phenominnal : **phe·nom·e·nal**
phenominnon : **phe·nom·e·non**
phenominon : **phe·nom·e·non**
phenommenal : **phe·nom·e·nal**
phenommenon :
  phe·nom·e·non
Pheonix : **Phoe·nix**
phesant : **pheas·ant**
phesible : **fea·si·ble**
phessant : **pheas·ant**
Philapino : **Fil·i·pi·no**
philibuster : **fi·li·bus·ter**
Philipino : **Fil·i·pi·no**
Phil·ip·pines
phillabuster : **fi·li·bus·ter**
Phillipines : **Phil·ip·pines**
Phillipino : **Fil·i·pi·no**
Phillippines : **Phil·ip·pines**
philoligy : **phi·lol·o·gy**
philollogy : **phi·lol·o·gy**
phi·lol·o·gy
philosiphy : **phi·los·o·phy**
phi·los·o·phy
philossophy : **phi·los·o·phy**
phinomenal : **phe·nom·e·nal**
phinomenon : **phe·nom·e·non**
phisical : **phys·i·cal**
phisician : **phy·si·cian**
phisics : **phys·ics**
phission : **fis·sion**
phobea : **pho·bia**
pho·bia
Phoe·nix
pho·net·ic
phonetick : **pho·net·ic**
phonettic : **pho·net·ic**
phosel : **fos·sil**
phosferris : **phos·pho·rous**
  (*adj.*) *or* **phos·pho·rus**
  (*noun*)

phosforus : **phos·pho·rous**
  (*adj.*) *or* **phos·phor·us**
  (*noun*)
phos·pho·rous (*adj.*);
  phos·pho·rus (*noun*)
phos·pho·rus (*noun*);
  phos·pho·rous (*adj.*)
phossil : **fos·sil**
photografy : **pho·tog·ra·phy**
pho·tog·ra·phy
physecal : **phys·i·cal**
phys·i·cal
phy·si·cian
physicion : **phy·si·cian**
physicks : **phys·ics**
physicle : **phys·i·cal**
phys·ics
physikal : **phys·i·cal**
physission : **phy·si·cian**
pianeer : **pi·o·neer**
piatza : **pi·az·za** (veranda) *or*
  piz·za (pie)
piaza : **pi·az·za** (veranda) *or*
  piz·za (pie)
pi·az·za (veranda); **piz·za** (pie)
piccalo : **pic·co·lo**
piccilo : **pic·co·lo**
pic·co·lo
pickal : **pick·le**
pickel : **pick·le**
pick·et
pickilo : **pic·co·lo**
pickit : **pick·et**
pick·le
picknic : **pic·nic**
picknick : **pic·nic**
picknicked : **pic·nicked**
pic·nic
picniced : **pic·nicked**
picnick : **pic·nic**
pic·nicked
picolo : **pic·co·lo**

pictoreal : **pic·to·ri·al**
pic·to·ri·al
picturial : **pic·to·ri·al**
pid·gin (language); **pi·geon** (bird)
piece (portion); **peace** (absence of conflict)
pierce
pierouette : **pir·ou·ette**
pietty : **pi·ety**
pi·ety
pi·geon (bird); **pid·gin** (language)
piggin : **pid·gin** (language) or **pi·geon** (bird)
pigion : **pid·gin** (language) or **pi·geon** (bird)
pigmy : **pyg·my**
pijamas : **pa·ja·mas**
pilar : **pil·lar**
pilet : **pi·lot**
pilgrem : **pil·grim**
pil·grim
pilgrum : **pil·grim**
pil·lar
pillary : **pil·lo·ry**
piller : **pil·lar**
pillery : **pil·lo·ry**
pillgrim : **pil·grim**
pil·lo·ry
pilory : **pil·lo·ry**
pi·lot
pinacle : **pin·na·cle**
pinchant : **pen·chant**
pindulem : **pen·du·lum**
pineer : **pi·o·neer**
pinguin : **pen·guin**
pin·na·cle
pinnecal : **pin·na·cle**
pinnical : **pin·na·cle**
pintagon : **pen·ta·gon**
pi·o·neer

pioneir : **pi·o·neer**
pionere : **pi·o·neer**
pi·ra·cy
pirassy : **pi·ra·cy**
pi·rate
pirce : **pierce**
piret : **pi·rate**
pirete : **pi·rate**
piricy : **pi·ra·cy**
pirissy : **pi·ra·cy**
pirl : **pearl** (gem) or **purl** (knitting stitch)
pirmeate : **per·me·ate**
piroette : **pir·ou·ette**
piromaniac : **py·ro·ma·ni·ac**
pir·ou·ette
pisston : **pis·ton**
pistal : **pis·til** (flower part) or **pis·tol** (handgun)
pistan : **pis·ton**
pisten : **pis·ton**
pis·til (flower part); **pis·tol** (handgun)
pis·tol (handgun); **pis·til** (flower part)
pis·ton
pitaful : **piti·ful**
pit·e·ous
pithon : **py·thon**
piti·able
piti·ful
pitious : **pit·e·ous**
Pitsburg : **Pitts·burgh**
pittiful : **piti·ful**
Pittsberg : **Pitts·burgh**
Pittsburg : **Pitts·burgh**
Pitts·burgh
pittuitary : **pit·u·itary**
pituetary : **pit·u·itary**
pit·u·itary
pituitery : **pit·u·itary**
pitunia : **pe·tu·nia**

pityable : **piti·able**
pityful : **piti·ful**
pityous : **pit·e·ous**
pivat : **piv·ot**
pivet : **piv·ot**
piv·ot
pivvot : **piv·ot**
piz·za (pie); **pi·az·za** (veranda)
plac·ard
placcid : **plac·id**
placed : **plac·id**
plac·id
plackard : **plac·ard**
plackerd : **plac·ard**
plagerism : **pla·gia·rism**
pla·gia·rism
plagierism : **pla·gia·rism**
plaguerism : **pla·gia·rism**
planed (leveled); **planned**
   (organized)
plan·et
planetariem : **plan·e·tar·i·um**
plan·e·tar·i·um
planetarrium : **plan·e·tar·i·um**
planeterium : **plan·e·tar·i·um**
planit : **plan·et**
planitarium : **plan·e·tar·i·um**
planned (organized); **planed**
   (leveled)
plannet : **plan·et**
plannetarium : **plan·e·tar·i·um**
plasstic : **plas·tic**
plastec : **plas·tic**
plas·tic
plastick : **plas·tic**
platanum : **plat·i·num**
platatude : **plat·i·tude**
pla·teau
platenum : **plat·i·num**
plat·i·num
plat·i·tude
pla·toon

platteau : **pla·teau**
plattinum : **plat·i·num**
plattitude : **plat·i·tude**
plattoon : **pla·toon**
plattow : **pla·teau**
platune : **pla·toon**
plausable : **plau·si·ble**
plauseble : **plau·si·ble**
plau·si·ble
playright : **play·wright**
play·wright
playwrite : **play·wright**
plead
pleas·ant
please
pleasent : **pleas·ant**
pleasint : **pleas·ant**
plea·sure
pleat
plebbisite : **pleb·i·scite**
pleb·i·scite
pledge
pleebiscite : **pleb·i·scite**
pleed : **plead**
pleese : **please**
pleet : **pleat**
pleez : **please**
plege : **pledge**
plenatude : **plen·i·tude**
plen·i·tude or **plen·ti·tude**
plentatude : **plen·i·tude**
plen·ti·tude or **plen·i·tude**
plentytude : **plen·i·tude**
pleshure : **plea·sure**
plessant : **plea·sant**
plessure : **plea·sure**
plesure : **plea·sure**
pli·able
pli·ant
plibiscite : **pleb·i·scite**
plible : **pli·able**
plient : **pli·ant**

Plimouth : **Plym·outh**
plum·age
plumb·er
plumb·ing
plumeage : **plum·age**
plumer : **plumb·er**
plumige : **plum·age**
plummer : **plumb·er**
plumming : **plumb·ing**
plu·ral
plurel : **plu·ral**
plurral : **plu·ral**
plurrel : **plu·ral**
plyable : **pli·able**
Plymath : **Plym·outh**
Plymeth : **Plym·outh**
Plym·outh
pneu·mat·ic
pneumattic : **pneu·mat·ic**
pneumoania : **pneu·mo·nia**
pneu·mo·nia
pnuematic : **pneu·mat·ic**
pnuemonia : **pneu·mo·nia**
pnumatic : **pneu·mat·ic**
pnumonia : **pneu·mo·nia**
poadium : **po·di·um**
poddium : **po·di·um**
po·di·um
po·em
pogoda : **pa·go·da**
poi·gnant
poignent : **poi·gnant**
poiniant : **poi·gnant**
poinsetta : **poin·set·tia**
poin·set·tia
poisen : **poi·son**
poi·son
poisson : **poi·son**
po·lar
polaritty : **po·lar·i·ty**
po·lar·i·ty
polarrity : **po·lar·i·ty**

polatics : **pol·i·tics**
polece : **po·lice**
po·lem·ic
polemick : **po·lem·ic**
polemmic : **po·lem·ic**
poleo : **po·lio**
poler : **po·lar**
polerity : **po·lar·i·ty**
po·lice
pol·i·cy
polimic : **po·lem·ic**
po·lio
polise : **po·lice**
polissy : **pol·i·cy**
polisy : **pol·i·cy**
politicks : **pol·i·tics**
pol·i·tics
pollanate : **pol·li·nate**
pollarity : **po·lar·i·ty**
pol·len
pollenate : **pol·li·nate**
pollice : **po·lice**
pollicy : **pol·i·cy**
pollin : **pol·len**
pol·li·nate
pollitics : **pol·i·tics**
pome : **po·em**
pomp·ous
pompus : **pomp·ous**
ponteff : **pon·tiff**
pon·tiff
pontive : **pon·tiff**
poodel : **poo·dle**
poo·dle
poperrie : **pot·pour·ri**
pop·lar (tree); **pop·u·lar**
  (accepted)
popler : **pop·lar** (tree) *or*
  pop·u·lar (accepted)
poporry : **pot·pour·ri**
poppulace : **pop·u·lace** (*noun*)
  or **pop·u·lous** (*adj.*)

poppulous : **pop•u•lace** (*noun*)
or **pop•u•lous** (*adj.*)
populace (*noun*); **pop•u•lous**
(*adj.*)
pop•u•lar (*accepted*); **pop•lar**
(*tree*)
populise : **pop•u•lace** (*noun*) or
pop•u•lous (*adj.*)
pop•u•lous (*adj.*); **pop•u•lace**
(*noun*)
popurrie : **pot•pour•ri**
por•ce•lain
porcelin : **por•ce•lain**
porcilain : **por•ce•lain**
poreous : **po•rous**
poridge : **por•ridge**
po•rous
porrage : **por•ridge**
porrege : **por•ridge**
por•ridge
porrige : **por•ridge**
porrous : **po•rous**
porselin : **por•ce•lain**
por•ta•ble
portaco : **por•ti•co**
por•tal
portel : **por•tal**
portfoleo : **port•fo•lio**
port•fo•lio
portfollio : **port•fo•lio**
portible : **por•ta•ble**
porticko : **por•ti•co**
por•ti•co
Porto Rico : **Puer•to Ri•co**
por•trait
portrate : **por•trait**
portrayt : **por•trait**
portret : **por•trait**
Portugeese : **Por•tu•guese**
Portugese : **Por•tu•guese**
Portugeze : **Por•tu•guese**
Por•tu•guese

posative : **pos•i•tive**
posess : **pos•sess**
posible : **pos•si•ble**
pos•i•tive
possable : **pos•si•ble**
pos•se
pos•sess
pos•si•ble
possitive : **pos•i•tive**
possy : **pos•se**
post•age
post•al
postarity : **pos•ter•i•ty**
postege : **post•age**
postel : **post•al**
posteritty : **pos•ter•i•ty**
pos•ter•i•ty
posterrity : **pos•ter•i•ty**
postige : **post•age**
po•ta•ble
po•ta•to
potatoe : **po•ta•to**
po•ta•toes
potatos : **po•ta•toes**
potible : **po•ta•ble**
potperrie : **pot•pour•ri**
pot•pour•ri
potpurrie : **pot•pour•ri**
pottable : **po•ta•ble**
povarty : **pov•er•ty**
pov•er•ty
povirty : **pov•er•ty**
poyson : **poi•son**
pracktical : **prac•ti•cal**
practacal : **prac•ti•cal**
prac•ti•cal
practicle : **prac•ti•cal**
prafer : **pre•fer**
prai•rie
prarie : **prai•rie**
preach

precareous : **pre·car·i·ous**
pre·car·i·ous
pre·cede (to go before);
  pro·ceed (to continue)
prec·e·dent (that which comes
  before); **pres·i·dent** (one who
  presides)
precepice : **prec·i·pice**
pre·cious
precipace : **prec·i·pice**
precipatation : **pre·cip·i·ta·tion**
prec·i·pice
pre·cip·i·ta·tion
precippation : **pre·cip·i·ta·tion**
predater : **pred·a·tor**
pred·a·tor
preditor : **pred·a·tor**
predjudice : **prej·u·dice**
preech : **preach**
pre-empt
preemptory : **pe·remp·to·ry**
preest : **priest**
pref·ace
pre·fer
prefface : **pref·ace**
preffer : **pre·fer**
prefice : **pref·ace**
prefiss : **pref·ace**
prefundity : **pro·fun·di·ty**
preg·nant
pregnent : **preg·nant**
pregnint : **preg·nant**
preimpt : **pre-empt**
preist : **priest**
prejewdice : **prej·u·dice**
prejudace : **prej·u·dice**
prej·u·dice
prejudiss : **prej·u·dice**
premeer : **pre·mier** (prime
  minister) *or* **pre·miere** (first
  performance)

premeir : **pre·mier** (prime
  minister) *or* **pre·miere** (first
  performance)
premere : **pre·mier** (prime
  minister) *or* **pre·miere** (first
  performance)
pre·mier (prime minister);
  pre·miere (first performance)
pre·miere (first performance);
  pre·mier (prime minister)
prepair : **pre·pare**
pre·pare
prescious : **pre·cious**
pre·scrip·tion
pres·ence (*noun,* being
  present); **pres·ents** (*verb,*
  introduces); **pres·ents** (*noun,*
  gifts)
pre·serve
pres·i·dent (one who presides);
  pre·ce·dent (that which
  comes before)
presious : **pre·cious**
presipice : **prec·i·pice**
presipitation : **pre·cip·i·ta·tion**
pressipice : **prec·i·pice**
presstige : **pres·tige**
prestege : **pres·tige**
presteze : **pres·tige**
pres·tige
pre·sume
presumetuous :
  pre·sump·tu·ous
pre·sump·tu·ous
presumtuous : **pre·sump·tu·ous**
pretence : **pre·tense**
pre·tense
pretsel : **pret·zel**
pret·zel
pretzell : **pret·zel**
pretzil : **pret·zel**
pre·vail

prevailent : **prev·a·lent**
prevale : **pre·vail**
prev·a·lent
prevelant : **prev·a·lent**
prevert : **per·vert**
previlent : **prev·a·lent**
priempt : **pre-empt**
prier : **pri·or**
priest
primative : **prim·i·tive**
prim·i·tive
primmitive : **prim·i·tive**
principal (*noun,* one in charge;
    adj., most important);
    prin·ci·ple (rule, standard)
principle (rule, standard);
    prin·ci·pal (*noun,* one in
    charge; *adj.,* most important)
pri·or
priorety : **pri·or·i·ty**
pri·or·i·ty
priorrity : **pri·or·i·ty**
prisen : **pris·on**
prism
pris·on
prisson : **pris·on**
pri·va·cy
privalege : **priv·i·lege**
pri·vate
privelege : **priv·i·lege**
privet (bush); **pri·vate** (personal)
privicy : **pri·va·cy**
priviledge : **priv·i·lege**
priv·i·lege
privilige : **priv·i·lege**
privissy : **pri·va·cy**
prizm : **prism**
prizzen : **pris·on**
prob·a·ble
probible : **prob·a·ble**
prob·lem
problim : **prob·lem**

problum : **prob·lem**
pro·ce·dure
pro·ceed (to continue);
    pre·cede (to go before)
proceedure : **pro·ce·dure**
procidure : **pro·ce·dure**
procktor : **proc·tor**
pro·claim
proclaimation : **proc·la·ma·tion**
proc·la·ma·tion
proclame : **pro·claim**
proclemation : **proc·la·ma·tion**
proclimation : **proc·la·ma·tion**
procrasstinate : **pro·cras·ti·nate**
procrastentate : **pro·cras·ti·nate**
pro·cras·ti·nate
procter : **proc·tor**
proc·tor
proddigal : **prod·i·gal**
prodegy : **prod·i·gy**
prodicle : **prod·i·gal**
prod·i·gal
prodigle : **prod·i·gal**
prod·i·gy
prodogy : **prod·i·gy**
pro·duce
produse : **pro·duce**
profacy : **proph·e·cy** (*noun*) or
    proph·e·sy (*verb*)
profain : **pro·fane**
pro·fane
profanety : **pro·fan·i·ty**
pro·fan·i·ty
profannity : **pro·fan·i·ty**
profesor : **pro·fes·sor**
professer : **pro·fes·sor**
pro·fes·sor
profet : **prof·it**
proffit : **prof·it**
prof·it
profoundity : **pro·fun·di·ty**
profundety : **pro·fun·di·ty**

pro·fun·di·ty
prohibbit : **pro·hib·it**
prohibet : **pro·hib·it**
pro·hib·it
proliffic : **pro·lif·ic**
pro·lif·ic
promanent : **prom·i·nent**
prom·e·nade
promice : **prom·ise**
prominade : **prom·e·nade**
prominant : **prom·i·nent**
prom·i·nent
prom·ise
promisory : **prom·is·so·ry**
promiss : **prom·ise**
prom·is·so·ry
prommenade : **prom·e·nade**
promminent : **prom·i·nent**
prommise : **prom·ise**
pronounciation :
   pro·nun·ci·a·tion
pro·nun·ci·a·tion
pro·pa·gan·da
propeganda : **pro·pa·gan·da**
propencity : **pro·pen·si·ty**
pro·pen·si·ty
prophacy : **proph·e·cy** (*noun*)
   or **proph·e·sy** (verb)
proph·e·cy (*noun*); **proph·e·sy**
   (*verb*)
proph·e·sy (*verb*); **proph·e·cy**
   (*noun*)
prophissy : **proph·e·cy** (*noun*)
   or **proph·e·sy** (verb)
propiganda : **pro·pa·gan·da**
propinsity : **pro·pen·si·ty**
proppaganda : **pro·pa·gan·da**
pros·e·cute
prosicute : **pros·e·cute**
pros·per·ous
prospirous : **pros·per·ous**
prossicute : **pros·e·cute**

protacol : **pro·to·col**
Prot·es·tant
Protestint : **Prot·es·tant**
Protistant : **Prot·es·tant**
protocall : **pro·to·col**
pro·to·col
prowace : **prow·ess**
prow·ess
prowice : **prow·ess**
prowiss : **prow·ess**
proximety : **prox·im·i·ty**
prox·im·i·ty
proximmity : **prox·im·i·ty**
psalm
psam : **psalm**
pseudanym : **pseu·do·nym**
pseudonim : **pseu·do·nym**
pseu·do·nym
psiche : **psy·che**
psichiatrist : **psy·chi·a·trist**
psichic : **psy·chic**
psichologist : **psy·chol·o·gist**
psichology : **psy·chol·o·gy**
psudonym : **pseu·do·nym**
psuedonym : **pseu·do·nym**
psychalogist : **psy·chol·o·gist**
psychalogy : **psy·chol·o·gy**
psy·che
psy·chi·a·trist
psy·chic
psycholagist : **psy·chol·o·gist**
psycholagy : **psy·chol·o·gy**
psychollogist : **psy·chol·o·gist**
psychollogy : **psy·chol·o·gy**
psy·chol·o·gist
psy·chol·o·gy
psychyatrist : **psy·chi·a·trist**
psycologist : **psy·chol·o·gist**
psycology : **psy·chol·o·gy**
ptarodactyl : **ptero·dac·tyl**
pteradactyl : **ptero·dac·tyl**
pteridactyl : **ptero·dac·tyl**

pterodactile : **ptero·dac·tyl**
pterodactill : **ptero·dac·tyl**
ptero·dac·tyl
ptomain : **pto·maine**
pto·maine
ptomane : **pto·maine**
Puarto Rico : **Puer·to Ri·co**
publacize : **pub·li·cize**
publicety : **pub·lic·i·ty**
publicise : **pub·li·cize**
pub·li·cist
publicitty : **pub·lic·i·ty**
pub·lic·i·ty
pub·li·cize
publisist : **pub·li·cist**
publisity : **pub·lic·i·ty**
puddel : **pud·dle**
pud·dle
pudle : **poo·dle** (dog) *or*
  pud·dle (water)
Puer·to Ri·co
pueter : **pew·ter**
pullmonary : **pul·mo·nary**
pulmanary : **pul·mo·nary**
pul·mo·nary
pulmonery : **pul·mo·nary**
pulpet : **pul·pit**
pul·pit
pumace : **pum·ice**
pum·ice
pumiss : **pum·ice**
pumkin : **pump·kin**
pummice : **pum·ice**
pumpken : **pump·kin**
pump·kin
pundet : **pun·dit**
pun·dit
punesh : **pun·ish**
pun·gent

pungint : **pun·gent**
pun·ish
punken : **pump·kin**
punkin : **pump·kin**
punnish : **pun·ish**
pupel : **pu·pil**
pu·pil
pup·pet
puppil : **pu·pil**
puppit : **pup·pet**
purety : **pu·ri·ty**
puriffy : **pu·ri·fy**
pu·ri·fy
pu·ri·tan
puriten : **pu·ri·tan**
puritty : **pu·ri·ty**
pu·ri·ty
purjury : **per·ju·ry**
purl (knitting stitch); **pearl**
  (gem)
purpetrate : **per·pe·trate**
purrify : **pu·ri·fy**
purritan : **pu·ri·tan**
purrity : **pu·ri·ty**
pursacute : **per·se·cute**
pursuade : **per·suade**
pur·sue
purterb : **per·turb**
putrafy : **pu·tre·fy**
pu·tre·fy
putriffy : **pu·tre·fy**
putrify : **pu·tre·fy**
puzle : **puz·zle**
puzzal : **puz·zle**
puzzel : **puz·zle**
puz·zle
pyg·my
py·ro·ma·ni·ac
py·thon

Q

Quabec : **Que•bec**
quack
quackary : **quack•ery**
quack•ery
quackry : **quack•ery**
quadrain : **qua•train**
quadrangel : **quad•ran•gle**
quad•ran•gle
quad•rant
quadrill : **qua•drille**
qua•drille
quadruble : **qua•dru•ple**
quadrublet : **qua•dru•plet**
qua•dru•ple
quaf : **quaff**
quafe : **quaff**
quaff
quaggmire : **quag•mire**
quagmier : **quag•mire**
quag•mire
quagmyre : **quag•mire**
quaik : **quake**
quail
quaint
quaisar : **qua•sar**
quaiver : **qua•ver**
quak : **quack**
quake
qualafication : **qual•i•fi•ca•tion**
qualafied : **qual•i•fied**
qualafy : **qual•i•fy**
qualaty : **qual•i•ty**
quale : **quail**
qualefy : **qual•i•fy**
qualifacation : **qual•i•fi•ca•tion**
qual•i•fi•ca•tion
qual•i•fied
qual•i•fy
qual•i•ty
quallification : **qual•i•fi•ca•tion**

quallified : **qual•i•fied**
quallify : **qual•i•fy**
quallity : **qual•i•ty**
qualm
quam : **qualm**
quan•da•ry
quandery : **quan•da•ry**
quandrent : **quad•rant**
quandry : **quan•da•ry**
quanity : **quan•ti•ty**
quantafy : **quan•ti•fy**
quante : **quaint**
quantety : **quan•ti•ty**
quan•ti•fy
quan•ti•ty
quantom : **quan•tum**
quan•tum
quaranteen : **quar•an•tine**
quar•an•tine
quarel : **quar•rel**
quareled : **quar•reled**
quareling : **quar•rel•ing**
quarentine : **quar•an•tine**
quarintine : **quar•an•tine**
quarl : **quar•rel**
quar•rel
quar•reled *or* **quar•relled**
quar•rel•ing *or* **quar•rel•ling**
quar•relled *or* **quar•reled**
quar•rel•ling *or* **quar•rel•ing**
quarrey : **quar•ry**
quar•ry
quart
quar•ter
quarts (*plur.*); **quartz** (mineral)
quartz (mineral); **quarts** (*plur.*)
quary : **quar•ry**
qua•sar
quasarre : **qua•sar**
quaser : **qua•sar**

237

quater : **quar·ter**
qua·train
quatrane : **qua·train**
quatrangle : **quad·ran·gle**
qua·ver
quawlified : **qual·i·fied**
quawlify : **qual·i·fy**
quay (wharf); **key** (for a lock)
quazar : **qua·sar**
Qubec : **Que·bec**
que : **queue** (pigtail; line) *or*
  cue (signal; poolstick)
quean : **queen**
quear : **queer**
queary : **que·ry**
queasaly : **quea·si·ly**
quea·si·ly
queasly : **quea·si·ly**
quea·sy
queazy : **quea·sy**
Que·bec
Quebeck : **Que·bec**
queeche : **quiche**
queen
queer
queery : **que·ry**
queesh : **quiche**
queesly : **quea·si·ly**
queesy : **quea·sy**
queezy : **quea·sy**
queishe : **quiche**
quene : **queen**
quere : **queer**
querie : **que·ry**
querry : **que·ry**
que·ry
questin : **ques·tion**
ques·tion
questionaire : **ques·tion·naire**
questionnair : **ques·tion·naire**
ques·tion·naire

queue (pigtail; line); **cue**
  (signal; poolstick)
quey : **quay**
quiche
quick
quicksotic : **quix·o·tic**
quiescant : **qui·es·cent**
qui·es·cent
quiesent : **qui·es·cent**
quiessent : **qui·es·cent**
qui·et (silent); **quite** (entirely)
quik : **quick**
quillt : **quilt**
quilt
quinntet : **quin·tet**
quintecence : **quin·tes·sence**
quintescence : **quin·tes·sence**
quintesence : **quin·tes·sence**
quin·tes·sence
quintessense : **quin·tes·sence**
quin·tet
quintette : **quin·tet**
quior : **choir**
quire : **choir**
quiseen : **cui·sine**
quisine : **cui·sine**
quis·ling
quite (entirely); **qui·et** (silent)
quivver : **quiv·er**
quix·ot·ic
quixottic : **quix·ot·ic**
quizacal : **quiz·zi·cal**
quizes : **quiz·zes**
quizical : **quiz·zi·cal**
quizine : **cui·sine**
quizling : **quis·ling**
quizotic : **quix·ot·ic**
quizzacal : **quiz·zi·cal**
quiz·zi·cal
quoat : **quote**
quoatable : **quot·able**
quoatient : **quo·tient**

quoff : **quaff**
quoram : **quo·rum**
quorom : **quo·rum**
quorrey : **quar·ry**
quorrum : **quo·rum**
quort : **quart**
quo·rum
quoshent : **quo·tient**
quotabile : **quot·able**
quot·able
quoteable : **quot·able**
quotent : **quo·tient**
quo·tient
qwack : **quack**
qwackery : **quack·ery**
qwadrangle : **quad·ran·gle**
qwadrant : **quad·rant**
qwadruple : **qua·dru·ple**
qwadruplet : **qua·dru·plet**
qwaff : **quaff**
qwagmire : **quag·mire**

qwaint : **quaint**
qwake : **quake**
qwalified : **qual·i·fied**
qwalify : **qual·i·fy**
qwality : **qual·i·ty**
qwandary : **quan·da·ry**
qwantify : **quan·ti·fy**
qwantity : **quan·ti·ty**
qwarantine : **quar·an·tine**
qwarrel : **quar·rel**
qwarreling : **quar·rel·ing**
qwarry : **quar·ry**
qwart : **quart**
qwarter : **quar·ter**
qwartz : **quartz**
qwasar : **qua·sar**
qwaver : **qua·ver**
qweasily : **quea·si·ly**
qweasy : **quea·sy**
Qwebec : **Que·bec**
qwote : **quote**

R

rabbed : **ra·bid**
rab·bi
rabbid : **ra·bid**
rabi : **rab·bi**
ra·bid
rac·coon
raccune : **rac·coon**
rac·ism
rack·et
rackit : **rack·et**
rackonteur : **ra·con·teur**
ra·con·teur
racontoor : **ra·con·teur**
racontuer : **ra·con·teur**
racoon : **rac·coon**
racunteur : **ra·con·teur**
raddish : **rad·ish**
radeator : **ra·di·a·tor**
radesh : **rad·ish**
radiam : **ra·di·um**
ra·di·ance
radianse : **ra·di·ance**
radiater : **ra·di·a·tor**
ra·di·a·tor
radience : **ra·di·ance**
radiense : **ra·di·ance**
rad·ish
ra·di·um
rag·ged
raggid : **rag·ged**
raign : **reign**
rai·ment
raindeer : **rein·deer**
rainment : **rai·ment**
raisen : **rai·sin**
rai·sin
rament : **rai·ment**
ram·pant
rampent : **ram·pant**
rampint : **ram·pant**

ranced : **ran·cid**
rancer : **ran·cor**
ran·cid
ran·cor
rancore : **ran·cor**
randam : **ran·dom**
randem : **ran·dom**
randim : **ran·dom**
ran·dom
randum : **ran·dom**
rangler : **wran·gler**
rankor : **ran·cor**
ransid : **ran·cid**
raon : **ray·on**
rap·id
raport : **rap·port**
rappid : **rap·id**
rappore : **rap·port**
rap·port
rappsody : **rhap·so·dy**
rapsady : **rhap·so·dy**
rapsody : **rhap·so·dy**
rarafied : **rar·efied**
rar·efied
rarety : **rar·i·ty**
rarified : **rar·efied**
raritty : **rar·i·ty**
rar·i·ty
rarrity : **rar·i·ty**
rasberry : **rasp·ber·ry**
ras·cal
rasen : **rai·sin**
rasin : **rai·sin**
rasism : **rac·ism**
raskal : **ras·cal**
raskel : **ras·cal**
rasor : **ra·zor**
raspbarry : **rasp·ber·ry**
rasp·ber·ry
raspbery : **rasp·ber·ry**

rasscal : **ras•cal**
rassel : **wres•tle**
rassle : **wres•tle**
ratafy : **rat•i•fy**
ratefy : **rat•i•fy**
ratiffy : **rat•i•fy**
rat•i•fy
ratler : **rat•tler**
rattify : **rat•i•fy**
rattlar : **rat•tler**
rat•tler
raught : **wrought**
rav•age
raveen : **ra•vine**
ravege : **rav•age**
ravene : **ra•vine**
raveoli : **rav•i•o•li**
ravesh : **rav•ish**
ravige : **rav•age**
ra•vine
raviole : **rav•i•o•li**
rav•i•o•li
ravioly : **rav•i•o•li**
rav•ish
ravvage : **rav•age**
ravvish : **rav•ish**
ray•on
razer : **ra•zor**
ra•zor
razzberry : **rasp•ber•ry**
razzor : **ra•zor**
reacter : **re•ac•tor**
re•ac•tor
read (book); **red** (color); **reed** (grass)
read•able
readible : **read•able**
readolent : **red•o•lent**
ready
reak : **reek** (to stink) or **wreak** (to inflict)
realise (*Brit.*) : **re•al•ize**

re•al•ize
realm
realter : **re•al•tor**
re•al•tor
reap
reasin : **rea•son**
rea•son
reath : **wreath** (*noun*) or **wreathe** (*verb*)
reathe : **wreath** (*noun*) or **wreathe** (*verb*)
rebelion : **re•bel•lion**
rebellian : **re•bel•lion**
re•bel•lion
re•but•tal
rebuttel : **re•but•tal**
rebuttle : **re•but•tal**
recalcetrant : **re•cal•ci•trant**
re•cal•ci•trant
recalcitrent : **re•cal•ci•trant**
recalsitrant : **re•cal•ci•trant**
reccognize : **re•cog•nize**
reccommend : **rec•om•mend**
recead : **re•cede**
re•cede
receed : **re•cede**
re•ceipt
receit : **re•ceipt**
re•ceive
recepe : **rec•i•pe**
re•cep•ta•cle
receptecle : **re•cep•ta•cle**
receptical : **re•cep•ta•cle**
recepticle : **re•cep•ta•cle**
recete : **re•ceipt**
receve : **re•ceive**
rech : **retch** (to vomit) or **wretch** (miserable one)
reciept : **re•ceipt**
recieve : **re•ceive**
rec•i•pe
recipiant : **re•cip•i•ent**

re·cip·i·ent
recippy : **rec·i·pe**
reciprical : **re·cip·ro·cal**
re·cip·ro·cal
reciprocitty : **re·ci·proc·i·ty**
re·ci·proc·i·ty
reciproety : **re·ci·proc·i·ty**
reciprosity : **re·ci·proc·i·ty**
reciprossity : **re·ci·proc·i·ty**
re·cit·al
re·cite
recitel : **re·cit·al**
recitle : **re·cit·al**
reck : **wreak** (to inflict) or
  wreck (to destroy)
reckage : **wreck·age**
reckondite : **re·con·dite**
reckonize : **rec·og·nize**
recognise (*Brit.*) : **rec·og·nize**
rec·og·nize
recomend : **rec·om·mend**
rec·om·mend
recompence : **rec·om·pense**
rec·om·pense
recompince : **rec·om·pense**
recompinse : **rec·om·pense**
rec·on·cile
recondight : **re·con·dite**
re·con·dite
reconsile : **re·con·cile**
recorse : **re·course**
recource : **re·course**
re·course
recovary : **re·cov·ery**
re·cov·ery
re·cruit
recrut : **re·cruit**
recrute : **re·cruit**
rectafy : **rec·ti·fy**
rectatude : **rec·ti·tude**
rectefy : **rec·ti·fy**
rectetude : **rec·ti·tude**

rectiffy : **rec·ti·fy**
rec·ti·fy
rectitood : **rec·ti·tude**
rec·ti·tude
recumpense : **rec·om·pense**
recurence : **re·cur·rence**
recurrance : **re·cur·rence**
re·cur·rence
red (color); **read** (book)
redalent : **red·o·lent**
reddolent : **red·o·lent**
reddress : **re·dress**
redduce : **re·duce**
reddy : **ready**
redeam : **re·deem**
re·deem
redeme : **re·deem**
rediculous : **ri·dic·u·lous**
red·o·lent
redolint : **red·o·lent**
re·dress
re·duce
re·dun·dant
redundent : **re·dun·dant**
reduse : **re·duce**
reed (grass); **read** (book)
reek (to stink); **wreak** (to
  inflict)
reelize : **re·al·ize**
reeltor : **re·al·tor**
reep : **reap**
reeson : **rea·son**
referance : **ref·er·ence**
ref·er·ee
ref·er·ence
referense : **ref·er·ence**
ref·er·ent
referie : **ref·er·ee**
referint : **ref·er·ent**
referrence : **ref·er·ence**
referrent : **ref·er·ent**
refery : **ref·er·ee**

refferee : **ref•er•ee**
refference : **ref•er•ence**
refirent : **ref•er•ent**
refrigarator : **re•frig•er•a•tor**
refrigerater : **re•frig•er•a•tor**
re•frig•er•a•tor
refriggerator : **re•frig•er•a•tor**
refrijerator : **re•frig•er•a•tor**
re•fus•al
re•fuse (*verb*); **ref•use** (*noun*)
refusel : **re•fus•al**
refussal : **re•fus•al**
regada : **re•gat•ta**
regadda : **re•gat•ta**
regail : **re•gale**
re•gal
re•gale
regamen : **reg•i•men**
re•gard
re•gat•ta
regaurd : **re•gard**
regeme : **re•gime**
regemen : **reg•i•men**
re•gen•cy
regensy : **re•gen•cy**
regergitate : **re•gur•gi•tate**
regester : **reg•is•ter**
reggale : **re•gale**
reggimen : **reg•i•men**
reggister : **reg•is•ter**
reggular : **reg•u•lar**
regiman : **reg•i•men**
re•gime
reg•i•men
regirgitate : **re•gur•gi•tate**
reg•is•ter
regle : **re•gal**
regotta : **re•gat•ta**
reguard : **re•gard**
reg•u•lar
reguler : **reg•u•lar**
regulir : **reg•u•lar**

regurgetate : **re•gur•gi•tate**
re•gur•gi•tate
regurjitate : **re•gur•gi•tate**
rehabilatate : **re•ha•bil•i•tate**
re•ha•bil•i•tate
rehabillitate : **re•ha•bil•i•tate**
rehearcel : **re•hears•al**
re•hears•al
re•hearse
rehearsel : **re•hears•al**
reherce : **re•hearse**
rehercil : **re•hears•al**
rehersal : **re•hears•al**
reherse : **re•hearse**
reign
reimberse : **re•im•burse**
reimburce : **re•im•burse**
re•im•burse
rein•deer
reitarate : **re•it•er•ate**
re•it•er•ate
reiterrate : **re•it•er•ate**
re•joice
rejoise : **re•joice**
rejoyce : **re•joice**
rejuvanate : **re•ju•ve•nate**
re•ju•ve•nate
rejuvinate : **re•ju•ve•nate**
reknown : **re•nown**
relagate : **rel•e•gate**
rel•a•tive
relavent : **rel•e•vant**
releace : **re•lease**
re•lease
releave : **re•lieve**
rel•e•gate
releive : **re•lieve**
relenquish : **re•lin•quish**
relese : **re•lease**
relesh : **rel•ish**
rel•e•vant
releve : **re•lieve**

relevent : **rel•e•vant**
reliabal : **re•li•able**
re•li•able
re•li•ance
relianse : **re•li•ance**
re•li•ant
relible : **re•li•able**
rel•ic
relick : **rel•ic**
relieble : **re•li•able**
relience : **re•li•ance**
reliense : **re•li•ance**
relient : **re•li•ant**
re•lieve
religate : **rel•e•gate**
relinquesh : **re•lin•quish**
re•lin•quish
rel•ish
relitive : **rel•a•tive**
relize : **re•al•ize**
rellative : **rel•a•tive**
rellavent : **rel•e•vant**
rellegate : **rel•e•gate**
rellevant : **rel•e•vant**
relliable : **re•li•able**
rellic : **rel•ic**
relligate : **rel•e•gate**
rellish : **rel•ish**
relm : **realm**
re•luc•tance
reluctanse : **re•luc•tance**
re•luc•tant
reluctense : **re•luc•tance**
reluctent : **re•luc•tant**
reluctince : **re•luc•tance**
reluctint : **re•luc•tant**
relyance : **re•li•ance**
remady : **rem•e•dy**
re•main
remane : **re•main**
remanisce : **rem•i•nisce**
re•mark•able

remarkible : **re•mark•able**
remeadial : **re•me•di•al**
remeddy : **rem•e•dy**
remedeal : **re•me•di•al**
re•me•di•al
rem•e•dy
remedyal : **re•me•di•al**
remeedial : **re•me•di•al**
remeidial : **re•me•di•al**
re•mem•brance
remembranse : **re•mem•brance**
remembrence : **re•mem•brance**
remembrense : **re•mem•brance**
remembrince : **re•mem•brance**
remiddy : **rem•e•dy**
remidy : **rem•e•dy**
reminice : **rem•i•nisce**
rem•i•nisce
reminiss : **rem•i•nisce**
remitance : **re•mit•tance**
re•mit•tance
remittanse : **re•mit•tance**
remittence : **re•mit•tance**
remittense : **re•mit•tance**
remittince : **re•mit•tance**
remminisce : **rem•i•nisce**
remmittance : **re•mit•tance**
remmoval : **re•mov•al**
rem•nant
remnent : **rem•nant**
remnint : **rem•nant**
re•mov•al
removel : **re•mov•al**
remunarate : **re•mu•ner•ate**
re•mu•ner•ate
remunnerate : **re•mu•ner•ate**
renagade : **ren•e•gade**
renavate : **ren•o•vate**
rench : **wrench**
rendavous : **ren•dez•vous**
rendevoo : **ren•dez•vous**
ren•dez•vous

ren·e·gade
re·new·al
renewel : **re·new·al**
renigade : **ren·e·gade**
rennagade : **ren·e·gade**
rennovate : **ren·o·vate**
renoun : **re·nown**
re·nounce
renounse : **re·nounce**
ren·o·vate
re·nown
renownce : **re·nounce**
renumerate : **re·mu·ner·ate**
reoccurrence : **re·cur·rence**
Reo de Janeiro : **Rio de Ja·nei·ro**
reostat : **rheo·stat**
re·pair
repare : **re·pair**
re·peal
re·peat
repeel : **re·peal**
repeet : **re·peat**
repele : **re·peal**
repelent : **re·pel·lent**
repellant : **re·pel·lent**
re·pel·lent
re·pen·tance
repentanse : **re·pen·tance**
repentence : **re·pen·tance**
rep·e·ti·tion
repintance : **re·pen·tance**
repitition : **rep·e·ti·tion**
repleat : **re·plete**
repleca : **rep·li·ca**
repleet : **re·plete**
re·plen·ish
replennish : **re·plen·ish**
re·plete
rep·li·ca
replicka : **rep·li·ca**
replinish : **re·plen·ish**

repplica : **rep·li·ca**
repprobate : **rep·ro·bate**
repramand : **rep·ri·mand**
repreave : **re·prieve**
reprehencible : **rep·re·hen·si·ble**
reprehensable : **rep·re·hen·si·ble**
rep·re·hen·si·ble
repreive : **re·prieve**
repremand : **rep·ri·mand**
repreve : **re·prieve**
repribate : **rep·ro·bate**
re·prieve
reprihensible : **rep·re·hen·si·ble**
rep·ri·mand
re·pri·sal
reprisel : **re·pri·sal**
reprissal : **re·pri·sal**
reprizal : **re·pri·sal**
re·proach
rep·ro·bate
reproch : **re·proach**
re·proof (*noun*); **re·prove** (*verb*)
reproove : **re·proof** (*noun*) *or* **re·prove** (*verb*)
re·prove (*verb*); **re·proof** (*noun*)
reptial : **rep·tile**
rep·tile
republec : **re·pub·lic**
re·pub·lic
republick : **re·pub·lic**
repudeate : **re·pu·di·ate**
re·pu·di·ate
rep·u·ta·ble
reputible : **rep·u·ta·ble**
requiam : **re·qui·em**
re·qui·em
requiset : **req·ui·site**
req·ui·site
requissite : **req·ui·site**
requium : **re·qui·em**
requizite : **req·ui·site**

resarrect : **res·ur·rect**
resavoir : **res·er·voir**
rescend : **re·scind**
re·scind
re·search
reseptacle : **re·cep·ta·cle**
reserch : **re·search**
resergence : **re·sur·gence**
res·er·voir
residdence : **res·i·dence**
res·i·dence
residense : **res·i·dence**
re·sign
resiliant : **re·sil·ient**
re·sil·ient
resillient : **re·sil·ient**
res·in
resine : **re·sign**
resipe : **rec·i·pe**
resipient : **re·cip·i·ent**
resiprocal : **re·cip·ro·cal**
resiprocity : **rec·i·proc·i·ty**
resipy : **rec·i·pe**
resirgence : **re·sur·gence**
re·sis·tance
resistence : **re·sis·tance**
resistense : **re·sis·tance**
resital : **re·cit·al**
resite : **re·cite**
resivoir : **res·er·voir**
reson : **rea·son**
resorce : **re·source**
resorse : **re·source**
re·source
resourse : **re·source**
re·spect·able
respectible : **re·spect·able**
resperator : **res·pi·ra·tor**
respirater : **res·pi·ra·tor**
res·pi·ra·tor
respit : **res·pite**
res·pite

responcible : **re·spon·si·ble**
responsable : **re·spon·si·ble**
responseble : **re·spon·si·ble**
re·spon·si·ble
ressel : **wres·tle**
ressend : **re·scind**
ressidence : **res·i·dence**
ressin : **res·in**
ressind : **re·scind**
ressle : **wres·tle**
restarant : **res·tau·rant**
restatution : **res·ti·tu·tion**
res·tau·rant
restetution : **res·ti·tu·tion**
res·ti·tu·tion
restle : **wres·tle**
restorant : **res·tau·rant**
resurect : **res·ur·rect**
re·sur·gence
resurgince : **re·sur·gence**
res·ur·rect
retacence : **ret·i·cence**
re·tail
retale : **re·tail**
retaleate : **re·tal·i·ate**
re·tal·i·ate
retalliate : **re·tal·i·ate**
retch (to vomit); **wretch**
  (miserable one)
ret·i·cence
reticense : **ret·i·cence**
ret·i·na
ret·i·nue
retisense : **ret·i·cence**
retreave : **re·trieve**
retreive : **re·trieve**
retreve : **re·trieve**
re·trieve
rettail : **re·tail**
retticence : **ret·i·cence**
rettina : **ret·i·na**
rettinue : **ret·i·nue**

revalation : **rev•e•la•tion**
revalry : **rev•el•ry**
revanue : **rev•e•nue**
revarence : **rev•er•ence**
revarent : **rev•er•ent**
revarie : **rev•er•ie**
re•veal
revecable : **re•vo•ca•ble**
reveel : **re•veal**
rev•eil•le
reveilly : **rev•eil•le**
rev•el
rev•e•la•tion
revele : **re•veal**
revell : **rev•el**
revellie : **rev•eil•le**
rev•el•ry
revennue : **rev•e•nue**
rev•e•nue
reverance : **rev•er•ence**
revercil : **re•ver•sal**
reveree : **rev•er•ie**
rev•er•ence
reverense : **rev•er•ence**
rev•e•rent
rev•er•ie
re•ver•sal
reversel : **re•ver•sal**
revery : **rev•er•ie**
revil : **rev•el**
revilation : **rev•e•la•tion**
reville : **rev•eil•le**
revinue : **rev•e•nue**
revirence : **rev•er•ence**
revirie : **rev•er•ie**
revirsal : **re•ver•sal**
re•vise
re•vi•sion
revission : **re•vi•sion**
re•viv•al
revivel : **re•viv•al**
revize : **re•vise**

revizion : **re•vi•sion**
re•vo•ca•ble
revoceble : **re•vo•ca•ble**
revocibal : **re•vo•ca•ble**
revokable : **re•vo•ca•ble**
revokeble : **re•vo•ca•ble**
rezervoir : **res•er•voir**
rezin : **res•in**
rhapsady : **rhap•so•dy**
rhapsiddy : **rhap•so•dy**
rhapsidy : **rhap•so•dy**
rhap•so•dy
rheo•stat
rhetaric : **rhet•o•ric**
rhet•o•ric
rhetorick : **rhet•o•ric**
rhettoric : **rhet•o•ric**
rhine•stone
rhi•noc•er•os
rhinocirus : **rhi•noc•er•os**
rhinoseros : **rhi•noc•er•os**
rhinosserus : **rhi•noc•er•os**
rhithm : **rhythm**
Rhode Is•land
rhu•barb
rhyme (poetry); **rime** (frost)
rhythem : **rhythm**
rhythm
rhythum : **rhythm**
rib•ald
ribbald : **rib•ald**
ribben : **rib•bon**
ribbin : **rib•bon**
rib•bon
ribon : **rib•bon**
ricachay : **ric•o•chet**
rickachet : **ric•o•chet**
rickashay : **ric•o•chet**
rick•ety
rickitty : **rick•ety**
rickity : **rick•ety**
ric•o•chet

ricoshay : **ric•o•chet**

ridacule : **rid•i•cule**

riddecule : **rid•i•cule**

riddicule : **rid•i•cule**

riddiculous : **ri•dic•u•lous**

rid•i•cule

ri•dic•u•lous

ridiculus : **ri•dic•u•lous**

rie : **rye** (grain) *or* **wry** (ironic)

riegn : **reign**

riendeer : **rein•deer**

rifal : **rif•fle** (to thumb through) *or* **ri•fle** (gun)

rifel : **rif•fle** (to thumb through) *or* **ri•fle** (gun)

rif•fle (to thumb through); **ri•fle** (gun)

ri•fle (gun); **rif•fle** (to thumb through)

rig•a•ma•role *or* **rig•ma•role**

riged : **rig•id**

riger : **rig•or**

riggamarole : **rig•ma•role**

riggid : **rig•id**

riggle : **wrig•gle**

riggor : **rig•or**

righ•teous

rightious : **righ•teous**

rightius : **righ•teous**

rig•id

rig•ma•role *or* **rig•a•ma•role**

rigmaroll : **rig•ma•role**

rigmerole : **rig•ma•role**

rig•or

rijid : **rig•id**

rime (frost); **rhyme** (poetry)

rimedial : **re•me•di•al**

rinagade : **ren•e•gade**

rinestone : **rhine•stone**

rinkle : **wrin•kle**

rinoceros : **rhi•noc•er•os**

rinovate : **ren•o•vate**

Rio de Ja•nei•ro

Rio de Janerro : **Rio de Ja•nei•ro**

Rio de Janiero : **Rio de Ja•nei•ro**

riostat : **rheo•stat**

riskay : **ris•qué**

risquay : **ris•qué**

ris•qué

rist : **wrist**

riter : **writ•er**

rithe : **writhe**

rithm : **rhythm**

rithum : **rhythm**

riting : **writ•ing**

rittual : **rit•u•al**

rit•u•al

rituel : **rit•u•al**

ri•val

rivel : **ri•val**

roadeo : **ro•deo**

Road Island : **Rhode Is•land**

robbot : **ro•bot**

ro•bot

robott : **ro•bot**

rock•et

rocketery : **rock•et•ry**

rock•et•ry

rockit : **rock•et**

rockitry : **rock•et•ry**

rodant : **ro•dent**

roddent : **ro•dent**

Rode Island : **Rhode Is•land**

ro•dent

ro•deo

rodio : **ro•deo**

roial : **roy•al**

roiel : **roy•al**

rollette : **rou•lette**

ro•mance

romanntic : **ro•man•tic**

romanse : **ro•mance**

ro·man·tic
romantick : **ro·man·tic**
rondavoo : **ren·dez·vous**
rondezvous : **ren·dez·vous**
roomate : **room·mate**
room·mate
rootabaga : **ru·ta·ba·ga**
rosarry : **ro·sa·ry**
ro·sa·ry
roserry : **ro·sa·ry**
rosery : **ro·sa·ry**
rotarry : **ro·ta·ry**
ro·ta·ry
roterry : **ro·ta·ry**
rotery : **ro·ta·ry**
rotory : **ro·ta·ry**
rough·age
roughege : **rough·age**
roughian : **ruf·fi·an**
roughige : **rough·age**
rought : **wrought**
rou·lette
routean : **rou·tine**
routeen : **rou·tine**
routene : **rou·tine**
rou·tine
roy·al
royel : **roy·al**
rubarb : **rhu·barb**
rubrec : **ru·bric**
ru·bric
rubrick : **ru·bric**
ruckas : **ruck·us**
ruckis : **ruck·us**

ruck·us
rudament : **ru·di·ment**
rudement : **ru·di·ment**
ru·di·ment
ruff : **rough**
ruffein : **ruf·fi·an**
ruf·fi·an
ruffien : **ruf·fi·an**
rufian : **ruf·fi·an**
rulette : **rou·lette**
rumage : **rum·mage**
rumanante : **ru·mi·nate**
rumer : **ru·mor**
ru·mi·nate
rum·mage
rummege : **rum·mage**
rummige : **rum·mage**
rumminnate : **ru·mi·nate**
rummor : **ru·mor**
ru·mor
rumpace : **rum·pus**
rumpis : **rum·pus**
rum·pus
Rushia : **Rus·sia**
Rusia : **Rus·sia**
Rus·sia
rus·tic
rustick : **rus·tic**
ru·ta·ba·ga
rutabaiga : **ru·ta·ba·ga**
rutabega : **ru·ta·ba·ga**
rutebaga : **ru·ta·ba·ga**
rutine : **rou·tine**
rye (grain); **wry** (ironic)
ryly : **wry·ly**

S

sabateur : **sab•o•teur**
Sabath : **Sab•bath**
sabatical : **sab•bat•i•cal**
sabatoor : **sab•o•teur**
Sab•bath
sab•bat•i•cal
sabbaticle : **sab•bat•i•cal**
Sabbeth : **Sab•bath**
Sabbith : **Sab•bath**
sabbotage : **sab•o•tage**
sabboteur : **sab•o•teur**
sa•ber *or* **sa•bre**
sabitage : **sab•o•tage**
sab•o•tage
sab•o•teur
saboture : **sab•o•teur**
sa•bre *or* **sa•ber**
sachel : **satch•el**
sacksiphone : **sax•o•phone**
sacrafice : **sac•ri•fice**
sac•ra•ment
sa•cred
sacrefice : **sac•ri•fice**
sacrement : **sac•ra•ment**
sacrid : **sa•cred**
sac•ri•fice
sacriment : **sac•ra•ment**
saddal : **sad•dle**
saddel : **sad•dle**
sad•dle
sa•fa•ri
safarri : **sa•fa•ri**
safe•ty
saffari : **sa•fa•ri**
saffire : **sap•phire**
safire : **sap•phire**
safty : **safe•ty**
Sahaira : **Sa•ha•ra**
Sa•ha•ra
Saharra : **Sa•ha•ra**

sail•er (ship); **sail•or** (one who sails)
sail•or (one who sails); **sail•er** (ship)
sal•able *or* **sale•able**
sal•ad
sal•a•man•der
sal•a•ry (wages); **cel•ery** (vegetable)
sale•able *or* **sal•able**
saleble : **sal•able**
salery : **cel•ery** (vegetable) *or* **sal•a•ry** (wages)
saliant : **sa•lient**
salible : **sal•able**
salid : **sal•ad**
sa•lient
salimander : **sal•a•man•der**
saliry : **cel•ery** (vegetable) *or* **sal•a•ry** (wages)
sa•li•va
sallable : **sal•able**
sallad : **sal•ad**
sallamander : **sal•a•man•der**
sallary : **cel•ery** (vegetable) *or* **sal•a•ry** (wages)
salled : **sal•ad**
sallid : **sal•ad**
sallient : **sa•lient**
salliva : **sa•li•va**
sallmon : **salm•on**
sallon : **sa•lon**
salloon : **sa•loon**
sallune : **sa•loon**
sallute : **sa•lute**
sallvage : **sal•vage**
salman : **salm•on**
salmin : **salm•on**
salm•on
sa•lon

sa·loon
salor : **sail·or**
sa·lute
sal·vage
salve (ointment); **save** (to
  rescue); **solve** (to find a
  solution)
salvege : **sal·vage**
salvige : **sal·vage**
Sambeezi : **Zam·be·zi**
Sambezi : **Zam·be·zi**
sammon : **salm·on**
sammurai : **sam·u·rai**
samon : **salm·on**
samouri : **sam·u·rai**
sampel : **sam·ple**
sam·ple
sampul : **sam·ple**
sam·u·rai
samuri : **sam·u·rai**
sanatarium : **san·a·to·ri·um**
sanatary : **san·i·tary**
san·a·to·ri·um *or* **san·i·tar·i·um**
san·dal
sandel : **san·dal**
sandle : **san·dal**
sandwhich : **sand·wich**
sand·wich
sandwitch : **sand·wich**
sanety : **san·i·ty**
San Fran·cis·co
San Francisko : **San Fran·cis·co**
San Fransisco : **San Fran·cis·co**
san·i·tar·i·um *or* **san·a·to·ri·um**
san·i·tary
saniterium : **san·a·to·ri·um**
sanitery : **san·i·tary**
sanitty : **san·i·ty**
san·i·ty
sannatarium : **san·a·to·ri·um**
sannatary : **san·i·tary**
sannity : **san·i·ty**

Sansibar : **Zan·zi·bar**
santer : **saun·ter**
Sanzibar : **Zan·zi·bar**
saphire : **sap·phire**
sap·phire
sarcasem : **sar·casm**
sarcasim : **sar·casm**
sar·casm
sarcasstic : **sar·cas·tic**
sar·cas·tic
sarcazm : **sar·casm**
sardeen : **sar·dine**
sardene : **sar·dine**
sar·dine
sarene : **se·rene**
sargent : **ser·geant**
sargient : **ser·geant**
sarrate : **ser·rate**
sassage : **sau·sage**
satalite : **sat·el·lite**
sa·tan·ic
satanick : **sa·tan·ic**
satannic : **sa·tan·ic**
satarize : **sat·i·rize**
satasfy : **sat·is·fy**
satch·el
satelite : **sat·el·lite**
sat·el·lite
Saterday : **Sat·ur·day**
saterize : **sat·i·rize**
Satern : **Sat·urn**
satesfactory : **sat·is·fac·to·ry**
satesfy : **sat·is·fy**
sat·in
sat·i·rize
satisfactery : **sat·is·fac·to·ry**
sat·is·fac·to·ry
sat·is·fy
sattelite : **sat·el·lite**
sattellite : **sat·el·lite**
satten : **sat·in**
sattin : **sat·in**

sattirize : **sat·i·rize**
sattisfactory : **sat·is·fac·to·ry**
sattisfy : **sat·is·fy**
Satturday : **Sat·ur·day**
Satturn : **Sat·urn**
Sat·ur·day
Sat·urn
saucege : **sau·sage**
sau·cer
saun·ter
sau·sage
sausege : **sau·sage**
sauser : **sau·cer**
sausige : **sau·sage**
sav : **salve** (ointment) *or* **save**
(to rescue)
sav·age
save (to rescue); **salve**
(ointment)
savege : **sav·age**
saveor : **sav·ior**
sav·ior *or* **sav·iour**
sav·iour *or* **sav·ior**
sa·vor
savour (*Brit.*) : **sa·vor**
sawcer : **sau·cer**
saxaphone : **sax·o·phone**
saxiphone : **sax·o·phone**
sax·o·phone
Saylon : **Cey·lon**
scabard : **scab·bard**
scab·bard
scabboard : **scab·bard**
scabbord : **scab·bard**
scaf·fold
scafold : **scaf·fold**
scairy : **scary**
scald
scalpal : **scal·pel**
scal·pel
scalple : **scal·pel**
scan·dal

scandel : **scan·dal**
Scandenavia : **Scan·di·na·via**
Scandinavea : **Scan·di·na·via**
Scan·di·na·via
Scandinnavia : **Scan·di·na·via**
scandle : **scan·dal**
scar·ab
scareb : **scar·ab**
scared (frightened); **scarred**
(having a scar)
scarey : **scary**
scarib : **scar·ab**
scar·let
scarlit : **scar·let**
scarred (having a scar); **scared**
(frightened)
scary
scauld : **scald**
scedule : **sched·ule**
sceme : **scheme**
sce·nar·io
scenarrio : **sce·nar·io**
scenary : **scen·ery**
sceneario : **sce·nar·io**
scenec : **sce·nic**
scenerry : **scen·ery**
scen·ery
sce·nic
scenick : **sce·nic**
scent·ed
sceptacism : **skep·ti·cism**
sceptecism : **skep·ti·cism**
scep·ter
scep·tic *or* **skep·tic**
scep·ti·cism *or* **skep·ti·cism**
sceptick : **skep·tic**
sceptisism : **skep·ti·cism**
sceptor : **scep·ter**
sceptre (*Brit.*) : **scep·ter**
scervy : **scur·vy**
scheam : **scheme**
scheddule : **sched·ule**

scheduel : **sched•ule**
sched•ule
scheme
schism
schissors : **scis•sors**
schisum : **schism**
schitxophrenia : **schizo•phre•nia**
schizm : **schism**
schizofrenai : **schizo•phre•nia**
schizophreania : **schizo•phre•nia**
schizo•phre•nia
schizzophrenia : **schizo•phre•nia**
scho•lar
scholasstic : **scho•las•tic**
scho•las•tic
scholer : **scho•lar**
schollar : **scho•lar**
schollastic : **scho•las•tic**
school
schoon•er
schuner : **schoon•er**
sciance : **sci•ence**
sci•ence
sciense : **sci•ence**
scientiffic : **sci•en•tif•ic**
sci•en•tif•ic
scimatar : **scim•i•tar**
scim•i•tar
scinted : **scent•ed**
scirry : **scur•ry**
scism : **schism**
scisors : **scis•sors**
scissers : **scis•sors**
scissophrania : **schizo•phre•nia**
scis•sors
scithe : **scythe**
scizzors : **scis•sors**
scolar : **scho•lar**
scolastic : **scho•las•tic**
scooner : **schoon•er**

scorpian : **scor•pi•on**
scorpien : **scor•pi•on**
scor•pi•on
scoundral : **scoun•drel**
scoun•drel
scoundril : **scoun•drel**
scourge
scrach : **scratch**
scral : **scroll**
scraped (rubbed); **scrapped** (discarded)
scrapped (discarded); **scraped** (rubbed)
scratch
screach : **screech**
scream
screan : **screen**
screech
screem : **scream**
screen
screne : **screen**
scrimage : **scrim•mage**
scrim•mage
scrimmege : **scrim•mage**
scroll
scrutanize : **scru•ti•nize**
scru•ti•nize
sculpter : **sculp•tor** (artist) *or* **sculp•ture** (work of art)
sculp•tor (artist); **sculp•ture** (work of art)
sculp•ture (work of art); **sculp•tor** (artist)
scurge : **scourge**
scur•ry
scur•vy
scythe (blade); **sigh** (deep breath)
seafairer : **sea•far•er**
sea•far•er
seafaror : **sea•far•er**
seamy

sé•ance
seap : **seep**
search
seasen : **sea•son**
seasin : **sea•son**
sea•son
seathe : **seethe**
Seattal : **Se•at•tle**
Seattel : **Se•at•tle**
Se•at•tle
secand : **sec•ond**
se•cede
seceed : **se•cede**
seceshion : **se•ces•sion**
se•ces•sion
secide : **se•cede**
seckular : **sec•u•lar**
sec•ond
secracy : **se•cre•cy**
secratary : **sec•re•tary**
se•cre•cy
secresy : **se•cre•cy**
se•cret
sec•re•tary
secretery : **sec•re•tary**
secrisy : **se•cre•cy**
secrit : **se•cret**
secritary : **sec•re•tary**
secter : **sec•tor**
sec•tor
sec•u•lar
seculer : **sec•u•lar**
secund : **sec•ond**
securety : **se•cu•ri•ty**
securitty : **se•cu•ri•ty**
se•cu•ri•ty
securrity : **se•cu•ri•ty**
sedament : **sed•i•ment**
se•dan
sedar : **ce•dar** (tree) *or* **se•der**
   (Passover meal)
sed•a•tive

seddan : **se•dan**
seddative : **sed•a•tive**
seddiment : **sed•i•ment**
seddition : **se•di•tion**
se•der (Passover meal); **ce•dar**
   (tree)
sedetive : **sed•a•tive**
sed•i•ment
se•di•tion
seditive : **sed•a•tive**
seefarer : **sea•far•er**
seege : **siege**
seemy : **seamy**
seep
seeson : **sea•son**
seethe
seeze : **seize**
segragate : **seg•re•gate**
seg•re•gate
segrigate : **seg•re•gate**
seige : **siege**
seis•mic
seismollogy : **seis•mol•o•gy**
seis•mol•o•gy
seive : **sieve**
seize
seizh : **siege**
seizmic : **seis•mic**
seizmology : **seis•mol•o•gy**
selary : **cel•ery** (vegetable) *or*
   sal•a•ry (wages)
seldem : **sel•dom**
sel•dom
selebrate : **cel•e•brate**
selebrity : **ce•leb•ri•ty**
se•lect
selery : **cel•ery** (vegetable) *or*
   sal•a•ry (wages)
selestial : **ce•les•tial**
selldom : **sel•dom**
sellect : **se•lect**
sellestial : **ce•les•tial**

selluloid : **cel·lu·loid**
Seltic : **Cel·tic**
sematary : **cem·e·tery**
sematery : **cem·e·tery**
sem·blance
semblanse : **sem·blance**
semblence : **sem·blance**
semenar : **sem·i·nar**
semenary : **sem·i·nary**
semesster : **se·mes·ter**
se·mes·ter
semeterry : **cem·e·tery**
semetery : **cem·e·tery**
sem·i·nar
sem·i·nary
seminerry : **sem·i·nary**
seminery : **sem·i·nary**
semmester : **se·mes·ter**
semminar : **sem·i·nar**
semminary : **sem·i·nary**
senario : **sce·nar·io**
sen·ate
senater : **sen·a·tor**
sen·a·tor
sence : **sense** (intelligence) *or*
  since (from that time)
sencery : **sen·so·ry**
sencible : **sen·si·ble**
senery : **scen·ery**
senet : **sen·ate**
senic : **sce·nic**
se·nile
senilety : **se·nil·i·ty**
se·nil·i·ty
senillity : **se·nil·i·ty**
senitor : **sen·a·tor**
sennate : **sen·ate**
sennator : **sen·a·tor**
sennile : **se·nile**
sensable : **sen·si·ble**
sensary : **sen·so·ry**
sensative : **sen·si·tive**

sense (intelligence); **cents**
  (money); **since** (from that
  time)
senseble : **sen·si·ble**
senser : **cen·ser** (incense
  container) *or* **cen·sor** (to
  remove objectionable
  material) *or* **cen·sure** (to
  condemn) *or* **sen·sor** (that
  which senses)
sensery : **sen·so·ry**
sensetive : **sen·si·tive**
sensibal : **sen·si·ble**
sen·si·ble
sensis : **cen·sus**
sen·si·tive
sen·sor (that which senses);
  cen·ser (incense container);
  cen·sor (to remove
  objectionable material);
  cen·sure (to condemn)
sen·so·ry
sen·su·al
sensuel : **sen·su·al**
sensus : **cen·sus**
sentament : **sen·ti·ment**
sentaur : **cen·taur**
sented : **scent·ed**
sentenal : **sen·ti·nel**
sen·ti·ment
sentimeter : **cen·ti·me·ter**
sentinal : **sen·ti·nel**
sen·ti·nel
sentinle : **sen·ti·nel**
sentrifugal : **cen·trif·u·gal**
sentripetal : **cen·trip·e·tal**
sentury : **cen·tu·ry**
sep·a·rate
sepea : **se·pia**
seperate : **sep·a·rate**
se·pia
sepirate : **sep·a·rate**

seppalcre : **sep·ul·cher**
seppalker : **sep·ul·cher**
sepparate : **sep·a·rate**
sepperate : **sep·a·rate**
seppia : **se·pia**
seppulchre : **sep·ul·cher**
Sep·tem·ber
Septembre : **Sep·tem·ber**
septer : **scep·ter**
Septimber : **Sep·tem·ber**
septor : **scep·ter**
sep·ul·cher or sep·ul·chre
sepulcre : **sep·ul·cher**
se·quence
sequense : **se·quence**
sequince : **se·quence**
sequinse : **se·quence**
Seracuse : **Syr·a·cuse**
seram : **se·rum**
seramic : **ce·ram·ic**
serate : **ser·rate**
serch : **search**
serean : **se·rene**
serebellum : **cer·e·bel·lum**
serebral : **cer·e·bral**
sereen : **se·rene**
seremony : **cer·e·mo·ny**
se·rene
serf (peasant); **surf** (waves)
serge (cloth); **surge** (to rise up)
ser·geant
sergent : **ser·geant**
sergeon : **sur·geon**
sergery : **sur·gery**
sergient : **ser·geant**
se·ri·al (in a series); **ce·re·al** (grain)
serine : **se·rene**
serman : **ser·mon**
sermin : **ser·mon**
ser·mon
ser·pent

serpint : **ser·pent**
serplus : **sur·plice** (vestment) or **sur·plus** (excess)
ser·rate
sertain : **cer·tain**
sertificate : **cer·tif·i·cate**
se·rum
servace : **ser·vice**
servaceable : **ser·vice·able**
ser·vant
servent : **ser·vant**
ser·vice
ser·vice·able
serviceble : **ser·vice·able**
servicible : **ser·vice·able**
servint : **ser·vant**
servise : **ser·vice**
servisible : **ser·vice·able**
serviss : **ser·vice**
servissible : **ser·vice·able**
ses·a·me
sesede : **se·cede**
seseed : **se·cede**
sesession : **se·ces·sion**
sesime : **ses·a·me**
sessame : **ses·a·me**
sessimy : **ses·a·me**
sesspool : **cess·pool**
sevarity : **se·ver·i·ty**
seveer : **se·vere**
sev·er·al
se·vere
severel : **sev·er·al**
severety : **se·ver·i·ty**
severitty : **se·ver·i·ty**
se·ver·i·ty
sevier : **se·vere**
seviral : **sev·er·al**
sevveral : **sev·er·al**
sew·age
sewige : **sew·age**
sex·tant

sextent : **sex·tant**
sextint : **sex·tant**
sex·u·al
sexuel : **sex·u·al**
seyance : **sé·ance**
Seylon : **Cey·lon**
shaddoe : **shad·ow**
shaddow : **shad·ow**
shadoe : **shad·ow**
shad·ow
shaffeur : **chauf·feur**
shaffure : **chauf·feur**
shampagne : **cham·pagne**
shampaign : **cham·pagne**
shampaine : **cham·pagne**
shampane : **cham·pagne**
sham·poo
shampu : **sham·poo**
shantie : **shan·ty**
shan·ty
shaparon : **chap·er·on**
shaperone : **chap·er·on**
sharade : **cha·rade**
shareff : **sher·iff**
shariff : **sher·iff**
sharlatan : **char·la·tan**
sharlaten : **char·la·tan**
sharletan : **char·la·tan**
shartreuse : **char·treuse**
shartroose : **char·treuse**
shartruese : **char·treuse**
shartruse : **char·treuse**
shateau : **cha·teau**
shatieu : **cha·teau**
shatoe : **cha·teau**
shatoue : **cha·teau**
shauffer : **chauf·feur**
shauvenism : **chau·vin·ism**
shauvinism : **chau·vin·ism**
sheaf
sheafs : **sheaves**
sheald : **shield**

shealf : **shelf**
sheaves
shedule : **sched·ule**
sheef : **sheaf**
sheeld : **shield**
sheepherd : **shep·herd**
sheeves : **sheaves**
sheif : **sheaf**
sheild : **shield**
shelac : **shel·lac**
shelf (*noun*); **shelve** (*verb*)
shel·lac
shellaced : **shel·lacked**
shellack : **shel·lac**
shel·lacked
shellter : **shel·ter**
shel·ter
sheltor : **shel·ter**
shelve (*verb*); **shelf** (*sing.*)
shelves (*plur.*)
shemise : **che·mise**
shepard : **shep·herd**
shephard : **shep·herd**
shep·herd
sher·bet
sherbit : **sher·bet**
shereff : **sher·iff**
sher·iff
Sheyenne : **Chey·enne**
shield
shillac : **shel·lac**
shillacked : **shel·lacked**
shingal : **shin·gle**
shingel : **shin·gle**
shin·gle
shirbet : **sher·bet**
shism : **schism**
shivalry : **chiv·al·ry**
shivelry : **chiv·al·ry**
shoalder : **shoul·der**
shoartage : **short·age**
shoffeur : **chauf·feur**

sholder : **shoul·der**
short·age
shortege : **short·age**
shortige : **short·age**
should·er
shov·el
shov·eled
shovelled : **shov·eled**
shovil : **shov·el**
shovilled : **shov·eled**
shovinism : **chau·vin·ism**
shrapnal : **shrap·nel**
shrap·nel
shrapnle : **shrap·nel**
shread : **shred**
shreak : **shriek**
shred
shreek : **shriek**
shreik : **shriek**
shrewd
shriek
shrival : **shriv·el**
shrivaled : **shriv·eled**
shriv·el
shriv·eled or shriv·elled
shriv·elled or shriv·eled
shrivil : **shriv·el**
shrivle : **shriv·el**
shrude : **shrewd**
shugar : **sug·ar**
shuger : **sug·ar**
shurbet : **sher·bet**
shute : **chute**
shutle : **shut·tle**
shuttal : **shut·tle**
shuttel : **shut·tle**
shut·tle
Siameese : **Si·a·mese**
Si·a·mese
Siameze : **Si·a·mese**
sianide : **cy·a·nide**
Siattle : **Se·at·tle**

Sibeeria : **Si·be·ria**
Si·be·ria
sibernetics : **cy·ber·net·ics**
Sibirea : **Si·be·ria**
Sicaly : **Sic·i·ly**
sicamore : **syc·a·more**
Sicely : **Sic·i·ly**
Sicili : **Sic·i·ly**
Sicilly : **Sic·i·ly**
Sic·i·ly
sickal : **cy·cle** (rotation) *or*
  sick·le (knife)
sickel : **cy·cle** (rotation) *or*
  sick·le (knife)
sick·le (knife); **cy·cle** (rotation)
siclone : **cy·clone**
sicomore : **syc·a·more**
sicophant : **sy·co·phant**
sidal : **si·dle**
sidan : **se·dan**
sid·le
siege
sience : **sci·ence**
siesmic : **seis·mic**
siesmology : **seis·mol·o·gy**
sieve
sieze : **seize**
sigar : **ci·gar**
sigh (deep breath); **scythe**
  (blade)
signafy : **sig·ni·fy**
sig·nal
signall : **sig·nal**
sig·na·ture
signefy : **sig·ni·fy**
signel : **sig·nal**
sig·net (ring); **cyg·net** (swan)
signeture : **sig·na·ture**
signifacant : **sig·nif·i·cant**
signifficant : **sig·nif·i·cant**
signiffy : **sig·ni·fy**
sig·nif·i·cant

sig·ni·fy
signiture : **sig·na·ture**
silacon : **sil·i·con**
silance : **si·lence**
si·lence
silense : **si·lence**
sil·hou·ette
sil·i·con
silince : **si·lence**
silinder : **cyl·in·der**
siliva : **sa·li·va**
sillable : **syl·la·ble**
sillabus : **syl·la·bus**
sillence : **si·lence**
sillhoette : **sil·hou·ette**
sillicon : **sil·i·con**
silloette : **sil·hou·ette**
silute : **sa·lute**
simalar : **sim·i·lar**
simblance : **sem·blance**
simbol : **cym·bal** (brass plate)
   or **sym·bol** (meaningful
   image)
Simese : **Si·a·mese**
simester : **se·mes·ter**
sim·i·lar
sim·i·le
similer : **sim·i·lar**
similiar : **sim·i·lar**
similie : **sim·i·le**
simitar : **scim·i·tar**
simmetry : **sym·me·try**
simmilar : **sim·i·lar**
simmulate : **sim·u·late**
simpathize : **sym·pa·thize**
simphony : **sym·pho·ny**
simplafy : **sim·pli·fy**
simplefy : **sim·pli·fy**
simpliffy : **sim·pli·fy**
sim·pli·fy
simposium : **sym·po·sium**
simptem : **symp·tom**

simptom : **symp·tom**
simtem : **symp·tom**
simtom : **symp·tom**
sim·u·late
sinagogue : **syn·a·gogue**
sinario : **sce·nar·io**
since (from that time); **sense**
   (intelligence)
sinceer : **sin·cere**
sinceir : **sin·cere**
sin·cere
sincerety : **sin·cer·i·ty**
sin·cer·i·ty
sinchronize : **syn·chro·nize**
Sincinnati : **Cin·cin·nati**
sindicate : **syn·di·cate**
sinema : **cin·e·ma**
sinemon : **cin·na·mon**
Singapoor : **Sin·ga·pore**
Sin·ga·pore
Singapour : **Sin·ga·pore**
singe·ing (burning); **sing·ing**
   (music)
sing·ing (music); **singe·ing**
   (burning)
Singopore : **Sin·ga·pore**
sing·u·lar
singuler : **sing·u·lar**
sinicism : **cyn·i·cism**
sinile : **se·nile**
sinility : **se·nil·i·ty**
sin·is·ter
sinnamon : **cin·na·mon**
sinnister : **sin·is·ter**
sinonym : **syn·o·nym**
sinphony : **sym·pho·ny**
sinsere : **sin·cere**
sinserity : **sin·cer·i·ty**
sinsual : **sen·su·al**
sinted : **scent·ed**
sintenal : **sen·ti·nel**
sinthesize : **syn·the·size**

sipher : **ci·pher**
sipress : **cy·press**
Siracuse : **Syr·a·cuse**
sirca : **cir·ca**
sircus : **cir·cus**
sirfeit : **sur·feit**
sirfiet : **sur·feit**
sirgeon : **sur·geon**
sirgery : **sur·gery**
sirgion : **sur·geon**
sir·loin
sirmount : **sur·mount**
sirname : **sur·name**
sirpent : **ser·pent**
sirplus : **sur·plice** (vestment) or
  sur·plus (excess)
sirrhosis : **cir·rho·sis**
sirum : **se·rum**
sirup or **syr·up**
Sisily : **Sic·i·ly**
sism : **schism**
sissors : **scis·sors**
sistem : **sys·tem**
sistern : **cis·tern**
sithe : **scythe**
sitrus : **cit·rus**
siv : **sieve**
sive : **sieve**
siz·able or **size·able**
size·able or **siz·able**
sizeble : **siz·able**
sizible : **siz·able**
sizmic : **seis·mic**
sizzel : **siz·zle**
siz·zle
skaffold : **scaf·fold**
skalpel : **scal·pel**
Skandinavia : **Scan·di·na·via**
skarlet : **scar·let**
skech : **sketch**
skedule : **sched·ule**
skelaton : **skel·e·ton**

skeletan : **skel·e·ton**
skeletin : **skel·e·ton**
skel·e·ton
skeliton : **skel·e·ton**
skelleton : **skel·e·ton**
skeme : **scheme**
skep·tic or **scep·tic**
skep·ti·cism or **scep·ti·cism**
skepticizm : **skep·ti·cism**
skermish : **skir·mish**
sketch
ski
skie : **ski**
skied
skiied : **skied**
ski·ing
skiis : **skis**
skilet : **skil·let**
skil·let
skillit : **skil·let**
sking : **ski·ing**
skirmesh : **skir·mish**
skir·mish
skirmush : **skir·mish**
skis
skolar : **schol·ar**
skool : **school**
skorpion : **scor·pi·on**
skulptor : **sculp·tor** (artist)
skulpture : **sculp·ture** (work of
  art)
skurmish : **skir·mish**
skurry : **scur·ry**
slagh : **sleigh**
slaghter : **slaugh·ter**
slaigh : **sleigh**
slaugh·ter
slauter : **slaugh·ter**
slavary : **slav·ery**
Slavec : **Slav·ic**
slaverry : **slav·ery**
slav·ery

Slav·ic
Slavick : **Slav·ic**
Slavvic : **Slav·ic**
slawter : **slaugh·ter**
slay (to kill); **sleigh** (sled)
sleak : **sleek**
sleap : **sleep**
sleapily : **sleep·i·ly**
sleasy : **slea·zy**
sleat : **sleet**
sleave : **sleeve**
slea·zy
sledge
sleek
sleep
sleep·i·ly
sleepyly : **sleep·i·ly**
sleesy : **slea·zy**
sleet
sleeve
slege : **sledge**
sleigh (sled); **slay** (to kill)
sleih : **sleigh**
sleive : **sleeve**
sleizy : **slea·zy**
slepe : **sleep**
slete : **sleet**
sleuth
slewth : **sleuth**
slice
sliceing : **slic·ing**
slic·ing
sliegh : **sleigh**
slimey : **slimy**
slimmy : **slimy**
slimy
slipery : **slip·pery**
slippary : **slip·pery**
slip·pery
slise : **slice**
slive : **sleeve**
slobenly : **slov·en·ly**

slo·gan
slogen : **slo·gan**
slogin : **slo·gan**
sloped (at an angle); **slopped** (spilled)
slopped (spilled); **sloped** (at an angle)
slouch
slov·en·ly
slovinly : **slov·en·ly**
slowch : **slouch**
sluce : **sluice**
slueth : **sleuth**
slugard : **slug·gard**
slug·gard
sluggerd : **slug·gard**
sluggird : **slug·gard**
sluice
sluise : **sluice**
sluth : **sleuth**
smear
smeer : **smear**
smithareens : **smith·er·eens**
smith·er·eens
smitherenes : **smith·er·eens**
smitherines : **smith·er·eens**
smoak : **smoke**
smoalder : **smol·der**
smoke
Smo·key (the Bear); **smoky** (filled with smoke)
smoky (filled with smoke); **Smo·key** (the Bear)
smol·der *or* **smoul·der**
smorgasboard : **smor·gas·bord**
smor·gas·bord
smorgesbord : **smor·gas·bord**
smorgisbord : **smor·gas·bord**
smoul·der *or* **smol·der**
smudge
smuge : **smudge**
smuggel : **smug·gle**

smugglar : **smug•gler**
smug•gle
smug•gler
smugle : **smug•gle**
snach : **snatch**
snatch
sneak
sneak•er
sneaky
snease : **sneeze**
sneaze : **sneeze**
sneek : **sneak**
sneeker : **sneak•er**
sneeky : **sneaky**
sneeze
sneke : **sneak**
snipet : **snip•pet**
snip•pet
snippit : **snip•pet**
sniv•el
sniv•el•ing *or* **sniv•el•ling**
sniv•el•ling *or* **sniv•el•ing**
snivil : **sniv•el**
snoarkel : **snor•kel**
snobbary : **snob•bery**
snob•bery
snobery : **snob•bery**
snobry : **snob•bery**
snorkal : **snor•kel**
snor•kel
snorkle : **snor•kel**
snuggal : **snug•gle**
snuggel : **snug•gle**
snug•gle
soak•ing
soap
soap•i•er
soapyer : **soap•i•er**
soarcerer : **sor•cer•er**
soarcery : **sor•cery**
soard : **sword**
soberiety : **so•bri•ety**

sobrietty : **so•bri•ety**
so•bri•ety
soccar : **soc•cer**
soc•cer
socciology : **so•ci•ol•o•gy**
soceable : **so•cia•ble**
soceology : **so•ci•ol•o•gy**
sociabal : **so•cia•ble**
sociabilety : **so•cia•bil•i•ty**
so•cia•bil•i•ty
so•cia•ble
socialibility : **so•cia•bil•i•ty**
socible : **so•cia•ble**
societty : **so•ci•ety**
so•ci•ety
sociollogy : **so•ci•ol•o•gy**
so•ci•ol•o•gy
sodder : **sol•der**
soddium : **so•di•um**
sodeum : **so•di•um**
sodiem : **so•di•um**
so•di•um
soffen : **soft•en**
sofisticated : **so•phis•ti•cat•ed**
sofmore : **soph•o•more**
sofomore : **soph•o•more**
soft•en
sojern : **so•journ**
sojorn : **so•journ**
so•journ
sojurn : **so•journ**
soking : **soak•ing**
so•lace
so•lar
solataire : **sol•i•taire**
solatary : **sol•i•tary**
solatude : **sol•i•tude**
sol•der (metal); **sol•dier**
  (fighter)
soldiar : **sol•dier**
sol•dier (fighter); **sol•der**
  (metal)

sole (only; fish; part of foot or shoe); **soul** (inner essence)
soled (having a sole); **sol•id** (not gas or liquid)
soledarity : **sol•i•dar•i•ty**
sole•ly
solem : **sol•emn**
sol•emn
soler : **so•lar**
solice : **so•lace**
solicet : **so•lic•it**
solicetor : **so•lic•i•tor**
solicetous : **so•lic•i•tous**
so•lic•it
so•lic•i•tor
so•lic•i•tous
solicitus : **so•lic•i•tous**
sol•id (not gas or liquid); **soled** (having a sole)
solidarety : **sol•i•dar•i•ty**
sol•i•dar•i•ty
solidefy : **so•lid•i•fy**
soliderity : **sol•i•dar•i•ty**
so•lid•i•fy
solilaquy : **so•lil•o•quy**
solilloquy : **so•lil•o•quy**
so•lil•o•quy
soliloqy : **so•lil•o•quy**
solise : **so•lace**
soliset : **so•lic•it**
solisetor : **so•lic•i•tor**
solisetous : **so•lic•i•tous**
soliss : **so•lace**
solissit : **so•lic•it**
solissitor : **so•lic•i•tor**
solissitous : **so•lic•i•tous**
sol•i•taire
solitare : **sol•i•taire**
sol•i•tary
solitery : **sol•i•tary**
sol•i•tude
sollace : **so•lace**

sollatude : **sol•i•tude**
sollemn : **sol•emn**
sollicit : **so•lic•it**
sollicitor : **so•lic•i•tor**
sollicitous : **so•lic•i•tous**
sollid : **sol•id**
sollidarity : **sol•i•dar•i•ty**
sollidify : **so•lid•i•fy**
solliloquy : **so•lil•o•quy**
sollitaire : **sol•i•taire**
sollitary : **sol•i•tary**
sollitude : **sol•i•tude**
solluble : **sol•u•ble**
sollvency : **sol•ven•cy**
sollvent : **sol•vent**
solstace : **sol•stice**
sol•stice
solstiss : **sol•stice**
soluable : **sol•u•ble**
sol•u•ble
soluible : **sol•u•ble**
solumn : **sol•emn**
solv•able
solve (to find a solution); **salve** (ointment)
sol•ven•cy
solvensy : **sol•ven•cy**
sol•vent
solvible : **solv•able**
solvincy : **sol•ven•cy**
solvint : **sol•vent**
soly : **sole•ly**
som•er•sault *or* **sum•mer•sault**
sommersault : **som•er•sault**
sonada : **so•na•ta**
so•na•ta
sonatta : **so•na•ta**
sonet : **son•net**
son•ic
son•net
sonnic : **son•ic**
sonnick : **son•ic**

sonnit : **son·net**
sonter : **saun·ter**
soparific : **so·po·rif·ic**
sope : **soap**
sophistacated : **so·phis·ti·cat·ed**
sophistecated : **so·phis·ti·cat·ed**
so·phis·ti·cat·ed
sophmoar : **soph·o·more**
sophmore : **soph·o·more**
soph·o·more
sopier : **soap·i·er**
soporiffic : **so·po·rif·ic**
so·po·rif·ic
sopranno : **so·pra·no**
so·pra·no
sor·cer·er
sorceror : **sor·cer·er**
sor·cery
sord : **sword**
sorded : **sor·did**
sor·did
soroarity : **so·ror·i·ty**
sororety : **so·ror·i·ty**
sororitty : **so·ror·i·ty**
so·ror·i·ty
sororrity : **so·ror·i·ty**
sorrority : **so·ror·i·ty**
sorserer : **sor·cer·er**
sorsery : **sor·cery**
sosiety : **so·ci·e·ty**
sosiology : **so·ci·ol·o·gy**
sosser : **sau·cer**
sossialibility : **so·cia·bil·i·ty**
sothern : **south·ern**
soufflay : **souf·flé**
souf·flé
souffley : **souf·flé**
soufle : **souf·flé**
soul (inner essence); **sole** (only;
  fish; part of foot or shoe)
sourcerer : **sor·cer·er**
sourcery : **sor·cery**

South Caralina : **South
  Car·o·li·na**
South Carlina : **South
  Car·o·li·na**
South Car·o·li·na
South Carrolina : **South
  Car·o·li·na**
South Dahkota : **South
  Da·ko·ta**
South Da·ko·ta
South Dakotah : **South
  Da·ko·ta**
south·ern
souveneer : **sou·ve·nir**
sou·ve·nir
souvineer : **sou·ve·nir**
souvineir : **sou·ve·nir**
soveregn : **sov·er·eign**
sov·er·eign
soveriegn : **sov·er·eign**
soviat : **so·vi·et**
so·vi·et
sovrin : **sov·er·eign**
spaceious : **spa·cious**
spacial : **spa·tial**
spa·cious
spacius : **spa·cious**
spagetti : **spa·ghet·ti**
spa·ghet·ti
spaghetty : **spa·ghet·ti**
Span·iard
span·iel
Spanierd : **Span·iard**
Span·ish
Spanniard : **Span·iard**
spanniel : **span·iel**
Spannish : **Span·ish**
sparce : **sparse**
sparcety : **spar·si·ty**
sparcity : **spar·si·ty**
sparow : **spar·row**
spar·row

sparse
sparsety : **spar•si•ty**
sparsitty : **spar•si•ty**
spar•si•ty
spasial : **spa•tial**
spasim : **spasm**
spasm
spatela : **spat•u•la**
spa•tial
spatiel : **spa•tial**
spattula : **spat•u•la**
spat•u•la
spatulla : **spat•u•la**
spaun : **spawn**
spawn
spazm : **spasm**
speach : **speech**
speak
spear
specafy : **spec•i•fy**
specamen : **spec•i•men**
specamin : **spec•i•men**
spechial : **spe•cial**
spe•cial
specifec : **spe•cif•ic**
speciffic : **spe•cif•ic**
speciffy : **spec•i•fy**
spe•cif•ic
specifick : **spe•cif•ic**
spec•i•fy
spec•i•men
specimin : **spec•i•men**
speckter : **spec•ter**
spectackular : **spec•tac•u•lar**
spec•ta•cle
spec•tac•u•lar
spectaculer : **spec•tac•u•lar**
spectater : **spec•ta•tor**
spec•ta•tor
spectecle : **spec•ta•cle**
spec•ter
spectical : **spec•ta•cle**

specticle : **spec•ta•cle**
spector : **spec•ter**
spectre (*Brit.*) : **spec•ter**
spedometer : **speed•om•e•ter**
speech
speedameter : **speed•om•e•ter**
speed•om•e•ter
speedomiter : **speed•om•e•ter**
speek : **speak**
speer : **spear**
speghetti : **spa•ghet•ti**
speir : **spear**
sperit : **spir•it**
speritual : **spir•i•tu•al**
spern : **spurn**
sperrow : **spar•row**
spert : **spurt**
spesafy : **spec•i•fy**
spesamen : **spec•i•men**
spesial : **spe•cial**
spesific : **spe•cif•ic**
spesify : **spec•i•fy**
spesimin : **spec•i•men**
spessify : **spec•i•fy**
spheer : **sphere**
spheir : **sphere**
sphenx : **sphinx**
sphere
sphinks : **sphinx**
sphinx
spicket : **spig•ot**
spicy
spigget : **spig•ot**
spiggit : **spig•ot**
spiggot : **spig•ot**
spighetti : **spa•ghet•ti**
spig•ot
spilled
spilt : **spilled**
spin•ach
spinaker : **spin•na•ker**
spi•nal

spindal : **spin·dle**
spindel : **spin·dle**
spin·dle
spinel : **spi·nal**
spinich : **spin·ach**
spinnacer : **spin·na·ker**
spinnach : **spin·ach**
spin·na·ker
spinnal : **spi·nal**
spinneker : **spin·na·ker**
spinnet : **spin·et**
spinnich : **spin·ach**
spinx : **sphinx**
spi·ral
spirel : **spi·ral**
spiret : **spir·it**
spiretual : **spir·i·tu·al**
spir·it
spir·i·tu·al
spirituel : **spir·i·tu·al**
spirrit : **spir·it**
spirritual : **spir·i·tu·al**
spirt : **spurt**
spisy : **spicy**
splean : **spleen**
spleen
splended : **splen·did**
splender : **splen·dor**
splen·did
splen·dor
splerge : **splurge**
splindid : **splen·did**
splindor : **splen·dor**
splirge : **splurge**
splurge
spoiled *or* **spoilt**
spoilt *or* **spoiled**
Spokan : **Spo·kane**
Spo·kane
sponser : **spon·sor**
spon·sor
spontaineous : **spon·ta·ne·ous**

spontainious : **spon·ta·ne·ous**
spon·ta·ne·ous
spread
spred : **spread**
spright·ly
sprily : **spry·ly**
spritely : **spright·ly**
sprock·et
sprockit : **sprock·et**
sproose : **spruce**
spruce
spruse : **spruce**
spry·ly
spu·mo·ne *or* **spu·mo·ni**
spu·mo·ni *or* **spu·mo·ne**
spumonie : **spu·mo·ni**
spureous : **spu·ri·ous**
spu·ri·ous
spurn
spurrious : **spu·ri·ous**
spurt
squadren : **squad·ron**
squadrin : **squad·ron**
squad·ron
squak : **squawk**
squaled : **squal·id** (filthy) *or*
    squalled (cried)
squal·id (filthy); **squalled**
    (cried)
squalled (cried); **squal·id**
    (filthy)
squall·er (one that cries);
    squal·or (filthiness)
squallid : **squal·id** (filthy) *or*
    squalled (cried)
squallor : **squall·er** (one that
    cries) *or* **squal·or** (filthiness)
squal·or (filthiness); **squall·er**
    (one that cries)
squawk
squeak
squeal

squeam·ish
squeaze : **squeeze**
squeek : **squeak**
squeel : **squeal**
squeemesh : **squeam·ish**
squeemish : **squeam·ish**
squeese : **squeeze**
squeeze
squerrel : **squir·rel**
squiar : **squire**
squier : **squire**
squire
squirl : **squir·rel**
squirral : **squir·rel**
squir·rel
squirrl : **squir·rel**
squirt
squize : **squeeze**
stabelize : **sta·bi·lize**
stabilety : **sta·bil·i·ty**
sta·bil·i·ty
sta·bi·lize
stabillity : **sta·bil·i·ty**
stableize : **sta·bi·lize**
stablize : **sta·bi·lize**
stacado : **stac·ca·to**
stacato : **stac·ca·to**
stacatto : **stac·ca·to**
stac·ca·to
stackato : **stac·ca·to**
stacotto : **stac·ca·to**
staddium : **sta·di·um**
stadiem : **sta·di·um**
sta·di·um
stag·nant
stagnent : **stag·nant**
stagnint : **stag·nant**
staid (set in one's ways);
   stayed (remained)
stair (step); **stare** (look)
stake (pointed piece of wood;
   to bet); **steak** (meat)

sta·lac·tite
sta·lag·mite
stalion : **stal·lion**
stallactite : **sta·lac·tite**
stallagmite : **sta·lag·mite**
stallian : **stal·lion**
stal·lion
stallwart : **stal·wart**
stal·wart
stalwert : **stal·wart**
stalwirt : **stal·wart**
sta·men
stamena : **stam·i·na**
stamin : **sta·men**
stam·i·na
staminna : **stam·i·na**
stammina : **stam·i·na**
stam·pede
stampeed : **stam·pede**
stampide : **stam·pede**
stan·dard
standerd : **stan·dard**
stapel : **sta·ple**
sta·ple
stapple : **sta·ple**
stare (look); **stair** (step)
stareotype : **ste·reo·type**
starile : **ster·ile**
statec : **stat·ic**
stat·ic
sta·tion·ary (fixed);
   sta·tion·ery (paper)
sta·tion·ery (paper);
   sta·tion·ary (fixed)
statisstic : **sta·tis·tic**
sta·tis·tic
statium : **sta·di·um**
stattic : **stat·ic**
stattistic : **sta·tis·tic**
stattue : **stat·ue**
statture : **stat·ure**
stattus : **sta·tus**

stattute : **sta·tute**

stat·ue

stat·ure

sta·tus

stat·ute

stayed (remained); **staid** (set in one's ways)

stead·fast

steady

steak (meat); **stake** (pointed piece of wood; to bet)

steal (to rob); **steel** (metal)

steaple : **stee·ple**

stear : **steer**

steddy : **steady**

stedfast : **stead·fast**

stedy : **steady**

steel (metal); **steal** (to rob)

steepal : **stee·ple**

steepel : **stee·ple**

stee·ple

steer

stelactite : **sta·lac·tite**

stel·lar

steller : **stel·lar**

stencel : **sten·cil**

sten·cil

stensel : **sten·cil**

stensil : **sten·cil**

steralize : **ster·il·ize**

ste·reo·type

stergeon : **stur·geon**

steril : **ster·ile**

ster·ile

sterilety : **ste·ril·i·ty**

sterilise (*Brit.*) : **ster·il·ize**

ste·ril·i·ty

ster·il·ize

sterillity : **ste·ril·i·ty**

sterillize : **ster·il·ize**

sternam : **ster·num**

ster·num

sterrile : **ster·ile**

stethascope : **steth·o·scope**

steth·o·scope

stew·ard

stew·ard·ess

stewardiss : **stew·ard·ess**

stewerd : **stew·ard**

stewerdess : **stew·ard·ess**

stewird : **stew·ard**

stifel : **sti·fle**

stiffle : **sti·fle**

sti·fle

stilactite : **sta·lac·tite**

stilagmite : **sta·lag·mite**

stileto : **sti·let·to**

sti·let·to

stilleto : **sti·let·to**

stimied : **sty·mied**

stimmulate : **stim·u·late**

stimmulus : **stim·u·lus**

stim·u·late

stimulis : **stim·u·lus**

stimulous : **stim·u·lus**

stim·u·lus

stincil : **sten·cil**

stipand : **sti·pend**

sti·pend

stippulate : **stip·u·late**

stip·u·late

stirep : **stir·rup**

stirrep : **stir·rup**

stir·rup

stirup : **stir·rup**

stoalen : **sto·len**

Stock·holm

Stockhome : **Stock·holm**

sto·len

stol·id

stollid : **stol·id**

stom·ach

stomache : **stom·ach**

stomack : **stom·ach**

stomich : **stom·ach**

stomick : **stom·ach**

stopige : **stop·page**

stop·page

stoppige : **stop·page**

straddel : **strad·dle**

strad·dle

straight (not crooked); **strait** (isthmus)

straight·laced or **strait·laced**

strait (isthmus); **straight** (not crooked)

strait·laced or **straight·laced**

straitlased : **strait·laced**

stratafy : **strat·i·fy**

strat·a·gem

stratajem : **strat·a·gem**

stratajy : **strat·e·gy**

stratasphere : **strat·o·sphere**

stratefy : **strat·i·fy**

strategem : **strat·a·gem**

strat·e·gy

strategy : **strat·e·gy**

stratiffy : **strat·i·fy**

strat·i·fy

stratosfere : **strat·o·sphere**

stratospheer : **strat·o·sphere**

strat·o·sphere

strattify : **strat·i·fy**

strattigem : **strat·a·gem**

strattigy : **strat·e·gy**

strattle : **strad·dle**

strattosphere : **strat·o·sphere**

streak

stream

streat : **street**

strech : **stretch**

streek : **streak**

streem : **stream**

street

strenghthen : **strength·en**

strength·en

stretch

strichnine : **strych·nine**

stricknine : **strych·nine**

stridant : **stri·dent**

stri·dent

strin·gent

stringient : **strin·gent**

stringint : **strin·gent**

striped (with stripes); **stripped** (pealed)

stripped (pealed); **striped** (with stripes)

stroake : **stroke**

stroaler : **stroll·er**

stroke

stroler : **stroll·er**

stroll·er

struggel : **strug·gle**

strug·gle

strugle : **strug·gle**

strych·nine

stubbern : **stub·born**

stub·born

stuboorn : **stub·born**

stuc·co

stucko : **stuc·co**

stuco : **stuc·co**

studant : **stu·dent**

studdio : **stu·dio**

stu·dent

studeo : **stu·dio**

studeous : **stu·di·ous**

stu·dio

stu·di·ous

stultafy : **stul·ti·fy**

stultefy : **stul·ti·fy**

stul·ti·fy

stupafy : **stu·pe·fy**

stuped : **stu·pid**

stupeffy : **stu·pe·fy**

stu·pe·fy

stuper : **stu·por**

stu•pid
stupify : **stu•pe•fy**
stu•por
stuppid : **stu•pid**
stur•geon
sturgion : **stur•geon**
sturgon : **stur•geon**
sty•mied
suacidal : **sui•cid•al**
suade : **suede**
suami : **swa•mi**
suarthy : **swar•thy**
suave
suavety : **sua•vi•ty**
sua•vi•ty
subblety : **sub•tle•ty**
subbtle : **sub•tle**
subcidize : **sub•si•dize**
suberb : **sub•urb**
suberban : **sub•ur•ban**
subgigate : **sub•ju•gate**
subjagate : **sub•ju•gate**
subjigate : **sub•ju•gate**
sub•ju•gate
sublamate : **sub•li•mate**
sub•li•mate
sub•merge
sub•merse
submirge : **sub•merge**
submirse : **sub•merse**
submishion : **sub•mis•sion**
submissian : **sub•mis•sion**
sub•mis•sion
submurge : **sub•merge**
submurse : **sub•merse**
subpena : **sub•poe•na**
subpina : **sub•poe•na**
sub•poe•na
subsadize : **sub•si•dize**
subsedize : **sub•si•dize**
sub•se•quent
subsequint : **sub•se•quent**

subservant : **sub•ser•vi•ent**
subservent : **sub•ser•vi•ent**
subserviant : **sub•ser•vi•ent**
sub•ser•vi•ent
subsiddy : **sub•sid•iary**
   (auxilliary) *or* **sub•si•dy**
   (assistance)
sub•side
sub•sid•iary (auxilliary);
   sub•si•dy (assistance)
sub•si•dize
sub•si•dy (assistance);
   sub•sid•iary (auxilliary)
subsiquent : **sub•se•quent**
sub•stance
substanse : **sub•stance**
substatute : **sub•sti•tute**
substence : **sub•stance**
substetute : **sub•sti•tute**
substince : **sub•stance**
sub•sti•tute
subtel : **sub•tle**
subteranean : **sub•ter•ra•nean**
sub•ter•ra•nean
sub•tle
sub•tle•ty (*noun*); **sub•tly** (*adv.*)
subturrainian : **sub•ter•ra•nean**
sub•urb (city outskirts);
   su•perb (superior)
sub•ur•ban
suburben : **sub•ur•ban**
succede : **suc•ceed**
suc•ceed
succeptible : **sus•cep•ti•ble**
suc•cess
suc•cinct
succulant : **suc•cu•lent**
suc•cu•lent
succulint : **suc•cu•lent**
suc•cumb
sucede : **suc•ceed**
sucess : **suc•cess**

sucidal : **sui·cid·al**
sucint : **suc·cinct**
suckulent : **suc·cu·lent**
sucsede : **suc·ceed**
sucum : **suc·cumb**
sucumb : **suc·cumb**
suecidal : **sui·cid·al**
suede
suffacate : **suf·fo·cate**
sufficate : **suf·fo·cate**
suf·fice
suffise : **suf·fice**
suffle : **souf·flé**
suf·fo·cate
sufice : **suf·fice**
sug·ar
suger : **sug·ar**
sugest : **sug·gest**
sug·gest
suggestable : **sug·gest·ible**
sug·gest·ible
sui·cid·al
sui·cide
suisidal : **sui·cid·al**
suiside : **sui·cide**
suit·able
suiter : **suit·or**
suitible : **suit·a·ble**
suit·or
sulfer : **sul·phur**
sullphur : **sul·phur**
sulltan : **sul·tan**
sulpher : **sul·phur**
sul·phur
sul·tan
sulten : **sul·tan**
sultin : **sul·tan**
su·mac
sumack : **su·mac**
sumary : **sum·ma·ry**
sumersalt : **som·er·sault**
sumit : **sum·mit**

sumlemate : **sub·li·mate**
summac : **su·mac**
sum·ma·ry
summen : **sum·mon**
summersalt : **som·er·sault**
summersault : **som·er·sault**
sum·mer·y (like summer);
 sum·ma·ry (synopsis)
summet : **sum·mit**
sum·mit
sum·mon
sumon : **sum·mon**
sun·dae (confection); **Sun·day**
 (day of week)
Sun·day (day of week);
 sun·dae (confection)
supeerior : **su·pe·ri·or**
supeeriority : **su·pe·ri·or·i·ty**
supeirior : **su·pe·ri·or**
supeiriority : **su·pe·ri·or·i·ty**
su·perb (superior); **sub·urb**
 (city outskirts)
su·per·cede *or* **su·per·sede**
superceed : **su·per·sede**
supercileous : **su·per·cil·ious**
su·per·cil·ious
supercillious : **su·per·cil·ious**
superentendent :
 su·per·in·ten·dent
su·per·fi·cial
superfishial : **su·per·fi·cial**
superfisial : **su·per·fi·cial**
superfissial : **su·per·fi·cial**
superier : **su·pe·ri·or**
superierity : **su·pe·ri·or·i·ty**
superintendant :
 su·per·in·ten·dent
su·per·in·ten·dent
su·pe·ri·or
superiorety : **su·pe·ri·or·i·ty**
su·pe·ri·or·i·ty
superiorrity : **su·pe·ri·or·i·ty**

su·per·sede
superseed : **su·per·sede**
supersilious : **su·per·cil·ious**
supersillious : **su·per·cil·ious**
su·per·vise
superviser : **su·per·vi·sor**
su·per·vi·sor
supervize : **su·per·vise**
supervizor : **su·per·vi·sor**
supirior : **su·pe·ri·or**
supiriority : **su·pe·ri·or·i·ty**
suplament : **sup·ple·ment**
suplant : **sup·plant**
suplement : **sup·ple·ment**
suplicate : **sup·pli·cate**
suply : **sup·ply**
suport : **sup·port**
suppena : **sub·poe·na**
suppina : **sub·poe·na**
supplacate : **sup·pli·cate**
supplament : **sup·ple·ment**
sup·plant
supplecate : **sup·pli·cate**
sup·ple·ment
sup·pli·cate
suppliment : **sup·ple·ment**
sup·ply
sup·port
sup·press
supreem : **su·preme**
su·prem·a·cy
supremasy : **su·prem·a·cy**
su·preme
supremicy : **su·prem·a·cy**
supremissy : **su·prem·a·cy**
supress : **sup·press**
suprimacy : **su·prem·a·cy**
suprime : **su·preme**
suprise : **sur·prise**
suprize : **sur·prise**
surch : **search**

sure·ly (with certainty); **sur·ly** (sullen)
surf (waves); **serf** (peasant)
sur·face
sur·feit
surfet : **sur·feit**
surfice : **sur·face**
surfiet : **sur·feit**
surfise : **sur·face**
surfiss : **sur·face**
surfit : **sur·feit**
surge (to rise up); **serge** (cloth)
sur·geon
sur·gery
surgion : **sur·geon**
surgirgy : **sur·gery**
surloin : **sir·loin**
sur·ly (sullen); **sure·ly** (with certainty)
sur·mise
surmize : **sur·mise**
sur·mount
sur·name
surogate : **sur·ro·gate**
surpent : **ser·pent**
sur·plice (vestment); **sur·plus** (excess)
sur·plus (excess); **sur·plice** (vestment)
surpreme : **su·preme**
surpress : **sup·press**
sur·prise
surprize : **sur·prise**
surragate : **sur·ro·gate**
surregate : **sur·ro·gate**
sur·ro·gate
surroget : **sur·ro·gate**
survaillance : **sur·veil·lance**
survallence : **sur·veil·lance**
survay : **sur·vey**
survayer : **sur·vey·or**
survayor : **sur·vey·or**

surveilance : **sur•veil•lance**
sur•veil•lance
survellance : **sur•veil•lance**
sur•vey
surveyer : **sur•vey•or**
sur•vey•or
surviellance : **sur•veil•lance**
sur•viv•al
survivel : **sur•viv•al**
surviver : **sur•viv•or**
survivil : **sur•viv•al**
sur•viv•or
susceptable : **sus•cep•ti•ble**
sus•cep•ti•ble
suscinct : **suc•cinct**
suspence : **sus•pense**
sus•pense
suspician : **sus•pi•cion**
sus•pi•cion
sus•pi•cious
suspince : **sus•pense**
suspinse : **sus•pense**
suspishious : **sus•pi•cious**
suspission : **sus•pi•cion**
suspissious : **sus•pi•cious**
suspition : **sus•pi•cion**
suspitious : **sus•pi•cious**
susseptible : **sus•cep•ti•ble**
sussinct : **suc•cinct**
sustainance : **sus•te•nance**
sustanence : **sus•te•nance**
sus•te•nance
sustenanse : **sus•te•nance**
sustinance : **sus•te•nance**
sutable : **suit•able**
suthern : **south•ern**
suttle : **sub•tle**
suvenir : **sou•ve•nir**
swade : **suede**
swammi : **swa•mi**
swamy : **swa•mi**
swar•thy

swasstika : **swas•ti•ka**
swastica : **swas•ti•ka**
swasticka : **swas•ti•ka**
swas•ti•ka
swave : **suave**
swealter : **swel•ter**
sweap : **sweep**
sweapstakes : **sweep•stakes**
sweat•er
Swedan : **Swe•den**
Swe•den
Swed•ish
Sweeden : **Swe•den**
Sweedish : **Swed•ish**
sweep
sweep•stakes
sweepsteaks : **sweep•stakes**
swel•ter
swerve
sweter : **sweat•er**
swetter : **sweat•er**
swindlar : **swin•dler**
swin•dler
Swisserland : **Switz•er•land**
Switzarland : **Switz•er•land**
Switz•er•land
swival : **swiv•el**
swiv•el
swiv•eled
swivelled : **swiv•eled**
Swizzerland : **Switz•er•land**
swoallem : **swol•len**
swolen : **swol•len**
swol•len
sword
sworthy : **swarthy**
swove : **suave**
swurve : **swerve**
syanide : **cy•a•nide**
sybernetics : **cy•ber•net•ics**
sycamoor : **syc•a•more**
syc•a•more

sycaphant : **sy·co·phant**

sycaphent : **sy·co·phant**

syckle : **cy·cle** (rotation) *or* **sick·le** (knife)

sycle : **cy·cle** (rotation) *or* **sick·le** (knife)

sycofant : **sy·co·phant**

sycomore : **syc·a·more**

sy·co·phant

sykamore : **syc·a·more**

sykophant : **sy·co·phant**

sylabus : **syl·la·bus**

sylalble : **syl·la·ble**

sylinder : **cyl·in·der**

syl·la·ble

syl·la·bus

sylleble : **syl·la·ble**

syllebus : **syl·la·bus**

symbal : **cym·bal** (brass plate) *or* **sym·bol** (meaningful image)

sym·bol (meaningful image); **cym·bal** (brass plate)

symetry : **sym·me·try**

symmatry : **sym·me·try**

sym·me·try

sym·pa·thize

sympethize : **sym·pa·thize**

sym·pho·ny

symposiem : **sym·po·sium**

sym·po·sium

symptam : **symp·tom**

symptem : **symp·tom**

symp·tom

symtom : **symp·tom**

syn·a·gogue

synanym : **syn·o·nym**

synchrinize : **syn·chro·nize**

syn·chro·nize

syncronize : **syn·chro·nize**

syndacate : **syn·di·cate**

syndecate : **syn·di·cate**

syndicat : **syn·di·cate**

syn·di·cate

synegogue : **syn·a·gogue**

synicism : **cyn·i·cism**

synonim : **syn·o·nym**

syn·o·nym

synpathize : **sym·pa·thize**

synphony : **sym·pho·ny**

synthasize : **syn·the·size**

synthesise : **syn·the·size**

syn·the·size

sypress : **cy·press**

Syr·a·cuse

syrep : **syr·up**

syrrup : **syr·up**

syr·up *or* **sirup**

systam : **sys·tem**

sys·tem

systum : **sys·tem**

sythe : **scythe**

T

tabarnacle : **tab·er·na·cle**
tabbernacle : **tab·er·na·cle**
tabbleau : **tab·leau**
tabblet : **tab·let**
tabbloe : **tab·leau**
tabboo : **ta·boo**
tabelware : **ta·ble·ware**
tabernacal : **tab·er·na·cle**
tabernackle : **tab·er·na·cle**
tab·er·na·cle
tab·leau
tab·let
ta·ble·ware
tablewear : **ta·ble·ware**
tablieu : **tab·leau**
tablit : **tab·let**
ta·boo
tabu : **ta·boo**
tacet : **tac·it**
taceturn : **tac·i·turn**
tac·it
tacitern : **tac·i·turn**
tac·i·turn
tackal : **tack·le**
tackel : **tack·le**
tack·le
tacktics : **tac·tics**
tactecs : **tac·tics**
tact·ful
tactfull : **tact·ful**
tac·ti·cal
tacticks : **tac·tics**
tacticle : **tac·ti·cal**
tac·tics
tactikal : **tac·ti·cal**
tafeta : **taf·fe·ta**
taf·fe·ta
taffita : **taf·fe·ta**
tafita : **taf·fe·ta**
Taheti : **Ta·hi·ti**

Ta·hi·ti
Tahitti : **Ta·hi·ti**
Tahity : **Ta·hi·ti**
Tailand : **Thai·land**
tailer : **tai·lor**
tai·lor
Talahassee : **Tal·la·has·see**
talant : **tal·ent**
talcem : **tal·cum**
tal·cum
talen : **tal·on**
tal·ent
tal·is·man
talissman : **tal·is·man**
talk·ative
talkitive : **talk·ative**
Tallahasee : **Tal·la·has·see**
Tal·la·has·see
tallant : **tal·ent**
tallcum : **tal·cum**
tallent : **tal·ent**
tallisman : **tal·is·man**
tallon : **tal·on**
Talmed : **Tal·mud**
Talmid : **Tal·mud**
Tal·mud
tal·on
talor : **tai·lor**
ta·ma·le
tamaly : **ta·ma·le**
tamborine : **tam·bou·rine**
tambourene : **tam·bou·rine**
tam·bou·rine
tamburine : **tam·bou·rine**
tamole : **ta·ma·le**
tamolle : **ta·ma·le**
tan·dem
tandim : **tan·dem**
tandum : **tan·dem**
tangarine : **tan·ger·ine**

275

tangeble : **tan·gi·ble**
tan·gent
tangerene : **tan·ger·ine**
tan·ger·ine
tangibal : **tan·gi·ble**
tan·gi·ble
tangient : **tan·gent**
tangierine : **tan·ger·ine**
tangint : **tan·gent**
tangirine : **tan·ger·ine**
tanjerine : **tan·ger·ine**
tannary : **tan·nery**
tan·nery
tantalise (*Brit.*) : **tan·ta·lize**
tan·ta·lize
tantallize : **tan·ta·lize**
tantelize : **tan·ta·lize**
tantilize : **tan·ta·lize**
tantrem : **tan·trum**
tantrim : **tan·trum**
tan·trum
tapeoca : **tap·i·o·ca**
tapestery : **tap·es·try**
tap·es·try
tap·i·o·ca
tapioka : **tap·i·o·ca**
tapistry : **tap·es·try**
tappestry : **tap·es·try**
tappioca : **tap·i·o·ca**
tappistry : **tap·es·try**
taranchula : **ta·ran·tu·la**
tarantoola : **ta·ran·tu·la**
ta·ran·tu·la
tareff : **tar·iff**
tar·get
targit : **tar·get**
tar·iff
tarnesh : **tar·nish**
tar·nish
tarpalin : **tar·pau·lin**
tarpaulen : **tar·pau·lin**
tar·pau·lin

tarpolin : **tar·pau·lin**
tarriff : **tar·iff**
tar·tan
tar·tar
tarten : **tar·tan**
tarter : **tar·tar**
tasel : **tas·sel**
taseturn : **tac·i·turn**
tasit : **tac·it**
tasiturn : **tac·i·turn**
tas·sel
tassit : **tac·it**
tassiturn : **tac·i·turn**
tassle : **tas·sel**
tatle : **tat·tle**
tatoo : **tat·too**
tattel : **tat·tle**
tat·tle
tat·too
tav·ern
tavurn : **tav·ern**
tavvern : **tav·ern**
tax·able
taxadermy : **taxi·der·my**
taxedermy : **taxi·der·my**
taxible : **tax·able**
taxi·der·my
taxidurmy : **taxi·der·my**
tea (drink); **tee** (golf)
teach
teadious : **te·dious**
tear·ful
tearfull : **tear·ful**
tease
technecal : **tech·ni·cal**
tech·ni·cal
technicle : **tech·ni·cal**
tech·nique
tecnical : **tech·ni·cal**
tecnique : **tech·nique**
tedeum : **te·di·um**
te·dious

te·di·um
tedius : **te·dious**
tee (golf); tea (drink)
teech : **teach**
teerful : **tear·ful**
teese : **tease**
teeth (*noun*); **teethe** (*verb*)
teethe (*verb*); **teeth** (*noun*)
Te·he·ran or **Teh·ran**
Teh·ran or **Te·he·ran**
telacast : **tele·cast**
telagram : **tele·gram**
telaphone : **tele·phone**
telascope : **tele·scope**
telavise : **tele·vise**
telavision : **tele·vi·sion**
tele·cast
tele·gram
tele·phone
tele·scope
tele·vise
tele·vi·sion
televize : **tele·vise**
tellecast : **tele·cast**
tellegram : **tele·gram**
tellephone : **tele·phone**
tellescope : **tele·scope**
tellevise : **tele·vise**
tellevision : **tele·vi·sion**
temblar : **tem·blor**
tembler : **tem·blor**
tem·blor
te·mer·i·ty
temmeritty : **te·mer·i·ty**
temmerity : **te·mer·i·ty**
tempachure : **tem·per·a·ture**
temparary : **tem·po·rary**
tempature : **tem·per·a·ture**
tem·per·ance
temperanse : **tem·per·ance**
tem·per·a·ture
temperence : **tem·per·ance**

temperince : **tem·per·ance**
temperment : **tem·per·a·ment**
temperture : **tem·per·a·ture**
tem·pest
tempirary : **tem·po·rary**
tempist : **tem·pest**
tem·po·rary
temporery : **tem·po·rary**
temprature : **tem·per·a·ture**
ten·a·ble
te·na·cious
tenacle : **ten·ta·cle**
tenament : **ten·e·ment**
tenamint : **ten·e·ment**
ten·ant
Tenasee : **Ten·nes·see**
tenat : **te·net**
tenatious : **ten·a·ble**
tenative : **ten·ta·tive**
tendan : **ten·don**
tendancy : **ten·den·cy**
tendansy : **ten·den·cy**
ten·den·cy
tendensy : **ten·den·cy**
tenderhook : **ten·ter·hook**
tendin : **ten·don**
tendincy : **ten·den·cy**
ten·don
tendrel : **ten·dril**
ten·dril
tendrill : **ten·dril**
ten·e·ment
tenent : **ten·ant**
tener : **ten·or**
Tenesee : **Ten·nes·see**
te·net
tenint : **ten·ant**
tenir : **ten·or**
tenis : **ten·nis**
Tenisee : **Ten·nes·see**
tenit : **te·net**
tennable : **ten·a·ble**

tennacious : **te·na·cious**
tennament : **ten·e·ment**
tennant : **ten·ant**
tennement : **ten·e·ment**
tennent : **ten·ant**
tennes : **ten·nis**
Tennesee : **Ten·nes·see**
Ten·nes·see
tennet : **te·net**
ten·nis
tennor : **ten·or**
tennuous : **ten·u·ous**
tennure : **ten·ure**
ten·or
ten·ta·cle
ten·ta·tive
ten·ter·hook
tentetive : **ten·ta·tive**
tentical : **ten·ta·cle**
tenticle : **ten·ta·cle**
tentitive : **ten·ta·tive**
ten·u·ous
ten·ure
teped : **tep·id**
tep·id
teppid : **tep·id**
terace : **ter·race**
teradactyl : **ptero·dac·tyl**
terain : **ter·rain**
terantula : **ta·ran·tu·la**
terban : **tur·ban** (headdress) *or*
  tur·bine (engine)
terbine : **tur·ban** (headdress) *or*
  tur·bine (engine)
terestrial : **ter·res·tri·al**
terible : **ter·ri·ble**
teridactyl : **ptero·dac·tyl**
terier : **ter·ri·er**
teriffy : **ter·ri·fy**
terific : **ter·rif·ic**
terify : **ter·ri·fy**
teritory : **ter·ri·to·ry**

terkey : **tur·key**
termenal : **ter·mi·nal**
ter·mi·nal
terminel : **ter·mi·nal**
terminnal : **ter·mi·nal**
ter·mite
termmite : **ter·mite**
ternip : **tur·nip**
terodactile : **ptero·dac·tyl**
terodactill : **ptero·dac·tyl**
terpentine : **tur·pen·tine**
terquoise : **tur·quoise**
terrable : **ter·ri·ble**
ter·race
terrafy : **ter·ri·fy**
ter·rain
terrane : **ter·rain**
terratory : **ter·ri·to·ry**
terrestial : **ter·res·tri·al**
ter·res·tri·al
terretory : **ter·ri·to·ry**
terribal : **ter·ri·ble**
ter·ri·ble
terrice : **ter·race**
ter·ri·er
terriffic : **ter·rif·ic**
ter·rif·ic
ter·ri·fy
terriss : **ter·race**
territorey : **ter·ri·to·ry**
ter·ri·to·ry
tesstify : **tes·ti·fy**
testafy : **tes·ti·fy**
tes·ta·ment
testamony : **tes·ti·mo·ny**
testement : **tes·ta·ment**
testemony : **tes·ti·mo·ny**
testiffy : **tes·ti·fy**
tes·ti·fy
testiment : **tes·ta·ment**
tes·ti·mo·ny
tetanis : **tet·a·nus**

tet·a·nus
tetnis : **tet·a·nus**
tetnus : **tet·a·nus**
tettanus : **tet·a·nus**
Teusday : **Tues·day**
Tex·as
textil : **tex·tile**
tex·tile
textill : **tex·tile**
Texus : **Tex·as**
thach : **thatch**
Thai·land
than (rather than); **then** (not
  now)
thatch
theaf : **thief**
thealogy : **the·ol·o·gy**
thearem : **the·o·rem**
theary : **the·o·ry**
theasaurus : **the·sau·rus**
the·a·ter *or* the·a·tre
the·a·tre *or* the·a·ter
theavery : **thiev·ery**
theaves : **thieves**
theef : **thief**
theevery : **thiev·ery**
theeves : **thieves**
theif : **thief**
their (belonging to them);
  there (not here); **they're** (they
  are)
theirem : **the·o·rem**
theirfore : **there·fore**
theirs (belonging to them);
  there's (there is)
theiry : **the·o·ry**
theiter : **the·a·ter**
theivery : **thiev·ery**
theives : **thieves**
then (not now); **than** (rather
  than)
theoligy : **the·ol·o·gy**

theollogy : **the·ol·o·gy**
the·ol·o·gy
the·o·rem
theorum : **the·o·rem**
the·o·ry
ther·a·peu·tic
therapuetic : **ther·a·peu·tic**
theraputic : **ther·a·peu·tic**
ther·a·py
there (not here); **their**
  (belonging to them); **they're**
  (they are)
therefor : **there·fore**
there·fore
therem : **the·o·rem**
therepeutic : **ther·a·peu·tic**
there's (there is); **theirs**
  (belonging to them)
theripy : **ther·a·py**
ther·mal
thermel : **ther·mal**
thermiss : **ther·mos**
ther·mos
thermus : **ther·mos**
therrapy : **ther·a·py**
Thersday : **Thurs·day**
thery : **the·o·ry**
the·sau·rus
thesoris : **the·sau·rus**
thesorrus : **the·sau·rus**
thesorus : **the·sau·rus**
theter : **the·a·ter**
thevery : **thiev·ery**
theves : **thieves**
they're (they are); **their**
  (belonging to them); **there**
  (not here)
Thialand : **Thai·land**
thief
thiefery : **thiev·ery**
thiefs : **thieves**
thievary : **thiev·ery**

thiev·ery
thieves
thievry : **thiev·ery**
thirmos : **ther·mos**
thiroid : **thy·roid**
Thirsday : **Thurs·day**
thirtean : **thir·teen**
thir·teen
thir·ti·eth
thirtine : **thir·teen**
thirtyeth : **thir·ti·eth**
thisel : **this·tle**
thissle : **this·tle**
this·tle
thoarax : **tho·rax**
tho·rax
thorogh : **thor·ough**
  (painstaking) *or* **through**
  (into and out of)
thor·ough (painstaking);
  through (into and out of)
thorow : **thor·ough**
  (painstaking) *or* **through**
  (into and out of)
thou·sand
thousend : **thou·sand**
thousind : **thou·sand**
thowsand : **thou·sand**
thread
thread·bare
thred : **thread**
thredbare : **thread·bare**
threshhold : **thresh·old**
thresh·old
through (into and out of);
  thor·ough (painstaking)
thru : **through**
thrugh : **thor·ough**
  (painstaking) *or* **through**
  (into and out of)
thum : **thumb**
thumb

thurmal : **ther·mal**
thurmos : **ther·mos**
Thurs·day
thy·roid
ti·ara
tiarra : **ti·ara**
tibbia : **tib·ia**
tibea : **tib·ia**
tib·ia
tickal : **tick·le**
tickel : **tick·le**
tick·le
tiera : **ti·ara**
tigar : **ti·ger**
ti·ger
tigeress : **ti·gress**
tigger : **ti·ger**
ti·gress
tigriss : **ti·gress**
tim·ber (wood); **tim·bre**
  (quality of sound)
tim·bre (quality of sound);
  tim·ber (wood)
Timbucktu : **Tim·buk·tu**
Timbuktoo : **Tim·buk·tu**
Tim·buk·tu
timerity : **te·mer·i·ty**
tim·id
timmid : **tim·id**
timpature : **tem·per·a·ture**
timperament : **tem·per·a·ment**
timperature : **tem·per·a·ture**
timperment : **tem·per·a·ment**
timperture : **tem·per·a·ture**
tinant : **ten·ant**
tinc·ture
Tinnessee : **Ten·nes·see**
tin·sel
tinsell : **tin·sel**
tinsill : **tin·sel**
tinsle : **tin·sel**
tinture : **tinc·ture**

tinuous : **ten·u·ous**
tipest : **typ·ist**
tipewriter : **type·writ·er**
tiphoid : **ty·phoid**
tiphoon : **ty·phoon**
tipical : **typ·i·cal**
ti·rade
tiraid : **ti·rade**
tiranny : **tyr·an·ny**
tirban : **tur·ban** (headdress) *or*
  tur·bine (engine)
tirmite : **ter·mite**
tirnip : **tur·nip**
tirrade : **ti·rade**
ti·tan
ti·tan·ic
titannic : **ti·tan·ic**
titen : **ti·tan**
tittan : **ti·tan**
toaken : **to·ken**
toast
to·bac·co
tobacko : **to·bac·co**
tobaco : **to·bac·co**
tobbacco : **to·bac·co**
tobogan : **to·bog·gan**
to·bog·gan
toboggen : **to·bog·gan**
toboggin : **to·bog·gan**
tobogin : **to·bog·gan**
tocan : **tou·can**
tocksic : **tox·ic**
tofee : **tof·fee**
tof·fee
toffy : **tof·fee**
toi·let
toilit : **toi·let**
to·ken
tokin : **to·ken**
tol·er·a·ble
tol·er·ance
toleranse : **tol·er·ance**

tol·er·ate
tolerence : **tol·er·ance**
tolerent : **tol·er·ance**
tolerible : **tol·er·a·ble**
tolirable : **tol·er·a·ble**
tollarance : **tol·er·ance**
tollerable : **tol·er·a·ble**
tollerance : **tol·er·ance**
tollerate : **tol·er·ate**
tollerense : **tol·er·ance**
tollerent : **tol·er·ant**
tollerint : **tol·er·ant**
tom·a·hawk
tomain : **pto·maine**
tomane : **pto·maine**
to·ma·to
tomatoe : **to·ma·to**
to·ma·toes
tomatos : **to·ma·toes**
tomb·stone
tommahawk : **tom·a·hawk**
tommorow : **to·mor·row**
tommorrow : **to·mor·row**
tomohawk : **tom·a·hawk**
tomorow : **to·mor·row**
to·mor·row
tonage : **ton·nage**
tonge : **tongue**
tongue
ton·ic
tonick : **ton·ic**
to·night
tonite : **to·night**
ton·nage
tonnege : **ton·nage**
tonnic : **ton·ic**
tonnige : **ton·nage**
tonsal : **ton·sil**
tonsel : **ton·sil**
tonsell : **ton·sil**
ton·sil
top·ic

topick : **top·ic**

toppic : **top·ic**

Toranto : **To·ron·to**

torchure : **tor·ture**

torent : **tor·rent**

torid : **tor·rid**

tornaddo : **tor·na·do**

tor·na·do

tornaido : **tor·na·do**

tornato : **tor·na·do**

To·ron·to

torpeado : **tor·pe·do**

tor·pe·do

torpeto : **tor·pe·do**

torpido : **tor·pe·do**

torrant : **tor·rent**

torrea : **tor·ti·lla**

torred : **tor·rid**

tor·rent

tor·rid

Torronto : **To·ron·to**

tort (civil wrong); **torte** (pastry)

torte (pastry); **tort** (civil wrong)

tortia : **tor·ti·lla**

tortice : **tor·toise**

tortila : **tor·ti·lla**

tor·ti·lla

tortise : **tor·toise**

tortiss : **tor·toise**

tor·toise

tor·tu·ous

tor·ture

torturous : **tor·tu·ous**

tost : **toast**

toste : **toast**

to·tal

totam : **to·tem**

totel : **to·tal**

to·tem

totil : **to·tal**

totim : **to·tem**

tottal : **to·tal**

totum : **to·tem**

tou·can

tough

tounge : **tongue**

toupay : **tou·pee**

tou·pee

toupey : **tou·pee**

tour·ist

tournakette : **tour·ni·quet**

tour·na·ment

tournamint : **tour·na·ment**

tournaquet : **tour·ni·quet**

tournement : **tour·na·ment**

tournequet : **tour·ni·quet**

tour·ney

tourniment : **tour·na·ment**

tour·ni·quet

tousalled : **tou·sled**

touselled : **tou·sled**

tou·sled

towal : **tow·el**

to·ward

tow·el

towerd : **to·ward**

towl : **tow·el**

towselled : **tou·sled**

toxec : **tox·ic**

tox·ic

toxick : **tox·ic**

tra·chea

trachia : **tra·chea**

trackia : **tra·chea**

trackter : **trac·tor**

tracktor : **trac·tor**

tracter : **trac·tor**

trac·tor

trad·er (one who trades);
    trai·tor (one who betrays)

traffec : **traf·fic**

traffecked : **traf·ficked**

traf·fic

trafficed : **traf·ficked**

traffick : **traf·fic**
traf·ficked
trafic : **traf·fic**
traficked : **traf·ficked**
tragectory : **tra·jec·to·ry**
trageddy : **trag·e·dy**
trag·e·dy
tragety : **trag·e·dy**
tragidy : **trag·e·dy**
traichea : **tra·chea**
traitor (one who betrays);
   trad·er (one who trades)
trajactary : **tra·jec·to·ry**
trajectery : **tra·jec·to·ry**
tra·jec·to·ry
trama : **trau·ma**
tramel : **tram·mel**
trammal : **tram·mel**
tram·mel
trancend : **tran·scend**
trancient : **tran·sient**
trancit : **tran·sit**
tranquel : **tran·quil**
tran·quil
tranquill : **tran·quil**
transam : **tran·som**
tran·scend
transcet : **tran·sit**
transcind : **tran·scend**
transem : **tran·som**
transferance : **trans·fer·ence**
trans·fer·ence
transferense : **trans·fer·ence**
transferrence : **trans·fer·ence**
transiant : **tran·sient**
tran·sient
tran·sit
tran·som
transsend : **tran·scend**
transum : **tran·som**
trapazoid : **trap·e·zoid**
trapeeze : **tra·peze**

trapese : **tra·peze**
tra·peze
trap·e·zoid
trappeze : **tra·peze**
trappezoid : **trap·e·zoid**
trau·ma
travasty : **trav·es·ty**
trav·el
travessty : **trav·es·ty**
trav·es·ty
travil : **trav·el**
travisty : **trav·es·ty**
travvel : **trav·el**
treacal : **trea·cle**
treachary : **treach·ery**
treacherry : **treach·ery**
treach·ery
trea·cle
tread
treakle : **trea·cle**
treashure : **trea·sure**
trea·son
trea·sure
treat
treatace : **trea·tise**
treatase : **trea·tise**
treatice : **trea·tise**
trea·tise
trebal : **tre·ble**
trebble : **tre·ble**
trebel : **tre·ble**
trebile : **tre·ble**
tre·ble
trechery : **treach·ery**
treck : **trek**
tred : **tread**
treecle : **trea·cle**
treeson : **trea·son**
treet : **treat**
treetise : **trea·tise**
trek
trekea : **tra·chea**

tremer : **trem·or**
trem·or
trenket : **trin·ket**
tres·pass
tresspass : **tres·pass**
tressure : **trea·sure**
tresure : **trea·sure**
trib·al
tribbutary : **trib·u·tary**
tribel : **trib·al**
tributarry : **trib·u·tary**
trib·u·tary
tributery : **trib·u·tary**
trilegy : **tril·o·gy**
triligy : **tril·o·gy**
trilligy : **tril·o·gy**
trillogy : **tril·o·gy**
tril·o·gy
trimor : **trem·or**
Trinadad : **Trin·i·dad**
Trin·i·dad
trin·ket
trinkit : **trin·ket**
Trinnidad : **Trin·i·dad**
tripal : **tri·ple**
tripel : **tri·ple**
tri·ple
trip·let
triplit : **trip·let**
tripple : **tri·ple**
tripplet : **trip·let**
triumf : **tri·umph**
tri·umph
trivea : **triv·ia**
triv·ia
trivvia : **triv·ia**
troley : **trol·ley**
trol·ley
trolly : **trol·ley**
troma : **trau·ma**
troop (organized group);
   troupe (group of actors)

tropec : **trop·ic**
trop·ic
trop·i·cal
tropicle : **trop·i·cal**
troppic : **trop·ic**
troppical : **trop·i·cal**
troubador : **trou·ba·dour**
trou·ba·dour
troubidor : **trou·ba·dour**
trou·ble
troul : **trow·el**
troupe (group of actors);
   troop (organized group)
trou·sers
trouzers : **trou·sers**
trow·el
trowl : **trow·el**
trowsers : **trou·sers**
tru·ant
trubadour : **trou·ba·dour**
trubble : **trou·ble**
truely : **tru·ly**
truent : **tru·ant**
trully : **tru·ly**
tru·ly
trum·pet
trumpit : **trum·pet**
trust·ee (*noun*); **trusty** (*adj.*)
trusty (*adj.*); **trust·ee** (*noun*)
tsar *or* **czar**
tucan : **tou·can**
Tues·day
tuff : **tough**
tulep : **tu·lip**
tu·lip
tullip : **tu·lip**
tumbstone : **tomb·stone**
tumer : **tu·mor**
tumestone : **tomb·stone**
tummor : **tu·mor**
tummult : **tu·mult**
tu·mor

tu·mult
tunec : **tu·nic**
tungue : **tongue**
tu·nic
tunnal : **tun·nel**
tun·nel
tunnic : **tu·nic**
tunnle : **tun·nel**
tupee : **tou·pee**
tur·ban (headdress); **tur·bine** (engine)
turbelant : **tur·bu·lent**
turben : **tur·ban** (headdress) *or* **tur·bine** (engine)
turbin : **tur·ban** (headdress) *or* **tur·bine** (engine)
tur·bine (engine); **tur·ban** (headdress)
tur·bu·lent
turet : **tur·ret**
turist : **tour·ist**
tur·key
turkoise : **tur·quoise**
turky : **tur·key**
turmite : **ter·mite**
turnament : **tour·na·ment**
turnep : **tur·nip**
turney : **tour·ney**
tur·nip
turniquet : **tour·ni·quet**
tur·pen·tine
turpintine : **tur·pen·tine**
turquoice : **tur·quoise**
turquois : **tur·quoise**

tur·quoise
tur·ret
turrit : **tur·ret**
Tusday : **Tues·day**
tuter : **tu·tor**
tu·tor
tux·e·do
tuxeto : **tux·e·do**
tuxido : **tux·e·do**
tweazers : **twee·zers**
tweesers : **twee·zers**
twee·zers
twelfth
twelth : **twelfth**
twelvth : **twelfth**
twen·ti·eth
twentyith : **twen·ti·eth**
tyfoid : **ty·phoid**
tyfoon : **ty·phoon**
typeriter : **type·writ·er**
type·writ·er
ty·phoid
ty·phoon
typhune : **ty·phoon**
typ·i·cal
typicle : **typ·i·cal**
typ·ist
typpical : **typ·i·cal**
typpist : **typ·ist**
tyr·an·ny
ty·rant
tyrenny : **tyr·an·ny**
tyrent : **ty·rant**
tzar : **czar**

U

ubiguitous : **ubiq·ui·tous**
ubiquitiss : **ubiq·ui·tous**
ubiq·ui·tous
ubiquitus : **ubiq·ui·tous**
Ucharist : **Eu·cha·rist**
ufemism : **eu·phe·mism**
Ugan·da
Ugganda : **Ugan·da**
ug·li·ness
uglyness : **ug·li·ness**
Ugonda : **Ugan·da**
ukalele : **uku·le·le**
ukelale : **uku·le·le**
ukelayle : **uku·le·le**
ukelele : **uku·le·le**
ukeley : **uku·le·le**
ukilele : **uku·le·le**
Ukrain : **Ukraine**
Ukraine
Ukrane : **Ukraine**
uku·le·le
ul·cer
ulogy : **eu·lo·gy**
ulser : **ul·cer**
ultearior : **ul·te·ri·or**
ulteerior : **ul·te·ri·or**
ultereor : **ul·te·ri·or**
ulterier : **ul·te·ri·or**
ul·te·ri·or
ul·ti·mate
ultimet : **ul·ti·mate**
ultimite : **ul·ti·mate**
ultirior : **ul·te·ri·or**
ultravilet : **ul·tra·vi·o·let**
ultravilot : **ul·tra·vi·o·let**
ul·tra·vi·o·let
ultraviolit : **ul·tra·vi·o·let**
ultreviolet : **ul·tra·vi·o·let**
umbrela : **um·brel·la**
um·brel·la

umpior : **um·pire**
um·pire
unabal : **un·able**
unabel : **un·able**
un·able
unacorn : **uni·corn**
unafy : **uni·fy**
unalatiral : **uni·lat·er·al**
unanamous : **unan·i·mous**
unanemous : **unan·i·mous**
unan·i·mous
unanimus : **unan·i·mous**
unannimous : **unan·i·mous**
unarring : **un·er·ring**
unason : **uni·son**
unatural : **un·nat·u·ral**
unaverse : **uni·verse**
unaversity : **uni·ver·si·ty**
unbeleavable : **un·be·liev·able**
unbeleevable : **un·be·liev·able**
unbeleivable : **un·be·liev·able**
unbelievabel : **un·be·liev·able**
un·be·liev·able
unbelieveble : **un·be·liev·able**
uncal : **un·cle**
un·can·ny
uncany : **un·can·ny**
un·cle
uncooth : **un·couth**
un·couth
uncuth : **un·couth**
undalate : **un·du·late**
undelate : **un·du·late**
un·de·ni·able
undenyable : **un·de·ni·able**
un·der·neath
underneeth : **un·der·neath**
underneith : **un·der·neath**
undertoe : **un·der·tow**
un·der·tow

underware : **un·der·wear**
un·der·wear
undulait : **un·du·late**
un·du·late
undully : **un·du·ly**
un·du·ly
unecorn : **uni·corn**
uneeke : **unique**
uneeque : **unique**
unefy : **uni·fy**
uneqivocal : **un·equiv·o·cal**
unequivacal : **un·equiv·o·cal**
unequivecal : **un·equiv·o·cal**
un·equiv·o·cal
unering : **un·err·ing**
un·err·ing
uneson : **uni·son**
unet : **unit**
unety : **uni·ty**
uneversal : **uni·ver·sal**
unfaigned : **un·feigned**
unfained : **un·feigned**
un·feigned
unfeined : **un·feigned**
unferl : **un·furl**
un·furl
unholesome : **un·whole·some**
uni·corn
uniffy : **uni·fy**
uni·fy
unike : **unique**
uni·lat·er·al
unilaterel : **uni·lat·er·al**
unilatiral : **uni·lat·er·al**
unilatteral : **uni·lat·er·al**
unint : **unite**
unique
unisen : **uni·son**
uni·son
unit (*noun*); **unite** (*verb*)
unite (*verb*); **unit** (*noun*)
uni·ty

univercity : **uni·ver·si·ty**
uni·ver·sal
universel : **uni·ver·sal**
universety : **uni·ver·si·ty**
universitty : **uni·ver·si·ty**
uni·ver·si·ty
univursal : **uni·ver·sal**
univurse : **uni·verse**
univursity : **uni·ver·si·ty**
unkanny : **un·can·ny**
un·kempt
unkimpt : **un·kempt**
unkle : **un·cle**
unkouth : **un·couth**
unkuth : **un·couth**
un·law·ful
unlawfull : **un·law·ful**
un·leav·ened
unlevened : **un·leav·ened**
un·mer·ci·ful
unmercifull : **un·mer·ci·ful**
unmersiful : **un·mer·ci·ful**
unmurciful : **un·mer·ci·ful**
unnateral : **un·nat·u·ral**
un·nat·u·ral
unnaturel : **un·nat·u·ral**
unnicorn : **uni·corn**
unnify : **uni·fy**
unnit : **unit**
unnite : **unite**
unnity : **uni·ty**
unniversal : **uni·ver·sal**
unniverse : **uni·verse**
unniversity : **uni·ver·si·ty**
un·pal·at·able
unpaletable : **un·pal·at·able**
unpalitable : **un·pal·at·able**
unpallatable : **un·pal·at·able**
un·prec·e·dent·ed
unprecidented :
    un·prec·e·dent·ed

unpresedented :
  un·prec·e·dent·ed
unpressidented :
  un·prec·e·dent·ed
unraval : **un·rav·el**
un·rav·el
unravil : **un·rav·el**
unravvel : **un·rav·el**
un·ready
unreddy : **un·ready**
un·re·li·able
unrelible : **un·re·li·able**
unrelieble : **un·re·li·able**
unrelyable : **un·re·li·able**
un·ri·valed *or* **un·ri·valled**
un·ri·valled *or* **un·ri·valed**
unriveled : **un·ri·valed**
unrivelled : **un·ri·valed**
unrivilled : **un·ri·valed**
unruley : **un·ruly**
unrully : **un·ruly**
un·ruly
unsanatary : **un·san·i·tary**
unsanetary : **un·san·i·tary**
unsanitarry : **un·san·i·tary**
un·san·i·tary
unsaniterry : **un·san·i·tary**
unsanitery : **un·san·i·tary**
unsavarry : **un·sa·vory**
unsaverry : **un·sa·vory**
unsavery : **un·sa·vory**
unsavorry : **un·sa·vory**
un·sa·vory
unscaithed : **un·scathed**
un·scathed
unseamly : **un·seem·ly**
unseemely : **un·seem·ly**
unseemily : **un·seem·ly**
un·seem·ly
unsheath : **un·sheathe**
un·sheathe
unsheeth : **un·sheathe**

unsheethe : **un·sheathe**
unsheith : **un·sheathe**
unsheithe : **un·sheathe**
unsoceable : **un·so·cia·ble**
unsochable : **un·so·cia·ble**
un·so·cia·ble
unspeakabel : **un·speak·able**
un·speak·able
unspeakible : **un·speak·able**
unspeekable : **un·speak·able**
un·steady
unsteddy : **un·steady**
un·til
untill : **un·til**
un·time·ly
untimly : **un·time·ly**
untootered : **un·tu·tored**
untudored : **un·tu·tored**
untutered : **un·tu·tored**
un·tu·tored
unuch : **eu·nuch**
unussual : **un·usu·al**
un·usu·al
unusuel : **un·usu·al**
unuzual : **un·usu·al**
unvail : **un·veil**
unvale : **un·veil**
un·veil
unviel : **un·veil**
unwealdy : **un·wieldy**
unweeldy : **un·wieldy**
unweildy : **un·wieldy**
un·whole·some
unwholesum : **un·whole·some**
unwhollsome : **un·whole·some**
unwholsome : **un·whole·some**
un·wieldy
upbrade : **up·braid**
up·braid
up·heav·al
upheavel : **up·heav·al**
upheeval : **up·heav·al**

upheevel : **up•heav•al**
upheival : **up•heav•al**
uphemism : **eu•phem•ism**
uphevel : **up•heav•al**
upholstary : **up•hol•stery**
upholsterry : **up•hol•stery**
up•hol•stery
upholstry : **up•hol•stery**
uphoria : **eu•pho•ria**
uppraid : **up•braid**
uproareous : **up•roar•i•ous**
up•roar•i•ous
uprorious : **up•roar•i•ous**
up•stream
upstreem : **up•stream**
Uraguay : **Uru•guay**
urainium : **ura•ni•um**
Urainus : **Ura•nus**
uraneum : **ura•ni•um**
uraniem : **ura•ni•um**
Uranis : **Ura•nus**
ura•ni•um
Ura•nus
urbain : **ur•ban**
ur•ban (of a city); **ur•bane**
  (witty)
ur•bane (witty); **ur•ban** (of a
  city)
urbanitty : **ur•ban•i•ty**
ur•ban•i•ty
urbannety : **ur•ban•i•ty**
urbannity : **ur•ban•i•ty**
urben : **ur•ban**
urchen : **ur•chin**
ur•chin
Ureguay : **Uru•guay**
urene : **urine**
ur•gen•cy
urgensy : **ur•gen•cy**
urgincy : **ur•gen•cy**
urginsy : **ur•gen•cy**
urine

urinn : **urine**
urn (vase); **earn** (work for gain)
Uroguay : **Uru•guay**
Urope : **Eu•rope**
urranium : **ura•ni•um**
Urranus : **Ura•nus**
Uru•guay
Urugway : **Uru•guay**
usabal : **us•able**
usabel : **us•able**
us•able *or* **us•eble**
usadge : **us•age**
us•age
usally : **usu•al•ly**
useable : **us•able**
us•eble *or* **us•able**
use•ful
usefull : **use•ful**
usege : **us•age**
useing : **us•ing**
userp : **usurp**
usery : **usu•ry**
usful : **use•ful**
usible : **us•able**
usidge : **us•age**
usige : **us•age**
us•ing
usirp : **usurp**
usserp : **usurp**
ussurp : **usurp**
ussury : **usu•ry**
usuage : **us•age**
usu•al•ly
usully : **usu•al•ly**
usuly : **usu•al•ly**
usurp
usury
Uta : **Utah**
Utah
utalize : **uti•lize**
utelize : **uti•lize**
utencil : **uten•sil**

utensel : **uten·sil**
uten·sil
uterice : **uter·us**
uteris : **uter·us**
uteriss : **uter·us**
uter·us
uthanasia : **eu·tha·na·sia**
utilatarian : **util·i·tar·i·an**
utiletarian : **util·i·tar·i·an**
utilety : **util·i·ty**
utilise (*Brit.*) : **uti·lize**
util·i·tar·i·an
utiliterian : **util·i·tar·i·an**
utilitty : **util·i·ty**
util·i·ty
uti·lize
utillety : **util·i·ty**
utillitarian : **util·i·tar·i·an**

utillity : **util·i·ty**
utillize : **uti·lize**
utilyze : **uti·lize**
utincil : **uten·sil**
utinsel : **uten·sil**
utinsil : **uten·sil**
utirus : **uter·us**
utopea : **uto·pia**
uto·pia
utoppia : **uto·pia**
Utta : **Utah**
ut·ter·ance
utteranse : **ut·ter·ance**
utterence : **ut·ter·ance**
utterense : **ut·ter·ance**
uttopia : **uto·pia**
utturance : **ut·ter·ance**
uturus : **uter·us**

V

vacacion : **va·ca·tion**
va·can·cy
vacansy : **va·can·cy**
vacasion : **va·ca·tion**
va·ca·tion
vaccancy : **va·can·cy**
vaccant : **va·cant**
vaccate : **va·cate**
vaccation : **va·ca·tion**
vaccene : **vac·cine**
vac·cine
vaccume : **vac·u·um**
vaccuous : **vac·u·ous**
vaccuum : **vac·u·um**
vacellate : **vac·il·late**
vacency : **va·can·cy**
vacilate : **vac·il·late**
vacillait : **vac·il·late**
vac·il·late
vacine : **vac·cine**
vacissitude : **vi·cis·si·tude**
vacseen : **vac·cine**
vacsene : **vac·cine**
vacsillate : **vac·il·late**
vacsine : **vac·cine**
vacuim : **vac·u·um**
vacuiss : **vac·u·ous**
vacume : **vac·u·um**
vac·u·ous
vac·u·um
vacuus : **vac·u·ous**
vadeville : **vaude·ville**
vag·a·bond
vagarry : **va·ga·ry**
va·ga·ry
vagebond : **vag·a·bond**
vagery : **va·ga·ry**
vaggabond : **vag·a·bond**
vaggery : **va·ga·ry**
va·grant

vagrent : **va·grant**
vagrint : **va·grant**
vagury : **va·ga·ry**
vaiporize : **va·por·ize**
vakcume : **vac·u·um**
valadictorian : **val·e·dic·to·ri·an**
va·lance (drapery); **va·lence** (in atoms)
valantine : **val·en·tine**
valece : **va·lise**
valed : **val·id**
valedictorean :
  val·e·dic·to·ri·an
val·e·dic·to·ri·an
valeece : **va·lise**
va·lence (in atoms); **va·lance** (drapery)
val·en·tine
valese : **va·lise**
valey : **val·ley**
val·iant
valice : **va·lise**
val·id
validdity : **va·lid·i·ty**
validety : **va·lid·i·ty**
validitty : **va·lid·i·ty**
va·lid·i·ty
valient : **val·iant**
va·lise
valladictorian :
  val·e·dic·to·ri·an
vallant : **val·iant**
vallantine : **val·en·tine**
valled : **val·id**
valledictorian :
  val·e·dic·to·ri·an
vallentine : **val·en·tine**
valler : **val·or**
val·ley
vallid : **val·id**

vallidity : **va·lid·i·ty**
vallient : **val·iant**
vallise : **va·lise**
vallor : **val·or**
valluable : **valu·able**
vally : **val·ley**
val·or
valour (*Brit.*) : **val·or**
valting : **vault·ing**
valuabel : **valu·able**
valu·able
valubel : **valu·able**
valuble : **valu·able**
valueble : **valu·able**
valuible : **valu·able**
valure : **val·or**
vampiar : **vam·pire**
vam·pire
vampyre : **vam·pire**
Vancoover : **Van·cou·ver**
Van·cou·ver
Vancuover : **Van·cou·ver**
Vancuver : **Van·cou·ver**
van·dal
vandel : **van·dal**
vandle : **van·dal**
vanella : **va·nil·la**
vanety : **van·i·ty**
vangard : **van·guard**
vangarde : **van·guard**
vangaurd : **van·guard**
van·guard
vanguish : **van·quish**
vanila : **va·nil·la**
va·nil·la
van·ish
vanitty : **van·i·ty**
van·i·ty
vannilla : **va·nil·la**
vannish : **van·ish**
vannity : **van·i·ty**
vanqish : **van·quish**

vanquesh : **van·quish**
van·quish
vantadge : **van·tage**
van·tage
vantege : **van·tage**
vantige : **van·tage**
vaperize : **va·por·ize**
va·pid
vaporise (*Brit.*) : **va·por·ize**
va·por·ize
vappid : **va·pid**
vapporize : **va·por·ize**
vaquous : **vac·u·ous**
varafy : **ver·i·fy**
varanda : **ve·ran·da**
varatious : **ve·ra·cious**
varcety : **var·si·ty**
varcitty : **var·si·ty**
varcity : **var·si·ty**
vareable : **vari·able**
vareance : **vari·ance**
vareation : **vari·a·tion**
varecose : **var·i·cose**
vareous : **var·i·ous**
variabal : **vari·able**
variabel : **vari·able**
vari·able
vari·ance
varianse : **vari·ance**
variasion : **vari·a·tion**
variatian : **vari·a·tion**
vari·a·tion
variatty : **va·ri·ety**
variaty : **va·ri·ety**
varible : **vari·able**
var·i·cose
varience : **vari·ance**
variense : **vari·ance**
varietty : **va·ri·ety**
va·ri·ety
varify : **ver·i·fy**
varily : **ver·i·ly**

var·i·ous
varnesh : **var·nish**
var·nish
varrecose : **var·i·cose**
varriable : **vari·able**
varriance : **vari·ance**
varriation : **vari·a·tion**
varricose : **var·i·cose**
varriety : **va·ri·ety**
varrious : **var·i·ous**
varsetty : **var·si·ty**
varsety : **var·si·ty**
varsitty : **var·si·ty**
var·si·ty
varyable : **vari·able**
varyation : **vari·a·tion**
varyis : **var·i·ous**
varyous : **var·i·ous**
vasal : **vas·sal**
vasel : **vas·sal**
vasillate : **vac·il·late**
vas·sal
vassel : **vas·sal**
Vatecan : **Vat·i·can**
Vat·i·can
Vatikan : **Vat·i·can**
Vattican : **Vat·i·can**
vaudaville : **vaude·ville**
vaudevile : **vaude·ville**
vaude·ville
vaudville : **vaude·ville**
vault·ing
vecinity : **vi·cin·i·ty**
veehicle : **ve·hi·cle**
Veetnam : **Viet·nam**
vegatable : **veg·e·ta·ble**
vegetabal : **veg·e·ta·ble**
veg·e·ta·ble
vegeteble : **veg·e·ta·ble**
vegetible : **veg·e·ta·ble**
veggetable : **veg·e·ta·ble**
vegitable : **veg·e·ta·ble**

vegtable : **veg·e·ta·ble**
vehamence : **ve·he·mence**
vehemance : **ve·he·mence**
vehemanse : **ve·he·mence**
ve·he·mence
vehemense : **ve·he·mence**
vehical : **ve·hi·cle**
vehicel : **ve·hi·cle**
vehickal : **ve·hi·cle**
vehickel : **ve·hi·cle**
ve·hi·cle
vehimence : **ve·he·mence**
Veinna : **Vi·en·na**
veinous : **ve·nous**
Veitnam : **Viet·nam**
veiw : **view**
vejetable : **veg·e·ta·ble**
veksatious : **vex·a·tious**
vellocity : **ve·loc·i·ty**
vellosity : **ve·loc·i·ty**
vellvet : **vel·vet**
velocety : **ve·loc·i·ty**
velocitty : **ve·loc·i·ty**
ve·loc·i·ty
velosity : **ve·loc·i·ty**
velvat : **vel·vet**
vel·vet
velvette : **vel·vet**
velvit : **vel·vet**
vemence : **ve·he·mence**
Venace : **Ven·ice**
venareal : **ve·ne·re·al**
venarial : **ve·ne·re·al**
venason : **ven·i·son**
Venazuela : **Ven·e·zu·e·la**
vendebta : **ven·det·ta**
vend·er *or* **vend·or**
vendeta : **ven·det·ta**
ven·det·ta
vendette : **ven·det·ta**
ven·dor *or* **vend·er**
venear : **ve·neer**

Venece : **Ven·ice**
ve·neer
veneir : **ve·neer**
ven·er·a·ble
ve·ne·re·al
venerial : **ve·ne·re·al**
venerible : **ven·er·a·ble**
veneson : **ven·i·son**
Venesuela : **Ven·e·zu·e·la**
Venezeula : **Ven·e·zu·e·la**
Venezuala : **Ven·e·zu·e·la**
Ven·e·zu·e·la
vengance : **ven·geance**
ven·geance
vengeanse : **ven·geance**
venge·ful
vengefull : **venge·ful**
vengence : **ven·geance**
vengense : **ven·geance**
vengful : **venge·ful**
vengiance : **ven·geance**
vengince : **ven·geance**
Ven·ice (city); **Ve·nus** (planet)
venicen : **ven·i·son**
venier : **ve·neer**
venigar : **vin·e·gar**
venim : **ven·om**
venimous : **ven·om·ous**
venirable : **ven·er·a·ble**
Venis : **Ven·ice** (city) *or* **Ve·nus**
  (planet)
Venise : **Ven·ice**
ven·i·son
Veniss : **Ven·ice** (city) *or*
  Ve·nus (planet)
Venizuela : **Ven·e·zu·e·la**
vennareal : **ve·ne·re·al**
Vennazuela : **Ven·e·zu·e·la**
venndetta : **ven·det·ta**
vennerable : **ven·er·a·ble**
vennereal : **ve·ne·re·al**
Vennezuela : **Ven·e·zu·e·la**

Vennice : **Ven·ice**
Vennis : **Ven·ice** (city) *or*
  Ve·nus (planet)
vennison : **ven·i·son**
vennom : **ven·om**
vennomous : **ven·om·ous**
vennum : **ven·om**
vennumous : **ven·om·ous**
Vennus : **Ven·ice** (city) *or*
  Ve·nus (planet)
ven·om
venomiss : **ven·om·ous**
ven·om·ous
venomus : **ven·om·ous**
venoo : **ven·ue**
ve·nous (having veins); **Ve·nus**
  (planet)
ventalate : **ven·ti·late**
ventelate : **ven·ti·late**
ven·ti·late
ventrilloquist : **ven·tril·o·quist**
ventriloquest : **ven·tril·o·quist**
ven·tril·o·quist
venue
venum : **ven·om**
venumous : **ven·om·ous**
Ve·nus (planet); **Ven·ice** (city);
  ve·nous (having veins)
veracety : **ve·rac·i·ty**
ve·ra·cious (truthful);
  vo·ra·cious (hungry)
veracitty : **ve·rac·i·ty**
ve·rac·i·ty
veracose : **var·i·cose**
verafiable : **ver·i·fi·able**
veraly : **ver·i·ly**
ve·ran·da *or* **ve·ran·dah**
ve·ran·dah *or* **ve·ran·da**
veranduh : **ve·ran·da**
verashious : **ve·ra·cious**
verasious : **ve·ra·cious**
verasitty : **ve·rac·i·ty**

verasity : **ve•rac•i•ty**
veratious : **ve•ra•cious**
verbage : **ver•biage**
verbaitim : **ver•ba•tim**
verbatem : **ver•ba•tim**
ver•ba•tim
verbatum : **ver•ba•tim**
verbeage : **ver•biage**
verbege : **ver•biage**
ver•biage
verbige : **ver•biage**
verboce : **ver•bose**
verbocity : **ver•bos•i•ty**
ver•bose
verbosety : **ver•bos•i•ty**
verbositty : **ver•bos•i•ty**
ver•bos•i•ty
verbossity : **ver•bos•i•ty**
verces : **ver•sus**
vercify : **ver•si•fy**
vercis : **ver•sus**
ver•dant
verdect : **ver•dict**
verdent : **ver•dant**
verdick : **ver•dict**
ver•dict
verdint : **ver•dant**
verefiable : **ver•i•fi•able**
verefy : **ver•i•fy**
verely : **ver•i•ly**
vergen : **vir•gin**
vergin : **vir•gin**
Verginia : **Vir•gin•ia**
vericose : **var•i•cose**
ver•i•fi•able
ver•i•fy
verifyable : **ver•i•fi•able**
verile : **vir•ile**
verillity : **vi•ril•i•ty**
ver•i•ly
verious : **var•i•ous**
verman : **ver•min**

vermen : **ver•min**
vermilian : **ver•mil•ion**
ver•mil•ion
vermillion : **ver•mil•ion**
ver•min
Ver•mont
vermooth : **ver•mouth**
Vermount : **Ver•mont**
ver•mouth
vermuth : **ver•mouth**
vernackular : **ver•nac•u•lar**
ver•nac•u•lar
vernaculer : **ver•nac•u•lar**
vernakular : **ver•nac•u•lar**
ver•nal
vernel : **ver•nal**
verracious : **ve•ra•cious**
verracity : **ve•rac•i•ty**
verraly : **ver•i•ly**
verranda : **ve•ran•da**
verrifiable : **ver•i•fi•able**
verrify : **ver•i•fy**
verrily : **ver•i•ly**
versafy : **ver•si•fy**
Ver•sailles
Versalles : **Ver•sailles**
ver•sa•tile
versatle : **ver•sa•tile**
versefy : **ver•si•fy**
versetile : **ver•sa•tile**
ver•si•fy
Versigh : **Ver•sailles**
Versilles : **Ver•sailles**
versis : **ver•sus**
versitile : **ver•sa•tile**
versitle : **ver•sa•tile**
versittle : **ver•sa•tile**
ver•sus
Versye : **Ver•sailles**
vertabra : **ver•te•bra** (*sing.*)
vertabrae : **ver•te•brae** (*plur.*)
vertacle : **ver•ti•cal**

vertago : **ver•ti•go**
ver•te•bra (*sing.*); **ver•te•brae** (*plur.*)
ver•te•brae (*plur.*); **ver•te•bra** (*sing.*)
vertebray : **ver•te•brae** (*plur.*)
vertecle : **ver•ti•cal**
vertego : **ver•ti•go**
vertibra : **ver•te•bra** (*sing.*)
vertibrae : **ver•te•brae** (*plur.*)
ver•ti•cal
verticel : **ver•ti•cal**
verticle : **ver•ti•cal**
vertiggo : **ver•ti•go**
ver•ti•go
vertikal : **ver•ti•cal**
vertue : **vir•tue**
vesel : **ves•sel**
vessal : **ves•sel**
ves•sel
vessle : **ves•sel**
vestabule : **ves•ti•bule**
vestage : **ves•tige**
vestebule : **ves•ti•bule**
vestege : **ves•tige**
vestiboole : **ves•ti•bule**
ves•ti•bule
vestidge : **ves•tige**
ves•tige
vestigeal : **ves•ti•gial**
ves•ti•gial
vetaran : **vet•er•an**
vetarinarian : **vet•er•i•nar•i•an**
vet•er•an
veteren : **vet•er•an**
veterenarian : **vet•er•i•nar•i•an**
veterin : **vet•er•an**
veterinarean : **vet•er•i•nar•i•an**
vet•er•i•nar•i•an
veterinerian : **vet•er•i•nar•i•an**
veternarian : **vet•er•i•nar•i•an**
veterran : **vet•er•an**

veterrinarian : **vet•er•i•nar•i•an**
vetiran : **vet•er•an**
ve•to
vetoe : **ve•to**
ve•toes
vetos : **ve•toes**
vettaran : **vet•er•an**
vetteran : **vet•er•an**
vetterinarian : **vet•er•i•nar•i•an**
vexacious : **vex•a•tious**
vexasious : **vex•a•tious**
vex•a•tious
vexatius : **vex•a•tious**
viabal : **vi•a•ble**
viabel : **vi•a•ble**
viabilety : **vi•a•bil•i•ty**
viabilitty : **vi•a•bil•i•ty**
vi•a•bil•i•ty
viabillity : **vi•a•bil•i•ty**
vi•a•ble
viablety : **vi•a•bil•i•ty**
viaduck : **via•duct**
via•duct
vi•al (container); vile (filthy)
vibility : **vi•a•bil•i•ty**
vible : **vi•a•ble**
vi•brant
vibrater : **vi•bra•tor**
vi•bra•tor
vibrent : **vi•brant**
vic•ar
vicareous : **vi•car•i•ous**
vi•car•i•ous
vicarrious : **vi•car•i•ous**
vicenity : **vi•cin•i•ty**
vicerious : **vi•car•i•ous**
vicinetty : **vi•cin•i•ty**
vicinety : **vi•cin•i•ty**
vicinitty : **vi•cin•i•ty**
vi•cin•i•ty
vicinnity : **vi•cin•i•ty**

vi·cious (immoral); **vis·cous**
(thick liquid)
vicisitude : **vi·cis·si·tude**
vicissatude : **vi·cis·si·tude**
vi·cis·si·tude
vicker : **vic·ar**
victary : **vic·to·ry**
victem : **vic·tim**
victer : **vic·tor**
victery : **vic·to·ry**
vic·tim
vic·tor
victorry : **vic·to·ry**
vic·to·ry
victum : **vic·tim**
viddeo : **vid·eo**
viddio : **vid·eo**
vid·eo
vidio : **vid·eo**
viduct : **via·duct**
viel : **vi·al** (container) *or* **vile**
(filthy)
Viena : **Vi·en·na**
Vienese : **Vi·en·nese**
Vi·en·na
Viennease : **Vi·en·nese**
Vi·en·nese
Vienneze : **Vi·en·nese**
Viet·nam
Vietnom : **Viet·nam**
view
vigalant : **vig·i·lant**
vigel : **vig·il**
vigelant : **vig·i·lant**
viger : **vig·or**
vigger : **vig·or**
vig·il
vig·i·lant
vigilent : **vig·i·lant**
vigill : **vig·il**
vignet : **vi·gnette**
vi·gnette

vig·or
vijil : **vig·il**
viker : **vic·ar**
vilafication : **vil·i·fi·ca·tion**
vilafy : **vil·i·fy**
vilage : **vil·lage**
vilain : **vil·lain**
vilan : **vil·lain**
vilate : **vi·o·late**
vile (filthy); **vi·al** (container)
vilefy : **vil·i·fy**
vile·ly
vilent : **vi·o·lent**
vilet : **vi·o·let**
vilifacation : **vil·i·fi·ca·tion**
vil·i·fi·ca·tion
vil·i·fy
vilin : **vi·o·lin**
villadge : **vil·lage**
vil·lage
vil·lain (evil one); **vil·lein**
(peasant)
villan : **vil·lain** (evil one) *or*
vil·lein (peasant)
villege : **vil·lage**
vil·lein (peasant); **vil·lain** (evil
one)
villen : **vil·lain** (evil one) *or*
vil·lein (peasant)
villidge : **vil·lage**
villification : **vil·i·fi·ca·tion**
villify : **vil·i·fy**
villige : **vil·lage**
villin : **vil·lain** (evil one) *or*
vil·lein (peasant)
vily : **vile·ly**
vinagar : **vin·e·gar**
vinager : **vin·e·gar**
vindacate : **vin·di·cate**
vindecate : **vin·di·cate**
vineer : **ve·neer**
vin·e·gar

vineger : **vin·e·gar**
vineir : **ve·neer**
vinel : **vi·nyl**
vinell : **vi·nyl**
vinette : **vi·gnette**
vine·yard
viniette : **vi·gnette**
vinigar : **vin·e·gar**
vinil : **vi·nyl**
vinill : **vi·nyl**
vin·tage
vintedge : **vin·tage**
vintege : **vin·tage**
vintelate : **ven·ti·late**
vintidge : **vin·tage**
vintige : **vin·tage**
vintilate : **ven·ti·late**
Vinus : **Ven·ice** (city) *or*
 Ve·nus (planet)
vinyard : **vine·yard**
vinyette : **vi·gnette**
vi·nyl
violant : **vi·o·lent**
vi·o·late
violen : **vi·o·lin**
vi·o·lent
vi·o·let
vi·o·lin
violint : **vi·o·lent**
virgen : **vir·gin**
Virgenia : **Vir·gin·ia**
vir·gin
Vir·gin·ia
Virginnia : **Vir·gin·ia**
vir·ile
virilitty : **vi·ril·i·ty**
vi·ril·i·ty
virill : **vir·ile**
virillity : **vi·ril·i·ty**
viris : **vi·rus**
virmooth : **ver·mouth**
virmouth : **ver·mouth**

virmuth : **ver·mouth**
virrus : **vi·rus**
vir·tue
vi·rus
visability : **vis·i·bil·i·ty**
visable : **vis·i·ble**
vis·age
viscious : **vi·cious** (immoral) *or*
 vis·cous (thick liquid)
viscositty : **vis·cos·i·ty**
vis·cos·i·ty
viscossity : **vis·cos·i·ty**
vis·cous (thick liquid); **vi·cious**
 (immoral)
viseble : **vis·i·ble**
visege : **vis·age**
viser : **vi·sor**
visibal : **vis·i·ble**
visibel : **vis·i·ble**
visibilety : **vis·i·bil·i·ty**
visibilitty : **vis·i·bil·i·ty**
vis·i·bil·i·ty
visibillity : **vis·i·bil·i·ty**
vis·i·ble
visige : **vis·age**
visinity : **vi·cin·i·ty**
visious : **vi·cious**
visissitude : **vi·cis·si·tude**
visiter : **vis·i·tor**
vis·i·tor
vi·sor
vissage : **vis·age**
vissitor : **vis·i·tor**
vis·u·al
visualise : **vis·u·al·ize**
vis·u·al·ize
visuel : **vis·u·al**
visule : **vis·u·al**
visulize : **vis·u·al·ize**
vi·tal
vitalitty : **vi·tal·i·ty**
vi·tal·i·ty

vitallity : **vi·tal·i·ty**
vitamen : **vi·ta·min**
vi·ta·min
vitel : **vi·tal**
vitemin : **vi·ta·min**
vit·re·ous
vitrious : **vit·re·ous**
vivacety : **vi·vac·i·ty**
vi·va·cious
vivacitty : **vi·vac·i·ty**
vi·vac·i·ty
vivasity : **vi·vac·i·ty**
vivassity : **vi·vac·i·ty**
vivatious : **vi·va·cious**
vix·en
vixin : **vix·en**
vizage : **vis·age**
vizer : **vi·sor**
vizitor : **vis·i·tor**
vocabularry : **vo·cab·u·lary**
vo·cab·u·lary
vocabulerry : **vo·cab·u·lary**
vocabulery : **vo·cab·u·lary**
vocal chords : **vo·cal cords**
vo·cal cords
vodca : **vod·ka**
voddville : **vaude·ville**
vod·ka
voiage : **voy·age**
vol·a·tile
volatle : **vol·a·tile**
volcanno : **vol·ca·no**
vol·ca·no
volentary : **vol·un·tary**
volenteer : **vol·un·teer**
voletile : **vol·a·tile**
voletle : **vol·a·tile**
volkano : **vol·ca·no**
vollatile : **vol·a·tile**

vol·ley·ball
vollume : **vol·ume**
vollyball : **vol·ley·ball**
volt·age
voltege : **volt·age**
voltige : **volt·age**
vol·ume
voluntarry : **vol·un·tary**
vol·un·tary
vol·un·teer
volunteir : **vol·un·teer**
voluntery : **vol·un·tary**
voluntier : **vol·un·teer**
vom·it
vommit : **vom·it**
vo·ra·cious (hungry);
   ve·ra·cious (truthful)
votarry : **vo·ta·ry**
vo·ta·ry
votery : **vo·ta·ry**
voudeville : **vaude·ville**
vow·el
vowl : **vow·el**
voy·age
voyege : **voy·age**
voyige : **voy·age**
vulcano : **vol·ca·no**
vul·gar
vulger : **vul·gar**
vulnerabal : **vul·ner·a·ble**
vul·ner·a·ble
vulnerble : **vul·ner·a·ble**
vulnerible : **vul·ner·a·ble**
vurbatim : **ver·ba·tim**
vurbose : **ver·bose**
vurbosity : **ver·bos·i·ty**
vurnacular : **ver·nac·u·lar**
vynel : **vi·nyl**
vynil : **vi·nyl**

W

wachful : **watch·ful**

wad (small mass); **wade** (to walk in water)

waddel : **wad·dle** (to move clumsily) *or* **wat·tle** (hut)

wad·dle (to move clumsily); **wat·tle** (hut)

wade (to walk in water); **wad** (small mass)

wadle : **wad·dle** (to move clumsily) *or* **wat·tle** (hut)

wafe : **waif**

waf·er (disk); **waiv·er** (relinquishment); **wav·er** (to hesitate)

waffer : **wa·fer** (disk) *or* **waiv·er** (relinquishment) *or* **wav·er** (to hesitate)

waf·fle

wafle : **waf·fle**

wagen : **wag·on**

wa·ger

waggon (*Brit.*) : **wag·on**

waght : **weight**

wag·on

wagur : **wa·ger**

waif

waifer : **wa·fer** (disk) *or* **waiv·er** (relinquishment) *or* **wav·er** (to hesitate)

Wai·ki·ki

wail (to cry); **whale** (mammal)

wain (cart); **wane** (to diminish)

wainscoat : **wain·scot**

wain·scot

wainscote : **wain·scot**

wairily : **wari·ly**

waist (part of body); **waste** (unused)

waistbasket : **waste·bas·ket**

waistbassket : **waste·bas·ket**

waistful : **waste·ful**

waistrel : **wast·rel**

wait (to stay for); **weight** (heaviness)

waiteress : **wait·ress**

wait·ress

waive (to forgo); **wave** (ridge of water; gesture)

waiv·er (relinquishment); **waf·er** (disk); **wav·er** (to hesitate)

wake·ful

wakefull : **wake·ful**

walet : **wal·let**

walit : **wal·let**

wallep : **wal·lop**

wal·let

wallip : **wal·lop**

wallit : **wal·let**

wallnut : **wal·nut**

walloe : **wal·low**

wal·lop

wal·low

wallris : **wal·rus**

wallrus : **wal·rus**

wal·nut

walow : **wal·low**

walris : **wal·rus**

walriss : **wal·rus**

wal·rus

walts : **waltz**

waltz

wane (to diminish); **wain** (cart)

wanescot : **wain·scot**

want (desire); **wont** (custom); **won't** (will not)

wanten : **wan·ton**

wan·ton

warant : **war·rant**

warbal : **war·ble**
war·ble
war·den
wardon : **war·den**
ware·house
warely : **wari·ly**
warent : **war·rant**
warf : **wharf**
wari·ly
warior : **war·rior**
war·rant
war·ran·tee (one who receives warranty); **war·ran·ty** (guarantee)
war·ran·ty (guarantee); **war·ran·tee** (one who receives warranty)
warrent : **war·rant**
warrentee : **war·ran·tee** (one who receives warranty) or **war·ran·ty** (guarantee)
warrier : **war·rior**
warrint : **war·rant**
warrintee : **war·ran·tee** (one who receives warranty) or **war·ran·ty** (guarantee)
war·rior
warsh : **wash**
Warshington : **Wash·ing·ton**
wash
washabel : **wash·able**
wash·able
washeble : **wash·able**
washible : **wash·able**
Washingten : **Wash·ing·ton**
Washingtin : **Wash·ing·ton**
Wash·ing·ton
Washinton : **Wash·ing·ton**
was·sail
wassal : **was·sail**
wassel : **was·sail**
wassell : **was·sail**

wasstrel : **wast·rel**
wastbasket : **waste·bas·ket**
waste (loss of use); **waist** (part of body)
waste·bas·ket
wastebaskit : **waste·bas·ket**
waste·ful
wastefull : **waste·ful**
wastful : **waste·ful**
wastral : **wast·rel**
wast·rel
wastrell : **wast·rel**
wastrill : **wast·rel**
watch·ful
watchfull : **watch·ful**
wa·ter
wateress : **wait·ress**
watermelan : **wa·ter·mel·on**
watermelin : **wa·ter·mel·on**
watermellin : **wa·ter·mel·on**
watermellon : **wa·ter·mel·on**
wa·ter·mel·on
waterry : **wa·tery**
watershead : **wa·ter·shed**
wa·ter·shed
wa·tery
watter : **wa·ter**
wattermelon : **wa·ter·mel·on**
wattershed : **wa·ter·shed**
wattery : **wa·tery**
wave (ridge of water; gesture); **waive** (to forgo)
wav·er (to hesitate); **waf·er** (disk); **waiv·er** (relinquishment)
wayfairer : **way·far·er**
way·far·er
waylade : **way·laid**
way·laid
waylayed : **way·laid**
way·ward
waywerd : **way·ward**

wayword : **way•ward**
weadle : **whee•dle**
weak•en
weakleng : **weak•ling**
weak•ling
weald : **wield**
wealp : **whelp**
wealterweight : **wel•ter•weight**
wealthy
weapen : **weap•on**
weap•on
wearas : **where•as**
wearhouse : **ware•house**
wearisom : **wea•ri•some**
wea•ri•some
weary
wearysome : **wea•ri•some**
wearysum : **wea•ri•some**
weasal : **wea•sel**
wea•sel
weasil : **wea•sel**
weath•er (atmospheric condition); **weth•er** (sheep); **wheth•er** (if)
weave
weavel : **wee•vil**
weavil : **wee•vil**
Weddnesday : **Wednes•day**
Wednes•day
weedal : **whee•dle**
weedle : **whee•dle**
weeken : **weak•en**
weekling : **weak•ling**
weel : **wheel**
weeld : **wield**
weerd : **weird**
weerisome : **wea•ri•some**
weerwolf : **were•wolf**
weerwulf : **were•wolf**
weery : **weary**
weerysome : **wea•ri•some**
weesel : **wea•sel**

weeval : **wee•vil**
weeve : **weave**
weevel : **wee•vil**
wee•vil
weght : **weight**
weight (heaviness); **wait** (to stay for)
weiken : **weak•en**
weild : **wield**
weird
weirwolf : **were•wolf**
weiry : **weary**
weirysome : **wea•ri•some**
weisel : **wea•sel**
weive : **weave**
weivil : **wee•vil**
welch (to cheat); **Welsh** (from Wales)
wel•come
welcume : **wel•come**
welfair : **wel•fare**
wel•fare
wellcome : **wel•come**
wellfair : **wel•fare**
wellfare : **wel•fare**
wellterweight : **wel•ter•weight**
wellthy : **wealthy**
welp : **whelp**
Welsh (from Wales); **welch** (to cheat)
wel•ter•weight
welterwieght : **wel•ter•weight**
welthy : **wealthy**
weman : **wom•en**
wemman : **wom•en**
wence : **whence** (from where) *or* **wince** (to flinch)
wendlass : **wind•lass**
Wendnisday : **Wednes•day**
Wendsday : **Wednes•day**
wendward : **wind•ward**
Wensday : **Wednes•day**

wepen : **weap·on**

wepon : **weap·on**

weppen : **weap·on**

weppin : **weap·on**

weppon : **weap·on**

were (*past of* to be); **we're** (we are)

we're (we are); **were** (*past of* to be)

were·wolf

werewulf : **were·wolf**

werl : **whirl**

wership : **wor·ship**

wersted : **wor·sted**

werthy : **wor·thy**

werwolf : **were·wolf**

Wesconsin : **Wis·con·sin**

West Verginia : **West Vir·gin·ia**

West Vir·gin·ia

west·ward

westwerd : **west·ward**

westword : **west·ward**

wet (moist); **whet** (to sharpen)

weth·er (sheep); **weath·er** (atmospheric condition); **weth·er** (if)

wetstone : **whet·stone**

whale (mammal); **wail** (to cry)

wharf

wharfs : **wharves**

wharves

wheadle : **whee·dle**

wheal : **wheel**

whealp : **whelp**

wheaze : **wheeze**

whee·dle

wheel

wheeze : **wheeze**

wheil : **wheel**

whelp

whemsical : **whim·si·cal**

whence (from where); **wince** (to flinch)

wheras : **where·as**

where as : **where·as**

where·as

wherehouse : **ware·house**

wherewolf : **were·wolf**

whet (to sharpen); **wet** (moist)

wheth·er (if); **weath·er** (atmospheric condition); **weth·er** (sheep)

whetstoan : **whet·stone**

whet·stone

which (what one); **witch** (sorceress)

whicked : **wick·ed** (evil) *or* **wick·et** (gate)

whicket : **wick·ed** (evil) *or* **wick·et** (gate)

whickit : **wick·ed** (evil) *or* **wick·et** (gate)

whim·per

whimsecal : **whim·si·cal**

whim·si·cal

whimsickal : **whim·si·cal**

whim·sy

whimzy : **whim·sy**

whince : **whence** (from where) *or* **wince** (to flinch)

whine (sound); **wine** (beverage)

whin·ny (neigh); **whiny** (given to whining)

whiny (given to whining); **whin·ny** (neigh)

whip

whipet : **whip·pet**

whipit : **whip·pet**

whipoorwill : **whip·poor·will**

whipperwill : **whip·poor·will**

whip·pet

whippit : **whip·pet**

whip·poor·will

whipporwill : **whip·poor·will**

whirl

whis·ker

whis·key or **whis·ky**

whis·ky or **whis·key**

whis·per

whissle : **whis·tle**

whisstel : **whis·tle**

whisteria : **wis·te·ria**

whistful : **wist·ful**

whis·tle

whith·er (to where); **with·er** (to shrivel)

whittal : **whit·tle**

whittel : **whit·tle**

whit·tle

whol·ly (completely); **hol·ly** (tree); **ho·ly** (sacred)

wholy : **ho·ly** (sacred) or **whol·ly** (completely)

who's (who is); **whose** (belonging to whom)

whose (belonging to whom); **who's** (who is)

wich : **which** (what one) or **witch** (sorceress)

wick·ed (evil); **wick·et** (gate)

wick·et (gate); **wick·ed** (evil)

wickit : **wick·ed** (evil) or **wick·et** (gate)

wieght : **weight**

wield

wierd : **weird**

wierwolf : **were·wolf**

wiery : **weary**

wiesel : **wea·sel**

wieve : **weave**

wievil : **wee·vil**

Wikeekee : **Wai·ki·ki**

wikked : **wick·ed** (evil) or **wick·et** (gate)

wildernes : **wil·der·ness**

wil·der·ness

wilderniss : **wil·der·ness**

wildurness : **wil·der·ness**

wil·ful or **will·ful**

wilfull : **will·ful**

wil·i·ness

willderness : **wil·der·ness**

will·ful or **wil·ful**

willfull : **will·ful**

wilyness : **wil·i·ness**

wiman : **wom·en**

wimen : **wom·en**

wimman : **wom·en**

wimmen : **wom·en**

wimper : **whim·per**

wimsical : **whim·si·cal**

wimsy : **whim·sy**

winary : **win·ery**

wince (to flinch); **whence** (from where)

windlas : **wind·lass**

wind·lass

windles : **wind·lass**

Windsday : **Wednes·day**

windsheald : **wind·shield**

windsheeld : **wind·shield**

windsheild : **wind·shield**

wind·shield

wind·ward

windwerd : **wind·ward**

windword : **wind·ward**

wine (beverage); **whine** (sound)

winerry : **win·ery**

win·ery

wintery : **win·try**

win·try

Wioming : **Wy·o·ming**

wip : **whip**

wippet : **whip·pet**

wippoorwill : **whip·poor·will**

wird : **weird**

wirl : **whirl**

Wisconsen : **Wis·con·sin**
Wis·con·sin
wis·dom
wisdum : **wis·dom**
wish·ful
wishfull : **wish·ful**
wisker : **whis·ker**
wiskey : **whis·key**
Wiskonsin : **Wis·con·sin**
wisky : **whis·key**
wisper : **whis·per**
wissel : **whis·tle**
wis·ta·ria *or* **wis·te·ria**
wis·te·ria *or* **wis·ta·ria**
wistfull : **wist·ful**
wistle : **whis·tle**
witch (sorceress); **which** (what one)
with·al
withall : **with·al**
with·draw·al
withdrawel : **with·draw·al**
withdrawl : **with·draw·al**
with·er (to shrivel); **whith·er** (to where)
with·hold
withold : **with·hold**
wit·ness
witniss : **wit·ness**
wit·ti·cism
wittisism : **wit·ti·cism**
wittle : **whit·tle**
wittness : **wit·ness**
wittycism : **wit·ti·cism**
wiz·ard
wiz·ard·ry
wizerd : **wiz·ard**
wizerdry : **wiz·ard·ry**
wizzard : **wiz·ard**
wizzardry : **wiz·ard·ry**
wizzerd : **wiz·ard**
wizzerdry : **wiz·ard·ry**

wod : **wad**
woddle : **wad·dle** (to move clumsily) *or* **wat·tle** (hut)
wofel : **waf·fle**
woffle : **waf·fle**
wofle : **waf·fle**
wolf (animal); **woof** (weaving)
wolfs : **wolves**
wollow : **wal·low**
woltz : **waltz**
wolves
wom·an (*sing.*); **wom·en** (*plur.*)
wom·en (*plur.*); **wom·an** (*sing.*)
womman : **wom·an**
wommen : **wom·en**
won·der·ful
wonderfull : **won·der·ful**
wonderous : **won·drous**
won·drous
wont (custom); **want** (desire); **won't** (will not)
won't (will not); **want** (desire); **wont** (custom)
woof (weaving); **wolf** (animal)
wool·en *or* **wool·len**
wool·len *or* **wool·en**
wool·ly
wooly : **wool·ly**
worbal : **war·ble**
worble : **war·ble**
word·age
wordege : **word·age**
wordige : **word·age**
world·li·ness
worldlyness : **world·li·ness**
wor·ri·some
worrysome : **wor·ri·some**
worrysum : **wor·ri·some**
wor·ship
wor·ship·ing *or* **wor·ship·ping**
wor·ship·ping *or* **wor·ship·ing**
worstead : **wor·sted**

wor·sted
wor·thy
worysome : **wor·ri·some**
wranglar : **wran·gler**
wran·gler
wrastle : **wres·tle**
wraught : **wrought**
wreak (to inflict); **reek** (to stink); **wreck** (to destroy)
wreath (*noun*); **wreathe** (*verb*)
wreathe (*verb*); **wreath** (*noun*)
wrech : **wreak** (to inflict) *or* **wreck** (to destroy) *or* **wretch** (miserable one)
wreck (to destroy); **wreak** (to inflict)
wreck·age
wreckege : **wreck·age**
wreckige : **wreck·age**
wreek : **wreak** (to inflict) *or* **wreck** (to destroy)
wreeth : **wreath** (*noun*)
wreethe : **wreathe** (*verb*)
wreith : **wreath** (*noun*)
wreithe : **wreathe** (*verb*)
wrekage : **wreck·age**
wrench
wressel : **wres·tle**
wrestal : **wres·tle**
wrestel : **wres·tle**
wres·tle
wretch (miserable one); **retch** (to vomit)

wriggal : **wrig·gle**
wriggel : **wrig·gle**
wrig·gle
wrigle : **wrig·gle**
wrily : **wry·ly**
winch : **wrench**
wrinkal : **wrin·kle**
wrinkel : **wrin·kle**
wrin·kle
wrist
writen : **writ·ten**
writ·er
writh : **writhe**
writhe
writ·ing
writ·ten
writter : **writ·er**
writting : **writ·ing**
wrought
wry (ironic); **rye** (grain)
wry·ly
wrythe : **writhe**
wufe : **wolf** (animal) *or* **woof** (weaving)
wulf : **wolf** (animal) *or* **woof** (weaving)
wunderful : **won·der·ful**
wundrous : **won·drous**
wursted : **wor·sted**
wurthy : **wor·thy**
wyerd : **weird**
Wykiki : **Wai·ki·ki**
Wy·o·ming
wyrd : **weird**

X

xe•non
xe•no•pho•bia
Xe•rox
xilophone : **xy•lo•phone**

xylaphone : **xy•lo•phone**
xylephone : **xy•lo•phone**
xy•lo•phone

Y

yacht
yack : **yak**
yaht : **yacht**
yak
yall : **yawl** (sailboat) *or* **yowl** (howl)
yamaka : **yar·mul·ke**
Yanckee : **Yan·kee**
Yan·kee
Yankey : **Yan·kee**
Yankie : **Yan·kee**
Yanky : **Yan·kee**
yard·age
yardege : **yard·age**
yardidge : **yard·age**
yardige : **yard·age**
yar·mul·ke
yat : **yacht**
yaught : **yacht**
yaun : **yawn**
yawl (sailboat); **yowl** (howl)
yawn
yeald : **yield**
year
yearn·ing
yeast
yeer : **year**
yeest : **yeast**
yeild : **yield**
yello : **yel·low**
yelloe : **yel·low**
yel·low
yelow : **yel·low**
Yeman : **Ye·men**
Ye·men
yeo·man
yerning : **yearn·ing**
yerself : **your·self**
yestday : **yes·ter·day**
yes·ter·day

yestoday : **yes·ter·day**
yesturday : **yes·ter·day**
yew (tree); **ewe** (female sheep); **you** (*pron.*)
Yid·dish
Yidish : **Yid·dish**
yield
yo·del
yodell : **yo·del**
yo·ga (Hindu philosophy); **yo·gi** (follower of yoga)
yogah : **yo·ga**
yogart : **yo·gurt**
yogert : **yo·gurt**
yogha : **yo·ga**
yoghi : **yo·gi**
yoghourt : **yo·gurt**
yoghurt : **yo·gurt**
yo·gi (follower of yoga); **yo·ga** (Hindu philosophy)
yo·gurt
yoke (harness); **yolk** (egg yellow)
yo·kel
yokle : **yo·kel**
yolk (egg yellow); **yoke** (harness)
yoman : **yeo·man**
Yoming : **Wy·o·ming**
yondur : **yon·der**
yool : **yule**
yor : **yore** (time past) *or* **your** (belonging to you) *or* **you're** (you are)
yore (time past); **your** (belonging to you); **you're** (you are)
Yosemety : **Yo·sem·i·te**
Yo·sem·i·te
Yosemitty : **Yo·sem·i·te**

Yosimete : **Yo•sem•i•te**
yot : **yacht**
you (*pron.*); **ewe** (female
  sheep); **yew** (tree)
young
youngstor : **young•ster**
your (belonging to you); **yore**
  (time past); **you're** (you are)
you're (you are); **yore** (time
  past); **your** (belonging to
  you)
yours
your's : **yours**
your•self
yoursself : **your•self**
youth
Yu•ca•tán
yuc•ca

Yuccatan : **Yu•ca•tán**
yucka : **yuc•ca**
Yucon : **Yu•kon**
yuel : **yule**
Yugaslavia : **Yu•go•sla•via**
Yu•go•sla•via *or* **Ju•go•sla•via**
Yugoslovia : **Yu•go•sla•via**
Yu•kon
yule
yull : **yule**
yung : **young**
yur : **yore** (time past) *or* **your**
  (*pron.*) *or* **you're** (you are)
yurning : **yearn•ing**
yurself : **your•self**
Yutah : **Utah**
yuth : **youth**

Z

Zambeezi : **Zam·be·zi**
Zam·be·si or **Zam·be·zi**
Zam·be·zi or **Zam·be·si**
Zambezy : **Zam·be·zi**
zaney : **za·ny**
Zansibar : **Zan·zi·bar**
za·ny
Zan·zi·bar
zar : **czar**
zeabra : **ze·bra**
zeal
zeal·ot
zeal·ous
zealus : **zeal·ous**
zearo : **ze·ro**
ze·bra
zeel : **zeal**
zeenith : **ze·nith**
zefer : **zeph·yr**
zeffer : **zeph·yr**
zefir : **zeph·yr**
zellot : **zeal·ot**
zellous : **zeal·ous**
zelot : **zeal·ot**
zeneth : **ze·nith**
zenia : **zin·nia**
ze·nith
zennith : **ze·nith**
zenon : **xe·non**
zenophobia : **xe·no·pho·bia**
zepelin : **zep·pe·lin**
zepher : **zeph·yr**
zephir : **zeph·yr**
zeph·yr
zep·pe·lin
zeppilen : **zep·pe·lin**
zercon : **zir·con**
ze·ro

Zerox : **Xe·rox**
zigote : **zy·gote**
zinc
zinck : **zinc**
zin·fan·del
zinfendel : **zin·fan·del**
zinfundel : **zin·fan·del**
zinia : **zin·nia**
zink : **zinc**
zin·nia
zinya : **zin·nia**
zippur : **zip·per**
zir·con
zirkon : **zir·con**
ziro : **ze·ro**
zoan : **zone**
zodeac : **zo·di·ac**
zo·di·ac
zodiac : **zo·di·ac**
zodiack : **zo·di·ac**
zodiak : **zo·di·ac**
zology : **zo·ol·o·gy**
zom·bie
zomby : **zom·bie**
zoolegy : **zo·ol·o·gy**
zo·ol·o·gy
Zooloo : **Zu·lu**
zuc·chi·ni
zuccini : **zuc·chi·ni**
zucheni : **zuc·chi·ni**
zukeeni : **zuc·chi·ni**
Zu·lu
zuology : **zo·ol·o·gy**
Zu·rich
Zurick : **Zu·rich**
zurkon : **zir·con**
Zurrich : **Zu·rich**
zy·gote
zylophone : **xy·lo·phone**

310

Guidelines for American English Spelling

1. *I* BEFORE *E* . . .

The most well-known spelling rule is

> *i* before *e*
> except after *c*
> or when sounded like *ay*
> as in *neighbor* and *weigh*.

This one works for many common words like *field, niece, receive*, and *ceiling*. The rule even works for some more unusual words like *sleigh* and *chow mein*. But there are a number of qualifications and exceptions.

  a. The rule applies only when the *c* is sounded like *see*. *Science* is spelled *ie*, because the *c* is not sounded *see*. When the *c* is sounded as *sh*, the spelling also remains "*i* before *e*," as in *efficient, proficient*, and *ancient*.

  b. The "*i* before *e*" rule applies after a *see* sound, even when the letter *c* is not actually present, as in *seize* and *seizure*.

  c. The following words are spelled *ei* even though they do not come after a *see* sound and are not sounded *ay*:

caffeine	*height*
codeine	*leisure*
counterfeit	*neither*
either	*protein*
forfeit	*sovereign*
heifer	*weird*

d. The following words follow a *see* sound, yet are spelled *ie*:

fancier   *financier*   *siege*

2. *-CEDE/-CEED/-SEDE*

There are scores of verbs that end with the sound *-seed*. All of these are spelled *-cede* except for four:

succeed   *exceed*   *proceed*

Only one *-seed* verb ends *-sede*:

supersede

3. *-IFY/-EFY*

There are likewise a great number of verbs ending *-ify*. Only five end *-efy*:

liquefy	*stupefy*
putrefy	*tumefy*
rarefy	

4. *-ND* BECOMES *-NSE*

When a verb ends *-nd*, some of the words derived from it will substitute *s* for *d*:

defend	→	*defense*
expand	→	*expansive*
offend	→	*offense*
pretend	→	*pretense*
suspend	→	*suspenseful*

5. *-DGE* ENDINGS

Words ending *-dge* drop the *e* before adding *-ment*:

abridge	→	*abridgment*
acknowledge	→	*acknowledgment*
judge	→	*judgment*

6. -ABLE/-IBLE

There are more words ending -able than -ible, so if it comes to a coin toss, choose -able. Generally, -able is added to words that could stand alone without a suffix:

agree	→	*agreeable*
break	→	*breakable*
depend	→	*dependable*
predict	→	*predictable*

-able also follows word stems ending *i*: *appreciable, reliable, sociable*.

The ending -ible is usually added to word parts that could not stand alone without the suffix:

aud	+	*ible*	=	*audible*
cred	+	*ible*	=	*credible*
feas	+	*ible*	=	*feasible*
vis	+	*ible*	=	*visible*

7. HARD C/SOFT C

The letter *c* can be sounded like a *k* (as in *cash*) or like an *s* (as in *city*). These are called "hard *c*" and "soft *c*," respectively.

Normally, when adding -able to a word ending in -e, drop the e:

desire	→	*desirable*
pleasure	→	*pleasurable*
use	→	*usable*

However, if a word ends soft *c* + *e*, retain the *e* befor -able (to retain the soft *c* sound):

notice	→	*noticeable*
peace	→	*peaceable*
service	→	*serviceable*

Word stems ending with a hard *c* sound take the -able suffix:

applicable
despicable
implacable

8. HARD *G*/SOFT *G*

Like the letter *c*, *g* can be sounded as a "hard *g*" (as in *gate*) or "soft *g*" (as in *gentle*). The spelling rules regarding hard *g* and soft *g* are similar to those concerning hard *c* and soft *c*.

Words ending soft *g* + *e* retain the *e* before adding *-able* or *-ous* (to retain the soft *g* sound):

change	→	*changeable*
knowledge	→	*knowledgeable*
manage	→	*manageable*
advantage	→	*advantageous*
courage	→	*courageous*
outrage	→	*outrageous*

Word stems ending hard *g* add *-able*:

indefatigable   *navigable*

Soft *g* may also be followed by *-ible* endings (see Rule 6 above):

eligible	*negligible*
intelligible	*tangible*

9. *C* ENDINGS

Words ending in *c* add a *k* (to retain the hard *c* sound) before adding a suffix:

bivouac	→	*bivouacked*
frolic	→	*frolicking*
panic	→	*panicking*
shellac	→	*shellacked*

10. *-Y/-EY*

In forming plurals, a final *-y* preceded by a consonant is usually replaced by *ie* before adding *s*:

baby	→	*babies*
caddy	→	*caddies*
poppy	→	*poppies*

But if the word ends *-ey*, simply add *s*:

alley	→	*alleys*
attorney	→	*attorneys*
chimney	→	*chimneys*
valley	→	*valleys*

(One exception here is *money* → *monies.*)

11. *PRIZE/-PRISE*

Prize ends *-ze*. But when part of another word, the ending is spelled *-prise*:

    comprise   *enterprise*   *surprise*

12. *-N + -NESS*

When adding *-ness* to a word already ending with an *n,* retain both *n*'s:

drunkenness	*greenness*
evenness	*thinness*

13. ADDING *-LY*

Most words ending in *e* retain the *e* when the ending *-ly* is added.

love	→	*lovely*
base	→	*basely*

There are three common exceptions, words in which the *e* is dropped when *-ly* is added:

true	→	*truly*
due	→	*duly*
whole	→	*wholly*

When adding *-ly* to words ending in *l,* retain the *l:*

brutal	→	*brutally*
cynical	→	*cynically*

14. WORDS ENDING IN SILENT *E*

Most words drop a silent final *e* before adding a suffix beginning with a vowel. The *e* is usually not dropped if the suffix begins with a consonant:

suffix begins with vowel	suffix begins with consonant
forgive → *forgiving*	*forgive* → *forgiveness*
confine → *confining*	*confine* → *confinement*

15. DOUBLING CONSONANTS

When adding *-ed* or *-ing* to words ending in *t* or *l* preceded by a single vowel, double the *t* or *l* if the last syllable of the word is accented. Use only one *t* or *l* if the last syllable is not accented:

last syllable accented	last syllable unaccented
commit → *committed*	*limit* → *limited*
control → *controlling*	*cancel* → *canceled*

Words ending in a single accented vowel and consonant usually double the consonant when a suffix that begins with a vowel is added. The consonant is usually not doubled if the suffix begins with a consonant:

suffix begins with vowel	suffix begins with consonant
fit → *fitting*	*fit* → *fitful*
regret → *regretting*	*regret* → *regretful*

16. *-ISE/-IZE*

In American spelling, there are hundreds of verbs ending in *-ize*. There are only ten common verbs ending in *-ise*:

advertise	*exercise*
advise	*improvise*
chastise	*revise*
despise	*supervise*
devise	*surprise*